THE BRITISH AND THE HELLENES

The British and the Hellenes

Struggles for Mastery in the Eastern Mediterranean 1850–1960

ROBERT HOLLAND
and
DIANA MARKIDES

OXFORD
UNIVERSITY PRESS

OXFORD
UNIVERSITY PRESS

Great Clarendon Street, Oxford OX2 6DP

Oxford University Press is a department of the University of Oxford.
It furthers the University's objective of excellence in research, scholarship,
and education by publishing worldwide in

Oxford New York

Auckland Cape Town Dar es Salaam Hong Kong Karachi
Kuala Lumpur Madrid Melbourne Mexico City Nairobi
New Delhi Shanghai Taipei Toronto

With offices in

Argentina Austria Brazil Chile Czech Republic France Greece
Guatemala Hungary Italy Japan Poland Portugal Singapore
South Korea Switzerland Thailand Turkey Ukraine Vietnam

Oxford is a registered trade mark of Oxford University Press
in the UK and in certain other countries

Published in the United States
by Oxford University Press Inc., New York

© Robert Holland and Diana Markides 2006

The moral rights of the authors have been asserted
Database right Oxford University Press (maker)

First published 2006

British Library Cataloguing in Publication Data

Data available

Library of Congress Cataloging in Publication Data

Data available

Typeset by Newgen Imaging Systems (P) Ltd., Chennai, India
Printed in Great Britain
on acid-free paper by
Biddles Ltd., King's Lynn, Norfolk

ISBN 0–19–924996–2 978–0–19–924996–1

3 5 7 9 10 8 6 4 2

For Mema Leventis, in memory of Deno

Acknowledgements

Inevitably in a book of this kind, the authors have incurred many debts along the way to institutions whose staffs have provided invaluable guidance. We would like to acknowledge the following: the National Archives of the United Kingdom, more fondly known as the PRO; the National Army Museum, Kensington; the much-loved London Library; Senate House Library and the Library of the Institute of Commonwealth Studies in London University; Rhodes House Library at Oxford; the excellent Genadius Library, Athens; the British School at Athens; the Archive of the Foreign Ministry of Greece; Rhodes Municipal Library, Greece; the State Archive of the Republic of Cyprus; and the Libraries of the Makarios III Foundation and the Cyprus Research Centre in Nicosia. The photographic images have been drawn from the collections of the National Historical Museum, the Benaki Museum, and, again, the Genadius Library in Athens; the Cultural Foundation of the Laiki Bank in Nicosia; and the Imperial War Museum and Hulton Archive in London. The image on the front cover has been used with the kind permission of the Corfu Reading Society, assisted by Mr Papadatos, and Mr Costas Tsiringakis of Capricorn Studios.

The authors have benefited from the labours of many scholars, present and past, incorporated in our bibliography. Two colleagues and friends should receive special mention: Dr John Darwin of Nuffield College, Oxford, and Dr Evanthis Hatzivassiliou of the Department of History, University of Athens. Extensive travel necessitated by research was relieved by the hospitality of family and friends. Giles and Angela Dixon, and their delightful home on Kew Green, provided a haven strategically close to the PRO. Behind most writers there are long-suffering partners. To Hillia Holland and Sophocles Markides go much love. First Ruth Parr, and then Anne Gelling, proved supportive and highly efficient editors at Oxford University Press. Generous and sustained financial support has been provided by the A. G. Leventis Foundation and the Cyprus Ministry of Education. The Hellenic Foundation in London provided a grant for photocopying.

Finally, and most importantly, this project would never have got off the ground without the personal interest and commitment of Constantine Leventis. Its fruition is just one more testimony to a life of remarkable philanthropy. The book is dedicated to his memory, and with much gratitude to Mema Leventis, whose support was characteristically unstinting.

R.H. and D.M.
April 2005

Contents

List of Illustrations

List of Maps

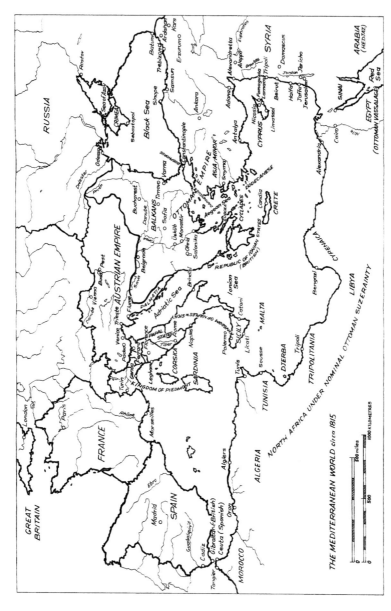

Map 1. The eastern Mediterranean in 1815.

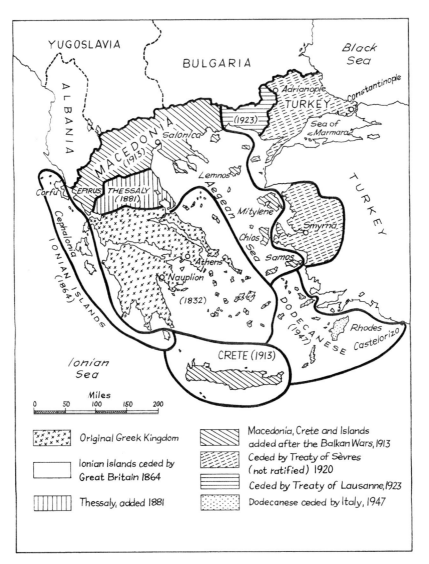

Map 2. The expansion of the Greek kingdom, 1830–1948.

Legend:

- ⊠ Original Greek Kingdom
- ☐ Ionian Islands ceded by Great Britain 1864
- ⊞ Thessaly, added 1881
- ⧄ Macedonia, Crete and Islands added after the Balkan Wars, 1913
- ⧄ Ceded by Treaty of Sèvres (not ratified) 1920
- ☰ Ceded by Treaty of Lausanne, 1923
- ⠿ Dodecanese ceded by Italy, 1947

Map labels: YUGOSLAVIA, BULGARIA, Black Sea, ALBANIA, Adrianople, Constantinople, TURKEY, MACEDONIA (1913), Salonica, (1923), Sea of Marmara, EPIRUS, THESSALY (1881), Lemnos, Corfu, Cephalonia, IONIAN ISLANDS (1864), Aegean Sea, Mitylene, Smyrna, Chios, TURKEY, Samos, Athens, Nauplion, (1832), DODECANESE (1947), Rhodes, Castelorizo, Ionian Sea, CRETE (1913)

Miles
0 50 100 150 200

1

The British and the Hellenes

Greece, Lord Palmerston once remarked, was 'an emotional word'.[1] His first intervention in foreign policy during 1827, indeed, took the form of a passionate statement that both expediency and principle dictated a more generous drawing of the boundaries of a new Greek state than the European powers were willing to grant. Hellenic themes remained emotional for many leading figures in British governments thereafter. William Gladstone became—despite some of his actions in office—a Hellenic icon, and his last notable outburst in public affairs during 1896 embraced the plight of Cretan Christians, alongside Armenians, under the despised rule of Sultan Abdul Hamid. Lord Salisbury swung between early sympathy for Hellenism, highly coloured by his High Church religiosity, to a withering contempt of Greece as 'the blackmailer of Europe'.[2] For Lloyd George, the promotion of that country as a new regional power under the leadership of the charismatic Eleutherios Venizelos became integral to his vision of a brave new world after 1918—though the Greeks were to pay a high price for taking this a shade too seriously. Winston Churchill developed an 'obsession' with Greek affairs during the Second World War.[3] Something of that obsession was shared by Anthony Eden, though one refracted through an overcharged reaction to the Cyprus Question as it unfolded during the early 1950s. The relationship at the heart of this book, with all its contradictory impulses, touched parts of British political culture that few others reached.

The extended range of British reactions to Hellenic aspirations (ultimately defined by what became known as the *Meghali Idhea,* or Great Idea[4]) was rooted in the very experience of the Greek Revolution after 1821. 'The British Cabinet was more surprised by the Greek Revolution', the historian George Finlay once wryly commented, 'and viewed the outbreak [against Ottoman rule] with more aversion than any other Christian government.'[5] Such an attitude was modified

---

[1] Kenneth Bourne, *Palmerston: The Early Years, 1784–1841* (London, 1982), 387.

[2] Quoted in Andrew Roberts, *Salisbury: Victorian Titan* (London, 1999), 647.

[3] See the essay by Richard Clogg on Greece in I. C. B. Dear (ed.), *The Oxford Companion to the Second World War* (Oxford, 1995), 504–10.

[4] The concept of the 'Great Idea'—that is, the 'redeeming' of the majority of Greeks who still remained outside the frontiers of the independent state—was first enunciated by Prime Minister Kolettis in a parliamentary debate in Athens during 1844 as the crux of the country's foreign policy.

[5] George Finlay, *A History of the Greek Revolution*, ii (London, 1861), 161.

by 1825 into George Canning's vision of a 'free' Greece as an engine of British
liberalism and a hoped-for barrier to Russian expansion. Yet Canning was soon
dead, and something of the aversion remained embedded in British thought. The
Duke of Wellington's notorious comment ('an untoward event') in Parliament
soon after the Battle of Navarino of 20 October 1827, which opened the way
towards an independent Greek state when the odds seemed stacked against it, indicated a bias among those of conservative disposition.[6] During the European discussions which followed as to the boundaries of a new Greece, British proclivities were
instrumental in keeping these within as narrow limits as possible. 'For her', a Greek
commentator observed of Britain, 'Hellas meant the Peloponnese', and little
more.[7] This was not surprising, since, according to the early biographer of Stratford
Canning, the British diplomatist whose career was so bound up with the Levantine
region, British ministers feared making a 'working state' out of a Greek polity
which it was soon anticipated would be 'if not wholly under the influence of
Russia, then at least sufficiently so to be irrevocably hostile to England'.[8]

In many ways the oscillations of British responses to Hellenic struggles, through
to Cyprus in the era of twentieth-century decolonization, simply repeated the fundamental gyrations of the original revolutionary saga. That revolution, nevertheless, was afterwards integrated into British historical understanding as the generator
of a philhellenic sentiment for which Lord Byron's death at Missolonghi provided a
sealing image. The fact that so many volunteers for that struggle returned home disillusioned with 'modern' Greece—just like their counterparts in Spanish struggles a
century later—was for some while less influential in shaping popular conceptions.
In reality, as we shall see, anti-Hellenism was to prove as powerful as philhellenism
in influencing the attitudes and actions of British governments when they increasingly collided with Greek aspirations. By the early 1860s it could be observed by the
Conservative politician Lord Stanley that 'Nobody much believes in the Turks, but
the old Philhellenism is dead, and cannot be revived.'[9] During the last two decades
of the nineteenth century the assertion of a moral equivalence between erring
Greeks and the 'unspeakable' Turk became almost a commonplace. By the 1890s it
was frequently stated in British diplomatic and political circles, for example, that in
south-eastern Europe 'the Christians murder the Mussulmans quite as freely as the
Mussulmans murder the Christians'.[10] Once a Graeco-Turkish war broke out in
1897, the young Winston Churchill, thirsting for action, was gripped by indecision
as to which side to join. He wrote to his mother:

Of course my sympathies are entirely with the Greeks, but on the other hand the Turks are
bound to win... If I go on this [Turkish] side it will be less glorious but much more safe,

---

[6] Wellington's famous comment was made during the opening of the British Parliament in Jan.
1828.   [7] Demetrios Bikelas, *Seven Essays on Christian Greece* (Edinburgh, 1890), 203.
   [8] Stanley Lane-Poole, *The Life of Stratford Canning*, i (London, 1888), 483.
   [9] Theodore Tatsios, *The Megali Idea and the Greek–Turkish War of 1897: The Impact of the Cretan
Problem on Greek Irredentism, 1866–1897* (Boulder, Colo., 1984), 36.
   [10] Quoted in David Steel, *Lord Salisbury: A Political Biography* (London, 1999), 250.

and I have no wish to be involved in the confusion of a defeated army. If you can get me good letters to the Turks—to the Turks I will go. If to the Greeks—to the Greeks.[11]

Here Churchill was parading his own cynicism for familial effect, and the events of 1896–7 with which we will be concerned below witnessed—in slightly contrived fashion—a final afterglow of humanitarian and anti-Ottoman sentiment for which the 'Bulgarian atrocities' of 1876 had provided the prototype. Yet clearly the spirit of Missolonghi had long since faded. As it turned out, the Graeco-Turkish war was over before Churchill could make up his mind whom to assist, and he soon found exciting action in the Sudan instead. Once Macedonia descended into bloody crisis after 1903, British liberals—in whose ranks Churchill still figured—were more likely to look with favour on the Bulgars than on the Greeks in that heart of darkness typified in contemporary British parlance as 'the Balkan cockpit'.

The changing nature and configuration of Greek aspirations is naturally central to our subject. Again, the founding revolution set the terms of transition. 'Even as late as 1821', a Greek commentator, Demetrios Bikelas, wrote in 1890, 'there was as much of the Byzantine tradition as the Hellenic idea in the minds of those who prepared the [Greek] National movement.'[12] The 'projet grec' of Empress Catherine II of Russia had fed off dreams of a restored Byzantine Empire. It was not accidental, therefore, that the first outbreak during 1821 took place in Moldavia and Wallachia, not on the shores of the Aegean. But in the Danubian marches the rebellion was swiftly snuffed out, and thereafter the revolution was prosecuted in the preponderantly Greek world of the Aegean. Demetrios Bikelas concluded with regard to late nineteenth-century conditions:

The Hellenic idea has now emerged and cleared itself from any necessary connection with schemes for restoring the Empire of Constantinople. It is still a Great Idea, and it is all the stronger because it is more concentrated. These aspirations are entirely confined within the limits of a possible and practical policy.

This book will focus on those 'concentrations' of political Hellenism in Mediterranean islands whose future was highly contested. What in Greek perspectives often appeared as a 'possible and practical policy' was viewed entirely differently from European vantage points. The consistent British proclivity to deflect the resulting tensions showed itself in an attempt to impose on the modern Hellenic idea a dreamlike quality of the purely provisional—'that cursed word', one observer of the newly established Hellenic kingdom remarked, '[which] is always injuring Greece'.[13] Here again the legacy of the founding revolution was crucial, since although it created a Hellenic kingdom with an ingrained consciousness of borders which excluded the *majority* of surrounding Greek-speaking

[11] Randolph Churchill, *Winston S. Churchill.* i: *Companion*, part 2: *1896–1900* (London, 1966), 740. [12] Bikelas, *Seven Essays*, 264.
[13] Entry for 21 Mar. 1834 in J. M. Hussey, *The Journals and Letters of George Finlay*, ii (Athens, 1995), 37.

populations, it did not bequeath any programmatic conception as to how this defect might be adjusted. 'The war of independence', John Koliopoulos has noted, '. . . became a guiding point of reference, but it did not provide a framework for the definition of national claims.'[14] Entangled in contrasting Balkan and Mediterranean imperatives within the Greek political imagination,[15] sometimes the dominant impulse was to expand northwards into Thessaly, Epirus, and Turkish Macedonia, whereas at others a habit prevailed of taking a line of least resistance by pursuing the 'Great Idea', or some version of it, southwards through the archipelago.[16] It was this latter tendency which most acutely entangled Hellenic aspirations with Great Britain's own expanding stake in and around the Mediterranean littoral.

The geographical plasticity of the Great Idea was mirrored by a certain confusion as to underlying strategy. Its proponents were caught between conflicting desires 'to inherit the Turkish Empire, and to disintegrate it'.[17] As late as the very eve of the Balkan war of 1912 there remained a school of thought, especially entrenched amongst the Greek community of Constantinople, that the Great Idea itself was a dangerous illusion, and obscured the real goal of 'Hellenizing the [Ottoman] state from many angles'.[18] British policy makers were struck by the resulting contradictions revealed by Greek actions, and attributed them to infantilism, or bad faith, without grasping the variety of forces at work. This was compounded by differing responses to the long-anticipated demise of Ottoman power. However disillusioned the British became with their Turkish ally, they invariably displayed a propensity to flinch from any final liquidation of the Sultan's dominion. 'We have everything to gain', Lord Salisbury once remarked, 'by postponing the catastrophe.'[19] The exact opposite was true of most opinion within the Hellenic kingdom, for whom an early 'catastrophe' was keenly desired whilst Greece enjoyed a head start in the scramble to exploit the post-Ottoman transition. British officials repeatedly impressed on Greek minds that 'time was on their side', and that as such they should do nothing which caused an awkward backwash within the international system. In Hellenic circles, however, time usually seemed only to favour some of their emerging and potentially aggressive rivals.

Whilst becoming more concentrated the Great Idea also became increasingly subject to intensive regional competition. The Western tendency to confuse

[14] John S. Koliopoulos, *Brigands with a Cause: Brigandage and Irredentism in Modern Greece, 1821–1912* (London, 1987), 306.

[15] For the Balkan/Mediterranean bifurcation in the growth of modern Greek consciousness see the introduction to Dimitris Tziovas (ed.), *Greece and the Balkans: Identities, Perceptions and Encounters since the Enlightenment* (London, 2003).

[16] From the 1840s onwards there was a tendency for Greek governments to allow 'volunteers' to sail to Crete without impediment, happily deflecting pressure from the northern frontiers of the Hellenic kingdom. See Koliopoulos, *Brigands with a Cause*, 117, 182.   [17] Tatsios, *The Megali Idea*, 14.

[18] For this strain in Hellenic thought, see Digenis Xanalatos, 'The Greeks and the Turks on the Eve of the Balkan Wars', *Balkan Studies*, 3 (1962).

[19] Quoted in W. N. Medlicott, *The Congress of Berlin and After: A Diplomatic Study of the Near Eastern Settlement, 1878–1880* (London, 1938), 345.

affiliation to Orthodoxy with Greek national feeling for some while obscured understanding that other peoples emerging from the ubiquitous 'Turkish yoke' had Great Ideas of their own, even if they were a bit slower off the mark than their Hellenic counterparts. Simultaneously the growth of Russian panslavism—ratcheted upwards during the war in the Crimea—undermined traditional Greek expectation of support from St Petersburg. A critical watershed turned out to be the calculated establishment by Sultan Abdul Aziz of the Bulgarian exarchate in 1870, after which challenges to the authority and prestige of the Greek Patriarch of Constantinople, on which Hellenic claims in Macedonia so critically depended, multiplied. Although the unending complexity of Macedonian issues will lie outside our scope, the fierce energy they transmitted will inevitably feed into our analysis. For the moment we need only observe that the growing pressure on Hellenic ambitions in the Balkans at large, especially emanating from Bulgaria and Serbia, constitutes a part of the backdrop to our subject.

British interactions with movements for *enosis* (or union) with Greece in the eastern Mediterranean were always to be subject to unpredictable shifts in the value attached in London to the Greek state itself. Those shifts could be intense over even very brief periods. There were interludes when a vision of the Hellenic kingdom as 'a model state in the East',[20] as in 1862, or 'a showpiece of western democracy', as at the time of the Truman Pact in 1947, might hold sway (though this itself reflected a perennial confusion as to whether Greece really did belong to the West or the East). In the former instance, Greece was deemed worthy—just about—of receiving the Ionian Islands, and in the latter instance of being granted the Dodecanese, the rationale on both occasions being to insulate Greece itself from elements hostile to Great Britain. Yet virtually instantaneously Greece could be reckoned to be 'fast on on the road to ruin' in 1863,[21] or, by 1949, 'economically and politically finished' and incapable of acting as a 'strong *point d'appui* in Southeastern Europe'.[22] The uneasy duality and contradictions in rapidly alternating images of Greece within the British official mind interacted with many of the fluctuations we shall describe below.

Powerful forces, nevertheless, operated from the mid-nineteenth century to effect a certain synergy in British and Hellenic expansiveness in the eastern Mediterranean. The British and the Hellenes, after all, shared some of the same fears and potential enemies. When the eminent Greek politician Charilaos Tricoupi referred at the end of the 1870s to 'the political necessity of the British Government to employ the rights of Hellenism as a weapon against panslavism',[23] he was driven by the keen hope that Great Britain might emerge as the alternative patron to Russia gravely needed if the hopes of Greek irredentism were to prove

[20] See below p. 71.
[21] Henry Elliott to Lord John Russell, 12 Jan. 1863, FO32/316, National Archives of the United Kingdom.
[22] Quoted in Ioannis D. Stefanidis, *Isle of Discord: Nationalism, Imperialism and the Making of the Cyprus Problem* (London, 1999), 164.   [23] Quoted in Tatsios, *The Megali Idea*, 52.

feasible. Increasingly, amongst the Great Powers, Britain became the only one likely to fulfil this role. French governments might occasionally espouse the most eloquent pro-Hellenism, as premier Waddington did at the Congress of Berlin in 1878,[24] but French influence in the wider region was too fitful, and mortgaged to continental dangers nearer home, to offer Greece a reliable mentor. As a result, the process whereby Hellenic political consciousness cleaved towards Great Britain as an idealized patron became increasingly central to the psychology of Anglo-Hellenic relations—though that psychology by its very nature was always liable to go into reverse as events dictated.

The place of the wider eastern Mediterranean in an evolving system of British imperial and world power also needs to be defined against this background. Sporadically during the nineteenth and twentieth centuries Great Britain sought to project power and influence onto the continental mainland of Europe—to be, that is, a fully fledged Great Power. Repeatedly that attempt foundered, or was deflected, at the hands of competitors (be it France, Russia, or Germany) better able to bring force to bear on land. By a principle of strategic compensation that became a recurring phenomenon, Britain's impulse towards a stake in continental paramountcy was partially displaced into a quest to make the Mediterranean into an English lake. The force of gravitation exerted by the significance of the route to its Indian Empire meant that for Great Britain the eastern portions of that lake came to possess a special resonance.

The outlines of these instinctive tendencies were already discernible during the great contest against Napoleonic France. In that founding drama of nineteenth-century Europe, the British were effectively shut out of the continental heartland. When the anti-Napoleonic allies finally beat their way into Paris on 31 March 1814, it was the Russian Emperor, Alexander I, who rode triumphantly into the city, with the King of Prussia at his side; the British contingents did not arrive for some days. Yet British military capacities *had* successfully found fruition at both ends of the Mediterranean, in the Iberian peninsula to the west, and amidst the islands and some of the adjoining littoral to the east. In this process, in addition to the critical seizure of Malta, the progressive occupation of the Ionian Islands—described by Napoleon as 'the key to the Adriatic'—after 1807 was particularly important; indeed, Malta and the Ionian Islands were to enjoy a natural symbiosis within the framework of the post-1815 British Empire, expatriate officials switching naturally between the two. Some forty years later, by which time a Russian emperor, Nicholas I, was cast in the guise of an inveterate enemy, Britain made another attempt to translate its potential into that of a land power, epitomized by the campaign in the Crimea. After all the blunders and sacrifices of that episode were over, however, it was France, not Britain, which emerged as the dominant military element in their shaky alliance.[25] Yet the scale of mobilization for the

---

[24] Although the French premier supported Greek territorial claims in principle at Berlin, he did nothing to further them in practice. See Medlicott, *Congress of Berlin*, 141.

[25] When the fighting ended in the Crimea, Britain provided less than one-quarter of the effective strength of the Allied armies.

Crimea, above all in its naval and logistical dimensions, enhanced the marginal 'weight' of the eastern Mediterranean in Britain's overseas engagements just as the age of its mid-Victorian supremacy (ambiguous and fragile though it always remained) entered its maturity.

In this setting the commencement of a study of Anglo-Hellenic relationships in the aftermath of the Crimean experience has a broad rationale, as well as a specific relevance, as we shall see, to the growing instability within the British Ionian Protectorate. Paradoxically, a war fought in defence of Ottoman integrity only served to erode British belief in the reformability of that empire. The early biographer of Stratford Canning, whose dominant role in British diplomacy at Constantinople climaxed at this juncture, emphasized his reaction against the Turkish polity, adding that in fact Canning 'had never been a Turcophil, but had always looked forward to the creation of a belt of practically autonomous Christian states, under the suzerainty of the Sultan, as the surest barrier against Russian aggression'.[26] In the wake of the Treaty of Paris (1856) there was a tendency amongst British observers of Levantine affairs to go a step further and anticipate a zone of completely *independent* Christian states, with Greece as the prototype, designed to secure the same object. Writing from Athens in October 1862 an agent sent out by John Delane, the highly influential editor of *The Times* deeply interested in Eastern affairs, stated with regard to the ineluctability of Turkish decline and the matching emergence of Christian races in south-eastern Europe:

They [the Christian states] are feeble, no doubt, but surely if watch there is to be kept over this part of the world, it ought to be more satisfactory for Europe to protect a cradle than to watch over a tomb.[27]

Delane was himself convinced that, even if the old *sentimental* philhellenism had evaporated, under contemporary conditions the Greeks remained the most pliable, and arguably the only available, proxy for British power in the eastern Mediterranean. This doctrine was rooted in naval experience, since the Royal Navy had been a founding partner in Greek statehood, and acted as a guarantor of the new kingdom for much of its early life. Navalism was reinforced by, and invariably interacted with, dynasticism once the brother of the Prince of Wales' Danish consort, himself a fledgling officer in the Danish Navy, was eased onto the Greek throne as King George I in 1863, a process which will loom large in Chapter 3. Queen Victoria and her immediate family circle always evinced a close interest in the ups and downs of their Danish-Greek relatives, and both Victoria and Edward VII responded instantly whenever those relatives' survival was sporadically threatened. This monarchical underpinning to Anglo-Hellenism continued well into the twentieth century, a longevity witnessed by the Greek consort of Queen Elizabeth II.

---

[26] Stanley Lane-Poole, *The Life of Stratford Canning*, ii (London, 1888), 462.
[27] F. Eber to J. T. Delane, 31 Oct. 1862, Delane Papers, News International Archive.

The archipelagic character of Greece, with its well-provided harbours and anchorages, then, defined the inherent attraction which the country had for those who worked the levers of British power overseas. Nevertheless, so long as the Royal Navy's Mediterranean Fleet, with its great Maltese base at Valetta, was kept up to full strength, capable of coping with all regional threats unilaterally, the British premium put on Greece remain capped. But once the Mediterranean Fleet began to be scaled down as part of the controversial reforms of the First Sea Lord, Sir John Fisher, after 1900, and became severely reduced after 1912 as a German threat close to home preponderated, the appeal of Greece as a regional partner rose *pro tanto*. That appeal was heightened by the new-found prestige of Greek naval and military arms after their success in the Balkan wars of 1912–13, and the doubling of the size of Greece which confirmed its control over much of the Aegean, now including the great port of Salonica (or Thessaloniki as it became). The critical significance ascribed to Greece by the Anglo-French Allies in the Great War of 1914–18, reflected in the antics of Western espionage portrayed in Compton Mackenzie's Athenian reminiscences,[28] and much more seriously in the determined sabotaging of Greek neutrality favoured by King Constantine I, testified to the transient emergence of Greece as a vital linchpin within an expanded system of British power in the region. It was to the Greeks and to the Zionists that Lloyd George subsequently looked as fellow stakeholders in the post-war British dispensation within what had become commonly labelled 'the Middle East' and its hinterlands.

Yet the sporadic interweaving of British and Hellenic interests in the eastern Mediterranean and its hinterland was also subject to powerful corrections in the opposite direction. Within the Eastern Question defined by the future of the Ottoman Empire there was wrapped up a separate Greek Question; and whilst in British perspectives Turkey was effectively subordinated within the framework of the former, it was accorded a persisting primacy in the latter. The complexity posed by such a 'question within the Question' will underlie a good deal of our account. Furthermore, after the 1860s it did not seem so clear-cut that the Ottoman Empire was locked into its gloomy mausoleum. The gritty resistance of Turkish arms during the Russian siege of Plevna during the war of 1877–78 became a symbol of what the British historian W. N. Medlicott once called 'the mysterious recuperative powers of the Porte'.[29] Plevna, in fact, entered powerfully into the British public imagination,[30] so that there are numerous Plevna Streets (just as there are matching 'Navarinos') still to be found on the street maps of the United Kingdom.[31] Twenty years later Lord Salisbury, locked into a bitter personal rivalry with Sultan Abdul Hamid, had arrived at the conviction that Turkey had been 'the wrong horse to

---

[28] For Compton Mackenzie's evocation of British officialdom in the wartime Greek capital see his *First Athenian Memories* (London, 1931).   [29] Medlicott, *Congress of Berlin*, 17.
[30] Joan Haslip, *The Sultan: The Life of Abdul Hamid* (London, 1958), 128.
[31] The Inner London *A to Z* street map, for example, includes a Plevna Crescent, Plevna Road, and Plevna Street, as well as a Navarino Grove and a Navarino Road.

back' in Eastern affairs,[32] but he by no means intended that henceforth the British should put all their money on the Greeks instead—only that English bets in the region should be more carefully hedged and circumscribed. Lloyd George's ambitions in the Eastern world later drove him to overlook this limitation, but he lost not only his money on the Greek horse amidst the Asia Minor disaster of 1922, but his premiership as well—though the Greek loss of the Great Idea, and the uprooting of nearly one and a half million Anatolian Hellenes, was much harder to bear.

In short, a hopefulness of British patronage firmly embedded in modern Hellenic political culture, and British expectations that the Greeks should subordinate and moderate their own aspirations whenever required, were often subject to a mutual disillusion all the greater because of the original expectations involved. Here again the benchmark of the founding revolution traced an inherent tendency to overlapping disappointments which was to repeat itself many times over. Thus George Finlay, in his Gibbonian way, wrote with regard to the Anglo-Irish General Sir Richard Church (the latter still alive in Athens during 1864 to entertain William Gladstone during the mission which forms the subject of our opening chapter):

Both Church and the Greeks misunderstood one another. The Greeks expected Church to prove a Wellington, with a military chest well supported from the British Treasury. Church expected the Greeks to execute his strategy like regiments of guards. Experience might have taught him another lesson.[33]

Such misunderstandings, reflecting Finlay's deep admiration for the Greek people and yet contempt for its narrow political class, was to provide the psychological problematic of most Anglo-Hellenic encounters during the decades ahead.

This was certainly the case in that other defining experience for the relationship, the Second World War. The fortitude and success of Greek arms when faced with Italian aggression in October 1940 led to the last ancestral upsurge of the Byronic impulse in British public culture. This episode helped to shape the evolution in Churchill's mind of that 'Mediterranean strategy' in which, as we shall see in Chapter 8, the Dodecanese was for a brief while to loom so large. In the 'soft underbelly of Europe' Churchill soon found the war with which he felt most comfortable, and the Greeks offered themselves as the most convenient ally with whom to fight it.[34] But first the latter had to be saved from the German onslaught which unfolded after the repulse of the Italians. Recording in his diary for 2 November 1940 a lunch hosted at Chequers by Churchill for Sir John Dill, Chief of the Imperial General Staff, the Prime Minister's personal secretary wrote: 'the P.M. is determined that all possible by land, sea and air, shall be done for

[32] This instantly renowned statement was made by Lord Salisbury at the opening of Parliament in Jan. 1897. [33] Finlay, *History of the Greek Revolution*, ii. 136.
[34] For the centrality of the 'Mediterranean Strategy' to Churchill's wartime statecraft see Robert Holland, *The Pursuit of Greatness: Britain and the World Role, 1900–1970* (London, 1991), 172–7.

Greece...when Dill drove away at teatime the P.M.'s last words were "Don't forget—the maximum possible for Greece".'[35]

Yet after things went wrong—and the British and Greek armies withdrew in disarray after mid-1941, first from Greece, and then from Crete, ending up in Egypt, amidst whose hothouse atmosphere many resentments festered—the emotional and political force-fields were apt to reverse themselves. After the mutiny within the Royal Hellenic Army in Egypt during April 1944, much of it was interned for the duration. Churchill even came to deny his earlier enthusiasm to help Greece in 1941, and when British troops, having reintervened on the Greek mainland in September 1944, were shortly faced with a spreading communist disturbance, Churchill's curt instruction to the British commander, General Scobie, was 'Treat Athens as a conquered city.'[36] Such recurring cycles in the nineteenth and twentieth centuries of hope, expectation, disillusionment, mistrust, and—on the Greek side—often of abandonment had a special relevance for the questions of *enosis* which form the precise focus of this book.

The conception of the Greek capital being *conquered* by returning British troops in 1944—though the implication of the British premier's remark was strenuously denied at the time—underlines the relevance of a colonial and quasi-colonial dimension to the treatment which follows, in which Hellenic populations were often to fall under British superintendence. Although it would require a more extended study than the current one to explore fully, the 'modern' state of Greece was itself caught up in the dynamics of colonialism. 'A really independent Greece is an absurdity', observed Edmund Lyons, the naval hero of Napoleonic days who was British minister in Athens between 1835 and 1849 (without, remarkably, ever once taking leave from his duties in the country).[37] The 'protected' and 'guaranteed', and therefore inherently subordinate, position which was accorded to Greece after 1830 continued in some degree throughout the nineteenth century.[38] Thus the finances of the Hellenic state were still subject to supervision by International Commission in the early twentieth century. And although Greek military successes in Macedonia during 1912/13, so unexpected to Western European opinion, made this suddenly seem anomalous, subsequent defeat of its army in Anatolia at Turkish hands during 1921/2, Germano-Italian occupation after 1941, and internal civil war dominating the latter half of that decade, resurrected and even intensified perceptions of the vulnerability and even inferiority of Greece. Such assumptions were to affect the development of the Cyprus Question in the 1950s, and by its climax, traced in Chapter 9, the British

---

[35] John Colville, *The Fringes of Power: Downing Street Diaries, 1939–45* (London, 2004), 240.

[36] Ibid. 386, 506. Churchill's instruction leaked through an American newspaper strongly critical of anything smacking of British colonialism, and helped to stir controversy surrounding British intervention in Greece.

[37] Quoted in Leonard Bower and Gordon Bolitho, *Otho I: King of Greece* (London, 1939), 106.

[38] For a comment on the term 'Protecting and Guaranteeing Powers' used in the treaties establishing independent Greece, see Mackenzie, *First Athenian Memories*, 233.

came to factor into their calculations the possibility of a complete implosion of Greek democracy.[39] Overall, the dependency of Greece, in varying degrees of intensity and overtness, will constantly intrude into our subject.

Yet if, in Palmerston's expression, the Greeks were not themselves a 'governing race,'[40] subordinacy never came naturally to them, so that if their forebears had made poor slaves in classical times, those Greeks 'unredeemed' from their Hellenic motherland were never anything but restless under the rule of other people—especially those who abjured the more drastic methods of the Ottomans. The history of the British Protectorate in the Ionian Islands testified to the pitfalls surrounding any attempt by Englishmen to govern Greeks from above, and the creeping staleness of later repetitions elsewhere only compounded the alienation. The writer, Lawrence Durrell, whilst director of publicity for the British military administration in the Dodecanese after May 1945, complained about the aloof 'colonial' attitudes displayed by his expatriate colleagues.[41] Yet Durrell's own interaction with the Greek intelligentsia sometimes showed how relationships were liable to be compromised wherever a degree of hierarchy intruded, and however 'liberal' the supposed intent might be. Thus, for all Durrell's immersion in Greek ways and inflections, his acceptance of the job as director of publicity in the Cyprus government in 1954 (offered to him, indeed, for the very reason that these traits would make him a subtle propagandist) only convinced the distinguished Greek poet-diplomat George Seferis that Durrell was not 'straight', and that his engagement with Hellenic culture was no more than 'stimulating games'.[42] Today the issues of cultural as well as merely political discrimination surrounding the proprietorship and location of the Elgin Marbles are just one sign that this 'colonial' dimension to Anglo-Hellenic discourse is not entirely dead and buried.[43]

It will not be our task to explore the wide terrain sketched out above. These remarks are simply intended to underscore the broader context of the more limited concerns that will follow. Our treatment will be confined to a study of those islands with Greek-majority populations where Great Britain played a leading role in climaxes leading either to union with Greece, or—in the case of Cyprus—to a rather different 'solution'. Indeed, it is integral to our theme that no other European power played a comparable role in relation to these various denouements. By focusing on the fates of the Ionian Islands, Crete, the Dodecanese, and Cyprus, the *longue durée* of Anglo-Hellenic relations in irredentist contexts may be conveniently covered from the mid-nineteenth century through to the mid-twentieth; that is, from the age of British mid-Victorian confidence through to the uncertainties of the 'end of empire' a century or so later. Although

---

[39] See below, 236.   [40] Quoted in H. L. F. Bell, *Lord Palmerston* (London, 1936), 83.

[41] Below, 205.

[42] Ian McNiven, *Lawrence Durrell: A Biography* (London, 1988), 412–13.

[43] William St Clair, *Lord Elgin and the Marbles* (Oxford, 1967), provides an excellent account of the origins of a controversy which still generates strong emotions.

these sequences are not rendered here for the first time, none of them—recent Cypriot history perhaps apart—have entered in a complex and detailed manner into the mainstream of English-language historiography. No apology is therefore required for a close, if necessarily episodic, reconstruction of events which in each case bore significantly on developments well beyond their insular limits.

Inevitably, there are close similarities but also important differences between the cases examined below. The place occupied by Britain in these islands was not ident-ical. The Ionian Islands constituted a British Protectorate (a territory, that is, whose inhabitants enjoyed 'protection' under the British Crown), but this polity was not a fully fledged colony. In Crete after 1897, and in the Dodecanese after 1945, British occupation took place under international authority. Cyprus provides one instance where a largely Greek population came to experience the formal trappings of British colonial status, though the ambiguities surrounding the occupation of 1878 were always to remain. Each of these places was held to be of considerable strategic value, but that value was to prove vulnerable to varying and acute shifts. The communal complexion of these societies differed. Crete and Cyprus had substantial Muslim minorities, though their fates were to prove contrasting. The Ionian and Dodecanesian archipelagos did not have a comparable presence, but their futures were both intimately connected to Ottoman and Turkish develop-ments. Despite such nuances, these assorted climaxes shared one overarching commonality: their narratives had an influence on wider international events disproportionate to their size, and impacted significantly on the British stake in the wider Mediterranean. They therefore provide a laboratory for exploring and comparing British involvements with Hellenic nationalism, and British interests in the region as a whole, during much of the nineteenth and twentieth centuries.

2

Gladstone and the Greeks: The Extraordinary Mission to the Ionian Islands, 1858–1859

> It may seem strange but so it is that my time & thoughts are as closely occupied and absorbed in the affairs of these little islands as they have been at almost any period in Parliamentary business ... The complexity of the case is inversely (so to speak) as the extent of the sphere.
>
> (William Gladstone, Diary, 31 Dec. 1858)

> One great genius had been sent out by another great genius, and had failed unmistakeably.
>
> (Viscount Kirkwall, *Four Years in the Ionian Islands*, 1864)

On the rainswept afternoon of Friday, 10 December 1858 the rising hope of British politics, William Gladstone, was attempting to cross the narrow bridge leading to the town of Argostoli,[1] on the island of Cephalonia in the Ionian archipelago. Gladstone had recently arrived in the Islands and had thrown himself energetically into his task as Extraordinary High Commissioner to investigate the ills and discontents of Ionian society after four decades under British protection. As his carriage clattered over the bridge, a crowd of about a thousand quickly gathered on the town side, and rushed to surround the prestigious visitor, the cry of 'Hurrah for union with Greece' (*zito i enosis*) being endlessly repeated.[2] Audible above this outburst, however, was another, more menacing assertion, with a clear anti-British meaning: 'Down with the Protection.' The hubbub panicked the horses, and they had to be taken in hand by the crowd. In this not very dignified way Gladstone's coach was slowly progressed to the house of the British resident, its occupant all the while gazing rigidly ahead, pointedly ignoring the leaflets advocating union with the Hellenic kingdom being thrust through the window. Gladstone's evolving relationship with crowds has attracted considerable attention from historians

---

[1] According to the current *Greece: The Rough Guide*, 'The stone bridge, connecting the two sides of ... [Argostoli] bay, was initially constructed by the British in 1813. A small obelisk remains, but the plaque commemorating "the glory of the British empire", has disappeared.'

[2] For Gladstone's account see his letter to Sir John Young, 13 Dec. 1858, CO136/162, National Archives of the United Kingdom.

concerned with analysing his relationship to wider democratic forces.[3] This was the only occasion when a large throng—albeit of Greeks rather than of fellow Britons—actually took possession of his person.

Gladstone might have appeared wholly impassive during this affair, but it is clear from his own account that he was busy drinking in the whole atmosphere. Although the experience helped to confirm his opinion that a strong sentiment of Greek nationality was almost universally shared by Ionians, including the most intelligent and respectable amongst them, he was convinced that only a handful in the crowd were responsible for the expression of anti-British feeling. Still, as Gladstone wrote a few days later, the demonstration was a fact which could not be ignored, and made him determined to use his mission to effect 'the undeceiving of the [Ionian] people on the subject of Union with Greece'.[4] The essentially psychological themes of mutual deception and the desire to 'undeceive' were to form a thread running through Gladstone's sole experience of the direct exercise of British authority overseas.

Gladstone's Extraordinary Mission to the Ionian Islands has a fascination at various levels. No leading British statesman in the nineteenth or twentieth centuries was ever to put himself in such close juxtaposition with the phenomenon of assertive Greek nationality. As such, certain traits and responses of close relevance to the preoccupations of this book can be clearly observed. More broadly still, by accepting the challenge of his Ionian commission, Gladstone—in the words of his most acute biographer—involved himself for the first time in 'questions of strategy, imperialism and nationalism, and in a crisis in which he had to act'.[5] We are therefore able to identify as the mission unfolded critical elements in the Gladstonian method, which was to be of great significance for the Eastern world of which Greek-populated societies were so vigorous a part.

Perhaps the most fundamental interest, however, of Gladstone's sojourn is in relation to the special meaning acquired by the Ionian question in the development of British overseas power and authority. This meaning was suggested by Sir John Young (a figure of some note in what follows) who, as Lord High Commissioner in the Ionian Protectorate, wrote to a government minister in London during December 1855 stating that the Islands were 'one of the very few, if not the sole dependency of the Crown which views with suspicion and dislike the terms of its connection with England'.[6] Certainly at the time it was widely assumed amongst British politicians and officials that in the Ionian Islands they were confronted with a unique challenge posed by a dependency unwilling to accept British control. That it was this Greek society which provided the first

---

[3] The most important example—also concerning aspects of the Eastern Question—was the meeting at Blackheath on 9 Sept. 1876. See Ann Pottinger Saab, *Reluctant Icon: Gladstone, Bulgaria, and the Working Classes, 1856–1878* (Cambridge, Mass., 1991), 81, 93–4.

[4] Gladstone to Young, 13 Dec. 1858, CO136/162.

[5] H. C. G. Mathew, *Gladstone, 1809–1874* (Oxford, 1988), 163.

[6] Young to Henry Labouchere, 1 Dec. 1855, Papers of Sir John Young, MS Add. 62940, British Library (henceforth BL).

prototype of Britain's classic engagement with 'modern' anti-colonial resistance or nationalism—and which finally provided a nineteenth-century model for later British 'decolonization'—is of profound interest in the morphology of Anglo-Hellenic relationships.

What, then, had gone so wrong with the Protectorate to require the remedial presence of Gladstone? The Ionian states—for in theory the main constituent islands formed separate entities—had a total population of approximately 230,000, and covered a land area of around 1,000 square miles. The Southern Islands in the group—principally Cephalonia, Zante, and Ithaca—lay off the western coast of the new Hellenic kingdom established in 1832, whilst Corfu, with its capital and historic fortifications, and its satellite of Paxo, lay opposite Ottoman territory. The Islands had for centuries been subject to Venetian rule, but after the Treaty of Campo Formio in 1797 they became a collection of independent but 'united' states, before falling under French and Russian influence. In 1807 British marines occupied the southern islands, though Corfu did not fall to them till 1815, following stiff resistance by French troops. Under a treaty signed in Paris on 5 November 1815, Great Britain was awarded the rights and obligations of a Protectorate over the archipelago. This treaty was ambivalent as to the true character of British Protection. Under various articles the independence of the Ionian states was explicitly re-established. On the other hand, it was clear that effective control was to be in British hands. From the start, the new system of government in the Ionian states was in practice modelled on Malta, another English acquisition during the recent wars against France. Ambiguity and contradiction were thus cemented into the very foundations of 'the Protection'.

This idiosyncratic Protectorate was once described by a senior British administrator as a 'sort of middle state between a colony and a perfectly independent country, without in some respects possessing the advantages of either'.[7] The modern history of British imperialism was often to show that it was precisely in such 'middle states'—halfway houses between external domination and local freedom—that misunderstanding and alienation was most rife;[8] the Ionian case here, too, helped to set a mould. Any latent instability in the Islands—connected, for example, to Ionian involvements in the Greek revolt against Ottoman rule after 1821—was suppressed so long as a dominant paternalism was imposed from the top. 'The subtlety of the system', one historian has written of the early history of the Protectorate, 'was that it always left the initiative with the Lord High Commissioner',[9] the latter being the portentous title attached to Great Britain's chief representative. The first such appointee, Sir Thomas Maitland—'King Tom'—bestrode the Ionian stage in the unlikely spirit of a pugnacious Irish doge.[10] Yet the more that the British sought to bypass constitutional complexities

[7] Michael Pratt, *Britain's Greek Empire* (London, 1978), 127.
[8] Egypt and Iraq at various times are prime examples.   [9] Pratt, *Britain's Greek Empire*, 107.
[10] For a biography see C. W. Dixon, *The Colonial Administrations of Sir Thomas Maitland* (London, 1969).

by routing power and responsibility through this office, the more opposition within the Protectorate sought to undermine its prestige. For this reason, successive Lord High Commissioners found themselves to be the eye of the storm.

Although Maitland died in 1824, shortly after leaving the Islands, his shadow lay heavily over them for some years. But through the 1840s the system of proconsular domination he invented started to shudder badly.[11] Difficulties intensified once Greece, under its first king, the Bavarian Otto I, was accorded the rough elements of constitutional government in 1843, a constitution which, under the guidance of Otto's leading minister, Kolettis, ran alongside the elaboration of the Great Idea of Hellenic expansion. Yet it was the way that Ionian opinion of Europe's 'Year of Revolutions' was caught up powerfully—albeit necessarily still at the margins—during 1848, which proved a psychological Rubicon. In an attempt to retain the initiative by 'one bold stroke of policy',[12] the current Lord High Commissioner, Lord Seaton, instituted a series of reforms during 1848–49. He granted freedom to the press, guaranteed that municipal elections would not be supervised, and, crucially, gave up controls over the composition and conduct of the Legislative Assembly. The aim of the reforms was to buttress the status quo by offering a counterpoint to the radical programme of union with Greece, with the prospect, Seaton hoped, that the Lord High Commissioner might at last be able to retreat into the background of Ionian political life.

Any hope that a cohort of 'moderate' Ionian politicians might be gathered around the banner of the Protectorate, however, was soon dashed. Instead a very different configuration was triggered. This was an alliance between, on the one hand, die-hard Ionian conservatives opposed to any widening of political life detrimental to their grip on existing patronage and their social interests, and, on the other hand, radical protagonists of union with Greece (or *rhizospastes*) hostile to English-led reform likely to deflect that aspiration and determined to blast their way into the perks of office. The complex pattern of local politics which emerged is not our concern; the effect, however, was that British Protection was more than ever incapable of effective action. Most damagingly, it was forced into systematic illegality as Seaton and his successors fell back on *atti di governo* approved by the upper chamber, or Senate, packed with Protectorate nominees, wholly bypassing the Legislative Assembly. The reforms quickly became as despised by the British as they were by most Ionians. A fatalistic and abrasive pessimism settled over the Ionian polity during the early 1850s, and never lifted thereafter, the vacuum being filled in Ionian political culture by the dream of union with Greece gratifying to the twin forces of shared Orthodox faith and Hellenic national feeling.

Was there any way out of this impasse? Sir John Young, as Lord High Commissioner from 1854, arrived at the grim conclusion that the problems facing the Protectorate were fundamentally intractable. In a dispatch to London dated 10 June 1857—the later leaking of which was to have a major impact on

---

[11] Pratt, *Britain's Greek Empire*, 104–42.   [12] Ibid. 137.

Gladstone's mission—Young told ministers in London that by acting with extreme caution, British authority in the Islands might benefit from a lull if they were lucky, but crucially added:

the truth is that no permanent benefit to England, or real satisfaction to the Ionians, can occur. England is in a false position here, and the Islands are too widely separated geographically, and their interests too distinct, ever to form a homogeneous whole, under foreign auspices.[13]

The only means that Young saw to resolve this unhappy situation was to act on the 'distinct' differences amongst the Islands. He advised that Corfu and Paxo—with their greater moderation and history of stability under British rule—should be fully integrated as colonies into the British Empire. The Southern Islands, including the disaffected states of Cephalonia (where British repression of two disturbances in 1848–49 had left lasting bitterness[14]) and Zante, should be allowed to join Greece. With the end of the recent Crimean War allowing a pause in the troubled Eastern Question, Young's considered view was that such disaggregrated unions offered the only prospect of extricating the British from the falsity of their position in the Islands as a whole.

Palmerston, still heading an essentially wartime administration, saw the merits of such a proposal. He cared little about overseas possessions, being more preoccupied with the sort of power that stemmed from diplomacy backed by the threat of force;[15] and he harboured little sentiment towards fragments of territory whose strategic utility was already widely regarded as suspect.[16] But this 'moment of opportunity', as Young portrayed it, soon passed. In the Cabinet any suggestion of 'Annexing Greeks' was regarded as 'unjust and impractical'—an early recognition that Greeks did not make pliable colonial subjects.[17] But more decisive for Palmerston was the confession of weakness in that moral influence on which his whole conception of British power hinged. To admit so openly the falsity of Britain's position on a matter bearing directly on the Eastern Question was impossible. The 'glamour' of victory, however costly, in the Crimea would have to be sustained somewhat longer before that became feasible. The Ionian question was therefore hedged about with imponderables of falsity and honour long before Gladstone appeared on the scene. Meanwhile the hapless Young could only fall back on that 'studied indifference' which was the psychological mask concealing the recognition that the British presence lacked legitimacy or the power to sustain itself over the long term.[18]

---

[13] Young to Labouchere, 10 June 1858, PRO22/6/69, National Archives of the United Kingdom.

[14] The rebellion of 1849 was most widespread, and during its suppression by British troops twenty-one executions were carried out. A recent acount is Miranta Paximapolou-Stavrinou, *I Exergerseis tes Kephallenias kata ta Etei 1848 kai 1849* (Rebellions of Cephalonia in the Years 1848 and 1849) (Athens, 1980).   [15] H. F. C. Bell, *Lord Palmerston* (London, 1936), 429.

[16] Malta had already emerged as Britain's critical naval station for its Mediterranean Fleet.

[17] See notes on Ionian policy in Papers of the 4th Earl of Carnarvon, MS Add. 60783, BL.

[18] Carnarvon note, 29 Nov. 1858, CO136/162.

A favourable Ionian lull nonetheless prevailed for a while. British and French troops continued to occupy Piraeus as punishment for the attack by Greece across the northern frontier with Turkey during the recent war with Russia, and Hellenic nationalists hesitated to give the allies any cause to prolong their stay on the mainland. In early 1858, however, the Anglo-French forces departed from Greece. One effect was a natural recrudescence of radical feeling against British Protection within the Islands. All political elements began to manoeuvre for position when the new Ionian Parliament should be convened in the spring of 1859. During the interim successive skirmishes raised the stakes, and, as so often in the politics of small islands, it was in the municipal arena that the tell-tale signs of looming confrontation surfaced.

In June 1858 an Ottoman warship visited Corfu, and the municipal councillors quickly passed a regulation which barred its provisioning. This was a transparent attempt to 'get at the English through their hated allies the Turks'.[19] A few weeks later an incident took place of even more concern. Festivities surrounding the patron saint of Corfu, St Spyridon, were especially important in the expression of local identities and precedence.[20] Indeed, during the early years of the Protectorate, British Army officers had helped to carry the relics in procession. In such ways a shaky co-operation between the Protection and the Greek Church had been fostered. Yet over time the English role in such religious occasions had become vestigial, pared down to the 'prayers' for Her Britannic Majesty offered by the Archbishop when the procession stopped briefly on the Esplanade opposite the Palace of St Michael and St George, duly acknowledged by the Lord High Commissioner from a balcony. In early August 1858, during such a processing of St Spyridon's remains, five municipal councillors absented themselves from their places behind the Archbishop at the point when these loyal prayers were offered. British prestige and Hellenic nationalism shared one thing in common: they fed on a diet of symbols conducive to their respective senses of power and authority. It was when the political contestation at elite and secular levels penetrated the world of symbols involving the masses and the Church that the danger point invariably beckoned.

The Conservative ministry in London now burdened with responsibility for Ionian problems was led by Lord Derby. In a period marked by ideological flux crossing party lines, keen differences emerged when Sir John Young requested not only to suspend the recalcitrant councillors from office, but if necessary to act outside the strict limits of the 1817 constitution. The questionable legality of this did not trouble Young, who told the Secretary of State for Colonies, Bulwer Lytton, that 'the restoration of Maitland's system is our only salvation'.[21] The Lord High

[19] Merivale to Carnarvon, 26 Aug. 1858, CO136/161.

[20] The relic of St Spyridon had been brought to the Ionian Islands after the fall of Constantinople in 1453. The power of this relic was held to be responsible for the successful resistance to subsequent Turkish invasions, including the Great Siege of 1716.

[21] Young to Lytton, 19 Aug. 1858, CO136/161.

Commissioner preferred a clear-cut solution along lines he had already trailed; but since this had not been allowed, he saw repression as the only logical and honest refuge. Like most Protection officials, he believed that unless swift action was taken, more insults to British authority would follow, 'resulting finally in lamentable disorders or bloodshed as in Cephalonia in 1848'.[22] The shadow of renewed rebellion was to hang heavily over ministerial minds, and to mark the whole rationale and conduct of the ensuing Gladstone mission.

Meanwhile Young's call for repressive action had supporters within the Colonial Office. The junior minister, Lord Carnarvon, was eager 'to strike the first blow' against the *Rhizospastes* faction.[23] But Bulwer Lytton's views as Colonial Secretary were diametrically opposed. He was a Tory of romantic sensibilities, destined for literary rather than political fame, harbouring a deep-seated belief that 'the first rule in the grammar of politics [is] ... the interests and wishes of the people governed'.[24] He instinctively shared the sentiment expressed by one senior official in Whitehall that 'much of our ill-success in these [Ionian] Islands has been owing to our misunderstanding and undervaluing the Greeks'.[25] It followed that his natural tendency (concurred in by Derby) was to ignore the insults levelled by Ionian politicians 'and to hasten at once to the announcement of our intention to send out a Special Commissioner to report on the best mode of healing those internal state maladies of which these disputes are but the outward symptoms. ... by this means we shall give all the strength and grace in our power to the arrival of our [new] Governor.'[26]

'Strength and grace'—whoever went out to the Islands on Britain's special behalf at this crucial moment had to incorporate those qualities. In fact a very delicate negotiation—replete with attempts to play on Gladstone's classical imagination[27]—proceeded from mid-September onwards, with Derby and Lytton struggling to cajole Gladstone into a Mediterranean role. 'I begin to think that he [Gladstone] really will go', Derby commented as late as 30 October 1858, 'but I

[22] Sir George Bowen to Merivale, 30 Aug. 1858, ibid.
[23] Carnarvon note, 27 Aug. 1858, ibid.
[24] The Earl of Lytton, *The Life of Edward Bulwer, First Lord Lytton,* ii (London, 1913), 358. A recent biography is Leslie Mitchell, *Bulwer Lytton: The Rise and Fall of a Victorian Man of Letters* (London, 2003).
[25] Merivale note, 22 June 1858, CO136/161.
[26] Lytton memorandum, 'Ionian Islands: Dispute with the Municipal Officers', CO136/161. The precedent in Lytton's mind was undoubtedly that of the mission by Lord Durham to Upper and Lower Canada in 1839.
[27] 'I have been studying your delightful volumes on Homer almost every afternoon', a British official in Corfu with close personal ties to the Colonial Office hierarchy was inspired to write temptingly to Gladstone, 'as I floated in my little yacht along the shores whom tradition identifies with the "Gardens of Alcinous", fragrant with groves of citrus, orange, lemon, pomegranate, olive and other fruit trees, interspersed with acacia, oleander and cypress.' See Sir George Bowen to Gladstone, 25 Sept. 1858, Papers of William Ewart Gladstone, MS Add. 44390, BL. Gladstone's three volumes entitled *Homer and the Homeric Age* had been published several months before, which was another reason why he had come so readily to the minds of Derby and Bulwer Lytton when pondering Hellenic issues.

shall not feel sure until he is on board.'²⁸ This eagerness has sometimes been
interpreted as a ploy to bring Gladstone back into the Tory fold. Certainly some
members of the Peelite faction to which Gladstone belonged warned him against
a trap—'self-immolation' was one expression.²⁹ But from a ministerial vantage
point the urgency of persuading Gladstone is explicable even without domestic
considerations. More information had been forthcoming about a possible breakdown
of law and order in the Islands at the next festivity of St Spyridon. The dispatch of
any ordinary representative would do little to avert such an outcome. Lytton had
earlier advocated a 'Hellenic Governor'—which leading Englishman was more
Hellenic than Gladstone, who wore his Homeric scholarship so heavily? If, as was
commonly assumed, the Ionian Greeks were above all suffering from a simple loss
of *amour propre* in the face of arrogance displayed by local British officials, then a
new start might be made by sending to them the best and the brightest in the
coming class of English leaders. So it was that the 'Special' Commissioner was soon
redesignated 'Extraordinary', to heighten the dazzle created in the eyes of the
Ionians—and also perhaps help to dazzle Gladstone himself into packing his bags
with the promptness that was required.

That Gladstone agreed to go to the Ionian archipelago is, indeed, more remarkable than that the offer was so zealously pressed on him by ministers. It was an
unusual move for an ambitious and still, at 47, relatively young politician to
remove himself from the centre of power. Colin Mathew has written that 'in
purely tactical terms the years 1855–59 were the most personally complex in
Gladstone's career'.³⁰ For some while he had remained undecided between the
great parties of the state, but had paid a price in doing so in absence from office—
'I am losing the best years of my life,' he had written to a friend in 1857.³¹ By the
early autumn of 1858 he was very eager for an executive position, but one which
did not yet definitively commit his own loyalties. Yet in entertaining the Ionian
proposition Gladstone had to take account of several dangers. One was that he
might be away when a vital political crisis erupted in London. Lytton therefore
assured Gladstone that he could return home at any point—though it was
expected that he would be in the Islands during the following March when the
new Ionian Parliament met, since the whole point of the exercise was to deflect the
danger of that moment. Another risk of the Ionian job was that it might tar
Gladstone with the brush of old-fashioned Toryism. For this reason he insisted as
part of the deal that whilst in the Islands there should be no acts of repression.
His task as incorporated in the royal warrant was made eminently limited and
practical—to consider and make recommendations for alterations to the Ionian
constitution or 'Chart' of 1817. The fact that his own situation dictated that he

²⁸ Derby to Lytton, 6 Sept., 30 Oct. 1858, Carnarvon Papers, MS Add. 60783, BL.
²⁹ F. Darrell Munsell, *The Unfortunate Duke: Henry Pelham, 5th Duke of Newcastle, 1811–1864*
(Colombus, Oh., 1985), 128.   ³⁰ Mathew, *Gladstone, 1809–1874*, 104.
³¹ Ibid. 105.

remain as ideologically neutral as possible *in relation to English politics*, however, was not necessarily helpful when it came to resolving Ionian dilemmas.

Yet the appeal of Derby's proposition to Gladstone should not just be seen in career terms. Gladstone was too earnest for that. In a more profound sense the Ionian matter transected some of the basic issues in his political thinking. Again, Mathew has described how, over time, Gladstone had accepted the irrelevance of his own original theocratic Toryism, and in seeking a new ideal of parliamentary secularism had concentrated on three themes: colonial affairs, the morality of international affairs, and faith in free trade. In 1858 the last of these still remained the least salient of the trio. During recent years Gladstone had made a close study of the problems of Responsible Government, especially as they had been experienced in the Australian and Canadian colonies, and this was to form a principal part of the intellectual baggage he took with him to the eastern Mediterranean—with, as we shall see, distorting effects. As for the morality of international affairs, the fact that England's 'honour' was so widely recognized to be entangled in the affairs of the Protectorate afforded an ethical, almost biblical, dimension which dug deep into Gladstone's psychology. The extraordinary commissionership therefore presented itself as a kind of laboratory for experimenting and highlighting his own mobile preoccupations and beliefs. The philosophical and the personal ran alongside each other, and were reflected in the temporary but blazing intensity which Gladstone was to give to Ionian problems.

There is one other dimension to Gladstone's selection—his very seniority as a statesman offered a potential means 'by which [Sir John] Young . . . could be eased out without a scene'.[32] Lytton would undoubtedly have preferred to sack the Lord High Commissioner without delay. But the latter still had powerful friends in England. Indeed, as Disraeli indicated the difficulty to Lytton, Young had been Gladstone's 'special friend and schoolfellow' at Eton,[33] and later colleague in the Peelite faction. Whilst negotiating the mission with ministers, Gladstone signalled that his close relations with Young made him 'an unfit and improper instrument' for effecting the latter's downfall.[34] Lytton deflected this slight complication by expressing confidence in Gladstone's 'high and pure conception' of the public good such that he 'would not scruple to advise . . . a change' in the Lord High Commissionership should enquiry prove one necessary.[35] The reality was that Young's stay of execution could only be temporary. He bitterly resented Gladstone's appointment to what was plainly 'an enquiry into his policy and conduct'.[36] His own conviction was that the whole initiative would prove fatal with regard to Ionian stability, for reasons which shall unfold. Meanwhile Gladstone's relationship to what was a hatchet job in the making

[32] Ibid. 163.
[33] Quoted in M. G. Wiede (ed.), *Benjamin Disraeli: Letters, 1857–59* (Toronto, 2004), 255.
[34] Gladstone to Lytton, 3 Oct. 1858, Gladstone Papers, MS Add. 44241, BL.
[35] Lytton to Gladstone, 9 Oct. 1858, ibid.
[36] Derby to Lytton, 30 Oct. 1858, Carnarvon Papers, MS Add. 60783, BL.

showed the feline counterpoint to his philosophical inclinations, and explains the brittleness of the mission in relation to the official world of the Protectorate as well as local Ionian politics.

Summarizing the dispatch of Gladstone to the Islands, the distinguished historian of ancient and modern Greece, George Finlay, who observed events from Athens throughout these years, concluded that it was made

> with the vain hope that the eloquence and candour which gave power in England would charm the subtle demagogues of Greece, and establish harmony between the British government and the Ionian people for the period that the Protectorate might still endure.[37]

This slightly facetious simplification does not do full justice to the situation. Nevertheless, Finlay's characteristically shrewd and elegant emphasis on the origins of the mission, its lack of clear thought for which Gladstone's own intellectual stature provided a screen, and its preoccupation with the purely provisional, was essentially just. The mission, despite the rhetoric and style at Gladstone's command, suffered from a hollowness at the centre at which its detractors, both English and Ionian, were eventually to take effective aim.

Having at last yielded to Derby's pleas, Gladstone set out on the journey to the Mediterranean on 8 November, accompanied by his wife and daughter,[38] along with two aides, James Lacaita and Arthur Gordon, the latter son of the ex-Prime Minister Lord Aberdeen. Lacaita was a prominent Italian scholar living in London for some years, and Gladstone had persuaded him to join the mission to help forge good relations with the Italianate aristocracy of Corfu, and check Gladstone's use of Italian when accurate meanings were at a premium.[39] But barely had they crossed the Channel when an event occurred which greatly complicated the whole venture. This was the theft from the Colonial Office and immediate publication in the *Daily News* of Sir John Young's earlier dispatch advocating the conversion of Corfu and Paxo into British colonies, and the transfer of the other Islands to Greece. A copy of this document had been amongst the batch given to Gladstone as background reading. Ironically, given later events, Gladstone's response had been that Young's plan might still offer the only viable method of escaping from an insoluble problem.[40]

The leaked document was picked up in the European press and, via Trieste, spread throughout the Balkans, where any infringement of existing treaty arrangements had disturbing implications. Meanwhile a rumour went round in London that the theft was a Tory ploy, so that having set Gladstone up as Extraordinary

---

[37] George Finlay, *A History of Greece*, vii (Oxford, 1877), 305.

[38] Mrs Gladstone's doctors had advised that the Ionian climate would be good for her health. See John Morley, *The Life of Sir William Ewart Gladstone*, i (London, 1903), 596.

[39] See Charles Lacaita, *An Italian Englishman: Sir James Lacaita, 1813–1895* (London, 1933), 113–14. During the subsequent *Risorgimento*, Lacaita served as a crucial intermediary between the British government and the Piedmontese leader, Count Camillo Cavour. See John Prest, *Lord John Russell* (London, 1972), 391.

[40] See H. C. G. Mathew (ed.), *The Gladstone Diaries*, v: *1855–60* (Oxford, 1978), 329 n. 10.

Commissioner, they promptly let him down with a thump. This scarcely fitted with Derby's style of aristocratic *hauteur* in politics. In fact the individual who was shortly tried for the offence seems to have had no motivation other than resentment at several unsuccessful applications for a clerkship in the Colonial Office.[41] Nevertheless, the atmosphere created was acrid. 'I can think of nothing else,' Lytton, always living on the edge of nervous exhaustion, told the cooler Carnarvon.[42]

Young was equally obsessed, claiming that in the Islands the publication had 'fallen like a thunderbolt', fuelling expectations that at least some of the Islands were about to be ceded to Greece, and crucially undermining the depleted band of loyal Ionians still standing by British Protection.[43] Later on it was to be convenient for Gladstone to claim that the leak had made the success of his mission impossible, and that he would have turned back in his tracks had that course of action not been highly injurious to the good name of England.[44] In this way he was to fend off, without further awkward examination, those who echoed Young's contention that the mission was flawed, and always bound to create the very uncertainty which made the Protectorate so hapless an institution. The leakage was therefore used from the start as a weapon by the various protagonists. What is unquestioned, however, is that as a result of the publication in London the political situation awaiting Gladstone in the Islands was far more febrile than it would otherwise have been.

Gladstone was in Vienna when the news of the theft broke, and the worried British Ambassador insisted that he go and see the Austro-Hungarian Foreign Minister, Count Buol. As the arch-apostle of a conservative European order based on quasi-sacred treaty, Austrian opinion was acutely sensitive to indications that other powers were about to renege on existing commitments. Whatever Gladstone's first attraction might have been to shuffling off the most troublesome of the Ionian Islands to Greece, and making Corfu and Paxo entirely British, he now poured out assurances to Buol that the contract for Ionian responsibility accepted by Great Britain in 1815–16 was immutable, and part of the Public Law of Europe.[45] Such susceptibility on Gladstone's part to ultra-conservative Austrian sensitivities might seem at odds with that championship of 'national principles' which later came to frame the classic Gladstonian element in Victorian political mythology. But as one historian has noted, closer examination shows that Gladstone always 'put more store on order and stability than on national liberty'.[46] In practice this meant that he only supported liberal national movements 'gradually and grudgingly', and only

[41] For details on the theft see Bruce Knox, 'British Policy and the Ionian Islands, 1847–1964: Nationalism and Imperial Administration', *English Historical Review*, 99(1984) 503–29.
[42] Bulwer to Carnarvon, 13 Nov. 1858, Carnarvon Papers, MS Add. 60783, BL.
[43] Young to Carnarvon, 23 Nov. 1858, ibid.
[44] *Hansard Parliamentary Debates*, 3rd series, vol. clxii (Commons), 7 May 1861, cols. 1679–80.
[45] Gladstone to Lytton, 20 Nov. 1858, CO136/162.
[46] Keith A. P. Sandiford, 'W. E. Gladstone and Liberal-Nationalist Movements', *Albion*, 13-1, (spring 1991), 22.

after the 'people' concerned had shown themselves capable of efficient government.[47] The resulting ambivalence characterized his attitude towards the evolution
of both the Italian and the Greek kingdoms, but it was most especially apparent in
the latter case, where there was no Cavour—that is, no dominating, European-
style leader—to provide the sort of guarantees and assurance required.

Although, therefore, the Ionian episode in Gladstone's career indicated how the
Public Law of Europe was emerging as a fixed point in his formidable armour, it
was a law which yet remained elastic in all directions. Much later it was to provide
the basis for a scintillating attack on Turkish conduct in Bulgaria. But in
November 1858 such European considerations still operated to buttress a regional
status quo recently secured by war in the Crimea, the original necessity for which
Gladstone had not questioned. He therefore reiterated to Buol whilst in Vienna
that as Extraordinary Commissioner to the Ionian states his sole task was to see if
Britain's responsibility could be better fulfilled, stressing that 'the contract itself
was not to be considered or reconsidered by me'. It was through this moral
emphasis on European engagement that Gladstone sought to stem the effects of
the *Daily News* leak, and which thereafter, whenever the pressure mounted, he
framed in such a way as to pin on Ionian radicals the damaging charge that in pursuing their Hellenic ideals they lost sight of the needs of wider European peace. It
was a charge always liable when it suited to get Hellenic nationalists a bad name.

As Gladstone steamed towards Corfu on an Austrian Lloyd steamer the tension
in the Protectorate increased. Young was on tenterhooks, since anything which
went wrong in the weeks ahead was sure to be held against him. He felt it politic,
given his stern instruction that 'every possible respect and honour should be paid
to national religious ceremonies',[48] to accede to the request of the Archbishop of
Corfu that the route of the procession for St Spyridon on 14 November should
bypass the palace altogether. The Lord High Commissioner and the Archbishop
were the two most prestigious figures in Corfu, and a subtle shift in favour of the
latter was exactly the sort of tendency which Young deprecated if indeed the aim
was to uphold Protection. Meanwhile any physical disturbance coincident with
the Extraordinary Commissioner's appearance would be disastrous. Young therefore ensured the presence in Ionian waters of Her Majesty's Ships *Terrible* and
Ariel, and reinforcements from the Malta station were arranged should trouble
occur. He bombarded the Colonial Office with reports from directors of police in
the various islands that 'tranquillity' prevailed. In short, everything was done to
ensure that if Gladstone's mission ran into the buffers, the blame could not easily
be put on local officialdom.

When Gladstone and his party stepped ashore in Corfu town[49] on Wednesday,
24 November, Young laid on the full works of a seventeen-gun salute and a big

---

[47] Keith A. P. Sandiford, 'W. E. Gladstone and Liberal-Nationalist Movements', *Albion*, 13-1,
(spring 1991), 28.   [48] Young to Lytton, 15 Nov. 1858, CO136/162.
[49] In 1858 the population of Corfu town was approximately 17,500, consisting of one-third
Greeks, one-third Jews, and one-third Mediterranean diaspora (Maltese, Albanians, Cyrenaicans,

reception in the elegant Palace of St Michael and St George, where the Gladstones were accorded their own suite of rooms. On 29 November, a levee was held in the palace grounds. Young assured Lytton in his report that to afford the Extraordinary Commissioner 'a full view and idea of Corfiote society' he had pressed leading citizens to attend[50]—a hint perhaps that Gladstone's magnetic power amongst Ionians was not quite what London assumed it to be. Even so, members of the mission complained privately to the Colonial Office that Young had been deficient in the welcome he had given. For one thing, an Extraordinary High Commissioner should not, it was felt, have been treated merely as a guest in the palace, but should have received separate accommodation. 'It was more like the conduct of a woman,' Carnarvon replied, and the fault was put down to Lady Young, whom Gladstone instantly disliked.[51] The Gladstones were quickly found an appropriate lodging in the town. But behind this banality the truth was that Sir John Young was already a marked man, and it served the mission's purpose to start off by laying down a line of criticism against him.

During his first days in Corfu, however, Gladstone could hardly do other than spend some time with Sir John mulling over Ionian affairs. Yet it was logical, too, that Gladstone—who had begun, after all, as a 'Hellenic' appointee—should seek to tap into more indigenous opinion. This was easier said than done. Gladstone did have interviews with leaders of the *Rhizospastes* but the atmosphere soon became strained—'the worst yet', Gladstone remarked after an interview with the prominent radical Signor Dandolo.[52] Some other means was required to explore hopefully 'moderate' Ionian attitudes. A solution offered itself in the form of a leading Protectorate official, Sir George Bowen, who some years before had married the daughter of Count Candiano Roma, one-time President of the Ionian Senate and leading aristocrat. Bowen was a classicist and Greek speaker, and his familial and social connections led to the assumption that he was an accurate source on Ionian opinion generally—Colonial Office officials had kept up a steady correspondence with him for some time. Bowen was intensely ambitious for preferment outside the Islands, and played up to the role expected of him, including a depreciation of Young's ability to handle the present surge in unionist sentiment in the Islands.[53] At first, Bowen helped Gladstone going through the daily Greek papers, but as the mission progressed he became a key adviser, and a conduit through whom to disseminate messages aimed at the local political class. But at various levels this dependency on Bowen as an accurate barometer of Greek feelings held dangers for Gladstone's grasp of Ionian realities.

Turks, etc.). Lord Rothschild, amongst others, tried to get Gladstone at this time to take up the complaints of the 'Hebraica' community in Corfu, but to no avail. For Gladstone's refusal see his letter to Lytton, 15 Dec. 1858, Gladstone Papers, MS Add. 44241, BL. The Jewish community ceased to exist in the Second World War. A lovely synagogue remains.

[50] Young to Lytton, 19 Dec. 1858, CO136/162.
[51] Carnarvon to Gordon, 8 Dec. 1858, Carnarvon Papers, MS Add. 60783, BL.
[52] Mathew, *Gladstone Diaries*, v. 344.
[53] Bowen to Herman Merivale, 9 Dec. 1958, Carnarvon Papers, MS Add. 60783, BL.

The first set-piece occasion for the mission was Gladstone's address to a meeting of the Senate on 13 November. His original intention had been to avoid any reference during his mission to the movement for union with Greece—to kill it with a mixture of aloofness and contempt. The renewed excitement stemming from the publication of the stolen dispatch forced his hand, and he now went out of his way to 'wholly exclude the question from the purview of the present mission'. To leave no mistake, the royal warrant for the mission, with its clear limitation, was read out in Italian by Lacaita as the secretary to the mission, and then in Greek by an Ionian official. Afterwards Gladstone made a brief speech in which he proceeded to state categorically that both the British Protectorate and the Ionian constitution formed 'a portion of the Public Law of Europe', and that any attempt to alter their fundamental relation to each other would founder on the will of the 'many Great States' which had underwritten the decisions of 1815–16.

From the start Gladstone's success depended on his words being believed by the Ionians. Was that likely? Simultaneously Young had forwarded to Lytton a radical newspaper which commented that all representatives of the Queen sent to them over the years had been 'Liars, Deceivers and Traitors', and that it would prove no different this time round. 'I fear', was Young's barbed comment, 'that words, however eloquent, only serve to arouse suspicion in these parts.'[54] Indeed, the essence of his critique of the mission was that in the end mere words, enshrined in speeches and eventually in a set of recommendations doomed to failure, would probably end up making things worse than they were to start with. The British government was banking on the belief that when the words were uttered by Gladstone, the outcome might be different. In the imponderability of words— their fluctuating force, persuasiveness, and credibility—lay the true test of success.

So long as Gladstone stayed in Corfu, he at least met with all due respect, and no unseemly demonstrations occurred. Corfu, however, was only one of the Illustrious Seven Islands, set apart by its distinctive Venetian imprint, a visible English presence (especially the soldiers and sailors whose petty expenditure was always welcome to Corfiote merchants) and the relatively moderate expression of Hellenic nationality. If Gladstone was to be able to claim to have fully investigated the Protectorate and the society around it, he had also to visit those islands to the south with a rather different history and pattern—islands which Sir John Young had once argued could have no other destiny (and sooner better than later) than union with Greece. These were societies with a record of unruliness towards English authority, and marked by a high incidence of personal violence.[55] Still, the reports flowing in from residents in those parts as to the 'tranquillizing effect' of Gladstone's speech to the Senate, which had been immediately printed and circulated through the archipelago, pacified concerns about Gladstone's safety.

[54] Young to Lytton, 23 Nov. 1858, CO136/162.
[55] For a sociological study of violence in Ionian society under British protection see Thomas W. Gallant, *Experiencing Dominion: Culture, Identity and Power in the British Mediterrranean* (New York, 2000).

On 7 December, leaving his family behind, but accompanied by Lacaita and Gordon, Gladstone set off on a tour aboard HMS *Terrible* to places whose classical relics he was intent on experiencing at first hand.

In Santa Maura and Ithaca Gladstone only stayed briefly. There were a few picnics at the main sites. He remained keen to avoid public speeches, at least until he was in a position to call a special meeting of the Ionian Parliament to consider whatever reforms he eventually decided to put forward. Although the legislators of Ithaca had begun on an awkward note with an address marked by radical enthusiasm, after a few stern glances they 'avowed their personal disinclination to union'.[56] Indeed, Ithaca, with its special Homeric association, was the personal highlight of what was arguably the most fascinating foreign tour that Gladstone ever made. 'The salute in this beautiful harbour', he wrote on leaving, 'was one of the grandest things from its regular circles of thundering echoes, that I ever heard.'[57]

On the morning of 10 December, he arrived in Cephalonia, and, as we saw at the outset of this chapter, was crossing the island to the capital of Argostoli when the progress of his coach was suddenly arrested by a crowd calling for union with Greece, and led into town.[58] Gladstone's response to this incident was to make sense of it in a way that was congruent with the more bashful representatives of Ithaca. He drew a sharp distinction between the mere handful of demonstrators who denounced British Protection outright—these were, he recalled, 'better dressed',[59] to imply the trouble-making lawyers and needy 'gentlemen' manning the ranks of the *Rhizospastes*—and the sober and thoughtful majority who aspired to union, but shrank from its premature and dangerous achievement. It was, in particular, the attitude of the local dignitaries whom Gladstone called to the residency the following morning which rooted into his mind the need for an 'undeceiving' of the Ionian people on the subject of union with Greece: for although they had apologized for any personal insult incurred, they refused to repudiate the previous day's demonstration.[60] A subtle but vital shift in the goal of the mission now occurred. Ostensibly reform remained the desired outcome. But even more desirable henceforth was a negative aim, without which reform itself could not be made to hold the stage—that of eradicating any 'deception' or illusion as to the possibility of union with Greece during the lifespan of the present generation.

The stakes had consequently been raised all round. Still, at least Gladstone's visit to Cephalonia was marked by no further commotion. But as Gladstone prepared to leave, the police warned that at his next destination of Zante he would

---

[56] Mathew, *Gladstone Diaries*, v. 346.   [57] Ibid.

[58] In approaching Cephalonia, Gladstone must have been conscious of the role played by the island in larger European controversies. As John Morley noted, the rebellion in that island during 1849 had provided the opportunity 'with which Prince Schwarzenburg [of Austria] had taunted Lord Aberdeen by way of rejoinder to Mr. Gladstone's letters on barbarous misgovernment in Naples'. He undoubtedly saw his new mission to the Ionian Islands as a natural extension of a controversy which had first made him prominent in continental affairs. See Morley, *Life*, 600.

[59] Gladstone to Young, 13 Dec. 1858, CO136/162.   [60] Ibid.

be met by 'a very strong exhibition of popular feeling'.[61] This warning had a special twist. Hitherto the Greek Church had not been in the forefront of appeals for union. The ambivalence was natural, since union might mean a similar fate for the Ionian clergy as had befallen the Church in Greece after 1830, their loyalty to the ecumenical patriarchate undermined, and clerical income subjected to state taxation. Yet to remain aloof from popular enthusiasms also carried dangers, and the police informed Gladstone that in Zante the Archbishop and clergy now intended to take the lead in the unionist demonstration being planned. This gave Gladstone a chance to work out how to respond to a second confrontation with a rowdy expression of Ionian ideals; on board he therefore closeted himself with Lacaita 'about a policy'—clearly Gladstone felt he did not have one yet.[62] As HMS *Terrible* approached Zante, it duly appeared that there were several thousands gathered about the principal mole, carrying placards and uttering slogans such as 'Long Live the Philhellene Gladstone' and the ubiquitous 'Long Live Union with Greece'. The important visitor was quickly landed at the stage of the residency, but the crowds besieged the outer gates of that building, and even penetrated to an inner courtyard, before being pushed out by armed soldiers. At the same time it was made known that if the demonstration for union continued, Gladstone—philhellene or not—would refuse to make any public appearance whilst on the island.

Gladstone had by now speedily clarified in his own mind where the limits of acceptability lay in his dealings with the movement for union with Greece. He had decided that where appeals were couched in sufficiently vague terms that they did not breach the laws of the Protectorate, needless conflict would be caused by failing to take any cognizance of them, an approach compatible with his own sympathy with that aspiration's fulfilment in some wholly indeterminate future. But where such appeals were couched in the language of demand—where, for example, they referred, however rhetorically, to the 'will of the Ionian People' as a higher authority—then they should be curtly and *decisively* dismissed. The crucial moment came with the inevitable levee on the following day, at which the Archbishop had let it be known that he would seek to put into Gladstone's hands a plea for union. This allowed Gladstone an opportunity to anticipate the Archbishop and set about the 'undeceiving' which was now the essence of the mission.

When, that afternoon in the residency grounds, the Archbishop was about to proffer the scroll carried ostentatiously around by one of his clerical entourage, Gladstone seized the moment to speak to the throng. He explained that it was on arrival in Cephalonia and Zante that he had realized how incumbent it was on him to dispel the illusions which clearly existed. He went on:

Notwithstanding the solemn and firm declaration made before the Senate, it seems that many persons still believe that in such times as these, in the present state of Europe and the

---

[61] Gladstone to Lytton, 13 Jan. 1859, PRO30/22/6, National Archives of the United Kingdom.

[62] Mathew, *Gladstone Diaries*, v. 347. According to the Ionian religious establishment under British Protection as fixed in 1823, there were archbishops in Corfu, Cephalonia, Zante, and Santa Maura.

Eastern Question, the idea of the union of these Seven islands, not with the whole Greek race, but with the actual Kingdom of Greece, is practicable, and that such an idea may be speedily realized by coupling it with my name as a supposed PhilHellene. They are deceived in this idea.[63]

The slight ambiguity here—that people might also be deceived by Gladstone's 'supposed' philhellenism—was entirely calculated. Lytton might once have seen Gladstone's Hellenic credentials as an advantage. What was seemingly an asset in London, however, often turned out to be a liability in the eastern Mediterranean. In this case assumptions about the Extraordinary Commissioner, true or false, had simply fuelled expectations and heightened the political risks. It was Gladstone's painful task to drive a stake into this process.

He had to be careful in doing so, however, not to fall headlong into reaction— the very reaction which Young himself had advocated. Gladstone knew that his movements in the Islands were closely followed in the British press; indeed, he went out of his way whilst travelling to boost the coverage of his activities.[64] He craved the publicity—but he could not afford to fall off the ideological and moral tightrope he found himself perched on. With several audiences, seen and unseen, before him in Zante, Gladstone was careful to add that he spoke 'with due respect for every sentiment of nationality, when restricted within the limits of possibility and justice'. With this caveat he proceeded:

But would not a person be out of his mind were he to take this subject of nationality as a rule or guide in the affairs of life, without taking into consideration time, manner, persons, means, consequences, and in short without regard to *facts*?

Doctrines of nationality of this sort could, he proceeded, prove a phantasm or a dream. But in the case of the Ionian Islands they were worse than a mere dream in their effect, since by clamouring for the impossible, they excluded the possible—that is, by refusing to consider the merits of useful reform, they left no option but the continuance of things exactly as they were, with all the defects clear to Britons and Greeks alike. 'This is the point', Gladstone drew towards an emphatic close, 'on which, so far as lies in my power, I undeceive you.' The real choice confronting Ionians, in short, was not the ideal one of Hellenic aspiration, but that made feasible by the immutable facts enshrined in the Public Law of Europe. Having made his point, Gladstone consented to the Archbishop reading out his own document, without himself actually receiving it, before disappearing inside the residency. Subsequently an address from the municipal councillors, couched in sweeping terms, was refused any recognition whatsoever—the open contempt shown to the lay politicians was telling. On 17 December at midnight (to avoid any further demonstration), Gladstone and the *Terrible* left for Athens—'and much rumination', he rather ruefully recorded.[65]

---

[63] 'Speech delivered by Mr. Gladstone at the Levée on Zante, 16 Dec. 1858', CO136/162.
[64] Mathew, *Gladstone, 1809–1874*, 136.   [65] Mathew, *Gladstone Diaries*, v. 348.

Before following Gladstone to Athens, more needs to be said about two factors with a special significance for the mission: language and religion. It had been assumed in London that, as an accomplished classicist, Gladstone would be able to make himself understood by educated Ionians. In Corfu this was not put to the test since Italian was the lingua franca of the leading classes—and in that tongue, especially under Lacaita's guidance, Gladstone was on firm ground. But however erudite his ancient learning, modern Greek was another matter. Lacaita used later to recount the story of how, on one occasion, Gladstone made a speech in the Islands purporting to be in the Greek tongue which, Lacaita remarked, was doubtless worthy of Demosthenes. Knowing no Greek himself, however, he turned to a distinguished Ionian standing nearby and asked what he had thought of the address. 'Oh, magnificent, magnificent!' the courteous Ionian responded. 'But I do not know what it was all about, for you see I know no English.'[66] There is in this something of the delicious comedy which, then and later, was also part and parcel of the Anglo-Hellenic encounter, but where—as in the Gladstonian mission—the plain meaning of words was vital, such potential obfuscation served to compound the difficulties.

Religion was a still more important variable than language. Lytton's original desire for a 'Hellenic Governor' compatible with the sympathies of Ionians implied one sensitive to the Greek faith. This was another reason why Gladstone seemed perfect for the job. He was the most ecclesiastical of all modern British politicians, and had taken a growing interest in Orthodoxy for some years. This has been ascribed to the appeal for him of 'any form of Catholicism that was unsullied by Rome'.[67] The appeal, however, also arose from Gladstone's trajectory as a political thinker. His early theocratic conceptions had imploded when confronted with the secular realities of contemporary Britain. But the residual idea of 'religious nationality' remained critical to his understanding of 'right' statehood. Few peoples offered a clearer example of a working 'religious nationality'—where, that is, the Church and its customs continued to encapsulate a society's ideals—than the Hellenes. Throughout his stay in the Islands, Gladstone showed a profound engagement with the Greek faith. Some aspects impressed him deeply. The senior priest at a Corfiote monastery visited by Gladstone bore all the physical marks of extreme self-denial. For an occasional self-flagellator like Gladstone, this meeting struck a very deep chord. 'I have not in the Latin countries', he wrote, 'seen any monastery like this'.[68] When, just over a week later, and having come to the end of his stringent attempt to 'undeceive' the Archbishop in Zante, Gladstone nonetheless stressed the veneration he felt for the local clergy, he was utterly sincere.

Such admiration was rare amongst British people. Those among them who had any dealings with Greek religion more stereotypically emphasized the ignorance

---

[66] Lacaita, *Italian Englishman*, 114.

[67] Mathew, *Gladstone, 1809–1874*, 156. For Gladstone's sympathy for Orthodoxy more generally, see Saab, *Reluctant Icon*, 69.   [68] Mathew, *Gladstone Diaries*, v. 344.

and squalor of ordinary priests and the materialism and sophistry of higher functionaries. Increasingly, the Greek Church was considered to be a source of instability in the eastern Mediterranean, encouraging dangerous manifestations of Hellenic nationality and irredentism. When it was therefore reported in the London newspapers that Gladstone had so demeaned himself as to make a practice of kissing the hands of senior Greek clerics, criticism mounted. Indeed, Lytton had second thoughts about how 'Hellenic' Gladstone should be, instructing that the Extraordinary Commissioner's attention should be drawn to the reports of the obeisance shown 'in case they had been exaggerated'.[69] Gladstone ignored this attempt to deflect him from what he considered an expression of proper Christian respect. Yet his earnest desire to effect a rapport with Ionian Orthodoxy was bound to be vulnerable. The story—so emblematic of cultural pitfalls—that Gladstone and the Bishop of Paxo, in bending simultaneously on one occasion to acknowledge each other, only succeeded in bashing their heads, was still in circulation during Lawrence Durrell's time in Corfu seventy years later.[70] Overall, Gladstone's belief in religious leadership as a source of 'moderation' in Ionian public life gradually dissipated as the mission proceeded, just as the Greek hierarchy was forced to react to the changing dynamics of their own circumstances.

So engaged, indeed, had Gladstone now become in Ionian problems that even in Athens—according to George Finlay, who met him in the household of the British minister Sir Thomas Wyse—he 'felt himself bound to devote all his... time to his mission as a statesman and not indulge his inclinations as a scholar'.[71] Considering the attractions of the ancient sites in the vicinity (somewhat offset by blustery weather) this was, perhaps, a nice comment on where Gladstone's real fascinations always lay. Inevitably, Gladstone received a courteous invitation from the palace, and whilst paying his respects there both King Otto and his formidable Queen, Amalia, discreetly avoided any mention of Ionian affairs.[72] Gladstone found Otto to be entirely moderate in his views, which led him to refute any idea that the Protectorate's problems arose from machinations in Athens—a conclusion consistent with a strong presumption that Ionian Hellenism was authentic, and not merely an artificial construct foisted on the islanders by outside forces. Yet this did not mean any diminution of Gladstone's gathering prejudice against any notion of cession, not least because, as he told Finlay, Russia and France 'are watching every pretext to bring England to the bar of the Congress of Vienna' for contravening its quasi-sacred settlement.[73]

During his few days in the Greek capital—still essentially a dusty Balkan town, though just beginning to assume an air of neoclassical sophistication—Gladstone

[69] Sir Henry Drummond Wolff, *Rambling Recollections*, i (London, 1908), 286.
[70] Lawrence Durrell, *Prospero's Cell: A Guide to the Landscape and Manners of Corfu* (London, 1945), 91. For a more contemporary account see Viscount Kirkwall, *Four Years in the Ionian Islands*, i (London, 1864), 210.   [71] Hussey, *Journals*, ii. 756.
[72] Gladstone to Lytton, 13 Jan. 1859, CO136/165.   [73] Hussey, *Journal*, 757.

was closeted with some leading Greek and Ionian residents to gain further insights into Hellenic views. None of these conversations, however, led him to differ markedly from the assessment which Wyse had recently provided for the British Foreign Office regarding attitudes in the Greek kingdom on union with the Ionian states, and which he successfully pressed on his guest.[74] This analysis stressed 'a divided sentiment' in Greek thinking on the matter, so that union was 'feared as well as desired'.[75] The desire sprang from a natural inclination to cohabit with fellow Hellenes; the fear from the prospect of incorporating a branch of their race whose competitive abilities and education were so finely honed. In sum, the Greeks of the kingdom were fearful that union would turn out to be 'an annexation of Greece to the Islands, not of the Islands to Greece'.[76] Such a version fitted neatly with Gladstone's new-found goal of 'undeceiving' the Ionians, since any undue enthusiasm for union could now be countered by the allegation that the mainland Greeks were themselves equivocal in their hopes. Suitably refreshed and reinforced in his assumptions, Gladstone retraced his steps to Corfu, where he arrived on 24 December.

Thereafter, Gladstone only left Corfu twice during his stay in the archipelago. He shortly visited Paxo, where, with relief, he found that 'the people behaved admirably'.[77] He also made an overnight trip to the coast of Albania. This was Gladstone's only visit in his lifetime to the Ottoman Empire. 'The whole impression', he wrote in his diary, 'is most saddening: it is all indolence, decay, stagnation: the image of God seems as if it were nowhere.'[78] To the extent that this minor foray helped fix a prejudicial image of the Ottoman realm in his mind, it has been suggested that this was a moment of some importance for Gladstone's development.[79] Other than these excursions, however, he now stayed in Corfu town, and over Christmas buckled down to completing the voluminous reports of his mission—even refusing the Youngs' dutiful invitation to Christmas lunch at the palace. On 28 December the first, and main, report was dispatched to Queen Victoria, whose personal representative he was.

At this point Gladstone's characteristic methodology and his natural intellectual bent become crucial. The climax of his Ionian interlude illustrate both to perfection. As for his method, Colin Mathew has written that:

Gladstone approached problems in two ways. First by massive and detailed analysis resulting in a practical solution and defended by overwhelming empirical argument, laborious correspondence, and dextrous institutional manipulation; second, if a problem moved him sufficiently, by a reflective article or book review, or in a major instance, by a book.[80]

---

[74] Wyse to Malmesbury, 2 Dec. 1859, FO32/263.
[75] Gladstone to Lytton, 13 Dec. 1859, CO136/165.
[76] Wyse to Malmesbury, 2 Dec. 1859, FO32/263.   [77] Mathew, *Gladstone Diaries*, v. 362.
[78] For Gladstone's visit to Albania see Morley, *Life*, 605–8.
[79] Mathew, *Gladstone Diaries*, v. 362.
[80] Mathew, *Gladstone, 1809–1874*, 61.

The Ionian Islands were never to merit the book, or even the review; they were, after all, mere dots on a map. But as a massive and detailed analysis, his three reports which were to make up the whole were superb specimens of the Gladstonian genre. They exemplify Gladstone's 'ferocity of consistent moderation'.[81] His basic instincts were always consolidatory and preservationist, but his style and mode of argument could be radical and unforgiving. Indeed, there was in the latter trait an intimidation of both those written about and those written to, which perhaps helps to explain Queen Victoria's aversion to Gladstone and his heavy analytical fare. Just as with regard to civil service reform in England, where Gladstone's primal instinct lay in the 'extending, confirming, cleansing, and legitimising an existing elite',[82] so in the Ionians it was to revise, cleanse, and legitimize the existing Protection. In essence Gladstone, consciously or unconsciously, approached the Islands and their government as a rather faded British institution in need of refurbishment. This tendency towards the imposition of English categories onto a Greek culture was part of a dislocating pattern in Anglo-Hellenic discourse which had been present at the very establishment of the modern Hellenic state. It was now to gain a characteristic Gladstonian flourish.

The first, and most important, of Gladstone's reports as Extraordinary High Commissioner amounted to well over 12,000 words, and arrived in London on 10 January.[83] There was not much time for a joyful Christmas in the Gladstones' Ionian household. This imposing state document put much emphasis at the outset on 'the particular solicitude' for the affairs of the Islands to which Britain was obligated under the Treaty of Paris. It was, indeed, this necessary 'solicitude' that invested them with a special moral dimension in the realm of European diplomacy and made English governments vulnerable to allegations of having fallen short. Whilst going out of his way to express the conviction that the Protectorate had been a benefit to Ionian society, he proceeded to examine what had gone wrong over many years. Most of these conclusions Gladstone culled from earlier Colonial Office papers. Thus the reforms of 1848–49 had made things worse, rather than better, and succeeded only in shattering the 'reform party' itself, leaving the way open for the monopoly of the cry for union with Greece. At the heart of this critique was the Senate, the proper role of which had been subverted by the way in which it had been exploited by successive Lord High Commissioners, and out of kilter in its relationship to the popular Assembly. The latter itself had been superseded by the unilateral acts of the Protectorate under the guise of *atti di governo* and left to founder amidst its own constitutional and moral irresponsibility. The result was that the very arrangements of the Ionian constitution had become 'an engine of corruption', and although these corruptions, Gladstone stressed, were not the fault of individuals, they had become endemic to the system.

---

[81] Ibid. 142.   [82] Ibid. 85.
[83] For Gladstone's first report see enclosure in PRO30/6/22.

Against this background, Gladstone posed a series of questions and answers. Could the status quo with all its blemishes be allowed to continue? The honour of the protecting power ruled this out. Was it possible to seek a solution by going back on the earlier reforms? Echoing what he knew to be the Colonial Secretary's strong feelings, Gladstone underlined the need for 'the strictest legality' and recognition of Ionian independence. There had, therefore, to be a way forward, not backwards. The issue, then, was whether an effort should be made 'to regulate the government of the islands by means of a popular but balanced constitution'. In answering this, Gladstone met the argument that the Ionians were not fit for truly free institutions with the retort that 'fitness is nowhere to be found perfect, but exists only in various grades of imperfection'; adding that only the gradual accretion of habit could foster true fitness, since 'in the Constitutional life of a people, the errors of today are the safeguards of tomorrow'. As John Morley observed, for Gladstone the Islands offered a conveniently oblique method of reflecting on problems of British, as much as Hellenic, governance.[84]

What clearly shaped Gladstone's judgement as much as these broad principles was the need to relate Ionian solutions to the general tendency in metropolitan colonial policy over recent decades. An extended quotation from his report is necessary here:

> In no one of your Majesty's Colonies did there exist, previously to the last twelve to fifteen years, any form of what is termed Responsible Government. But within that period it has been extended generally to the North American and Australian Colonies, as well as the Cape of Good Hope, with great advantage and satisfaction on all sides, and it may now be said to form the fixed rule of the policy of the British Empire in all your Majesty's Possessions which are not stamped with an exceptional character, either as military Possessions, or as being in mere infancy, or as being too critically divided between dominant and subject races. In the absence of evidence to the contrary, presumptions of no inconsiderable weight arise out of the general tenor of British policy, in favour of the extension of similar advantages to the Ionian Islands.

There were various problematical aspects to this (for example, regarding the military utility of the Islands) which Gladstone passed over silently, but there was one which he could not avoid. Did the Ionian people actually *want* Responsible Government English style? Would they not use free institutions to demand more vociferously union with Greece? The biggest obstacle to the proposal taking shape in Gladstone's report lay, as he confessed, in 'the spirit of Hellenic nationality', and the critical portion of his text dealt with that theme.

Gladstone proceeded to recognize that spirit arising as it did from ties of 'blood, religion, language, vicinity, and predominating intercourse'. He even went so far as to admit that when it was asked what bound together the very disparate Ionian Islands 'the answer can be but one. It is this very Hellenic feeling: They [the Islanders] are Ionians because they are Greeks.' Such broad assertions of Hellenic

---

[84] Morley, *Life*, 620.

sentiment eventually entrenched Gladstone in the philhellenic pantheon. The fact that the Gladstonian hand that gave also took away often seemed to matter less. Certainly Gladstone's report made clear that under Ionian circumstances a good deal of subtraction was required from ideals of nationality. He argued that most Ionians understood 'that there are the strongest reasons against the accomplishment of their wish at the present epoch'; whilst in Greece itself—here he re-echoed the views of Sir Thomas Wyse—the attitude towards union was ambivalent. Yet such observations were only the prelude to Gladstone's main emphasis on the Public Law of Europe which made it a criminal act of folly on Britain's part were it to allow the legitimate aspiration of Ionians to slide into premature reality. He banged the point home as remorselessly as he could:

What would be the position of Corfu, with its great strategical importance, in the hands of a Power so unable as Greece must be to defend it? What would be the condition of the Ottoman dominion in Albania, with Corfu an appendage to Greece? What obedience the inhabitants of Candia [Crete], Thessaly, Macedonia, the [Aegean] Islands, could, as Greeks, be expected to pay to Turkish sovereignty, after the Ionians of the Seven Islands had, as Greeks, been relieved of British Protection?

It was this danger that Ionian union with Greece might trigger bloody rebellions against Ottoman authority elsewhere, entailing heavy Christian losses and potentially setting the powers at odds with each other, combined with the associated recognition that the matter was in fact 'the narrow corner of a very great question . . . the reconstruction of all political society in South-Eastern Europe', which Gladstone felt was the insuperable obstacle to abandoning the Protectorate, however gross its faults might be.

The practical problem was how to impress the absoluteness of this truth so that not only was it transparent to ordinary Ionians, but that even the most inveterate radical would fear to challenge it, in case their obliviousness to the public good was revealed. This was the point where Gladstone the clear-eyed political analyst gave way to the slippery tactician. He unveiled the idea that the Assembly might be led to frame a petition, couched 'in terms of due respect', asking for union with Greece. If this petition should receive a prompt and unyielding rejection directly from the British sovereign to 'the regularly elected organ of the Ionian people', there was a possibility that the unionist movement would at last be stopped dead in its tracks, and an opportunity created for the benefits of practical reform to be accepted. Thus could be engineered that 'undeceiving' on which Gladstone had set his sights ever since he had been so amiably kidnapped by the good, if misguided, townspeople of Argostoli.

Yet did it make sense to recognize so clearly the moral force of Hellenic aspirations in the Ionian states, and yet close the door to their fulfilment in any practical sense so definitively? Since the very ties that held the Protectorate together as a unity were so ephemeral, could Ionians really be asked to accept its continuance far into the future—until those Greek *Kalends* when the problems of Crete,

Thessaly, and Macedonia were also solved? Would not some over-subtle attempt to propagandize the necessity for this only heighten an aversion to Britain? Gladstone did not deal with these objections, but, since a get-out might be needed, he did admit that the chances of success were not assured. 'In any case', Gladstone concluded in the event of failure to inveigle the Ionians to drink at the pool of colonial reform, 'they will then better learn that England is not the friend of abuses, nor the enemy of freedom; and your Majesty's Government will cease to be responsible in the eyes of Europe for the political and administrative evils the prevalence whereof in the Seven Islands is so much to be lamented.' In this portentous rhetoric was detectable a hint of the view held by the mission's critics that its real object had really always been simply a buffing-up of the tarnished honour of Britain under the guise of ministering to the real needs of the Ionians. Certainly there seems little doubt that the coldness which now suddenly grew up between Gladstone and his young liberal and aristocratic aide, Gordon, was related to the latter's realization that the mission's goals had subtly changed along the way.[85]

Whatever the underlying problems, Gladstone was in no mood to dwell upon them. The Islands had already consumed enough of his time, and he had pressing reasons for going home—it had appeared that unless he returned soon his eligibility at the looming general election for his Oxford University seat would be jeopardized. 'This is a great blow. The difficulty and the detriment are serious,' Gladstone wrote to Bulwer Lytton, though the urgency this gave for escaping from an increasingly invidious situation was probably not, in truth, unwelcome.[86] Even in forwarding his report to the Queen, Gladstone had impressed on the Colonial Secretary that the situation should be 'brought to a crisis without loss of a day that can be spared',[87] and on 1 January he started drafting Her Majesty's reply to the envisaged petition that was now the key to the psychological puzzle of the Ionian problem. It was remarkable metaphorical testimony to the exercise that Gladstone saw himself as engaged upon that the following period covered by his diary was entitled 'The Circumcision'.[88] Yet before this sensitive operation could be carried out, there had to be one surgical preliminary: the dismissal of Sir John Young. Once accomplished, it would fall to Gladstone to call the Legislative Assembly into an extraordinary session, and nudge that body towards the 'prayer' to the British sovereign, the decisive crushing of which was critical to the desired outcome. Here was a fine example of the 'dextrous institutional manipulation', and lack of scruple under pressure, central to Gladstone's methods and personality.

The reason Gladstone gave for his brisk advice was that unless Young was got rid of, it could not be unequivocally understood by Ionians that union was impossible 'with reference to the present and all proximate times and circumstances', since the publication of the stolen dispatch had made it known that Young had

---

[85] See Diary of James Lacaita, 4 Jan. 1859, quoted in Lacaita, *Italian Englishman*, 114. In referring to Gordon's 'slackness', Roy Jenkins, *Gladstone* (London, 1995), 192 merely reflects Gladstone's bias.
[86] Quoted in Morley, *Life*, 612.   [87] Gladstone to Lytton, 27 Dec. 1858, CO136/162.
[88] Mathew, *Gladstone Diaries*, v. 360.

at one time himself supported such an outcome. In fact, as we saw earlier, Lytton had always intended Young's recall. Nor did he spare the latter's feelings in a private letter on 7 January, telling him that any confidence in his judgement had long since vanished.[89] He was then formally dismissed, and on 12 January Gladstone temporarily assumed the full range of conventional as well as extraordinary duties in the Protectorate as Lord High Commissioner.[90] The Youngs only stayed some days to pack their bags—the farewell reception at the palace, necessarily attended by Gladstone, must have been an excruciating event.[91]

For the British, everything now hinged on the extraordinary session of the Legislative Assembly to be opened on 25 January. In the interim, Lytton and his colleagues in the Colonial Office were busy studying Gladstone's proposed package. The devil, as always with reform, lay in the detail. Ironically, the analogy between British colonies and the Ionian states so critical to Gladstone's thinking was no more persuasive to ministers and officials in the metropole than it was to most Ionians, albeit for very different reasons. The tell-tale sign was found in an error of fact in Gladstone's report. Responsible Government *had* been applied in British North America and Australasia, but *not*, as Gladstone had asserted, at the Cape. Its track record was therefore only credible with regard to what were deemed to be 'healthy' populations principally composed of British settlers, and where, crucially, the imperial Parliament had the power if necessary to suspend the constitution if things went wrong.[92] Neither of these preconditions existed in the Ionians. In failing to say what recourse there might be should a Lord High Commissioner find himself confronted with local ministers still bent on union with Greece, Gladstone had glossed too easily over a very serious problem.

The other worry in London concerned Gladstone's recommendation for a blanket abolition of the coercive powers of the high police.[93] This was in tune with Lytton's liberal predilections. But such predilections had to engage with certain realities. Lytton advised his colleagues:

suppose a case, not improbable, in which persons may be fomenting an insurrection—the Executive may have proofs of guilt—but no jury would convict—A crafty and ruthless Lord High Commissioner would allow ... the insurrection to run its course, martial law

---

[89] Lytton to Young, 7 Jan. 1859, CO136/165.

[90] In *The Times* (18 Jan. 1859) it was speculated that Gladstone had clearly given up political ambitions at Westminster 'should he really settle down into the administration of a third-rate dependency'. In reality, he was already plotting his imminent re-entry into the metropolitan fray. The fact that Gladstone's disappearance into the obscurity of service overseas was taken at all seriously at this time remains of some biographical interest.

[91] At Gladstone's urging, Young was soon made a Knight Commander of the Bath in an attempt to assuage his resentment, and that of his fellow Peelites.

[92] Merivale note, 12 Jan. 1859, CO136/165.

[93] This recommendation was influenced by the separate and very detailed report on the history of the Cephalonian rebellion of 1849 submitted by Gladstone. The latter contained a scathing criticism of the suppression then carried out by Sir Henry Ward. Its composition marked a watershed in Gladstone's own thinking about disorder and public policy, and as such suggestively pre-echoes his later evolution over Ireland. See enclosure in Gladstone to Lytton, 27 Jan. 1959, PRO30/22/6.

would step in, blood be shed, executions follow—But all might have been prevented . . .
by a few sentences under the High Police.[94]

A repeat, possibly in extended form, of the Cephalonian rising and repression ten
years before was clearly in Lytton's mind—a precedent which the recent Mutiny in
India, with its bloody aftermath, can only have underscored. He queried whether
the gaining of a 'momentary lull' would be worth the price of running such risks
of breakdown in a reformed, but dangerously disarmed, Protectorate. These and
other matters were put directly to Gladstone in a full dispatch on 18 January.[95]
But from the start Gladstone's extraordinary powers had invested him with discretion over his own recommendations. Anyway, it was not really expected in
London that what was to be put forward would ever actually be implemented.
The green light was therefore given despite the obvious pitfalls identified. A high
degree of dissimulation, even of farce, now marked events. That what Gladstone
was about to unveil in Corfu as conducive to the public welfare was seen in
Whitehall as full of pitfalls, in the unlikely event of its ever being accepted, gave an
extra twist to an episode whose moral flexibility was always its distinguishing
characteristic.

For Gladstone, it was the petition, not the reforms, which held the key to the
end-game of his mission. Afterwards Ionian politicians were to allege that they
had been lured into a sucker punch, and in this they were not far from the truth.
Certainly ahead of the Assembly the suggestion for a 'prayer' for union with
Greece addressed to Queen Victoria was already being deftly put about through
Sir George Bowen's contacts with the Ionian political world. For the *Rhizospastes*
there were great dangers in allowing the Assembly to be drawn into a process
brokered by a Lord High Commissioner. On the other hand, Ionians had to weigh
the cost in snubbing anything Gladstone proposed—his future enmity was not to
be lightly incurred. When the Assembly opened on 25 January, therefore, the
petition issue emerged as the chief dividing line in local Ionian politics.

In opening the Assembly, Gladstone's tactic was to see that it moved promptly
to the framing of a national desire for union. He waited for his moment before, on
28 January, intervening directly in the debate with a message from the palace to
advise the Assembly that the 'one and only legal method of expressing the desires
of the Assembly is by a "petition, memorial, or representation", in conformity
with the Constitutional Charter', not omitting that he felt confidence in the 'pru-
dence' of such action[96]—the last remark deflecting the arguments of those who
felt that to be drawn into the process would be fatal to the real prospects of union.
A Lord High Commissioner actually encouraging the expression of the national
desire was remarkable. After some further argument, the Assembly decided, rather
nervously, to act in the sense of Gladstone's message. That evening (29 January) a
public illumination of Corfu town as a good augury for union was decreed by the

[94] Lytton note, 12 Jan. 1859, CO136/165.   [95] Lytton to Gladstone, 18 Jan. 1859, ibid.
[96] Gladstone to Lytton, 31 Jan. 1859, ibid.

municipal authorities. Whether the patchy response indicated, as Gladstone believed, that most Ionians had no real desire to see union implemented in the foreseeable future, or whether it rather reflected a suspicion that all was not quite as it seemed, is best determined in the general light of events.

Once decided on sending a petition, the Assembly turned to the matter of its framing. Inevitably, the wording itself became the focus of acute controversy, the outcome being a composite of the varying suggestions put forward. On the one hand, there was due recognition of loyalty to the British Queen—the people of the Seven Islands, it was stated, 'approaches with reverence your Most Mighty Throne'.[97] On the other hand, the petition stated that the Ionian people through their representatives 'proclaimed with one voice the single and unanimous will of the Ionian people' for union with the kingdom of Greece, language more in keeping with the popular sovereignty inherent in Ionian radicalism. This petition was formally adopted by the Assembly on 30 January, and handed by its President to Gladstone, who had been impatiently awaiting the text all afternoon. In rushing the document to the Colonial Office for presentation to Her Majesty, Gladstone gave an assurance that he had consulted persons 'highly skilled in modern Greek' (predictably the pliable Bowen) who provided the convenient advice that in this case the rendering from the original text in relation to Ionian desires should be 'disposition', with its less imperious overtones, rather than 'will'. This got over the problem of Gladstone's earlier principle that any request for union with Greece expressed in peremptory form could not even be considered. The truth was that Gladstone was bent on the unhindered transmission of a petition for his own purposes, and was not to be denied by mere forms of language.

In the Colonial Office the answer that Gladstone wished to be provided with in reply to the Ionian 'prayer' for union—that is, 'a brief but unmistakable negative'[98]— was understood and accepted. There was a niggling problem that the Colonial Office's own legal advisers were aware of no precedent for a direct message from the monarch to a legislature other than that at Westminster. So complete was Gladstone's control of Ionian policy, however, that he was in effect told that if this legal scruple did not worry him, then ministers and officials in London were not disposed to mind either.[99] Gladstone was simply provided with the proposed formula of Her Majesty's crushing reply with blanks left for him to fill in as required. Gladstone was now armed for the climax he anticipated which, according to his own analysis at least, stood a chance of dishing the radicals, and rallying moderates back into a 'Party for the Protectorate'—that elusive precondition for the survival of British authority in the Islands. At this crucial point Gladstone tendered his resignation to London on 1 February, his designated replacement being Sir Henry Storks, a senior military officer who had for some months been attending the Colonial Office's premises waiting for an opportunity of employment

[97] 'Petition of the Ionian Assembly', enclosed, ibid.   [98] Carnarvon note, 9 Feb. 1859, ibid.
[99] Lytton to Gladstone, 12 Feb. 1859, Gladstone Papers, MS Add. 44241, BL.

to arise.[100] Storks at once set off for Malta. Meanwhile Gladstone remained in post, the news of his impending disappearance becoming known in Corfu on 5 February—not accidentally the day when Gladstone, speaking in Italian, unveiled to the Assembly both the Queen's answer to the Ionian petition, and his own proposals for constitutional and political reform.

The profound local surprise caused by Gladstone's resignation was grist to the mill of pressurizing Ionian legislators. The imminence of his departure for England, where he would regain his position as a figure of great influence, was thereby calculated to reinforce his leverage over local opinion. From this position, Gladstone handed down his various *obiter dicta*. He first had printed in the Ionian *Gazette*, on 5 February, Her Majesty Queen Victoria's gracious response, in which it was starkly asserted that she could not possibly consent to abandon the obligations she had undertaken in the Protectorate and that, where necessary, 'the sacred duty of obedience to the laws' would be enforced. The covering instruction to Gladstone, also published in the *Gazette*, was to make this determination known 'without loss of time, and in the most solemn manner, to the Legislative Assembly, and to the Ionian people, in order that both one and the other may fully and clearly comprehend their actual position'. This was unmistakably to lay down an anchor to which future Lord High Commissioners might cleave as the starting point and legitimization of their policies.

This psychological coup aimed at the radical faction, and any fellow travellers, formed the background against which Gladstone set out in a lengthy speech before the Assembly his plans for reform. The details we need not relate here, except to say that Gladstone stuck by his commitment to Responsible Government as a solution for the Protectorate's ills. The only amendment to the recipe of his report to the Colonial Office was a somewhat more qualified allusion to the reduction in the powers of the high police. The British colonial analogy—with its pitfalls in relation to the Ionian states—was omitted, it being merely stated that they were invited 'to follow the example of the nations, great and free, which have been content to establish effectually for themselves the great principles and guarantees of Constitutional Government'. The resolutions which Gladstone now put before the Assembly were, he stressed, offered to the legislators as a whole, not as parts which could be rejected or accepted according to preference. 'Her Majesty has now done her part,' Gladstone concluded, putting on his mantle as the sovereign's Extraordinary Envoy, 'and the rest, Mr President and Gentlemen, is in your hands.' Shunting the onus of responsibility—above all, the moral responsibility—over to the Ionians themselves was the essence of Gladstone's purpose as he now began to manœuvre towards his own exit from the scene.

---

[100] It was common practice for officials seeking colonial preferment whilst on furlough in London to be given daily access to the Colonial Office for lobbying purposes. In fact Storks had been reading up the Ionian papers in the Office alongside Gladstone on the eve of the mission, and it seems likely that even at that point he had been pencilled in as Lord High Commissioner once Gladstone's job was done. See Drummond Wolff, *Rambling Recollections*, 282.

As soon as these resolutions were in the public domain, they were fiercely attacked by the *Rhizospastes*, who depicted them as 'deadly gifts' the acceptance of which could only mean 'national suicide'.[101] It was undoubtedly a critical moment for Ionian Hellenism. The previous reforms of 1848 might have failed, but a new programme, once implemented under the lustre of Gladstone, might well throw up permanent obstacles to *enosis*. With the stakes thus raised, the possibility loomed that the more extreme radical factions would launch an appeal, not to the British sovereign, but to the other powers. Such unilateral excursions into European diplomacy were, as Gladstone realized, the real 'point of danger' for the future of British Protection,[102] and to prevent it he pronounced himself ready to use the full powers of the high police. His preparedness at this juncture—somewhat to Lytton's dismay—to fall back on repression was typical of Gladstone's glorious self-contradiction, but was also highly paradoxical in relation to the mission's origins.

On 9 February Sir Henry Storks arrived in Malta. But the moment he set out on the last leg of his journey to Corfu, Gladstone's authority as Lord High Commissioner would effectively pass into commission. Gladstone therefore instructed Storks to stay in Valetta whilst the political struggle in the Ionian Islands— one in which his prestige needed every gloss it could muster—was resolved one way or the other. From 5 February onwards the Assembly had procrastinated, desultory discussion of the resolutions punctuated by successive adjournments. The real discussions were going on in private villas and the ubiquitous coffee houses. At first, Gladstone entertained the hope that these delaying tactics indicated that the balance was swinging towards those too fearful to reject what was on offer.[103] To counter the impressions still circulating of his not entirely successful visits to Cephalonia and Zante, he even made a visit to a village close to Corfu town, Old Perithia, at which, in a rather staged demonstration, loyal inhabitants garlanded the great statesman, and told him of their ready acceptance that union remained an impossible dream.[104]

Within a few days, however, Gladstone's hopes had been dashed. 'It was clear . . .', he confessed, 'that the Assembly . . . were now able to play against me the game of time, with the certainty of winning.'[105] Instead of the Ionian politicians falling into a Gladstonian trap, it suddenly became clear that Gladstone was caught in a snare himself—kept dangling by the Assembly, his authority superseded by the waiting Storks, and his prestige waning by the hour. 'I did not feel justified', Gladstone told the Colonial Office, 'in requesting Sir H. Storks further to retard his journey for the chance of being able to give to the Assembly explanations [about the reforms] which they show so decided a disposition not to ask for.'[106] On 13 February he therefore telegraphed Storks to make his way promptly to Corfu, and set the following Saturday as the day of his own departure. In the

---

[101] See translation of Zante newspaper (*Pinas*), 5 Feb. 1858, in CO136/165.
[102] Gladstone to Lytton, 7 Feb. 1859, ibid.
[103] Gladstone to Lytton, 10 Feb. 1859, ibid. [104] Ibid.
[105] Gladstone to Lytton, 14 Feb. 1859, ibid. [106] Ibid.

circumstances it was far better for Gladstone to get out fast, before any degree of personal humiliation should become too transparent.

By the same token, however, it was absolutely necessary for Gladstone at this point to set out clearly the case for judging his mission—with its seemingly abortive outcome—as a success. Staring defeat in the face, he told Lytton, in a dispatch that was likely to be published in due course, that he did not regret his recent actions as Lord High Commissioner.[107] He stated categorically of the resolutions:

They were necessary in order to vindicate the policy and character of England. They were necessary in order to clear the ground for an earnest attempt at improved administration. They were necessary in order to test the ordinary quality of Ionian patriotism ... [and] to supply the people with some means of judging ... the conduct of their Representatives, and of deciding for themselves whether they will or will not be dupes.[108]

That the Extraordinary Mission to the Seven Islands had vindicated British honour, whilst testifying to the follies of Ionian patriotism, had indeed been the essential goal more or less from the start, and nothing evoked this truth more clearly than Gladstone's exculpatory analysis.

Storks duly arrived in Corfu on 16 February, and the following day the ceremony of his inauguration as Lord High Commissioner took place before the Senate. It was part of the underlying logic that simultaneously the tempo of unionist rhetoric went up a notch. Above all concerned to put the best possible gloss on things, Gladstone considered this effervescence 'eminently favourable to England', since it showed how the Ionian politicians had been manoeuvred into adopting 'an entirely false position'.[109] When a vote was taken in the Assembly on a radical motion, only six members out of thirty-eight lined up firmly on the Protectorate side. Especially galling was the fact that more than half of this majority was made up of individuals who had supposedly been tied to the British by virtue of patronage they had previously received. Exacting a price for this betrayal was afterwards to be amongst Sir Henry Storks's principal tasks.

On the morning of Saturday, 19 February, Mr and Mrs Gladstone received their own farewell in the Palace of St Michael and St George, attended by the President and members of the Senate, and the leading civil functionaries; 'The Archbishop [also] came, which I rather regretted,' Gladstone noted, an index of how his appreciation of the Greek Church had become more strictly political, and therefore prejudicial.[110] The Legislative Assembly did not bother to suspend its sitting or even to send a deputation, though a couple of loyal representatives attended of their own volition. On the other hand, there was no unionist demonstration at the harbour, as there certainly would have been had Gladstone left from the Southern Islands. The great man was allowed by the polite Corfiotes to take his leave with a reasonable degree of decorum. All senior officers of the garrison

[107] Gladstone to Lytton, 7 Feb. 1859, in CO136/165.   [108] Ibid.
[109] Gladstone to Lytton, 17 Feb. 1859, ibid.   [110] Mathew, *Gladstone Diaries*, v. 370.

were present as the Gladstones were taken aboard HMS *Terrible*, bound for Trieste. 'The sympathy and good feeling expressed towards Mr. Gladstone', Storks sought to add a positive spin, 'were certainly sincere and well merited, for no one had ever worked more laboriously or with greater sincerity to secure the welfare of the Ionian people, and the improvement of their institutions, than the distinguished man who has just left these shores.'[111]

It was not only Ionian radicals, however, who took a more jaundiced view than Storks of Gladstone's conduct. The fact was that even British expatriates in Corfu suspected his intentions—Gladstone, for example, was never invited to any garrison mess during his stay. Such implied suspicion was frequently taken up back in Britain, and had a clear focus in criticisms of the Ionian resolutions, the object being to wound the great man before he re-entered domestic English politics.[112] The prominent Whig Lord Grey put down a motion on Ionian affairs for debate in the House of Lords, stating that the rejection of Gladstone's resolutions was 'in the highest degree desirable—that there could be no such great public misfortune as that they should be accepted'.[113] The reason given was the weakness already identified within the government—that in the Islands British ministers would have no power to reassume control if a democratic experiment spun out of control. Lord Derby, as Prime Minister, succeeded in putting off any parliamentary debate, but he reluctantly afforded the pledge that no Act of the Ionian legislature would be applied in practice until it had been approved in Westminster. In short, even if Ionian politicians had experienced a last-minute conversion to the rapidly receding echo of Gladstone's entreaties, there was no certainty that the resolutions would have survived the gauntlet of the British Parliament.

The fate of Gladstonian reform in the Ionian states was anyway already determined. On 25 February it fell to Storks to receive the overwhelming rejection of the proposals by the Ionian chamber. Though respectful in tone, Storks reported that only one thought now pervaded the formal reply—'a revival of the question of Union with Greece'.[114] This was hardly what had been hoped for when Gladstone had set out for the eastern Mediterranean four months before. Storks found solace in the prospect of being able to fall back on the abrupt terms of Her Majesty's rejection of the recent petition, permitting him to assert that the whole matter of union 'is finally settled, and that I cannot at any time, or under any circumstances, hold any conversations with the Assembly on the subject'. Indeed, the very purpose of Gladstone's tactics as they had evolved was to clear the path of obstacles for future Lord High Commissioners. But even in the Colonial Office there was no belief that the petition saga had effectively capped the union movement, and a fresh wave of pessimism pervaded Whitehall.

111 Storks to Lytton, 20 Feb. 1859, CO136/165.
112 'Ah', Lord Aberdeen famously responded when one colleague speculated that Gladstone had been damaged by his Ionian diversion, '*but he is terrible in the rebound.*' Quoted in Morley, *Life*, 613.
113 *Hansard's Parliamentary Debates*, 3rd series, vol. clii (Lords), 21 Feb. 1859, col. 597.
114 Storks to Lytton, 28 Feb. 1859, CO136/165.

Meanwhile the outcome of the mission constituted a weakness in the defences of the ailing government back at home. A campaign got under way to force the tabling of Gladstone's dispatches. In the Lords on 11 March Derby argued rather feebly that any publication of documents from the mission remained undesirable because it would produce facts which would 'cast considerable censure on some persons not here to explain or defend their proceedings'.[115] This was taken to be an unsavoury attempt to use Sir John Young's battered reputation as the pretext for a cover-up. But even after Derby's Tories finally left office a couple of months later, the new English ministers remained adamantly opposed to any public inspection of the papers arising from Gladstone's period in the Islands. The truth was that the latter's dispatches had been so devastating in their frank description of the paralysis within the British Protection that no government in London could contemplate lifting the lid on it,[116] and that lid was kept firmly shut for the duration of the Protectorate—after which, of course, the episode lost all conceivable interest for practising politicians.

What, then, might be a final judgement on the mission and its fruits? Gladstone was sent to the Islands to remedy the faults of the Protectorate without prejudicing its future. Whilst there he developed an analysis and prescriptions which fitted with this goal. These included a theory of Hellenic nationality which sought to be sympathetic without being incompatible with the continuance of British rule. The underlying realpolitik in this approach lay in the need to identify and exploit divisions amongst the Ionian political class. That Gladstone failed in this latter respect was not due to the lack of social and ideological fractures within the Islands but because those fractures lay outside the range of his prescriptions and tactics—or those of British officialdom more generally.[117] The basic truth was always that the Protection could either be kept going as a semi-veiled military autocracy, or it could be got rid of *tout court*. Any attempt to find a middle way was bound to become trapped in contradictions, and encourage ever more desperate gambits, such as Gladstone's manipulation of the unionist petition to Queen Victoria. Sir John Young would not, of course, have framed matters precisely in these terms, but many of them were embedded in his own critique. As so often in the buried history of public policy, it was an interpretation defeated and condemned in its own time which was, on balance, somewhat closer to the truth.

A French historian, in dealing with these Ionian events, once referred to the 'erreur de psychologique' behind Gladstone's failure to see the black hole separating Hellenic nationality and British reform in the Protectorate.[118] If so, it was an error

---

[115] *Hansard Parliamentary Debates*, 3rd series, vol. clii (Lords), 11 Mar. 1859, col. 23.

[116] See Carnarvon to Gladstone, 7 May 1859, Gladstone Papers, MS Add. 44391, BL.

[117] Divisions within local Ionian politics can be traced in Eleni Calligas, 'The "Rizopastoi": Politics and Nationalism in the British Protectorate of the Ionian Islands, 1815–1864' (doctoral dissertation, London School of Economics, 1994).

[118] Édouard Driault, *Histoire diplomatique de la Grèce*, ii: *La Règne d'Othon: la grande idée (1830–1862)*, (Paris, 1926), 469.

driven inexorably by the higher necessities of a Public Law of Europe as refracted through the prism of British interests in the contemporary Levantine world. Although Gladstone ended up disillusioned with 'the Greeks in general and the Ionians in particular',[119] he did not alter his views on Hellenic national sentiment as a purely platonic ideal—in a parliamentary debate during 1861 he said that it still grieved him 'when I see that sentiment ... treated in this country with ridicule and scorn'.[120] Yet during the years which remained to British Protection in the Islands he remained implacably of the view that it was not for the Ionians to decide their own future, but for the British and others to decide it for them in the light of the requirements of a stable international concert. Oddly enough, Gladstone's prestige amongst Eastern Christians, and especially the Hellenes, did not suffer unduly as a consequence. They needed his sympathy too much—and often in circumstances more strained than they had been in the Ionian archipelago—for this 'blip' as a practising philhellene to loom large; it has therefore been left for the occasional historian (usually but not exclusively Greek) to puncture with gently ironic asides.

As for the wider Anglo-Hellenic paradigm with which we are critically concerned, the sequence we have followed captured certain compelling traits. Its dilemmas were never more acute than in contexts where British 'masters' ruled over Greek colonial (or quasi-colonial) 'subjects'. It is a truism that such colonial mastery is belied by complicated reality; and few instances offer such a rich illustration of this subversion than the Ionian Islands. If British versions of Hellenic statehood were necessarily bent to fit with their own local and regional stake, the Greeks were themselves impelled by a political culture in which the 'Great Idea' provided one of the few effective binding agents. In this perspective the British were always measured according to the 'legend' they helped to create at Navarino. They were usually found wanting; and against that benchmark Greek experience appeared to prove conclusively that the British were never more suspect than when they came bearing their 'deadly gifts' of compromise and reform. Here was a paradox within a conundrum from which Anglo-Hellenism could never quite escape in the Ionians or, as we shall see, elsewhere. For the moment, however, we must return to the difficulties faced by Sir Henry Storks once HMS *Terrible*, with the Gladstones aboard, had steamed away past the great fortress of Corfu whose fate, curiously, was also to be bound up with the eventual foundering of British Protection.

[119] Kirkwall, *Four Years*, 236.
[120] *Hansard's Parliamentary Debates*, 3rd series, vol. clii (Commons), 7 May 1861, col. 1683.

3

The Abandonment of the Ionian Protectorate, 1859–1864

Ionia will be the Ireland of Greece.

(Sir Henry Storks, 28 Jan. 1863)

A wonderful world is this Corfu, but—we leave it!

(Edward Lear, *Journal*, 14 Feb. 1864)

In appointing Sir Henry Storks as Lord High Commissioner, the British government had selected somebody with previous experience of the Islands, since he had served there as a Royal Engineer twenty years before. In fact, as we noted earlier, even before Gladstone had begun his own mission, Storks seems to have already been designated his eventual successor.[1] He enjoyed a high reputation after a distinguished record in the Crimean conflict, being responsible for much of the logistics in the eventual withdrawal of the British Army from that peninsula.[2] But his intended task in the Islands was not to preside over another evacuation. Although Gladstone's reform plan had failed, his reports contained many suggestions for the proper conduct of affairs. In essence, the challenge facing Storks was to play the role already envisaged by Gladstone as an ideal Lord High Commissioner, one who rooted out petty corruption, who acted vigorously and implacably up to the limits of British responsibility *but no further*, and who occupied the narrow but Olympian heights of a more efficient and cleansed Protection.

This was to be reform without the reforms, and Storks approached the task with a British regimental zeal. Hopeful that the recent mission had put the Protectorate's opponents on the defensive, he reconvened a normal session of the local Parliament on 2 March 1859. Any illusions were quickly dashed. The legislators sought to adopt an 'improper and insulting' rule that the Lord High

---

[1] See above 40.

[2] In the Crimea Storks had commanded the garrison at Scutari, and done much to assist the labours of Florence Nightingale, to the extent that the latter, in a testament drawn up in case of her own death, entrusted her legacy to Storks as the senior officer who 'had given the most sterling and consistent support to the work entrusted to me by Her Majesty's Government'. Sir Edward Cook, *The Life of Florence Nightingale*, i: *1820–1861* (London, 1913), 294.

Commissioner had no authority to address the Assembly.[3] Whilst the *Rhizospastes* had feared to insult Gladstone, they had no inhibitions about snubbing his successor. Storks promptly prorogued the legislators, telling the Colonial Office that 'the time has come for making the Assembly aware that they are not to insult the Protectorate with impunity'.[4] Those issues of honour and dignity embedded in the Gladstone mission, far from easing, intensified until the day over four years later when Storks (exhausted, disillusioned, but, in his own eyes, thoroughly vindicated) presided over a second major withdrawal in his military career.

After cutting Parliament short, Storks set off on a tour of the southern Protectorate. One of Gladstone's recommendations had been that Lord High Commissioners should break out of a fixed circle of Corfiote advisers. As a result, no previous occupant of his post travelled more extensively through the archipelago than Storks. He was struck by the fact that even in supposed hotbeds of 'disaffection and *Rhizospastism*' he met with great courtesy.[5] He interpreted this not only as reflecting the much-lauded amiability of the general population, but as an expression of a strong reaction of Ionian opinion in favour of the Protection. The 'tranquillity' he was able to report in his official dispatches could conveniently be repeated in Westminster, and thereby broadcast to the whole of Europe. There was a pattern here that was to be endlessly recycled. For British authority in the Protectorate, 'tranquillity' had always possessed a grail-like quality—so seemingly tangible and yet ultimately so elusive—and this was never to be more so than in the mounting crisis of its final years.

Above all, what Storks felt he needed for success was a prolonged period during which, after all its Gladstonian excitements, the Ionian public mind might 'lie fallow'.[6] But any chance that Ionian opinion would do so disappeared even before Gladstone himself had got back to Britain. 'Bad signs and menacing accounts meet us', the latter noted on 26 February as his family party travelled through Tuscany, 'of the political condition of this country',[7] and almost immediately the Italian *Risorgimento* began to break its banks. In April 1859 France and Piedmont went to war against Austria. The 'canon of Magenta' (4 June 1859) not only turned the tide against Austrian rule in Italy, but reignited questions of nationality eastwards and southwards as well.[8] The vibrations were powerfully felt in the Ionian Islands, integrated into the web of European politics not least through the linkages of 'Mazzinian' secret societies characteristic of both Italian and Ionian radicalism.[9]

---

[3] After Storks had left the Assembly chamber, a priest appeared to 'purify and bless' the house after alleged desecration by a 'heretic'. See Kirkwall, *Four Years*, 249.

[4] Storks to Lytton, 10 Mar. 1859, CO136/165.   [5] Ibid.

[6] Storks to Lytton, 10 Mar. 1859, CO136/165.   [7] Mathew, *Gladstone Diaries*, v. 372.

[8] See Driault, *Histoire*, 450–460 on the effects of Italian events in south-eastern Europe.

[9] Ionian political clubs and societies—such as the 'Sacred Struggle' which featured prominently at this time in the demonology of British Protection in the Ionians—operated as a conduit between Italian popular organizations and 'political committees' in the Greek kingdom. Critics saw them as playing a notable part in destabilizing the affairs of south-eastern Europe. See Eleftherios Prevalakis, *British Policy towards the Change of Dynasty in Greece* (Athens, 1953), 19–30.

The Greek kingdom bore a more oblique relationship to events and forces in Europe. Nevertheless, rumours recurred of a landing by Garibaldi and his bands on Greek soil, usually said to be assisted by Ionian money. In this manner 'national questions' in both West and East were increasingly thrust up against each other. Given the swirl of events, very few political minds lay fallow thereafter.

A merger of Western and Eastern Questions was exactly what the new ministry in London led by Lord Palmerston after June 1859 wished to avoid. The allegedly pro-Austrian tendencies of the previous Derby government had been a prime focus of the attacks made on it by opponents. The coming together of Whigs, Liberals, and Peelites which brought Palmerston back to the premiership, with Lord John Russell as his Foreign Secretary and Gladstone as Chancellor of the Exchquer, was a watershed in British politics during the nineteenth century: it spawned the Liberal Party of the future. As yet, however, this incipient liberalism remained deeply divided on domestic issues—above all, over the extension of the suffrage. Anti-absolutism, and the championing of oppressed nationality abroad, provided the most effective rallying points within the new government's ranks. None could exploit that shared feeling better than Palmerston, who had long cultivated a species of braggishly patriotic moral leadership. Suggestively that style and ideology, culminating in the most distinctive parliamentary evocation of the ideal of *Pax Britannica*, had been forged some years before on a Greek anvil— the famous 'Don Pacifico affair' of 1850.[10] Palmerston's supremacy in British politics through to his death in 1865 hinged on sustaining the credibility and *brio* of this approach to European affairs.

Over the dominating Italian Question, Palmerston and Russell emerged as unambiguous advocates of national liberation. Yet south of Trieste British policy appeared in a different, even 'Austrian', light—one opposed to any readjustments to those treaty structures on which the European status quo was based. Indeed, Palmerston was more committed than any other British politician to shoring up the existing scheme of things in the Eastern world, whatever course his instincts took elsewhere. To do otherwise would have tarnished those Crimean memories on which his own personal record hinged. The inconsistency between Palmerstonian proclivities so ostentatiously displayed in favour of national principles in northern Europe, but which appeared so flaccid when they arrived on Europe's south-eastern marches, was exploited by critics, whether in the Westminster Parliament, the French Chamber, or at the Habsburg court in Vienna. Sarcasm was frequently

---

[10] During the celebration of the Eastern Easter in 1847, an Athenian crowd ransacked the house of a Maltese Jew, Don Pacifico. As the latter was a British subject, Palmerston as Foreign Secretary championed his claim for compensation from the Greek authorities. In Jan. 1850, a Royal Navy squadron enterered Piraeus and seized forty Greek merchantmen. Subsequently Palmerston refused French mediation and secured his demands. His actions were immensely controversial in British politics, but the impassioned debate in the House of Commons 'gave Palmerston the opportunity of securing the triumph of his life in a five hour speech ending with the resonous peroration, *civis romanus sum*'. See G. P. Gooch (ed.), *The Later Correspondence of Lord John Russell, 1840–1878*, ii (London, 1925), 67.

reinforced by special allusion to the Ionian Islands, where the policy of the Palmerston government was so clearly at odds with an expressed national feeling. The ideological and moral sensitivity of the Ionian issue within wider British diplomacy was in inverse proportion to the physical size and significance of the Islands themselves, and crucially affected the ending of the Protectorate.

As Gladstone had come to appreciate whilst in the Islands, the real 'point of danger' for Britain was that its Ionian opponents would find in the evolving Italian crisis an international vent for their grievances. From the summer of 1859 the possibility loomed that Emperor Napoleon III of France might call a European congress. Had this happened, the *Rhizospastes* would undoubtedly have attempted to insert themselves into the process.[11] Although such a congress never met, the shadow of such an occasion hung over Palmerston and Russell. They therefore looked to Sir Henry Storks to keep the Ionians as quiet as possible. It mattered very little to them what humiliations and insults the Lord High Commissioner incurred, providing he succeeded in preventing any external seepage. Conversely, signs that Storks was not in control, that the Protectorate might suddenly implode, strained ministerial nerves and gradually exhausted the reserves of commitment on which the Protectorate was dependent for its life.

The most basic requirement for tranquillity in the Islands was the avoidance of any episode which might trigger physical disturbances on the lines of 1848–49. To this end, Storks adopted 'a policy of wise concessions', typical of which was a new compromise with the Archbishop of Corfu over the conduct of the annual festivities of St Spyridon.[12] Stabilizing the Protectorate, however, required more than the avoidance of rebellion. Storks faced the challenge of nurturing a positively pro-British feeling amongst the population. In his early days he toyed with such ideas as encouraging a 'moderate' newspaper to challenge the pro-unionist monopoly of the local press,[13] and with such symbolic tokens as installing a picture of Queen Victoria in the Palace of St Michael and St George to underpin a more 'loyal' atmosphere—the latter suggestion rejected in the Colonial Office as 'not dignified'.[14] More subtle was the conception of deflecting Ionian energies into cultural and commercial, rather than political, patriotism. It was Storks's ambitious private secretary, Henry Drummond Wolff, who got the Ionian Association off the ground, though the British government's refusal to provide a subsidy did little to help.[15] Ministers and officials in London were distinctly patronizing towards such efforts, which they felt underestimated 'the ... forces

[11] Ionian radicals were especially preoccupied with the possibility of a new European congress because the manner in which their representatives had been excluded from the Congress of Vienna in 1815 was a major grievance from the commencement of British Protection. See Calligas, 'The "Rizopastoi"', 28.   [12] Storks to Lytton, 18 Apr. 1859, CO136/165.
[13] Storks to Lytton, 14 Mar. 1859, ibid. In London Gladstone sought to arrange £50,000 from secret service funds to establish such an organ. See Wiede (ed.), *Disraeli*, 400.
[14] Lytton note, 12 Mar. 1859, CO136/165.
[15] Storks to Newcastle, 4 Feb. 1862, CO136/177.

which really impel political action in the islands'.[16] But the alternative for local British authority was to sink back into a wave of defeatism. That was not Storks' personal style.

The dilemmas of British Protection continued to be defined most acutely in relation to the Ionian Parliament. There was a crude physical dimension to this. The Assembly chamber in Corfu town was confined, and when the Lord High Commissioner came to deliver his opening address, he was repeatedly hemmed in by the throng, including the benches open to the public rising above the floor of the legislators. The fear of 'insult'—eyeball to eyeball—was real and present in such circumstances. Storks' predecessors had long sought compensating support from the more dignified upper house, or Senate. But even there the recent uproar surrounding Gladstone's proposals had undermined the British grip. No wonder Storks—like most of his predecessors—tried every excuse to keep Parliament out of session. The ideological and moral consistency of British governments might require that all the forms of Ionian constitutionalism be maintained, but for a military man like Storks the prospect of direct exposure to Ionian politicians was excruciating—like being sent into a battle with a key flank wholly unprotected.

In fact, when Storks reluctantly convened the Assembly in December 1859, things turned out not so badly. His address was not boycotted, and met a more 'moderate and respectful' response than any Lord High Commissioner had enjoyed for some years.[17] The interpretation that the forces of *Rhizospastism* were in retreat was, however, misplaced. The tactic of the radical leadership was to ensure that, with events still flowing strongly in Italy, the Ionian Parliament should remain in session in case a European congress be called at any moment. When the Parliament had run its course by February 1860, no such opportunity had arisen. Thereafter the less likely it became that Ionian unionism would be able to tag itself onto wider shifts of nationality in Europe, the more the contest within the Protectorate returned to its established rhythm of bitter if usually bloodless confrontation.

By January 1861 Storks repeatedly signalled to the Colonial Secretary, the Duke of Newcastle, that the approaching new Parliament was likely to be marked by a fresh surge of unionist demands. Storks' request for authority to prorogue was predictable enough; less so was his sardonic request for precise instructions as to how to carry out his ordinary tasks should such prorogation be denied.[18] Since Whitehall had no idea on the latter subject it much disliked having the question raised. Bureaucratic friction was always a mark of a 'colonial' regime sinking lower in the water. Noting that failure once more to call an assembly would only 'proclaim to the world the embarrassing state of things' in the Islands, Newcastle's junior minister, Chichester Fortescue, proceeded to frame the central question:

---

[16] Note by Herman Merivale, 12 Jan. 1860, CO136/169.
[17] Storks to Newcastle, 22 Dec. 1859, CO136/166.
[18] Storks to Newcastle, 18 Jan. 1861, CO136/171.

'But are there not friends of the Protectorate', he cryptically asked, 'on whose assistance Sir Henry Storks can rely as the safest course?'[19]

Here was the nub of the matter—there were hardly any such friends left. They had been deserting the Protection for decades. After the 'disillusioning' of Gladstone's mission, the drift quickened. The risks run by those who remained in overt relationship with British authority rose. 'We are living', Storks once noted in an observation that caught the flavour of things, 'in the worst times of the old Venetian republic. The same suspicion, the same fear of friends and foes, the same apprehension of being denounced as an enemy, and an absolute want of moral and political courage, are the leading characteristics of Society here.'[20] Social contact between British officialdom and expatriates and the Ionian classes, once reasonably free and easy at such venues as the Corfu racetrack, now tailed off almost completely.[21] Storks' emphasis on a lack of moral courage on the part of leading Ionians was central to his own understanding of the challenge he faced; the local intelligentsia saw only the black hole separating British libertarian rhetoric and political reality in the Ionian states.

Storks' political strategy as Lord High Commissioner bore the twin hallmarks of indignant passion and tactical manoeuvring. He had no hope of making headway with the long-standing champions of union with Greece. His target was reserved for the cadre which had received British favours, but had increasingly deserted the Protection at vital points, most recently in the parliamentary vote on Gladstone's resolutions; those who took British bread, but who also tried to insure themselves with unionism as the wave of the future. What Storks termed his 'policy of strict neutrality', therefore, amounted to a denial of favours to those who had wavered, in effect exposing office holders—especially at elections—to the cold blast of the political marketplace. In this way the Lord High Commissioner hoped to elevate himself above the fray, in the expectation that those now left to fend for themselves would return to the British fold, suitably chastened. As for unreliable Senators, Storks cut their perks, exposed their petty corruption to investigations, and upbraided any residents who hesitated to execute his instructions.[22] This drive to put into place under Ionian conditions a new system of supposedly neutral supervision was eventually to have considerable significance on a much larger plane, since it proved a formative influence on one of Storks' principal aides in Corfu, Liuetenant Evelyn Baring, who later—as Lord Cromer—was to preside for many years over British rule in Egypt.[23]

[19] Chichester Fortescue to Newcastle, 8 Feb. 1861, CO136/173.

[20] Storks to Lytton, 11 Apr. 1859, CO136/165.

[21] For the growing gulf between Ionian and British society in Corfu, see Storks to Newcastle, 26 Aug. 1861, CO136/170.

[22] Dixon, *Colonial Administrations*, 191 relates how Sir Thomas Maitland, in establishing the residency system, had allowed for minimal supervision of post holders. A series of peculiarly corrupt petty autocracies emerged. For the asperity with which Storks set about hauling residents back into line see his letter to Baron d'Everton (Resident, Santa Maura), 29 Aug. 1859, Storks Papers, National Army Museum (hereafter NAM).

[23] As Lord Cromer, Baring's practical philosophy as British High Commissioner in Egypt after 1885 reflected the 'non-interventionism' which Storks had pioneered in the Ionian Islands. In Cairo, however, this method proved just as prone to contradiction and ultimate failure as it had in Corfu.

Instead of chasing some Ionian politicians back into the Protectorate camp, however, the result was to drive them definitively over to the unionists. Storks' actions reinforced the very configuration of forces which had doomed Gladstonian reform. At some indistinct point in this process the political balance tilted danger-ously. The British Protection had never succeeded in rooting itself into the social foundations of the Islands, as even the old Venetian primacy, with all its failings, had.[24] Yet now the movement for union with Greece, despite its own internal frac-tures, was soldered into a powerful social and cultural force. There was a conscious-ness of this cracking in the edifice of Protection when, faced with Storks' acid request for 'precise instructions', the Colonial Office in London insisted that the Lord High Commissioner should provide 'a full account ... of the present state of the parties and of public opinion and feeling on the subject of Union with Greece and towards the Protection', including the prospects for the looming elections—in short, an assessment of the viability of the existing regime.[25] Such a demand for comprehensive political accounting indicated that a watershed was approaching.

The document Storks produced was his testament as Lord High Commissioner.[26] Its finer detail need not concern us. In it he described all Ionian parties as 'ropes of sand without discipline or cohesion', and unionism as a blackmailing tactic to obtain official bribes. The fact that at elections the vast majority of Ionians voted for the *Rhizospastes* needed explaining. But this caused Storks little difficulty. Protagonists for union with poor and overtaxed Greece which 'could only bring ruin to these [Ionian] states' did so safe in the expectation, he alleged, that it would never happen. As for the lower orders and peasantry, brought within the force-fields of nationality and religion through 'national' propaganda, their hatred for a grinding proprietorial and business class was thereby controlled and deflected. 'I feel convinced', Storks stated, 'that if British Protection were withdrawn from these States, an attack would be made on the *signori*, and bloodshed would be the conse-quence'.[27] The reason for this stalling of economic improvement Storks found in the impossibility of constructive legislation after the reforms of the later 1840s. 'The machine', Storks stated baldly, 'will not progress.' It was against such a depressing background that he told ministers there was little to be done except to turn a blind eye to unionist agitation so long as it stayed within constitutional bounds, and otherwise to seek to ensure that the Protectorate remained wrapped in 'quiet obscurity'.

This assessment was received in London with intense disquiet. 'It looks ... as if the L[ord] H[igh] C[ommissioner] did not see his way,' the Duke of Newcastle commented;[28] and there was always the lurking danger that Storks, like Young before him, might try to confront ministers at some inconvenient juncture with a painful and unwanted choice. Newcastle himself had no solution to offer, other

---

[24] Calligas, 'The "Rizopastoi"', 12.   [25] Newcastle to Storks, 19 Feb. 1861, CO136/173.
[26] Storks to Newcastle, 5 Mar. 1861, CO136/171.   [27] Ibid.
[28] Note by Duke of Newcastle, 25 Apr. 1861, CO136/173.

than that 'the only mode left of operating on the mind of the [Ionian] people is . . . by leading them to the acquisition of wealth as an object of desire'.[29] The idea that the commercially supple Ionians needed lessons in acquisitive materialism was hardly persuasive. When a new session of the Assembly was convened, and the legislators speedily drew up 'a Bible of indictment against the Protection', the British government reluctantly authorized its suspension. Yet this move was attended with a novel degree of tension and ill feeling. There was a demonstration in the chamber itself; and matters were not improved when HMS *Orion* accidentally landed two explosive shells on a passing Greek steamer bearing the provocative name of *Enosis Panhellinion* (Pan-Hellenic Union). Through the summer of 1861 the atmosphere surrounding the Protectorate assumed a new brittleness.

Already, then, British Protection in the Ionian Islands was irreparably broken. The life force had gone out of it. It was friendless, paralysed, and exposed. Although Storks still insisted the Islands were 'perfectly tranquil' on his customary perambulation in the autumn, he had to confess that the *Rhizospastes* 'were in possession of the field';[30] and when elections to a new Parliament took place in early February 1862, not one member returned was opposed to union with Greece. Quiet obscurity was not to be had. But now something happened to shake the kaleidoscope. On 17 February news reached Corfu of a serious outbreak at Nauplion, the old Greek capital, against the rule of King Otto. At that juncture two young Bavarian princes, both possible heirs to the childless monarch, had arrived in Corfu, en route to Athens; and at the urgent request of the Greek consul-general, they were turned back in their path before their presence could intensify disaffection in both the Islands and Greece. It was the interaction of British dilemmas in the Protectorate and the Greek kingdom which thereafter shaped events.

King Otto's problem was similar to that of Sir Henry Storks: the desertion of fair-weather friends to add to the challenge of incorrigible enemies.[31] The reason for his unpopularity, however, was keenly disputed between Otto and his British detractors. The latter lambasted him for not being a good constitutional ruler in the English style. This was the constant refrain of Sir Thomas Wyse as British minister at Athens.[32] In doing so he avoided taking into account the view—expressed, for example, by one experienced foreign observer of Greek affairs—that if Otto had simply reigned and not ruled he would never have lasted half as long as he had.[33] Otto believed that he was unpopular with his people because, after an

[29] Note by Duke of Newcastle, 22 Mar. 1861, ibid.

[30] Storks to Newcastle, 8 Nov. 1861, CO136/175.

[31] For a sympathetic biography of a monarch usually maligned by British commentators see Bower and Bolitho, *Otho I.*

[32] The appointment of Sir Thomas Wyse, an Irish 'reform' politician, to be the British government's representative to Greece in 1849 was the first senior diplomatic post to be held by a British Catholic after the emancipation legislation of 1829. His other claim to fame—and a source of deep personal unhappiness—was that he was married to a Bonaparte. See James Auchmuty, *Sir Thomas Wyse, 1791–1862: The Life and Times of an Educator and Diplomat* (London, 1939).

[33] See Memorandum by George Finlay, 'Must the Constitutional King of Greece reign and not govern?', FO32/323.

attempt in 1854 to grab a slice of Thessaly whilst other people were preoccupied with the Crimean conflict, he had caved in to British and French pressure and cracked down on those forces behind the Thessalian adventure. Otto and his formid-able Queen Amalia sought to screen themselves from the resulting Anglo-French occupation of the Piraeus, never once going near the European encampments; but the humiliation of this alien presence rubbed off on them nonetheless. Otto's foreign race and Catholic religion made him all the more vulnerable to the tag of 'traitor', not least when firm action was taken to impose better control over the northern frontier, including the prosecution and occasional execution of the klephts and brigands of an evolving 'modern' Greek legend.

Stabilization and reform on the Ottoman land frontier, indeed, encapsulated a tension between generations, classes, and ideals at the heart of the fragile Greek state—between an old system symbolized by the picturesqueness of the traditional *palikari*, and the shock of the new epitomized by bourgeois decorum in politics and society.[34] This was one reason why the Great Idea of Hellenic expansion tended increasingly to relieve pressure on itself by sliding sideways to focus on islands, where the risks and tensions could be better controlled. Yet the Crimean War also introduced a long-term crisis within Hellenic ideology since it emerged that the Slavic peoples might challenge any Greek monopoly of the post-Ottoman succession, and in so doing win Russian favour. A gathering apprehension that destiny was not necessarily on the side of Hellenism was symbolized by the visit to Athens of Tsar Nicholas I's brother, the Grand Duke Constantine, in the spring of 1859. The latter went out of his way to be cold to his hosts, failed to provide the usual *doucements*, and refrained from the accustomed rhetorical flourishes about a new Byzantium.[35] Russophile sentiments in Greece were by no means to disap-pear in the future, if only because the community of Orthodox feeling was to prove resilient. Nevertheless, a certain vulnerability in the Great Idea, mixed with a sense that other patrons might prove more reliable and potent, made themselves felt. British awareness of these vibrations was reflected in the comment of one diplomat, referring to the growing Greek 'dread' of Russian aims in Macedonia, that it was 'not desirable that this uneasiness should entirely cease'.[36]

The swelling tide of popular opposition to Otto's rule led to student demonstra-tions as Palmerston's new ministry took office in London. Wyse's assessment was that it would take 'a mere trifle' to touch off a decisive explosion.[37] Yet without any guarantee as to who would follow in Otto's footsteps, the minister warned Lord John Russell that Britain might prejudice one of the few points of leverage it pos-sessed in Eastern politics 'which we have spent so much blood and treasure to secure'.[38] Such language reflected that what was at stake for Britain in Greece was the legacy of the Crimean conflict and the shaky gains enshrined in the Treaty of

---

[34] For an excellent study of these themes, see Koliopoulos, *Brigands with a Cause*.
[35] Wyse to Malmesbury, 12 May 1859, FO32/268.
[36] Cornwallis Elliot to Russell, 17 July 1860, FO32/275.
[37] Wyse to Malmesbury, 16 June 1859, FO32/268.   [38] Ibid.

Paris of 1856. Wyse's advice that, in addition to a naval reinforcement in Greek waters, 'we [the British] must make up our minds as to a successor, in case of an Abdication',[39] was all very well, but the trouble was that other people began to do the same, sucking Greece back into an old-fashioned competition between *soi-disant* British, French, and Russian 'parties'. When students demonstrated in Athens, it was pictures of the French Emperor, his prestige boosted by his leading role in *Risorgimento* diplomacy, and of King Victor Emmanuel, that they carried aloft. The British had to begin to deploy what local assets they had in an incipient struggle for preponderance. Wyse's wish for more Royal Navy ships was granted, but ships cannot sail far inland. Gladstone as Chancellor gave important concessions to Greek agricultural products in his 1860 budget—trading towns along the Gulf of Corinth were lit up in his honour—but modern Greeks did not live by currants alone.[40] Yet among the Great Powers only Britain had a very tangible gift at its disposal sure to gratify Hellenic aspirations: the Ionian Islands. It is the relationship of the Protectorate's future to this much larger context that is therefore crucial to our perspective.

The visit of Queen Victoria's second son, Prince Alfred, to the Ionian Islands and Athens in late 1859 marked a conscious British attempt to regain some ground. He showed himself receptive to all things Hellenic, whether walking with Storks through Corfu town to the fascination of the locals, or when sightseeing the ruins of Athens.[41] Wyse was struck by the 'moral effect' of the Prince's visit;[42] and the manner in which opposition figures in the Greek Assembly praised British constitutional models was, Wyse felt, evidence that 'the policy of England has begun to be better understood in Greece' than for many years past. This better understanding had less to do with constitutional proclivities than with the growing conviction in Greek political circles that British sympathy— itself rebounding from disillusionment with Ottoman reform—might offer them the European mentor they required. Such a prospect was recycled through the influential London Greek community, situated as it was in that classic Victorian niche where banking and politics met.[43] The Greek government's young and fluent representative in London, Charilaos Tricoupi, was a favoured protégé of Russell, and thereby able to gain access at critical moments even to Palmerston himself.[44] In this milieu the idea that the Islands were in fact a burden to Britain best disposed of when an opportunity arose became commonplace; nor was it surprising that such a notion was exaggerated when transmitted back to Greece.

---

[39] Ibid.   [40] Wyse to Russell, 16, 28 Feb. 1860, FO32/274.

[41] For Prince Alfred's visit to Corfu see Storks to Newcastle, 9 Dec. 1859, CO136/166.

[42] Wyse to Russell, 7 Jan. 1860, FO32/274.

[43] For the role of the London Greek press see Stefanos Xenos, *East and West* (London, 1865), 18–20.

[44] Prevalakis, *British Policy*, 24. In 1863 Tricoupi was elected as the delegate of the Greek community in Britain at the Parliament in Athens. After his election as Prime Minister of Greece in 1882, he emerged as the dominant figure in Greek national politics during the rest of the century, noted above all for a bias towards internal 'improvement' and against dangerous irredentist adventures. He died in 1896. See Thanos Veremis and Mark Dragoumis, *Historical Dictionary of Greece* (London, 1995), 92.

During 1860 and into 1861 the expectation that the British government was about to cede unilaterally the Ionian Islands to Greece surfaced more and more frequently. Such rumours invariably sent a frisson through the suggestible world of Athenian politics, and even when disproved left a residue behind. They also took on more ambitious forms as instability in the Balkan provinces of the Ottoman Empire—principally in Montenegro, Serbia, and the Danubian principalities—rose.[45] One widely touted conception was that of a new Eastern and Hellenic throne, to which Prince Alfred would be raised, composed of the Ionian Islands, parts of European Turkey, Thessaly, and possibly Crete. Passed on through Trieste newspapers to the Ionian press, it was assumed that this composite entity would be under Ionian leadership, and that very shortly it would 'swallow up the present Kingdom of Greece'.[46] Who would end up swallowing whom was to prove an important variable in the minds of all parties involved in a looming enlargement of Greece. Meanwhile there now appeared a conjuncture in which protagonists of the Great Idea could see a real possibility of winning British favour, expanding Greek frontiers, *and* getting rid of King Otto, all in one go.

In Athens Otto's grip on affairs proceeded to slip badly, and Wyse did little to help him recover his poise. When the King sought a British guarantee of help in an emergency, Wyse acknowledged the original commitment to him in 1832 was 'clear and binding on the Powers, but how far its maintenance by force was obligatory was another matter'.[47] These were weasel words, since Greece remained a society where without force any principle was wholly nugatory. Nor did the attempted assassination during September 1861 of Queen Amalia, whose bearing won her sympathy in some quarters, affect Wyse's stance. His only new suggestion was that plans should be laid for the Royal Navy to protect the Bank of Greece if necessary—the security of bullion was always the first consideration of both the British and French representatives. It was a mark of Otto's panic that, under European pressure to clarify the muddled matter of the succession, he at last summoned to Athens the two Bavarian princes who had reached Corfu only to be sent back, as we have already seen, when news of the Nauplion mutiny in February reached the ears of Storks.

But it was not only Otto who was made to look into the void by the Nauplion insurgents. So too were the powers. If Otto fell with tension high on the northern frontiers, the chances of a controlled transition to a successor were thin. European officials played a part in negotiating an end to the revolt, and the request made by the ringleaders that they should be taken off by a Royal Navy warship was said by one commentator to be the first sign of a growing orientation towards Britain in Greek politics generally.[48] Another indication was the funeral in Athens of

---

[45] For the wider Balkan context at this time see Barbara Jelavich, *History of the Balkans: Eighteenth and Nineteenth Centuries* (Cambridge, 1983), 235–99.

[46] Elliot to Russell, 25 Nov. 1860, FO32/276.

[47] Wyse to Russell, 25 Apr. 1861, FO32/294.   [48] Finlay, *History of Greece*, vii. 264.

Sir Thomas Wyse in mid-April with the highest state honours, the much respected and venerable Archbishop of Athens (himself with only weeks to live) and various heroes of the independence war amongst the mourners.[49] Meanwhile, it was universally believed that 'the next outbreak [against Otto] will have more serious consequences'.[50]

Whilst the insurgency had raged, Palmerston and Russell were sufficiently rattled to dispatch a special mission to Greece in the form of Lord Russell's son-in-law Sir Henry Elliot.[51] His tasks included guiding Otto into more constitutional paths, and towards a clarification of the succession—the latter especially delicate, since it was assumed that the one thing keeping Otto on his shaky throne was the 'dread of disorder' which uncertainty about the future guaranteed. What British ministers wanted to scotch was a scramble amongst the powers to slide one of their own candidates onto the Greek throne—a competition Britain might too easily lose. There was a danger that the allegation that the British government was angling to elevate Prince Alfred, his popularity buttressed with the cession of the Ionian Islands, might trigger just what British ministers were seeking to avoid. In addition to persuading Otto that his mission bore him no personal ill will, Elliot therefore went about Athens after arrival trying to dissolve dangerous expectations attached to the name of Alfred.

The special envoy, however, had another task: to explore an understanding with the Greek government on the enlargement of the kingdom's frontiers, and (by natural extension) on relations with Turkey. On this matter British standing in Greece still suffered in comparison with other powers because of its intimate attachment to the Ottoman Empire. In Elliot's analysis, France especially

might not be more loved or respected than Great Britain, but she is looked to with more hope by the ambitious Greeks who, though knowing she is bound by the same obligations to Turkey, feel doubt as to whether she is equally desirous [as Britain] of maintaining the integrity of that Empire.[52]

Elliot had a very tricky hand to play. If an impression leaked out that Britain's obligation to Turkey was being diluted, the repercussions could be very serious in relations with Constantinople and within domestic British politics. On the other hand, Palmerston was beginning to apprehend that British policy needed to make provision should the Ottoman plank in its Eastern arrangements snap apart. Throughout his discussions Elliot therefore reiterated that his country's interest in the integrity of the Ottoman Empire 'was at least equally strong' as its commitment

[49] Wyse's family problems, combined with overwork at a time of high political tension, contributed to his death. His biographer notes, suggestively, on the condolences that '... the sympathy of the Sublime Porte was perhaps the most noteworthy'. See Auchmuty, *Sir Thomas Wyse*, 293.

[50] Drummond to Russell, 7 May 1862, FO32/302.

[51] Sir Henry Elliot had recently conducted a prolonged mission to Naples where his task had been to prod the much-criticized regime in the kingdom of the Two Sicilies towards better government. He was therefore seen as a logical person to send to the Greece of King Otto.

[52] Elliot to Russell, 27 May 1862, FO32/312.

to Greece. He told the King that 'there was only one way ... in which he [Otto] might attack Turkey', and that was by providing a model of good government which would *gradually* draw the Christian populations of Turkey within the Hellenic orbit.[53]

Yet to speak of 'attacking' Turkey at all was new, and obviously impressed Otto, because at their last meeting he returned to the theme. He told Elliot that he hoped, in the event of the Turkish Empire collapsing *from within*, that 'the sympathies of Great Britain would be on the side of Greece' in the ensuing reorganization.[54] Elliot nudged matters further by giving the assurance that providing Greece improved her internal economy 'there could be no doubt of what the feelings of Great Britain would be' in the unlikely event of the Ottoman Empire suffering some fearful disruption—an event, in truth, everybody expected at any time.[55] For his part, Otto ended by promising to pay more heed to constitutional principles *à l'anglaise*, and to settle the succession issue as soon as Greece settled back into normality.

Ultimately abortive in themselves, these discussions shed much light on what followed. A clear impression had been left by Elliot that Greece was being invited to develop herself as the prime legatee *under British aegis* of the ailing Ottoman Empire. He was too astute a diplomat to have left such an impression by mistake, though in his memoirs—by which time the vision had long faded—he was to cover his tracks by describing his talks with Otto as 'a pretty flight of fancy'.[56] At the time, however, some concrete token was required to embody the potentiality of a reinforced Anglo-Hellenic link. This was where the fate of the Ionian Protectorate entered the reckoning—as a potential makeweight to hold the balance pending the emergence of a more fundamental equilibrium.

In fact over the following months conditions in Greece did not settle down. When Wyse's successor as British minister, Campbell Scarlett, stopped off en route in Corfu, Storks warned him that Otto was 'in greater danger than at the time of Mr. Elliot's departure'.[57] His enemies were closing in—including some on the British side. These included *The Times* newspaper, whose famous editor, Delane, was a frequent and privileged visitor to Palmerston's home at Broadlands, and whose correspondence at this time was dominated by Greek affairs.[58] One of Delane's journalists sent out to Corfu and Greece to cover events wrote back that those plotting against Otto 'wanted the courage to strike. We gave the cheer, which emboldened them to charge.'[59] The 'cheer' was a series of editorals aimed at Otto, long one of Delane's special targets. What can be said with some certainty is that Palmerston could have saved Otto, and chose not to do so. The value put on

---

[53] Elliot to Russell, 28 May 1862, ibid.   [54] Elliot to Russell, 30 June 1862, ibid.
[55] Ibid.   [56] Henry Elliot, *Diplomatic Recollections* (privately printed, 1900), 172.
[57] Scarlett to Russell, 7 Aug. 1862, FO32/303.
[58] See Arthur Dasent, *John Thadeus Delane: His Life and Correspondence*, ii (London, 1908), 59.
[59] F. Eber to Dasent, 6 Nov. 1862, JTD/11/67, Delane Papers, News International Archive (hereafter NIA).

Greece as a partner in regional politics might be rising, but it could not be a Greece with Otto and his Byzantine-dreaming Queen at its head.

The facts of Otto's fall need not detain us.[60] On 16 October the royal couple embarked on a tour of the provinces. A few days later a revolution broke out at Vonitza, and spread rapidly. The European representatives decided that Otto's life would be in danger if the royal couple returned to Athens, and the diplomats met with the King on a Greek frigate at Piraeus. An incipient British primacy in Greek politics showed itself when the King turned to Scarlett for salvation. It was not forthcoming. 'A revolution of so rapid and general a character ... was not foreseen', Scarlett professionally lied, '... I did not conceal from the King my belief that there was no alternative for him but his immediate departure.' Since even the loyalty of the Greek sailors could not be trusted, Otto and Amalia were taken off to safety in HMS *Scylla*.[61] When they arrived in Corfu on 22 October, the Queen spoke bitterly in an interview with Storks of how they had been let down. Storks listened politely, but commented afterwards that Otto and Amalia merited little sympathy 'for I believe that he [Otto] had little love for us, and was mixed up in a good deal of the intrigue and agitation which have been going on so long in the Ionian Islands'.[62] Whether that agitation would cease now Otto was gone, however, seemed unlikely.

The struggle to fill the vacuum in Athens got under way immediately. European marines landed to protect the legations, and the Royal Navy was reinforced in Salamis Bay. A 'party' in favour of the Duke of Leuchtenburg, related by marriage to the Tsar, became active. But both in the Ionian Islands and in Greece a pro-British tendency surged powerfully. 'In these Islands', Storks reported, taken aback by such a phenomenon amongst Ionians, 'the cry is all for Prince Alfred.'[63] When he visited the island of Santa Maura and attended a dinner at the casino, memorabilia of the British Prince covered the walls and, rather touchingly, even 'the decorations on the Tables'. It was, indeed, widely believed that Alfred was already on his way to accept the throne, and would appear at Patras any moment. 'The Greeks', commented Storks, for whom apparent *naïveté* could only be a cover for Hellenic super-subtlety, 'with their habitual acuteness see where their interests lie and act accordingly.'

Storks' interpretation of the movement for Alfred—'absolutely fanatic' as it became—was simplistic. The extremity of the phenomenon was dictated by recent Greek experience of what the costs of disorder and revolution could be. George Finlay, the great historian of Greece, and long-time resident of Athens,

---

[60] For full accounts see Scarlett to Russell, 24 Oct. 1862, FO32/304 and especially 'The Fall of Otho', Papers of George Finlay, E. 23, British School at Athens.

[61] There was a certain appropriateness to this departure under the Royal Navy's auspices, since Queen Amalia had first arrived in Greece on board HMS *Portland* following her marriage to King Otto during Nov. 1838—one more testimony to the interweaving of British naval power and Greek statehood.   [62] Storks to Scarlett, 3 Nov. 1862, Storks Papers, NAM.

[63] Storks to Newcastle, 4 Nov. 1862, Storks Papers, NAM.

observed that after Otto's departure the Greeks were 'at sea without a compass', and Alfred—like HMS *Icarus*, cruising up and down the Maniote coast pacifying minor outbreaks—offered the prospect of a British anchor in stormy times.[64] Precisely because the name (one might say the metaphor) of Alfred was already circulating when the new revolution occurred, it became a rallying point for those who saw both safety and advantage if they could 'place their future destinies... under the direction of the greatest constitutional power in the world'.[65]

Yet there was some truth in Storks' belief that the movement was essentially artificial. Greeks had not been converted to unqualified Anglophilia overnight. From the start, there was a menacing strain that, should the proffered Greek embrace be spurned, the direction of popular sympathies might be rapidly reversed. Palmerston understood this danger very well. For him, the revolution became a major preoccupation. He stood firmly on the principle that the Greek people had every right to change their sovereign, stating that the country had 'clearly come of age, and can no longer be deemed *in statu pupillari*'.[66] An old ideological inconsistency in Palmerstonian libertarianism towards 'national' questions in Europe might be partially corrected. The principle of dumping monarchs, unsurprisingly, was not approved by Queen Victoria, who was determined that her second son 'must not and shall not' wear the tarnished crown of Greece.[67] The premier's tangled relationship with his sovereign quickly got caught up in Greek affairs. But if Alfred was not to reign in Greece, who would? It was to block any French or Russian alternative that the British premier pressed for a quick reaffirmation by the powers of the 'self-denying principle' whereby members of the principal ruling families of Europe were barred from accepting the Greek throne. Initial failure to extract such a statement made Palmerston nervous about being outwitted by European rivals—an outcome likely to highlight his own failing grip in British politics as his health at last began to break up.

In the interim, therefore, the Alfred proposition attracted Palmerston as potentially the only means at his disposal to protect the British stake in Greece.[68] When Charilaos Tricoupi visited Palmerston at Broadlands on 4 November, he played on this theme, telling his host that the great object of all Greeks was 'to be well with England and to increase their territory, and that they thought both objects might be attained by electing Prince Alfred who ... would bring with him the Ionian Islands'.[69] Palmerston kept aloof, saying that Alfred 'was out of the question', and that, although the rest of the Ionian states were of no interest to Britain, Corfu remained 'a military and naval station of some importance, and

---

[64] 'The Fall of King Otho', Finlay Papers.

[65] Scarlett to Russell, 1 Dec. 1862, FO32/305.

[66] Palmerston to Russell, 4 Nov. 1862, PRO30/22/14D. In fact at no point during or after his flight did Otto formally abdicate, adding a legal complication to the management of the succession.

[67] Palmerston to Russell, 17 Nov. 1862, PRO30/22/14D.

[68] Lord Malmesbury reported to this effect, though others were sceptical as to the premier's real views at the time. See Dasent, *Delase*, 60.   [69] Palmerston to Russell, 6 Nov. 1862, PRO30/22/14D.

that Greece ... would be unable to hold ... [the island] if it was given to her'.[70] Yet with the names of French, Russian, and even Italian candidates proliferating, the temptation grew. By mid-November, Palmerston was swinging round, telling Russell that Prince Alfred 'ought to accept', and that if Greece was 'bent on an increase of territory', then it should have it.[71] But he also knew that when and if these matters were put to the House of Commons, they had to be watertight; and nothing could be more watertight than if they appeared to 'solve', in part at least, the Eastern Question. Such a prospect was, intriguingly, now opened up by the Ottoman chargé in Athens, Photiades Bey. Photiades had stated that the Porte would warmly welcome a British prince going to Greece with an Ionian dowry. But he was reported to have gone further in stating that

Even if at the expense [to Turkey] of the Imperial loss of Thessaly and Epirus a Greek Kingdom were thus constituted and placed under British Power, he had no doubt that the Sultan would gladly submit to some diminution of territory to ensure thereafter infinitely more security from further territorial invasion.[72]

In other words, as the price for underpinning a new dispensation in Greece dominated by his British ally, Sultan Abdul Aziz might throw a chunk of Ottoman territory—territory which anyway was not defensible in the longer term—into the bargain. It was not likely that Photiades would have raised such a controversial prospect without encouragement from within the Porte, where the notion that there had to be 'some ballast dropped overboard' to save the empire began to be heard. Palmerston latched onto the prospect of a real *coup de théâtre*. His rationalization was revealing. He had previously argued that if the Ionian islands were ceded alone to Greece, the Greek kingdom would be afforded scope for twenty years of internal development. Now he argued that if Thessaly and Epirus were included, that figure rose to fifty.[73] Palmerston was no developmental economist. But he grasped that if Ionian cession could be put into an expanded framework, not only would the dangers of a Greek revolution be safely navigated, but his own statecraft in the East—never quite free from the stain of Crimean blunders—might be brought to a resounding conclusion.

Here, then, was an outline of a Greece Anglified, expanded, commercialized, and constitutionalized—in short, the perfect inheritor for the bulk of Turkey's European territories, should that empire finally come to grief. The stakes were high—too high to be entrusted to the hands of such a junior diplomatist as Scarlett. A new mission was called for, and it was a mark of its significance that the most eminent practitioner of British oriental politicking, Lord Stratford de Redcliffe, was considered for the task, only to be discarded for his excessively brusque ways in dealing with Eastern peoples—not something proud Athenians

[70] Palmerston to Russell, 4 Dec. 1862, ibid.   [71] Palmerston to Russell, 17 Nov. 1862, ibid.
[72] Elliot to Russell, 25 Dec. 1862, FO32/313.
[73] Palmerston to Russell, 16 Nov. 1862, PRO32/22/14D.

were likely to tolerate for long.[74] Instead, in mid-December 1862 the smoother and suppler Sir Henry Elliot was packed off back to the Greek capital.

Elliot's fresh mission was even more difficult than its predecessor. Panicked by the Alfred movement, France and Russia had at last signed up under British insistence to a new self-denying agreement over the succession to the Hellenic crown. There was a danger, however, that in the first flush of disappointment at an agreement which necessarily ruled out Alfred, the Greeks might veer off at a tangent: that is, elect a king entirely of their own choosing, and almost certainly of their own faith. A combination of religious Orthodoxy and political unreliability would hold substantial dangers for British interests. Elliot's task, then, was to finally 'disillusion' (or, in Gladstonian terms, 'undeceive') Greek opinion in its apparent passion for the succession of Alfred, yet in such a way which kept the revolution on moderate and above all Anglophile lines. To achieve this Elliot had to be armed with something of real value for the Greeks.

This was where Ionian cession moved back into the foreground. Whatever Palmerston may have said to Tricoupi, in strategic terms the British stood to lose little of consequence—in the war of 1859, new steam technology had allowed a French fleet to enter the Adriatic without the British authorities in the Islands noticing the smoke.[75] The Protection itself was dead in the water politically. The Greek crisis fortuitously provided Palmerston with a screen for escaping from a problem which could only get worse. That the British troops tied down in garrisoning the Islands could be diverted to India, where the numbers required had increased markedly since the Mutiny in 1857, was an advantage also present in Palmerston's mind.[76] These were the considerations which opened the way to a memorandum appearing conveniently under Elliot's name in the *London Gazette*. This stated that if Greece chose a sovereign 'against whom no well-founded objection could be raised', the British government would announce to the Ionian Parliament its wish to see those states united to Greece, and to take the necessary steps for securing the concurrence of the European powers who were parties to the treaties of 1815. Since, however, it was imperative that there should be no misunderstanding, the memorandum ended with the explicit threat that if the new Greek authorities adopted a sovereign 'who shall be the precursor of revolutionary disaffection, or of the adoption of an aggressive policy towards Turkey', then the Ionian Islands would remain indefinitely under British occupation.

Such a statement opened up Palmerston and his colleagues to attack at home if things nonetheless went wrong. Many would point out that to back an erratic Greek horse was a fatal misjudgement, spiced up by continuing claims as to the

---

[74] Stratford de Redcliffe (as Canning had become following his peerage in 1859) later emerged as a critic of Ionian cession. See *Hansard Parliamentary Debates* (3rd series), vol. cxii (Lords), 27 July 1863, cols. 1440–4.   [75] Eber to Delane, 6 Nov. 1862, JTD/11/67, Delane Papers, NIA.
[76] E. D. Steele, *Palmerston and Liberalism, 1855–1865* (Cambridge, 1991), 246.

exceptional character of the Islands as military bases.[77] Fellow ministers were at best lukewarm when Palmerston and Russell pushed the decision through Cabinet.[78] In another warning sign, Queen Victoria argued that Corfu at least should be retained. 'The Corfu people would be very discontented if they were to be kept when the other Islands were given,' Palmerston countered, 'and when a gift is to be given it is as well to make it a handsome one.'[79] The problematical 'handsomeness' of the gift was in the end to underlie much of its complex meaning within Anglo-Hellenic relations. Meanwhile Elliot repeated the 'offer' verbatim to the provisional government of Greece in an interview immediately after his arrival in Athens on 23 December. For the moment he said nothing about his secret instruction to go at short notice to Constantinople for discussions about Thessaly and Epirus. 'But you will not go there', Palmerston had severely qualified his command, 'without a fair prospect of success.'[80] This was an indication that Elliot's superiors were not themselves going to run too many risks to ensure his mission's success.

Almost from Elliot's arrival in Athens, things began to fall apart. Previously Scarlett had been the target of criticism (including that of Queen Victoria) for not unreservedly quashing any notion of Alfred's elevation. In truth, the ambiguity and deception was embedded in British policy, since it had not been convenient to close down that possibility altogether. Now this had to be done, Elliot found that Alfred had an 'absolute hold' over Greek minds; when he first met the provisional leaders, Boulgaris and Diantopoloulos, they had told him that Alfred was 'the only possible King'.[81] Although Elliot reiterated that he had 'spared no pains' in telling bitter truths to the Greeks, it seemed to do no good. Preparations were already under way for the popular plebiscite which on 3 February 1863 unilaterally declared Alfred as sovereign by the biggest—if unavailing—plurality in Greek political history. Yet even before that point was reached, the real truth of the matter was sinking in. Hidden from view at first, the Alfred movement began to swing dangerously round. Elliot, like Gladstone, might have 'undeceived' the Greeks, but the effects were again not those intended.

Nor was the prospect of territorial largesse as effective in taking the edge off Elliot's sour pill as had been hoped. An experienced British official in the Greek provinces told him that 'even the promise of the Ionian Islands *and increased frontiers* [in Thessaly and Epirus] will scarcely sweeten it down'.[82] Certainly Elliot complained that with regard to the Islands he had found 'no appreciation of the importance of the boon to Greece'. To make things worse, the chance of additional frontier rectifications evaporated. Far from being secret, such rumours

---

[77] Lord Derby argued, not very convincingly, that the introduction of steam had made Corfu *more* important than before. *Hansard Parliamentary Debates*, 3rd series, vol. cxii (Lords), 29 May–30 June 1863, col. 1719.   [78] Palmerston to Russell, 4 Dec. 1862, PRO30/22/14D.

[79] Ibid.   [80] Russell to Elliot, 31 Dec. 1862, FO32/313.

[81] Elliot to Russell, 25 Dec. 1862, ibid.

[82] Vice-Consul Wood to Merlin, 22 Dec. 1862, FO32/305.

preceded Elliot to the region. Publicity was enough to scupper the proposal. Photiades Bey began to sound a different tune, voicing the Sultan's anger at being urged by Britain 'on one side to cut off a leg and on the other an arm'.[83] The British Embassy in Constantinople was anything but enthusiastic.[84] Not only was the British premier's anticipation of fifty years of Hellenic self-improvement consequently cut back to twenty, but the view that Palmerston and Russell had been gravely premature to proffer Ionian cession began to gain ground at home.

Most alarmingly, however, the loss of Greece suddenly reared up as a prospect in British diplomacy. Russian attention had fortuitously been diverted to Poland, where a bloody repression was in progress.[85] But a French candidacy for the Hellenic crown began garnering support around the Duc d'Aumale, and there-after other names were successively thrown into the ring—varieties of German and Italian princelings, whose very obscurity and ties of blood and marriage boded ill.[86] Elliot's task now was to fend off these suggestions whilst the British government fulfilled its new pledge to Boulgaris and his colleagues to come up with an acceptable alternative to Alfred. It was the manner in which Palmerston and Russell started to hawk the Greek throne around the minor royal courts of Europe like a cheap trinket which first imported an air of vulgarity into the matter, never to dissipate thereafter.

This would not have mattered so much if they had rapidly discovered a king 'to whom no well-founded objection could be raised'. Ferdinand of Portugal seemed interested, but backed out in January 1863, preferring to co-reign in Brazil. Swiftly pressure was directed to secure the agreement of Duke Ernst of Saxe-Coburg, who would have gratified the Greeks as the brother of Victoria's deceased consort, thus guaranteeing British patronage and money. But the Duke flatly declined, on the grounds that if a new king of Greece only brought the Ionian Islands in his baggage, he was bound to share the fate of Otto.[87] This may only have been an excuse, but its leakage into European newspapers was not helpful. The Greek succession was becoming a game of musical chairs—and nobody could tell who might be sitting on the rickety throne when the music stopped.

As the game proceeded, furthermore, the condition of Greece worsened. 'I have seen Greece before Capodistrias,' a British resident remarked 'and the interregnum between him and Otto, but nothing to be compared to the present state.'[88] This was probably an exaggeration, but Boulgaris's warning to Elliot that the Athenian

---

[83] Elliot to Russell, 28 Dec. 1862, FO32/313.

[84] Horace Rumbold, *Recollections of a Diplomatist* (London, 1902), 107.

[85] The Russian government traded a British 'blind eye' to the severity with which insurgents were then being crushed in Poland for their own abstention from exploiting disruption in Greece.

[86] If the Duc d'Aumale became King of Greece, Palmerston told Russell, 'all the *Orleans* Frenchmen would flood there, and it [Greece] would become a centre of intrigue of all kinds against England'. Quoted in Gooch (ed.), *Correspondence*, 75.

[87] Russell telegram to Elliot, 8 Feb. 1861, FO32/315.

[88] Vice-Consul Black to Dr Hall (Chaplain, British Legation), 10 Jan. 1863, FO32/316.

treasury would soon be empty was all too convincing.[89] After that, the revolution was likely to take a radical, perhaps a republican, turn. Until his superiors came up with a likely king, all Elliot could do was spread around a bit of secret service money, send Royal Navy ships around the coasts, and hold out the bait of the Ionian Islands. This quickly assumed an undignified air, and a sad contrast to the height of Alfredian enthusiasms.

The situation of Sir Henry Storks in the Ionian Islands was even worse than that of Elliot in Athens. He, after all, had actually to govern an occupied and increasingly disturbed territory. No advance warning was given to him concerning the publication of the British government's readiness to abandon the Protectorate. There are few types of polity more prone to distress than colonial or quasi-colonial regimes branded with the mark of impending death. In the Ionian Islands this distress was to take many forms. Immediately there was a fall in the value of Ionian securities. Whether the Protectorate could remain solvent through to its own demise remained henceforth an important consideration in both Corfu and London. Morale plummeted amongst expatriate officials facing unemployment. Storks was soon having to pass on to the Colonial Office pleas for compensation and new jobs—the latter not readily forthcoming when it was felt that most employees of the Protection were 'fit only for Levantine life'.[90] Even Storks himself had to calculate where his future employment might lie. In short, the Protectorate entered a state of suspense, and the always choppy water surrounding it started to lap over the side.

The agitation was naturally felt most intensely by Ionians. An excitement last experienced during the Gladstone mission took hold.[91] Storks told Elliot that when the news of a likely change of sovereignty reached Corfu there had been a feeling of consternation, soon giving way to disbelief, and doubt as to whether cession could be satisfactorily effected.[92] This was hardly surprising since the 'offer' had been highly conditional. Although the Archbishop of Corfu, in presiding over the ubiquitous festivities of St Spyridon, maintained the usual decorum—even including a short rendition of 'God Save the Queen'—the nervousness of the occasion was apparent.[93] News coming in from the other islands was still less tranquil. In notoriously disaffected Zante, demonstrators adopted such slogans as 'Long Live Russia', 'Down with Alfred', and, even worse, 'Down with England'.[94] Far from defusing the tension between Storks and his radical opponents, the prospect of cession merely intensified it. The former accused the latter of trying, though their inflated demands, to *avoid* union, whilst radicals accused the British of using cession as a 'snare' to harm the interests of Greece. What was really plain

---

[89] Elliot to Russell, 12 Jan. 1863, ibid.
[90] Storks to Sir Austen Layard, 19 Feb. 1864, Storks Papers, NAM.
[91] Storks to Newcastle, 10 Apr. 1863, CO136/181.
[92] Storks to Newcastle, 26 Dec. 1862, CO136/179.
[93] Storks to Newcastle, 26 Dec. 1862, ibid.
[94] Storks to Newcastle, 2 Jan. 1863, Storks Papers, NAM.

was that the two sides were as determined as ever to damage each other. 'When Greece gets the Ionian Islands', Storks wrote privately to a Colonial Office colleague, 'I wish them joy of the association. Ionia will be the Ireland of Greece.'[95] This reflected a *schadenfreude* embedded deep in the ending of the Protectorate.

Well ahead of cession, then, the draining of British power and prestige in the Protectorate and Greece merged into a single process. For Elliot, the fall of Boulgaris at the head of the provisional government was a turning point. Feeling 'abandoned by the Powers',[96] and above all by England, the possibility that Greek politicians might strike out in directions of their own could no longer be discounted. After the 'state of despondency' created in Athens by the Saxe-Coburg refusal, Elliot sent a string of urgent messages to London emphasizing the desperate need to fill the vacuum in Athens. Finally, in early March 1863 he told Russell flatly that there were only a few weeks, perhaps only days, left, after which the British government would no longer retain the leverage to determine who occupied the Greek throne *unless they had French support in doing so.*[97] In raising the spectre of Emperor Napoleon's growing influence, Elliot knew well he was touching Palmerston's most sensitive point.

British ministers, therefore, now had to look around in desperation for a suitable individual on whom to place the Greek crown. Inevitably, the requirement got watered down. It had been assumed that to survive in the internecine world of Athenian politics, the new king had to be of mature years and some experience of responsibility.[98] Now even a boy would do. Fortunately, one came very conveniently to hand. This was the 17-year-old Prince William George of Slesvig-Holstein. He had been included in the Greek plebiscite in early February as a column filler, and received six votes, after which he disappeared from view. He swiftly reappeared, however, at the wedding of his elder sister Princess Alexandra to the Prince of Wales the following March, where he made a good impression. This connection to British royalty made all the difference as to how such a candidacy could be sold to the Greeks.

An even bigger problem was how to sell it to the Danes. Otto's fall had devalued the Greek throne; the way it had been traded at a discount forced it down further. However, the Danish monarchy had its own problems as Prussia circled ominously around the duchy of Slesvig-Holstein. The Danes were not well placed to deny Palmerston a favour if he asked for one. The British premier called Tricoupi and Russell to Broadlands for a weekend on 18–19 March, after which the Foreign Secretary was able to reassure a tense and frustrated Elliot that 'our young Prince William is a trump card'.[99] After preliminary soundings in Copenhagen, Elliot formally put the proposal to the Greek government at the end of the month, and on 3 April the National Assembly, precipitate as always, proclaimed Prince William as their monarch-elect.

---

[95] Storks to Merivale, 10 Feb. 1863, Storks Papers, NAM.
[96] Elliot to Russell, 12 Mar. 1863, FO32/316.   [97] Elliot to Russell, 19 Mar. 1863, ibid.
[98] Russell to Elliot, 5 Feb. 1863, PRO30/22/108.   [99] Russell to Elliot, 26 Mar. 1863, ibid.

William was not yet king of Greece. There remained a good deal of haggling to do in Copenhagen in which the Ionian Islands figured principally as political currency. Still, Elliot had seemingly brought off what his father-in-law Russell described as a 'brilliant finish' to his mission in Athens. Historians have sometimes concurred.[100] 'En fait, c'était l'Angleterre qui triomphait', a French writer once wrote of this episode, 'et elle triomphait non seulement de la France et de la Russe, mais aussi encore de la Grèce'.[101] But was this outcome so brilliant, and whose triumph was it? Who needed to be grateful, and to whom, as the shadow of a new dynasty in Greece appeared? The Greeks, for having their tawdry throne filled? The Danish royal house, for having acquired an exotic cadet line despite its other troubles? Palmerston and Russell, for having their embarrassing search for a candidate ended? Misunderstanding on the slippery theme of gratitude was seriously to distort the process of Ionian cession and the simultaneous reconstitution of Greek statehood.

For the moment, the important point for everybody was to strike a deal which would definitively clinch William's accession. The House of Glücksburg needed an assurance that its amiable scion would not end up like Otto. Here final confirmation that the new King would be boosted by the transfer of the Ionian Islands was vital. Any suggestion that there might be snags was therefore highly inconvenient. But such a snag existed in the military fortifications, principally on Corfu. As soon as the Greek Assembly had 'elected' William, warnings started to flow from Constantinople that the Islands must not become a source of disaffection in the Ottoman Empire—the Sultan, it was said, 'would not hesitate to risk a war' if that happened.[102] Similar noises began to be sounded in Westminster. Indeed, it was the interconnection of Ottoman sensitivity and parliamentary opposition which posed a danger to the British ministry. The surest way to turn this corner was to guarantee the destruction of the Ionian forts, or to inflict what a British critic termed 'devastation in the bidding of farewell'.[103] Such destruction now became a fixed assumption in London. Nothing at all was said, however, on this matter whilst the negotiations on the new dynasty proceeded.

Another snag was money—or, rather, the trade-off between territory and cash in kitting out the new King. If he was to have less territory than had been hoped, then he had to have more cash as an alternative means to popularity amongst his new and potentially fickle people. An increased civil list was therefore required. Since the powers were not prepared themselves to pay the full amount, a premium had to come from somewhere. It seemed natural to take it from the rich Ionians—as a kind of tax on their unionist aspirations. A significant hike in the Greek civil

[100] Ibid.
[101] Michael Lhéritier, *Histoire diplomatique de la Grèce à nos jours*, iii: *La Règne de Georges I avant le traité de Berlin (1862–1878): Hellénisme et Slavisme* (Paris, 1925), 278. This book, as well as giving a French pespective, is of interest for being based on special access to the Greek state archive.
[102] Scarlett to Russell, 19 Apr. 1863, FO32/319.
[103] *Hansard Parliamentary Debates* (3rd series), vol. clxxxiv (Commons), 18 Mar. 1864, col. 344.

list was, with very doubtful legality, therefore hypothecated on future Ionian revenues. Here, too, Palmerston and Russell kept a discreet silence about what Storks continued to tell them—that those revenues might be completely exhausted by the time transfer took place. With these sleights of hand, the various protocols and agreements had all been signed by 5 June 1863, and on the following day the ceremony of proclamation took place at Christiansborg Castle near Copenhagen.

This ceremony was attended by the delegation of leading Greek politicians who had been there for some weeks.[104] Their leader presented to King Frederick of Denmark the decree of the Greek National Assembly on a silk cushion emblazoned in the blue and white colours of Greece; King Frederick then duly invested the Prince, henceforth to be King George I, with his new status. His title was to be not 'King of the Greeks', to which the Ottoman Sultan had objected, but 'King of the Hellenes', and although it was obscure what possible significance this might have, it proved that the Sultan could affect the very nomenclature of the Greek sovereign. At the ceremony King George formally adopted as his royal motto that of the Glücksburgs: 'The Love of my People will be my Strength.' This was not mere rhetoric, for the very nature of the accession embodied a profound issue— whether as king in a distant land he had yet to visit, George I would be safer basing his security and legitimacy on Greek hopes and ideals, or on the goodwill of those powers (above all Great Britain) who had put him where he was.

These events made Storks's situation almost unmanageable in the Islands. When the Greek delegation to Denmark had stopped off en route in Corfu, they had omitted to pay any respects at the palace, and instead allowed themselves to be 'completely kidnapped' by the *Rhizospastes* and drawn about the island in carriages amid much local unionist fervour.[105] This was a humiliation for those struggling to maintain calm. Even those few Ionians who had remained 'loyal' to the Protection were now deserting the sinking ship, driven by the necessity to limit the damage to their own futures. The proclamation at Christiansborg Castle made this into a final scramble. A huge demonstration, to be crowned by a Te Deum in the cathedral, was called for 18 April. Storks feared that the Ionian police could no longer be trusted to keep the peace, warning the Duke of Newcastle that the force was 'not exempt from certain extraneous influences', and that their confidence had slumped.[106] A regime which can no longer rely on its own policemen is perched above an abyss. In Storks' nightmare, it only needed some 'hostile allusion' to British honour by demonstrators to make British soldiers run amok, and so ensure that the last days of the Protectorate should be marked by violence and a lasting bitterness.[107]

The episode which followed encapsulates the flavour of contemporary Corfu. Storks sent his most senior Ionian official (and future Foreign Minister of Greece), Sir Peter Brailla, to the Archbishop to impress on him the need for order, and to

104 For a description of the ceremony see Lhéritier, *Histoire*, iii. 79–80.
105 Note by G. Barrow, 22 Apr. 1863, CO136/181.
106 Storks to Newcastle, 19 June 1863, Storks Papers, NAM.   107 Ibid.

ask that Britain 'should have the principal place in the thanks to be offered up' in the cathedral (the Lord High Commissioner had clearly forgotten about God). Such a plea by Storks for the help of the Archbishop in running the Protectorate marked a further loss of power. The Archbishop was magnanimous but supple, inviting Storks to attend the service 'as Representative of that [British] sovereign to whom the whole Greek Race owes so much, and towards whom he was most anxious to show every mark of respect and gratitude'. Storks was not prepared to go to his Canossa—to sit in the cathedral, amidst his radical enemies, and remain silent through an archiepiscopal address not likely to be limited to merely spiritual matters. Instead he sent Liuetanant Evelyn Baring and his other key aide, Henry Drummond Wolff,[108] to suffer any indignity that might be sprung on them.

At the gathering in the cathedral on 18 April, the entrance of Wolff and Baring was to their surprise met with cries of 'Long Live England', 'Long Live Queen Victoria', and, most unusually of all, 'Long Live the Lord High Commissioner'.[109] Startlingly, some of the more extreme radicals even offered greetings. The two Britons were placed in the centre of the church, though hemmed in by a swathe of Greek flags (this was what Storks had feared). On their exit, however, they were strewn with flowers, and when the crowd proceeded to the palace in good humour, Storks felt compelled to go out onto the balcony and acknowledge the acclaim. That night the town was illuminated, and British soldiers were fêted in the taverns with free beer. As at other times and places in the Hellenic world, Anglophobia and Anglophilia had a capacity for revolving with bewildering and even inexplicable rapidity. 'Everything plainly showed', Storks was pleased to be able at last to give some good news to Newcastle, 'that the tide of popularity had set in towards England.'[110] His ability to keep this tide flowing again was why his reputation in London now rose steadily. Yet the nightmare of some chance event sending everything into a renewed slide did not go away.

Violence was already breaking out in Athens. Here, too, the new King's proclamation in Copenhagen simply ratcheted up the pressure. Factions mobilized to dominate affairs at the crucial moment when George I arrived.[111] In early July the Acropolis was occupied; fighting erupted around the Bank of Greece, which had to be defended by the landing of British, French, and Russian marines. Over 200 Greeks were killed, and many more wounded. European representatives did what they could to quieten things down. A British naval squadron appeared off the Gulf on 9 July; bullion was taken aboard the ships at Patras; Scarlett pulled on the Ionian lever, warning that the Islands could not be handed over whilst such conditions continued. Although an uneasy calm descended, even the necessity for a British reoccupation of the Piraeus began to be broached. So far the Tory

---

[108] Drummond Wolff went on to a series of British diplomatic posts in the Ottoman Empire, before serving as a Tory M P 1874–85, becoming a leading light in Randolph Churchill's 'Fourth Party'. [109] Storks to Newcastle, 19 June 1863, CO136/181.
[110] Storks to Newcastle, 19 June 1863, CO136/181.
[111] Finlay, *History of Greece*, vii. 292–6.

opposition at Westminster had refrained from an outright attack on Palmerston's Ionian policy, on the grounds that it was a 'bad party fight'[112]—that is, one that had no real resonance with British opinion. But there were signs that this calculation might change, and on 28 July the Tory leader, Lord Derby, tested the waters by referring to cession as a 'crime of the gravest character'.[113]

There was no possibility of King George leaving for Athens whilst violence was raging. Indeed, there was even a fear that the Danes might withdraw from the whole deal. They sent a special commissioner of their own to make sure that the Ionian population was not turning against any idea of joining the troubled Greek kingdom. Storks himself was convinced that the unionist movement was now too entrenched to go back on itself. But the delay in getting George to Athens, and putting cession into motion, risked unravelling. Finally, under sustained pressure from Palmerston and Russell, King George and his key political adviser, Count Sponneck, set out on their long journey in mid-September.[114] They did so by a circuitous route via St Petersburg, and forgoing the invitation to visit London, an indication that King George and his minders were determined not to be seen as British stooges. The main reason why the progression had to be slow, however, was to give Storks time to go through the necessary motions to secure Ionian approval for their transfer to Greek sovereignty.

That Ionians should have the opportunity to formally express their own views had found a place in the original 'Elliot Memorandum'. Indeed, the British government was adamant that all the due forms of the Ionian constitution must be kept—a kind of final riposte to allegations that British conduct in the Protectorate had always lacked a proper legal and moral foundation. Palmerston had contemptuously ruled out a plebiscite—which at least had the advantage of speed—as a European fad with no place in British policy. The Ionian Parliament would therefore have to meet and express its view. In thinking about how to handle this, however, Storks saw a way of ensuring that even in the termination of the Protectorate the tables could be turned on those who had contributed to its demise. He calculated that an election might be called to send legislators to a new Parliament, the sole purpose of which would be to provide an immediate and authoritative answer on the issue of union with Greece. Once that answer was given, the Parliament would be promptly dissolved, leaving the incoming King 'a clear field' to select his own office holders, and arrange the methods by which Ionian legislators would be selected in future.[115] In short, Ionian politicians were to be marginalized and their privileges put at the mercy of the new sovereign. In their dependence would lie Storks's parting triumph, and proof of his own theories of Ionian affairs.

Ionian elections were consequently set in motion, though the very dispersion of the archipelago made them a protracted affair. That the opponents of union

---

[112] Quoted in Drummond Wolff, *Rambling Recollections*, i. 394.
[113] *Hansard Parliamentary Debates*, 3rd series, vol. clxxii (Lord's) 17–28 July 1863, col. 1451.
[114] For the selection of Sponneck, see Lhéritier, *Histoire*, iii. 91–2.
[115] Storks to Newcastle, 23 Oct. 1863, Storks Papers, NAM.

remained 'pusillanimous and abject'—that is, largely invisible—now hardly mattered.[116] Right at the end of September the legislators finally gathered in Corfu. Even to bring the Parliament into session, however, Storks had to solicit fresh help from the Archbishop, and it was only his intervention which persuaded enough delegates to accept nomination to the despised Senate to ensure a quorum.[117] It had been Storks' hope that he might be saved one final unpleasantness: that of personally appearing before the Assembly in its moment of victory, by simply sending a message inviting them to approve a resolution of cession. But his bosses in London insisted that he drink the cup to the very bottom, and in making his address direct to the packed and fervent Assembly, instructed him to find no 'cause of quarrel' whatever verbal brickbats came his way.

In fact, when Storks opened Parliament on 3 October, he met no real discourtesy, and on his way back along the Esplanade was greeted with affability on all sides. He felt able to assure Newcastle that 'the whole transaction would pass off creditably'.[118] In a way it did, but it also testified to continuing ideological differences. Instead of passing the resolutions Storks had left embedded in his address, the Assembly drew up a decree declaring union 'immediate and complete' by virtue of the sovereign will of the people. This decree was then solemnly carried through the town and presented at the palace door. There was considerable excitement at this news in Athens, though not, Scarlett had to report, 'any manifestation of gratitude towards England'.[119] The Anglophilia so powerfully generated by the Alfred movement on the mainland was now extinguished. Still, there was at least a good deal of celebratory firing of arms in Greek towns, whilst the shots which peppered the hull of HMS *Icarus* at anchorage in Patras were conceivably an accident.

Ionians had now approved their own transfer, and the way was open for King George to enter Athens. As he, and Sponneck, neared the city on board the frigate *Hellas*, considerable European pressure was brought to bear to prevent armed men flooding back into town. At last, on 30 October, George arrived to an ecstatic welcome, the King humbly approaching the cathedral on foot. With the British Navy lying offshore as a tangible expression of where power really lay at this crucial moment, George's address held out the vision of Greece as a 'model state in the East'—a calculated echo of what Sir Henry Elliot had once trailed before the unlamented Otto. Yet the new monarch could not afford to appear merely as a manifestation of British favour, and although he could never be 'complètement grec', as he had recently promised, he knew he had to appear as Greek as possible.[120] One way was by going promptly to the Ionian Islands to take possession of a fine extension to the kingdom. Scarlett was therefore informed that the monarch and his entourage wished to depart for Corfu without more ado.

---

116 Storks to Newcastle, 25 Sept. 1863, Storks Papers, NAM.
117 Storks to Newcastle, 3 Oct. 1863, Storks Papers, NAM.
118 Storks to Newcastle, 3 Oct. 1863, Storks Papers, NAM.
119 Scarlett to Newcastle, 8 Oct. 1863, FO32/234.   120 Lhéritier, *Histoire*, iii. 72.

To this there could be no ready agreement. There were several reasons. The information reaching London about the condition of Greek politics became more alarmist just as George had arrived. Scarlett reported that in Athens there was 'a perfect chaos, with the scum on the surface'.[121] By 'scum' was really meant politicians whom the British either did not know, or did not trust, and it was true that the revolution in Greece was throwing up a new cadre with whom the European legations were not acquainted. These currents were fully mirrored in the Ionian Islands, where one Protectorate official, on returning after some months, found that local opinion had 'returned to their former hatred' of the British.[122] Such unpropitious circumstances inevitably fed back into British politics, where any outbreak in Greece or the Islands coinciding with cession could be used to attack Palmerston in Parliament. The Russian Ambassador warned Tricoupi, when the latter got back to London from Greece, how the atmosphere had darkened, and that this was liable to be exploited by the Tories.[123]

There was one other reason why the Protectorate could not yet be abandoned. The forts of Corfu were still intact. Storks had earlier warned that their destruction was capable of opening up 'an immense field for disaffection'. Indeed, there was even disaffection in British circles in Corfu. The most senior British Army engineer did not believe 'in the probability or even possibility of Corfu being used for aggressive purposes', and deprecated the 'discredit for leaving this picturesque town flanked by two hideous ruins'; the special correspondent sent out by *The Times* shared the judgement.[124] Edward Lear, the landscape painter and poet resident in the island, called the demolition 'a most singular folly, done ... simply to aggravate and vex an impressionable people'.[125] This was close to the mark. 'We must demolish the fortifications to satisfy Austria,' was how Russell sought to persuade Count Sponneck when insisting that a Greek delegate be sent quickly to London to approve the protocol, though adding the gentler assurance, 'we shall do it gently and without defacing the beautiful town of Corfu'.[126] But in truth the motive for this controversial action, whilst having something to do with Austrian sensitivities, also derived from the desire to throw a sop to those in the British Parliament who were prepared to swallow the ending of the Protectorate, providing that the Ionians received a parting swipe.

Frantic Greek attempts to prevent a European agreement on demolition— including a plea to Gladstone—got nowhere. The stark choice was put by the powers to Tricoupi in London: Greece could accept the Ionian Islands without the forts, or have no Islands at all. There was therefore no alternative but to swallow what was an international affirmation of the inferiority of Greece. King George

---

[121] Scarlett to Russell, 20 Oct. 1863, FO32/234.   [122] Kirkwall, *Four Years*, 277.

[123] Xenos, *East and West*, 14.

[124] Chief Engineer to Commander-in-Chief, Corfu, 1 Oct. 1863, WO30/127, National Archives of the United Kingdom. Also see Dasent, *Delane*, ii. 73.

[125] Philip Sherrard, *Edward Lear: The Corfu Years* (Athens, 1988), 213.

[126] Russell to Scarlett, 26 Nov. 1863, PRO30/22/108.

complained bitterly to Scarlett that 'he was asked and persuaded to come here [to Greece] without delay but nothing was said about the conditions of annexation [of the Islands]'.[127] Scarlett, indeed, had done what he could, suggesting to ministers in London that the forts be retained under British occupation—'a second Gibraltar', he had phrased it, seeking to add a patriotic gloss—which the Greeks could subsequently prove themselves worthy of possessing.[128] But he, too, was rebuffed. Russell was adamant that the Islands were 'a very handsome present to Greece, and the Greeks ought to accept it as such'.[129] But it was a present cracked in the giving. Due to the sheer massiveness of the Venetian masonry, much heavy explosive turned out to be required to bring the edifices down.[130] If this provided 'a most absorbing spectacle to witness' for some British officials,[131] it was viewed differently by locals. 'I wish Lord Roosel were on top of it', one Englishman allegedly heard a Corfiote remark as a rampart was seen exploding in an orange puff of smoke and cordite.[132]

It was, amidst all these currents, Storks' job to keep on top of what he called 'the difficulties and dying struggles' of the British Protectorate.[133] At least, along with the final decision on the forts, came the instruction to begin packing up. But for ministers in London the way that a 'bad and ungrateful spirit' in the Islands was now interacting with an analogous spirit in Greece was highly perturbing. The linkage between the two—only intensified by the saga of the forts—indicated the nature of the danger. A prospect now loomed in which the old anti-Protection, anti-British cry in the Ionian states would be translated into a reinforced call to arms against Turkey within the expanded kingdom—exactly the opposite of Palmerston's intentions. Effecting that translation was alleged to be the new game of Ionian radicals.[134] Certainly it was true that the calculations of all political actors hinged on what would *follow* union, and specifically the entry of Ionian deputies into the Assembly. 'At present the bone of contention [in Athens] is the possession of power at the time when the Ionian deputies join the Assembly', a British observer explained the underlying dynamics, 'and when the permanent bases of the [expanded] State are to be laid.'[135]

It was the sense that the permanent bases of a new Greek state were in flux which underlay the acute nervousness all round. This process had an intimate connection with the wider Eastern Question, a point accentuated by a rash of new troubles in Serbia and Montenegro. Nor were things helped by Count Sponneck. He seemed to veer towards politicians in Athens known to be hostile to Britain; worse, in conversation with Scarlett he referred to a possible Russian

[127] Scarlett to Russell, 18 Dec. 1863, FO32/326
[128] Scarlett to Russell, 20 Dec. 1863, ibid.
[129] Russell to Scarlett, 3 Dec. 1863, PRO30/22/108.
[130] Storks to Newcastle, 1 Mar. 1864, CO136/184.
[131] Drummond Wolff, *Rambling Recollections*, i. 390.
[132] Kirkwall, *Four Years*, 250.
[133] Storks to Fortescue, 2 Mar. 1864, Storks Papers, NAM.
[134] Fortescue minute, 5 Mar. 1864, CO136/184.
[135] Horace Rumbold to Russell, 19 May 1864, FO32/335.

marriage for George.[136] A shot across the Greek bow was delivered in the form of a warning that if the King did not act constitutionally (if, that is, he fell into Otto's bad ways) then the British government would not guarantee the dynasty or even assist in 'protecting the person of the sovereign'.[137] That there was already a question about the future safety of George testified to the fragility of the transition.

The dangerous spin in Greek politics coincided with the resolution of the modalities of Ionian cession. Of the successive protocols made necessary by the elaborate rituals of European treaty culture we need not take account. The last such protocol arrived in Athens for signature in mid-March 1864. A few concessions had been included to meet continuing Greek protests—for example, on the sweeping neutralization of the Islands which had previously been inserted. The Assembly in Athens was in no mood to quibble more. What public opinion in Greece wanted was the Islands—they, along with George himself, were the symbol of a brighter future. The instruments of cession were therefore approved, and the Minister of Foreign Affairs wasted no time in telling Scarlett that Greek troops would be ready to leave for Corfu in a couple of days, that it was expected that the British soldiers would by then have left, and that the King and his entourage would follow immediately afterwards.[138]

All was more or less ready in Corfu for the handover. Handling the complicated details came naturally to Storks. There continued to be a worry about a collapse of Ionian finance, but Gladstone agreed to guarantee Treasury support to fend this off; on a matter of a few pennies, Gladstone's Hellenism found an outlet.[139] Some troops left early. The 2nd Battalion of the 5th Regiment did so in early March— one British resident noting, however, that as the troops marched off to embarkation, the watching crowd pointedly failed to return the cheers of the soldiers.[140] Although the Ionians were 'behaving rather well',[141] despite the provocation of the explosions around the forts, Storks still worried about a collision. This was why it was vital to maintain vigilant control right up to the last, not least with the help of a beefed-up presence by the Royal Navy. The logistics of departure were vital. In particular, Storks insisted that instead of troops leaving the various Islands in penny packets, they should be progressively withdrawn to Corfu as a position of strength. The whole force would then leave in one go, once—and only once—a regular Greek force arrived to take possession. Amidst all these departures and arrivals there should be no hiatus allowing Ionian 'demagogues' to seize the initiative. Storks's conception of what he called 'the historic closing scene' of the

---

[136] In Oct. 1867 King George was to marry Grand Duchess Olga Konstantinovna, the daughter of the Tsar.   [137] Scarlett to Russell, 29 Jan. 1864, FO32/333.

[138] Scarlett to Russell, 15 Apr. 1864, FO32/334.

[139] 'It would be a great pity if our administration of these Islands', it was stated within the Colonial Office, 'were to finish with a bankruptcy' (T. F. Elliot note, 22 Feb. 1864, CO136/184). In the end, Gladstone stumped up enough cash from the Exchequer to ensure this did not happen.

[140] Kirkwall, *Four Years*, 252.   [141] Storks to Newcastle, 1 Mar. 1864, CO136/184.

Protectorate was revealed in his statement to the Duke of Newcastle's successor as Colonial Secretary, Lord Cardwell:

At Corfu especially, it is very important that so great an event as the spontaneous cession . . . of the Ionian States to Greece, and the withdrawal of the British Protectorate after a period of nearly fifty years' duration, should be marked by such a display as will not lead the people of these countries to suppose that we have been driven away or have yielded to any pressure which the Ionians have been able to impose upon us.[142]

In this first *de facto* decolonization in British imperial history was evident a theme which was to recur so much in the twentieth century—a preoccupation with arranging and fabricating the very moment of demission.[143] Above all there should be no *impression* of defeat. For Storks, this priority was set in stone through his experience and preconceptions in the Islands. Just as a very British concern with 'honour' had suffused the mission of Gladstone, so it returned with full force at the climax. All these things catered for, Storks signalled to the government in London that he was ready, and indeed intensely eager, to depart from the Islands on 16 April.

Everybody was now ready for the handover—except Palmerston and Russell. Once they looked cession in the face, they drew back. This had nothing to do with sentiment about the Islands, and everything to do with the expectation that George—'the poor unfortunate King of the Hellenes'[144]—would not long remain in the saddle. The debate on Ionian policy in the House of Commons on 18 March had passed off without upset for the British government, if only because it was so poorly attended, but certain dangerous markers had been laid down. One speaker, for example, echoed the recent statement by M. Thiers in the Paris Chamber, to the effect that the British and French positions in relation to the new Greek Revolution were now reversed, with the British regarded with 'peculiar aversion' for their meddling and duplicity.[145] If Britain's 'trump card' in the form of King George was any further devalued, the Greek game might end with Palmerston framed as a dupe of foreigners. At the end of March, therefore, Storks received the surprise instruction that any departure should be put on hold for two months.[146] The only reason given was that 'plots were ready to explode in Greece', though no further details of what these consisted of were provided.

For Storks, this was an imposition too far. He no longer believed in Greek 'plots'.[147] Any further delay in going would only confirm the truth of what some Ionians alleged, that the British had never had any intention of departing in the first place. Storks was dismissive of the argument that postponement would allow the Greeks to 'prepare some force which would enable them to step quietly into

---

[142] Storks to Newcastle, 15 Mar. 1864, ibid.

[143] The loss of America at the end of the 18th century resulted from Britain's military defeat, not a political decision to abandon sovereignty.

[144] Storks to Scarlett, 2 May 1864, Storks Papers, NAM.

[145] *Hansard Parliamentary Debates* (3rd. series), vol. clxxiv (Commons), 18 Mar. 1864, col. 344.

[146] Storks to Scarlett, 18 Apr. 1864, Storks Papers, NAM.   [147] Ibid.

our shoes', since in his view the Greek Army was in such a mess that it did not matter whether one hung on for two months or two years. Yet there was something more fundamental.[148] 'The Islands', he insisted to Cardwell, 'have been annexed in all but the fact.' This was true. Power and authority over the Ionians had slipped from his hands. Any prolongation of 'termination' would increase, not diminish, the likelihood that cession would be accompanied by violence. It was difficult and even dangerous to reject such advice from their own principal agent, so that Palmerston and Russell had little choice but to screw up their courage, and name the day for the Ionian transfer. This was to be Saturday, 2 June.

The final timetable for the Protection now unfolded. The demolition of the forts—in the end, restricted to the fortifications on the islet of Vido, and the New Fortress in the Town itself—was noisily completed at the end of April.[149] On 19 May a leading Greek official, M. Zaimis, arrived in Corfu to act as Commissioner Extraordinary of the King of the Hellenes. As if to mark an occasion which brought home to ordinary Greeks the reality of what was about to occur, the British royal arms on the Palace of St Michael and St George were taken down by a party of Royal Engineers, and the massive stone fragments 'sold to eager competitors at fancy prices'.[150] Storks and Zaimis co-operated closely in fixing the last details of transfer. They made preparations for a dissolution of Parliament, although the following elections were already the subject of an agreement between the King and a delegation of Ionian politicians to Athens; thus was Storks denied his parting victory over the legislators. Instead his very last transaction as Lord High Commissioner was not to punish enemies, but to protect a few remaining old friends: he provided Zaimis with a list of persons resident in the Islands whose pension had been guaranteed under Ionian law, just in case the new regime should overlook their claims.[151]

At the end of May King George set out on an extensive tour of his kingdom, of which the arrival in Corfu was to be merely the climax. He visited Hydra, Nauplion, Argos, Tripoli, and Kalamata, before boarding the familiar frigate *Hellas*. To underpin the King's sketchy knowledge of recent Greek history, it was agreed that this vessel should rendezvous with a European naval squadron at Navarino, symbol of the role of the powers in the creation of the Hellenic state. The entire diplomatic body of Athens was carried in the ships, though it was a relatively junior British diplomat, Horace Rumbold, who travelled in Scarlett's place on the Royal Navy flagship HMS *Revenge*. George and Sponneck had only provided an assurance that there would be no anti-British demonstrations in Corfu on condition that Scarlett—who made no secret of his disillusionment with the new regime, and even hankered after Otto—was

---

[148] Storks to Scarlett, 11 Apr. 1864, Storks Papers, NAM.
[149] The Old Fortress of Corfu was therefore largely spared. For more detail see Maria Camonachou et al., *The Old Fortress of Corfu* (Corfu, 1994).   [150] *The Times*, 14 June 1864.
[151] Note by T. F. Elliot, 25 June 1864, CO136/184. The Greek government was still meeting obligations to pensioners of the old British Protectorate at the end of the 19th century.

replaced.[152] After meeting at Navarino, the assortment of British, French, Russian, and Greek vessels pottered around whilst the historic day of 2 June should come and go.

On 1 June, 830 Greek soldiers and a few gendarmes arrived off Corfu harbour in 'a clumsy paddlewheel steamer' which made a curious contrast with powerful British warships anchored nearby.[153] All British women, children, and the garrison's personal baggage were taken off by a strong Royal Navy force. On the following morning the British soldiers began boarding at 10 a.m. Only after this was completed were Greek troops allowed to begin disembarking themselves. Around noon British soldiers of the 4th King's Own marched for the last time out of the famous citadel, whilst Storks proceeded to give a formal farewell to the assembled Ionian public functionaries in the throne room of the palace. He spoke in fluent Italian, his voice apparently breaking with emotion, and indeed this ceremony marked the end of that special Anglo-Italian-Hellenic blend which had characterized leading Ionian society for a considerable period.[154]

It was when Storks left the palace for the harbour that he set eyes on the largest crowd he had ever seen in the Islands.[155] Spectators crammed every spot, filling the Esplanade, including its balconies, to overflowing, whilst pleasure boats plied just offshore. The high spirits and good fellowship of the occasion were striking. Storks later reported that he was so much overcome that 'it required all one's self-command and "*sang froid*" not to break down completely'. This has the touch of sincerity. According to Edward Lear, in whose company Storks frequently sought relief, the latter had been 'bothered out of his life' that the climax of the British departure would go badly wrong.[156] When, instead, there appeared a sudden frisson of reconciliation between Britons and Greeks his relief was intense. Characteristically, despite the 'running fire' of acclamations for *enosis* which

[152] For Scarlett's 'blackballing' at the hands of the new dynasty see his letter to Russell, 12 May 1864, in FO32/335. Scarlett's subsequent career suggests an unexpected shadow cast by recent Greek experience. He was next sent to troubled Mexico as British minister, where his task was to look after another European monarch—the Emperor Maximilien—put on a shaky throne. At the climax of that saga, Scarlett advised Maximilien not to flee from insurgency but to stay and fight for his crown. Maximilien stayed, and afterwards his fate before a firing squad was laid by some on Scarlett's shoulders. It seems highly probable that in his dealings with the beleaguered Emperor, Scarlett was influenced by his belief that in Greece Otto had let his throne go too easily. See Bertita Harding, *The Phantom Crown: The Story of Maximilien and Carlotta of Mexico* (London, 1935), 307–9.

[153] *The Times*, 14 June 1864.

[154] Storks, whose deceased wife had been Neapolitan, was fluent in the language. As for the Anglo-Italian flavour in the Islands, Edward Lear—who, after leaving in 1864, made two subsequent visits to Corfu before his death in 1885—later found it more or less eradicated by Hellenic influences. See Pratt, *Britain's Greek Empire*, 172.

[155] For Storks's accounts see his letters to Lord Cardwell, 2 June 1864, CO136/184 and 6 June 1864, Storks Papers, NAM.

[156] Sherrard, *Edward Lear*, 213. Lear himself had left on 4 Apr. 1864 in the company of Evelyn Baring. The image of the author of the *Book of Nonsense* and the man who was to be Britain's most masterful Eastern proconsul sitting together, as Lear described it, stargazing as Corfu town finally dipped on the horizon, is surely piquant. For the close friendship of Baring and Lear in Corfu, see Marquis of Zetland, *Lord Cromer* (London, 1931).

marked his progress to the quayside,[157] he could not resist afterwards drawing the conclusion that the behaviour of the ordinary Ionians reflected their sadness at seeing the British go. That there was at least a scintilla of this feeling is not, perhaps, wholly incredible—after all, without the cash flow of an British military presence, the prosperity of the islands was highly uncertain.[158]

Immediately Storks arrived aboard the flagship HMS *Marlborough*, the British military guards still ashore were formally relieved by their Greek counterparts. British colours were lowered over the palace and what remained of the fortifications, and taken off in a guard of honour. The Islands were Greek at last. Most of the British garrison headed for Malta, but Storks in his flagship detoured to the Bay of Katacolo, off Patras, where the *Marlborough* and the frigate *Hellas*, sailing in the opposite direction, both hove to. Storks personally took the old Protectorate colours aboard the King's vessel and laid them, theatrically, at his feet.[159] Their ensuing conversation may be passed over, except for Storks's parting shot that when the King and his counsellor arrived in the Islands they 'should not expect a bed of roses there'.[160] For all the good feeling at the last, it was this exhausted cynicism and frustration which was the authentic spirit permeating the end of British Protection in the Ionian Islands.

This analysis has to end, however, not with the 'closing scene' of the Protectorate, but the overture to an enlarged, if not quite 'greater', Greece. On Monday, 6 June the King's squadron, having steamed through the channel separating Zante and Cephalonia, came within sight of Corfu. Rumbold felt a surge of emotion at a vista which 'had been so dear to many of our English race'.[161] For the last stretch the European warships held back, whilst *Hellas* sailed past the harbour walls and docked. King George—whose special connection with the Islands was to last throughout his reign—was received with much jubilation, the Philharmonia Band at last relieved of the necessity for the British anthem, with its excruciating tempo. The monarch was taken by carriage to the cathedral, where the Archbishop presided over a Te Deum. So began a tour which Rumbold, for whom the episode was distasteful as a mark of British retreat, and yet exciting in its tangible significance, described as 'one continuous triumph'.[162] But, as always in the minefield of Anglo-Hellenic relations, it was not entirely clear to whom the triumph really belonged. Rumbold told Russell that everything had been done to 'enhance the pomp and circumstance of the Royal progress', and that the King

[157] *The Times*, 14 June 1864.
[158] Corfu town may have been a bit poorer in the wake of the British garrison's departure, but it was a lot safer for locals, since, according to a British writer, no 'respectable' woman had been secure so long as drunken British 'jolly tars' sporadically cruised the harbour area. Zetland, *Lord Cromer*, 31.
[159] Walter Christmas, *The Life of King George I of Greece* (London, 1914), 66.
[160] Storks to Cardwell, 6 June 1864, Storks Papers, NAM. After his return to England, Storks was shortly appointed Governor of Malta. In Dec. 1865 (having a track record of successfully averting disorder in a discontented island) he was appointed to head an inquiry into the controversial actions of Governor Eyre of Jamaica in suppressing a rebellion.
[161] Rumbold to Russell, 25 May 1864, FO32/335.
[162] Rumbold to Russell, 2 July 1864, ibid. Also Rumbold, *Recollections*, 134–7.

had been accompanied by British warships on all his perambulations between the Islands. 'He has never once left or rejoined the ship that bore him', Rumbold concluded, 'but to the thunder of our guns.'

The 'thunder' of European (mainly British) guns and 'The Love of his People'—these formed the sometimes jarring parameters within which the rule of King George was to be confined over the next fifty years until he was assassinated in Salonica amidst the turmoil of a great Balkan war.[163] Meanwhile a formal dinner at the Palace in Corfu on 8 June 1864 the dashing young King was a 'picture of happiness', enthusing over the beauty of his new dominions.[164] He was fulsome in his gratitude to Her Majesty Queen Victoria for her handsome gift, though pointedly saying nothing of her government, without whom the present might have been more handsome still. Further down the table Rumbold and Sponneck spoke confidentially of the future. The Dane assured Rumbold that the long crisis unleashed in Greece by the fall of Otto was at last over. Suggestively, he alluded several times to the determination that henceforth the Archbishop of Corfu would be forced back into a purely religious sphere. Rumbold's account of Sponneck's analysis went on:

Alluding more generally to the 'Great Idea' ... [he] said it were well for this country if the Greeks could understand that the most important step towards its realisation would be first to establish a sound and lasting order of things at home. There was plenty to be done in that direction to utilize the activity of the Greeks and it was to that the King had alluded to when he had said that it was his ambition to found 'a model state of the East'.[165]

All this was reassuring for Rumbold, and also for Palmerston and Russell, for whose consumption it was really intended. But was the long Greek crisis really over? The British knew that even whilst in the Ionian Islands the King received a stream of messages from Montenegro and Serbia seeking to entice him into a joint attack on Turkey.[166] The penalties attached to King Otto's adventurism in 1854 were too fresh for such invitations to be tempting. Yet the new King went out of his way before long to refute any suggestion that he was just a Palmerstonian poodle. 'He has kicked English policy out of his palace', George Finlay reported, with some exaggeration, in July 1865, 'as decidedly and openly as ever Otto did.'[167] Finlay saw only advantage in a development inimical to the recent 'embarrassing tendency' for Great Britain to take *both* the Ottoman Empire and the Hellenic kingdom under its protection—in his view, not a trick that could ever be successfully pulled off. As Britain's restraining power dwindled, however, Greek aspirations were all the more likely to drift into directions where they impinged on British maritime interests. In 1866 a Christian insurrection broke out in Crete and

---

[163] Rumbold to Russell, 2 July 1864, ibid. Also Rumbold, *Recollections*, 134–7.
[164] Rumbold to Russell, 8 June 1864, FO32/335.   [165] Ibid.
[166] Rumbold to Russell, 18 June 1864, FO32/335. These messages, mostly from Prince Michael of Serbia, are significant as the first concerted attempt at a 'Balkan front' against Turkey which did not finally come into being until the First Balkan War of 1912.   [167] Hussey, *Journals*, 816.

blazed fiercely and bloodily for two years before grinding to a temporary halt. In explaining the roots of that revolt Finlay, now ensconced as *The Times'* correspondent in Greece, reflected that

The cession of the Ionian Islands to the Hellenic Kingdom [had] caused a fermentation of the minds of the whole Greek race ... It was believed that the British government was awed into conceding the demands of Greek nationality ... The cession therefore became an incitement to fresh agitation in the provinces of the Ottoman empire where the Greeks form a large part of the population.[168]

In short, Sir Henry Storks' determination that, in departing from the Islands, no impression should be left behind that 'we [the British] have been driven away' was crucially belied by subsequent events.[169] Instead the Hellenic legend of Ionian cession subtly reinstated the primacy of a national struggle for freedom. The long and crisis-ridden reign of George I never did achieve 'a model kingdom in the East' as nineteenth-century Britons conceived it, although by the time of King George's death a new, more prosperous, and diversified Greece had indeed emerged. But along the way there were many setbacks, and most of them touched, one way or another, on the tortuous and violent path by which Crete finally followed in the wake of the Ionian Islands into Greek statehood. If the British expected that in abandoning the Ionian Protectorate they were freeing themselves from Hellenic complications, they were therefore sorely disappointed. As we are about to see, during the later and concluding stages of the bitter Cretan Question it was Great Britain, amongst all the Great Powers, who came inexorably to bear the brunt of the risks and responsibilities which fell on Europe.

---

[168] 'The History of the Cretan Insurrection', E. 27, Finlay Papers.

[169] Even at the time the British abandonment of the Ionian Protectorate was widely interpreted in Europe as compounding a weakness simultaneously displayed by the Palmerston government's inability to make its influence felt during the current Danish–Prussian war. 'Un pays qui a cessé de prendre et commencé a rendre est dans sa décadence,' was Bismarck's alleged remark on hearing of the British exit from Corfu. Zetland, *Lord Cromer*, 36.

4

The End of Ottoman Power
in Crete, 1894–1898

If the wretched island catches fire again and fresh soldiers come from
Anatolia, and guns as well as gallows and fresh pashas, the Franks will again
mix themselves up in it: curse them too! And it won't do me any good—I
shall simply have more trouble.

(The Pasha of Megalokastro, in Nikos Kazantzakis, *Freedom and Death*)

To England, more than any other Power, the liberation of Crete has been due.

(*The Times*, 22 Dec. 1898)

Nikos Kazantzakis' great novel was set against the backdrop of renewed insurrection
by Cretan Christians against Ottoman domination at the end of the 1880s. The
worsening troubles his fictional Pasha foresaw came to a climax on 5 November
1898, when British troops of the 2nd Battalion of the Rifle Brigade in the port of
Candia (today's Heraklion) forcibly disembarked the remaining Ottoman soldiers
onto military transports. So ended effective Turkish rule in Crete stretching back to
1669. A few days later the Orthodox Archbishop of Crete ordered Te Deums to be
chanted throughout the island in honour of the up to 800 Christians (overwhelmingly Greek, although including some Armenians) who had been massacred in
the city on 6 September. But during those services special mention was made of the
British soldiers and sailors who were victims of the outbreak, and whose deaths were
described as 'the real cause of the ending of the Turkish rule in the island'.[1] Our task
is to explain why a relatively small number of *British* deaths triggered a change of
regime which had been the cause of fluctuating struggle for over thirty years; and to
explore what that meant—and did *not* mean—for the aspirations of the island's
majority to join Greece. In doing so our treatment must be related to the larger
Eastern Question as processes of ethnic confrontation, regional conflict, and
international rivalry collided at the end of the nineteenth century.[2]

[1] Sir Alfred Biliotti to Lord Salisbury, 16 Nov. 1898, FO78/4969, National Archives of the
United Kingdom.
[2] Previous accounts dealing with these events in a wider context include Douglas Dakin, *The
Unification of Greece* (London, 1972) and W. L. Langer, *The Diplomacy of Imperialism, 1890–1902*

Writing to the Duke of Wellington in mid-1830, Prince Leopold of Saxe-Coburg, briefly the prime candidate for the occupancy of the Hellenic throne, sought to influence Britain's distinguished premier on the subject of the addition of Crete to the territories designated for inclusion in the new kingdom of Greece. The Prince argued that

The exclusion [of Crete] will cripple the Greek state, morally and physically, will make it weak and poor, expose it to constant danger from the Turks, and create from the beginning innumerable difficulties for him who is to be at the head of that Government.[3]

Leopold's entreaty, however, left Wellington unmoved. The 'Iron Duke' had for some while been absolutely intent that Crete should constitute the most significant exception to the general principle which otherwise shaped the making of independent Greece: that its frontiers should enclose those Greek populations, and only those populations, which had participated most keenly in the revolt against Turkish rule. For this reason the British premier had insisted on the raising of the European blockade of the island, much to the consternation of Britain's own negotiator on the spot, Stratford Canning, who complained that the reimposition of Ottoman authority this would allow presaged severe retribution for local Christians. The ensuing coldness between Wellington and Canning, the latter destined to be a pivotal figure in Eastern diplomacy for decades thereafter, was a foretaste of the peculiar capacity of Cretan questions to trigger internal fractures amongst British cadres.[4]

In one respect at least, however, Wellington bowed to pressure in both Great Britain and Europe from those who declared that the Cretan Christians should not be left to the vengeance of Sultan Mahmud II, for whom the Greek revolt was the greatest blight on his reign. Although Crete was therefore excluded from Greece, its administration was transferred from the responsibility of the Porte to that of Mehmet Ali, the Albanian Viceroy of Egypt, then extending his claims on outlying provinces of the Sultan. During the ensuing years of Egyptian administration the situation of the Christian Greeks in Crete gradually improved. A process began in which the Turkish landholding classes were pushed back towards the hinterlands of the port towns where Ottoman military and civilian administration was based. The underlying shift was reflected in a demographic revolution. Whereas the total population of Crete in 1834 was estimated at 128,650, of which 35.6 per cent were Muslims, by 1881 the first formal census recorded a total of 279,165, of which the Muslim component had fallen to just over 26.2 per cent.[5] Yet Crete was by no means

(New York, 1935). For background on the earlier phases of the Cretan Question see Kenneth Bourne, 'Great Britain and the Cretan Revolt, 1866–1869', *Slavonic and East European Review*, 35 (1956–7), 137–52. Useful contemporary accounts in French are Victor Bérard, *Les Affaires de Crète* (Paris, 1898) and Lieut. H. de La Martinière, *La Marine française en Crète* (Paris, 1911).

   [3] Quoted in Bikelas, *Seven Essays*, 210.   [4] Lane-Poole, *Stratford Canning*, i. 479.
   [5] For an excellent survey of Crete's demography in modern times see Émile Kolodny, 'La Crète: mutations et évolutions d'une population insulaire grecque, *Revue de géographie de Lyon*, 43/3 (1968).

characterized by unrelenting communal division. Unlike many of their Cypriot co-religionists, Cretan Muslims were Greek speakers.[6] A recent study of Cretan society in the long wake of Ottoman conquest has, indeed, stressed the 'shared world' of the main religious communities.[7] That sharing had not been obliterated into the nineteenth century, and not even repeated insurrections were to liquidate it entirely—a facet captured in the tortured affinity of the great Greek captain and agonized Pasha of Kazantzakis' imagination.

With the break-up of Mehmet Ali's mini-empire under European pressure in 1840–1, Crete had been returned to the authority of the Sultan. The setback this represented to incipient Christian domination in the island, however, accentuated political tensions.[8] These were most acutely felt in the extensive mountainous districts in the west—their peaks towering above the capital, Canea (today's Khania)—where the almost complete absence of Muslims made the status quo seem especially anomalous.[9] Crete remained quiet during the Crimean War, as Hellenic populations waited, unavailingly, for the triumph of Russian Orthodoxy in the East. Only at the end of the 1850s did Christian grievances coalesce into a militant movement—though one viewed with little sympathy by Britain's consul in the island.[10] In mid-1866 a Christian revolt finally erupted, and although this fizzled out after much bloodshed two years later, it established what a subsequent French observer identified as the distinctive Cretan 'insurrection-type': successive phases of agitation and quiescence, a Muslim retreat into the towns, destruction of crops and homes, cordons separating the sides, and a European proclivity to become involved *without* effecting any resolution of fundamental conflicts.[11]

For our purposes one aspect of Cretan events during 1866–8 stands out: British determination that Christian militancy—seen principally as a manifestation of the ambitions of Russia and Greece—should not cause a new explosion of the Eastern Question. A critical assessment of the recently installed regime in Greece—whose 'cardinal sin' was perceived to be an alleged undoing of all the achievements of British rule in the Ionian Islands—was just one expression of this bias.[12] The Conservative Foreign Secretary, Lord Stanley, looked expectantly for a Turkish

[6] The Greek used by Cretan Muslims was in the demotic form, however, not the pure *kathevarousa* of high Greek culture. For example, on the arrival of Sawas Pasha as Governor-General in 1885, the *firman* of appointment had to be read out by a secretary who had accompanied him from Constantinople, 'as no Cretan Mussulman knows literary Greek'. See Thomas Sandwith to Sir William White (Ambassador, Constantinople), 6 June 1885, FO78/3774. Note that in our discussion of Cretan affairs below, we shall use the more modern term 'Muslim' rather than the contemporary British usage of 'Mussulman', except in original quotations.

[7] Molly Green, *A Shared World: Christians and Muslims in the Early Mediterranean World* (Princeton, 2000).

[8] In fact during the 1840s the Ottoman Governor of Crete, Mustapha Pasha, looked to local Christians for support in governing the unruly island. He was dismissed by the Sultan in 1851. See David Barchard, 'The Princely Pasha of Crete', *Cornucopia*, 5 (2003/4), 23–6.

[9] Canea had replaced Candia as the island capital with the return of Ottoman rule in 1841.

[10] See 'Memorandum Relative to the Island of Candia, 1821–1862', FO195/853.

[11] Martinière, *La Marine française*, 15–21.

[12] Bourne, 'Great Britain and the Cretan Revolt, 1866–1869', 82.

victory over Christian insurgents, and British officials encouraged Ottoman generals in Crete to act *more* firmly than they seemed disposed to do, providing that they kept 'within the limits of humanity'.[13] Even these limits could be fudged, so that whereas other European navies took off starving Christian women and children at the height of the troubles, British warships were under instructions to hold aloof, on the grounds that humanitarian intervention simply prolonged needless agony.[14] Whereas the Russians and the French for a while supported Crete's annexation to Greece, Lord Stanley identified Cretan autonomy under continuing Ottoman sovereignty—but with greater provision for Christian rights—as the best prescription.[15] This was the essence of the Organic Statute imposed on Crete by the Sultan in 1868, and approved not only by Stanley's Tories, but—despite Hellenic hopes—by Gladstone's Liberal government which shortly assumed office in London. In analysing later events, the fact that the concept of Cretan autonomy had its roots in British preferences is highly pertinent.

Crete remained exhausted and undisturbed until 1877, when communal violence was renewed, stimulated by the regional tremors fanning out from the bloody unrest in Bulgaria. When the Congress of Berlin was convened during the summer of the following year in the wake of a Russo–Turkish war, the Greek government incorporated the annexation of Crete in the list of its own desiderata. The manner in which the British premier, Benjamin Disraeli, kept the Greeks at arm's length in Berlin, however, put paid to any hope this aspiration might be met. Disraeli (or Lord Beaconsfield, as he had quite recently become) had already annoyed Sultan Abdul Hamid by grabbing Cyprus, and was not going to rub Cretan salt in the Ottoman wound. Instead, Article 23 of the Berlin Treaty decreed that the Organic Law of 1868 should be scrupulously executed, and it was a mark of Britain's deepening engagement with Crete that its modification in what was termed the Halepa Pact was duly signed in the presence of the British consul, Thomas Sandwith.[16] An Ottoman Christian, Photiades Pasha, was duly dispatched from Constantinople in November 1878 as Governor-General, and in the spirit of a new Turkish constitutionalism the Pasha not only sought his advisers from those who commanded a majority in the Cretan Assembly,[17] but accorded to the Christians 'the influence which their superior education and their numbers entitled them'.[18]

[13] For Stanley's attitudes to the Cretan crisis see John Vincent (ed.), *Disraeli, Derby and the Conservative Party: Journals and Memoirs of Edward Henry, Lord Stanley, 1849–1869* (London, 1978), 301–33.

[14] See J. Hilary Skinner, *Roughing it in Crete in 1867* (London, 1868), 33, for an eyewitness account by a British 'volunteer'. [15] Bourne, 'Great Britain and the Cretan Revolt, 1866–1869', 90–1.

[16] Tatsios, *The Megali Idea*, 49.

[17] An Ottoman constitution had been proclaimed on 23 Dec. 1876 at the start of the Constantinople Conference, attended by Lord Salisbury.

[18] Thomas Sandwith to Salisbury, 5 Sept. 1885, FO78/3774. It was symptomatic of the ironies in Anglo–Ottoman relations 'on the ground' that when Photiades Pasha pronounced his enthusiastic conversion to constitutional methods, Sandwith, as the representative of the most self-consciously liberal of the Great Powers, proved anything but encouraging on the matter.

The Halepa system, though short-lived, had critical effects on Cretan affairs. An authentic legislature brought with it the 'real' politics that the wider availability of public spoils implied. One effect was that sharper divisions opened up *within* the Christian community, suggestively assuming English tags as 'Liberal' and 'Conservative'. Furthermore, such divisions showed a capacity to cut *across* religious lines. Within a couple of years Sandwith was reporting the 'unusual spectacle ... of a mixed mob of Christians and Mussulmans cheering a successful Christian candidate, and hooting his Christian opponent'.[19] Yet already an incipient process whereby religious and cultural differences were subsumed in 'modern' forms of politicization was counteracted by other variables. For Sultan Abdul Hamid the loss of Egypt to his overlordship in 1882 following British occupation cut to the quick of his sultanate as the loss of Greece had to that of his grandfather, Mahmud II. A deep reaction set in from which Crete was unlikely to remain exempt. The appointment of a new Muslim Governor, Sawas Pasha, in mid-1885 indicated a return 'to the old days of Mussulman ascendancy', all the more pointed since the Pasha's personal involvement in the Cretan insurrection of the 1860s had been associated with extreme violence.[20] Sawas Pasha's arrival in the island on the early morning of 6 June testified to the latent polarity in Cretan society. The Pasha landed, Sandwith reported,

under a salute of artillery and proceeded to the Konak through streets lined with Turkish troops. A small detachment of native gendarmes was also on duty, and groups of Mussulmans were gathered on the line of route, but no Christian policemen or private citizens were to be seen. The sound of cannon died away only to render audible that of Church bells tolling forth ... to express the mournful feelings of the inhabitants.[21]

Shortly afterwards, Sandwith was himself replaced as British consul by Sir Alfred Biliotti, and it fell to the latter to become embroiled in the rising tension of the following years. It was inherent in the complexity of Cretan conditions that although the essential dispute was, in the formulation of a British naval observer, 'drifting into the more regularly defined channel of enmity between the Christian and the Mussulman population', the intensity of intra-Christian competition did not die away *pari passu*.[22] For some time the two principal fault-lines in Cretan politics ran alongside each other. They interacted in barely perceptible but profound ways, and it was no accident that it was a smashing Liberal win at elections in August 1889 which produced a disturbance mutating immediately into a confessional and ethnic struggle. This bout of fighting was only extinguished in mid-1890, by which time 30,000 Ottoman troops had been drafted into the island under the stern leadership of Shakir Pasha—the last time Constantinople was able

[19] Sandwith to Lord Granville (Foreign Secretary), 24 Apr. 1885, FO78/3774.
[20] Sandwith to White, 6 June 1885, ibid.   [21] Ibid.
[22] Commander Brenton (HMS *Fearless*) to Vice-Admiral Hoskyns, 1 Aug. 1889, *State Papers*, lxxxvii: *Correspondence Relating to the Affairs of Crete*, 112.

to stifle Cretan problems in this way.[23] Meanwhile, the Halepa arrangements had been suspended, and it remained to be seen whether there could be any way back to the opportunities so fleetingly witnessed in the wake of the Berlin Congress.

In Biliotti's analysis, the Halepa Pact possessed one central flaw: for it to work successfully 'the Imperial [Ottoman] Government required the hearty co-operation of the Christian population which they have never had and will never obtain'.[24] The British consul remained a strong advocate of reform in the fields of the judiciary and taxation, and a greater Christian presence in the gendarmerie, but he was under no illusions that such actions could produce anything more than a 'temporary rest' to Cretan struggles.[25] As usual during interludes of passivity, Christian and Muslim deputies joined in common demands in precisely the fields which Biliotti defined as most requiring action.[26] But if the latter had little real faith in the payback of reform for Ottoman authority, it is hardly surprising that Abdul Hamid shared the pessimism. Under the pressure from European ambassadors in his capital, he did dispatch a distinguished Ottoman Christian, Karatheodory Pasha, a veteran of the great meeting in Berlin, as Governor-General. But the circumstances were very different from the aftermath of 1878. Karatheodory was not, like Photiades Pasha before him, authorized to employ quasi-constitutional principles, or to recognize the facts of Christian superiority. The Sultan no longer recognized such facts anywhere in his realm. No reform legislation was consequently admitted to the Cretan legislature. Yet although the Ottoman Army had extinguished the fighting of 1889–90, it had not succeeded—as in 1867–8—in doing so for almost a generation. Instead there appeared a new Christian Revolutionary Committee, or *Epitropi*. The aim of this body was not to evict Ottoman troops—since it could hardly do that—but to 'remain under arms until the coming spring in the hope that external complications may offer an occasion to promote the interests of the island according to their own notions'.[27] Whether these 'notions' might be satiated by a revived and expanded Halepa agreement, or necessarily implied full annexation to Greece, remained, however, unclear.

When a fresh wave of violence occurred during early 1896, involving mostly but not exclusively Christian victims, Consul Biliotti sought to explain to his superiors in London a polarization within Crete which showed signs of plumbing new depths. He told Lord Salisbury, the Conservative leader who combined the British premiership with the position of Foreign Secretary, of the desperate feelings of Cretan Christians that the situation must be resolved by a 'final decisive

---

[23] Although Shakir Pasha was widely criticized in Europe for his repressive actions, it is notable that Commander Brenton, who was in a position to make the comparison, stated that 'he did not believe the Vali acted in suppressing disorder with anything like the sharpness which our [British] Government found necessary in dealing with Egypt in 1882'. See Brenton to Hoskyns, 2 Dec. 1889, *State Papers*, lxxxii: *1890: Correspondence Relating to the Affairs of Crete*, 137–8.

[24] Biliotti to Salisbury, 3 Mar. 1891, *State Papers*. xcvii: *1890–91: Further Correspondence Relating to the Affairs of Crete*, 32.   [25] Biliotti to Salisbury, 17 Mar. 1891, ibid.

[26] Tatsios, *The Megali Idea*, 67.   [27] Biliotti to Salisbury, 18 Jan. 1896, FO78/4736.

blow', and the contrasting apprehension of the Muslims that their only safety lay in martial law.[28] The gulf was accentuated by the replacement of Karatheodory by a Muslim Governor, Turkhan Pasha, whose suspension of the Cretan General Assembly appeared as the abolition of the very last residue of the Halepa system. Biliotti, suspecting a breakdown of unprecedented proportions, now pressed the Vali to reinforce key points in the island. He was not alone in seeking to avert disaster. Several Greek Orthodox bishops appealed to leaders of the *Epitropi* not to descend upon the strategic point of Vamos, since the only effect would be to make Christians elsewhere in the island more vulnerable.[29] Their advice was disregarded. On 24 May a Muslim mob ransacked the Christian quarter of Canea. By the following day it had the aspect of a 'dead city', though Biliotti discounted any 'preconceived scheme of massacre' by regular Turkish troops.[30] The event inaugurated the last great insurrection in the history of Ottoman Crete.

Several consequences flowed from the Canea disturbance. An impulse to direct European intervention surfaced. HMS *Hood* was the first to arrive, followed by Russian and French gunboats, fuelling Christian 'hopes of an interposition' by Europe.[31] They were disappointed, and it was left to Biliotti to join senior Orthodox clergy in seeking to calm the worst affected sections of the town. A widespread flight of terrified Cretans of both faiths started. The growing concentration of Turkish troops left rural Muslims without protection, and they fled towards the coasts. Christians caught in the ports often fanned out into the countryside where their co-religionists predominated, or took boats to mainland Greece and nearby islands such as Syra. These migrations were of great local complexity. Elements of communal coexistence survived. Christian chiefs sometimes provided escorts so that Muslim villagers could pass in safety. Here, too, began an economic war of religions epitomized by the destruction of olive groves—in Cretan insurrections there was an 'olive line' in patterns of violence beyond which normality was irretrievable. The outcome was an extreme form of Cretan disintegration in which the Muslims shut themselves up with Ottoman troops in the 'fortified places' on the coast, whilst the Christians—their internal differences inevitably in abeyance— dominated much of the rest of the country.

The instability around Canea spread rapidly to other towns, especially Candia, with its large hinterland of rural Muslims. Turkish reinforcements drove inland to relieve the besieged garrison at Vamos, and if, having done so, they had dug in, the possibility of a viable Ottoman statelet in Crete—that is, the basis of some future partition—might have emerged. Instead, the column traced a route back to the coast leaving 'a stream of fire' in its wake.[32] A retreating tide of Muslim civilians

28 Biliotti to Salisbury, 22 Feb. 1896, ibid.

29 S. B. Chester, *The Life of Venizelos* (London, 1921), 23.

30 Biliotti to Salisbury, 1 June 1896, FO78/4736.

31 The Royal Navy's eastern Mediterranean flotilla had recently been reinforced during the Armenian crisis, so that it was always British ships which were first to arrive in Crete during ensuing events.   32 Biliotti to Salisbury, 14 June 1896, FO78/4736.

followed, climaxing in a final headlong rush to safety offered by the walls of Candia. The problem immediately arose as to how these refugees were to be fed and housed. Sultan Abdul Hamid established a flow of relief from Constantinople which continued through resulting crises—though it did not eliminate the threat of starvation. As for accommodation, Biliotti helped to devise arrangements whereby the abandoned houses of Christian families were appropriated for the use of displaced Muslims. Such appropriation on an ethnic basis indicated how Europe was compromised by its deepening engagement in the Cretan struggle— one which was to have special vibrations for the British involvement in anguished Candia.

Biliotti was to remain central to the evolving British dilemma in Crete. He com- plained about this time of 'the inexplicable suspicion which is always hovering over this [British] Consulate'.[33] It was a very personal suspicion. Significantly, an experi- enced French commentator, Victor Bérard, stated that the island was afflicted not so much by a Cretan Question as by a 'Biliotti Question', a view not wholly to be discounted as characteristic of French Anglophobia in the Levant.[34] Born in Ottoman Rhodes to a Catholic Levantine family rooted in British consular service, Biliotti had gained great experience in various posts in the empire before becoming consul in Canea. He played a key personal role in negotiating the termination to the violence of 1889–90. By the mid-1890s he was indubitably 'The Boss' in the European suburb of Halepa—even the French consul was his son-in-law—and his influence extended well beyond consular circles. 'Absolutely saturated in oriental ways' was how a British journalist characterized Biliotti's persona.[35] Inevitably, he became susceptible to allegations by protagonists inside and outside the island. King George of Greece complained of his 'extreme Turkish bias'.[36] Others thought he favoured Greeks, and in posterity he emerged as a philhellene.[37] As usual in the complex late Ottoman world, the truth was not so crystalline.

Biliotti was, in fact, neither phil- nor anti-Hellene, Turcophile nor Turcophobe. But he did have distinctive views on Cretan society and politics. He believed that Cretans of all faiths 'longed for peace', but were driven to extremities by the inter- play between their own too-vivid imaginations and the cynical manipulation of the few. The island's passions were all the more corrosive because they were yet more frightening than 'the real known danger'. Reflecting on a recent panic, Biliotti remarked as follows:

The more futile the causes, the more the impending danger is serious, for it rests not on an incident which can be controlled or explained ... but in the imagination of the whole population which has gradually grown to that state of nervousness and excitability that the general feeling seems to be to 'kill and not be killed'.[38]

[33] Biliotti to Salisbury, 31 Mar. 1896, ibid.   [34] Bérard, *Les Affaires,* 91.
[35] R. A. H. Bickford-Smith, *Cretan Sketches* (London, 1898), 87.
[36] Sir Edwin Egerton to Salisbury, 5 Dec. 1896, FO32/678.
[37] J. Dawkins to Athens Embassy, 26 Sept. 1922, FO286/818.
[38] Biliotti to Salisbury, 3 July 1896, FO78/4736.

Here was the primal instinct which for Biliotti explained the grim scale of Cretan violence. His principal notion of how to improve matters involved the supersession of contested religious feeling by 'a union of the honest elements amongst Christians and Muslims' sharing identical interests in the flow of olives and wine—concerns nicely congruent with British commerce. In crude political terms this vision amounted to a renewed accommodation between the customary social leadership of Muslim pashas and Christian chiefs and merchants. Biliotti pressed such a political strategy, allied to the crushing use of force whenever required, on successive *valis*. 'How can I believe', Turkhan Pasha once exclaimed, 'that a Consul who gives such advice is intriguing against the tranquillity of the island?' The Pasha's gentle irony evoked the complex psychology in which Cretan reform and Biliotti were both caught up.

Yet the 'inexplicable suspicion' attached to Biliotti's consulate was also bound up more widely with British actions in the eastern Mediterranean. There was an Egyptian blot on British good faith, since Gladstone's promise during the occupation of that country in 1882 that the troops would soon depart had not been fulfilled. The possibility from the late 1880s that the British might be diplomatically crowbarred out of Egypt afforded credence to rumours that they aimed to add Crete to their empire as an alternative. Rumours of a British seizure of the island went back some fifty years. Suda Bay offered a better anchorage than either Alexandria or Cyprus, and as Secretary of State for India in 1876 Lord Salisbury had indeed raised the prospect at Cabinet. Two years later Britain occupied Cyprus, but at the time Crete had been considered as an alternative, only to be rejected as too challenging a proposition. When Salisbury, having formed a new Conservative administration in June 1895, sought to drag the Concert into sanctions against Sultan Abdul Hamid for a massacre of his Armenian subjects, opinion in Europe interpreted the British premier's zeal as simply a front for Britain's meddling in the Levant.[39] Britain's espoused 'disinterest' in the region as a whole, in short, was widely discounted, not least with regard to Crete.

Over the Armenian affair, however, Abdul Hamid inflicted a searing political defeat on Salisbury by exploiting divisions amongst the Powers. Although the British premier sought to play down this outcome by famously pointing out that the Royal Navy 'could not sail across the Taurus mountains', it weakened him severely.[40] At home those critics which traditionally looked to the break-up of the Ottoman polity afterwards urged him to wound the Sultan over Crete where he had failed over Armenia. An attempt was made to whip up a feverish anti-Ottoman climate of the sort that had accompanied the Bulgarian atrocities of the mid-1870s. 'The heather', one radical veteran impressed on Salisbury, referring obliquely to Gladstone's tirades of the Midlothian hustings at that time, 'is on fire all over the country.'[41] Salisbury retorted that in 1876 the other powers had

[39] Langer, *Diplomacy*, 379–80.   [40] Haslip, *The Sultan*, 218.
[41] Malcolm MacColl to Salisbury, 16 Sept. 1896, quoted in G. W. E. Russell, *Malcolm MacColl: Memoirs and Correspondence* (London, 1914), 163.

also been bent on punishing Turkey, whereas Russia and Austria had now become defenders of the Eastern status quo.[42] The nonconformist and liberal ferment through the summer of 1896 certainly had an artificial air, since Crete could not really be made to replicate the 'symbolic grievance' which had earlier allowed Bulgaria to reverberate in British politics. Nevertheless, Salisbury had to tread carefully, since even influential Conservative organs—such as *The Spectator*—criticized his tendency to follow a Concert supine before Ottoman depredations.[43] For the British premier, visibly championing an extension of Cretan autonomy represented the most convenient means of fending off such pressures.

Sultan Abdul Hamid, whose subtlety as an Eastern diplomatist was not in doubt, knew he had to tread very carefully himself, and it was no accident that a fresh pogrom in September 1896 against the Armenians coincided with a new schedule for Cretan reform, including a reduction in the Turkish military garrison.[44] Biliotti stressed the need for speedy implementation, and Salisbury latched onto the programme as a personal project. Central to these proposals was a reorganization of the Cretan gendarmerie under European officers. Without such a reliable law and order agency, the paralysis of free movement in the island—stopping Christians and Muslims returning to their homes—was bound to continue. In the following December an International Gendarmerie Commission arrived, composed of European military attachés from Constantinople. The British member, Sir Herbert Chermside—like Biliotti, steeped in Ottoman experience, and a fluent Turkish speaker—was to loom large in the history of the insurrection.[45] The Commission, however, was not followed by field officers, and although Salisbury lobbied for a British appointee at the head of a refurbished gendarmerie, this was blocked by the other powers as tantamount to an English takeover.[46] With the reforms reduced to yet another paper exercise, a cycle of refugee movement and political implosion restarted. 'A harmless looking lot', a British naval officer described Muslim families streaming sadly into Candia in early January 1897, 'with their pack donkeys, a few cattle, women and children', driven on by 'a kind of universal dread of some unknown calamity'.[47]

---

[42] Salisbury to MacColl, 12 Sept. 1896, ibid. 150

[43] G. H. Perris, *The Eastern Question of 1897 and British Policy in the Near East* (London, 1897), 104.

[44] The massacre followed an assault by Armenian revolutionaries on the Imperial Ottoman Bank in the capital. The incident marked a crucial watershed in the development of the Armenian Question.

[45] Chermside had served as military attaché in Constantinople during the Turco–Russian war of 1877–8, and subsequently sat on the Commission for the Delimitation of Turkish Frontiers. He was in the Egyptian Army 1883–88, before returning as attaché to the Embassy in Constantinople.

[46] Salisbury telegram to Queen Victoria, 9 Feb. 1897, in G. A. Buckle (ed.), *The Letters of Queen Victoria*, iii: *1896–1901* (London, 1932), 129. Salisbury tried to get the British High Commissioner in Cyprus to offer some of his British police officers for service in Crete, only for the request to be turned down on the grounds that it would prejudice law and order in Cyprus—a mark of the insecurity bedevilling British authority throughout the eastern Mediterranean.

[47] Commander Francis Noel to Captain Custance, 27 Jan. 1897, FO78/4831.

The sense of Greek Christians *and* Muslims of being 'abandoned by the Powers' fuelled the ensuing violence.[48] An Albanian, George Berovich Pasha, was made acting Vali, but he enjoyed no real authority over the Ottoman commander-in-chief. On 3 February the Pasha appealed to the consuls for intervention to avert a catastrophic collapse. Two days later a mob rampaged through the Christian quarter of the capital, this time to devastating effect. 'Massacre in Canea which is burning,' Biliotti telegraphed desperately and the first task of HMS *Barfleur* as it quickly descended on the town was to fight the conflagration.[49] When on the 6th the British consul and an Orthodox bishop visited the Christian neighbourhoods, they found the inhabitants 'in great dread', though Biliotti added that they 'praised the conduct of the Turkish soldiers surrounding them'.[50] 'We are ... face to face', the consul bleakly warned London, 'with [the situation] that if conciliatory measures fail, the matter may have to be fought out ... over a wide area, including Rethymno and Candia.'[51] It was already so. In Sitia province a 'sort of frenzy' took hold in which hundreds of isolated Muslim villagers, already disarmed, were killed, unleashing a final surge of frightened refugees towards Candia town. The breakdown of Crete was complete.

The effects resonated powerfully in Greece. The plight of Cretan Christian refugees in Athens was all too plain. In the Cretan troubles of 1888–89 King George had refrained from action.[52] But it would not be easy to keep 'the love of his people' by doing so again. If the monarchy proved powerless to pursue Greek claims over that island, where there was at least no other feasible successor to the Ottomans, there could be no hope of defending the Hellenic stake in Macedonia which since the 1870s had become so central to the Great Idea.[53] On 8 February 1897 a Greek naval squadron was sent into Cretan waters announcing its purpose to save Christians from massacre and 'assist the revolution' in the island (though Biliotti was adamant that in fact this put local Christians in even *greater* danger). It certainly threatened to trigger Ottoman reinforcements from other Turkish provinces. A Greek torpedo flotilla under the command of the King's second son, Prince George, was dispatched amidst scenes of delirious enthusiasm from Piraeus. A few days later a force of Greek regular troops also departed for Crete, and a British diplomat—otherwise scathing about Greek hopes and ambitions—who saw them go admitted that 'it was impossible not in some degree to sympathize' with the expedition.[54] On 15 February, 1,000 men under the command of Colonel Vassos went ashore in western Crete, and—having swiftly

[48] Biliotti telegram to Constantinople Embassy, 18 Jan. 1897, FO78/4832.
[49] Biliotti telegram to Constantinople Embassy, 5 Feb. 1897, ibid.
[50] Biliotti telegram to Constantinople Embassy, 6 Feb. 1897, ibid. One English eyewitness was the newly arrived archaeologist D. G. Hogarth. 'To this day,' Hogarth wrote years later, 'when I smell burning oil, I see Canea as I saw it first.' See his *Accidents of an Antiquary's Life* (London, 1910), 22.
[51] Biliotti to Constantinople Embassy, 6 Feb. 1897, FO78/4832.
[52] For background on the dilemmas of the dynasty see George J. Markopoulos, 'King George I and the Expansion of Greece, 1875-1881', *Balkan Studies*, 9 (1968), 21–39.
[53] Bérard, *Les Affaires*, 174.   [54] Sir Vincent Corbett, *Reminiscences* (London, 1927), 253.

secured control over the central portion of the island—prepared to march on the capital.

For the first time, Cretan union with Greece loomed as an imminent *fait accompli*. But its fruition under current circumstances could only be very bloody, and a blow to the credibility of the Concert as a guarantor of regional stability. When the consuls met together in Canea on 11 February Muslim mobs were 'masters of the situation' in the towns, passions ignited by news that Greek troops were on the move inside the island. Biliotti and Berovich Pasha together tried to make contact with Colonel Vassos's advance guard to tell them they were risking a 'last struggle' in which there would be many losers, but they were turned back by gunfire. Afterwards the British consul told Salisbury that only the forced evacuation of the Greek soldiers, the implementation of reforms, and European occupation could avert an implosion which not even Christian monasteries in the island would escape (thus deftly implying how inaction might feed political dangers in Britain).[55] 'These few measures', Biliotti grimly concluded his advice, 'should be taken immediately and simultaneously.'[56]

It was not Biliotti's reportage, vivid as it was, which decided things, however, but Abdul Hamid's intervention. He could not easily pacify Crete himself. But he could manoeuvre Europe into doing it for him. He signalled that otherwise Turkey would take 'extreme measures'—and there was little doubt that this entailed further massacres of Christian minorities in the empire.[57] The Concert of Europe had nearly split apart over Armenia. None of the powers relished a repeat. The Tsar sent his own flagship to Crete as a mark of his determination to calm things down. On 14 February the European embassies in Constantinople added their own call for prompt action. The following day 400 marines drawn equally from Britain, Russia, France, and Italy, and fifty Austrians, went ashore at Canea—the more belated arrival of fifty Germans indicating that Berlin was semi-detached from this newly activated local Concert. The international occupation of the island was under way.

That occupation had not been set in motion to further Christian aspirations, as Greek opinion supposed, but to stuff the genie back into its bottle. Misunderstanding on this point had profound implications. Clarity was not helped by the joint European statement that Crete was to be held *en dépôt* under the Concert's protection. But where was it to be *en dépôt* to? A Council of Admirals was set up and immediately called on Cretans to 'quietly await' the decision of the powers. To an English observer this was 'ridicuously vague', a criticism not surprisingly felt even more keenly by native Cretans.[58] Salisbury was bent on

---

[55] There were fierce attacks in Parliament on Salisbury's stance over Crete. 'The Greeks have joined the Cretans,' the Liberal leader, Sir William Harcourt, scoffed at the Tory benches, 'and you have joined the Turks.' Quoted in A. G. Gardiner, *The Life of Sir William Harcourt*, ii (London, 1923), 439.   [56] Biliotti to Salisbury, 11 Feb. 1897, FO78/4832.

[57] Sir Philip Currie (Constantinople) to Salisbury, 11 Feb. 1897, FO78/4815.

[58] See handwritten letter dated 20 Mar. 1897, in FO78/4800.

instituting 'absolutely effective autonomy', but whether the other Powers were prepared to help make it effective was another matter. Amidst the confusion Berovich Pasha suddenly vanished to Albania, and the Sultan did not appoint a successor—chaos had become his main ally in Crete, as it sometimes was elsewhere. Such chaos was assisted by the fact that this occupation was to be conducted by admirals whose writ did not penetrate far inland. Biliotti might have meddled dangerously in local politics, but he had provided a form of mediation between warring elements; for some while he was now pushed to the margins, whilst the European admirals blundered about lacking any political compass to guide them.[59] In Crete, the cost of the resulting vacuum was to be measured in lives.

More immediately transparent was a European backlash against Greece the venom of which had not been matched since the time of Otto. Of no Power was this more true than Germany, the Kaiser's mother (the English-born Empress Victoria) complaining of his 'unjust and blind dislike' of Greece.[60] But Salisbury was also contemptuous of Hellenic intervention driven, as he saw it, by mob emotions and heedless of the threat to regional and European peace.[61] When Colonel Vassos' force tentatively approached Canea it was stopped in its tracks by a combined cannonade of the Turkish Army and the warships of the Concert—a sort of little 'Navarino reversed' which roused fresh indignation amongst some British Liberals.[62] As the battered Greeks retired into the interior, Crete was divided up into European *secteurs*: Sitia was allocated to France, Rethymno to Russia, Canea to international control under an Italian commandant, and Candia—now with its 50,000 Muslim refugees—to Great Britain. When 500 Seaforth Highlanders, under the command of Colonel Chermside, arrived in Candia town, Turkish guards and a band accompanied them to their barracks, with much hailing by the crowds of a British Protectorate with a special obligation to the Muslim community.[63] After five more Highlander companies arrived in early April, met by a similar manifestation, Biliotti reported approvingly on the tie which had quickly sprung up between British peacekeepers and Cretan Muslims.[64]

Chermside's instruction was 'to get control of the situation', but there could be no control until Colonel Vassos and his men were evacuated. Their very presence, it was felt, explained why Christian opinion had swung wildly from support for 'moderate' autonomy towards full annexation to Greece.[65] Kaiser Wilhelm was 'wild' for a blockade of Piraeus to impose an immediate evacuation of Vassos' force.[66] Salisbury

[59] For a widely shared critique of the admirals see Bickford-Smith, *Cretan Sketches*, 220–1.
[60] One source of the Kaiser's prejudice was his opposition to the marriage of his sister Sophie to the Greek monarch, and his bitterness at her subsequent adoption of the Orthodox faith.
[61] Roberts, *Salisbury*, 650.   [62] Perris, *The Eastern Question*, 185.
[63] Biliotti telegram to Constantinople Embassy, 30 Mar. 1897, FO78/4832.
[64] Biliotti telegram to Constantinople Embassy, 11 Apr. 1897, ibid.
[65] Bickford–Smith, *Cretan Sketches*, 115–22. Muslim opinion was divided between those who thought that autonomy represented their best hope for future safety, and those who cleaved to direct Ottoman rule as the sole guarantee that was dependable.
[66] Hannah Pakula, *An Uncommon Woman: The Empress Frederick* (London, 2002), 568.

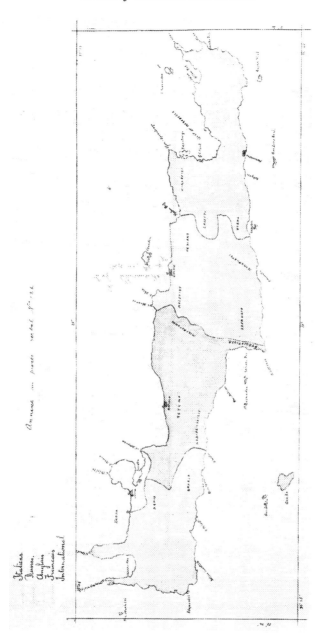

Map 3. Colonel Chermside's map showing the international occupation of Crete, 1898. (European sectors from left to right: Italian, Russian, English, French. The capital, Canea, and its hinterland came under collective international supervision.)

shared his intent on such swift eviction, but for slightly different reasons. Experience had taught him that autonomy within the Ottoman Empire only worked—as it had in the Lebanon—when Ottoman troops had already been removed from the scene.[67] There was no chance of that so long as Greek soldiers remained in strength. Yet the complicity of British warships in punishing those purporting to save vulnerable Christians from slaughter remained sensitive. Several members of Salisbury's Conservative Cabinet were 'very Hellenic', including Joseph Chamberlain, clinging to his own nonconformist past.[68] A blockade of Crete alone, rather than one encompassing the Hellenic kingdom, was the most that Salisbury could drive through the British Parliament. In some quarters in Europe, where hostility to Great Britain was rising sharply, it was claimed that this drag on decisive action helped intensify the slide to war between Greece and Turkey.

Neither King George of Greece nor Sultan Abdul Hamid wanted war, but neither could risk confronting the forces around them. Mediation between them had anyway been complicated by the suggestion that the Greek monarch's second son, Prince George, should be made Vali or 'High Commissioner' of Crete as a counterweight to the withdrawal of Vassos. Significantly, this idea was contested by some Athenian factions, for whom it smacked of a ploy to degrade the Great Idea into petty fiefdoms under royal aegis—here were the traces of future ideological and political stress.[69] But it was above all opposed by Abdul Hamid, for whom a non-Ottoman in the role was anathema. At first the Sultan restrained the militant impulse amongst his own advisers,[70] but on 18 April 1897 an incursion of Greek irregulars across the northern border sparked hostilities. The Turkish Army might no longer be able to pacify Crete, but it could hit hard on the mainland. A Greek Army under Crown Prince Constantine was defeated in the plains of Thessaly, and the road to Athens lay open. Badgered by Queen Victoria, Salisbury dispatched HMS *Nile* to the area, ready to take the Greek royal family into exile. To Turkish assault, however, was added a diplomatic battering by Europe, with the Kaiser insisting that the Greeks be made to 'beg' before being saved from their fresh mistakes.[71] Insofar as King George looked to England to shield him from this onslaught, he was largely disappointed.

Abdul Hamid exploited these events with his usual adroitness. For once the powers had to supplicate him, not vice versa. Only when Tsar Nicholas promised his 'lifelong gratitude' did the Sultan stop his army's advance on Athens. He ensured, however, that the resulting occupation of much of Thessaly was not marked by the usual excesses—a British military observer congratulated the Ottoman commander-in-chef, Edhem Pasha, on his 'humanity, good sense and generosity'.[72] Abdul

[67] Salisbury to Currie 14 Apr. 1897, FO78/4810.   [68] Buckle (ed.), *Letters*, iii. 133.
[69] George J. Markopoulos, 'The Selection of Prince George of Greece as High Commissioner in Crete', *Balkan Studies*, 10 (1969), 338–9.   [70] Haslip, *The Sultan*, 228.
[71] Tatsios, *The Megali Idea*, 116.
[72] C. Bigham to Salisbury, 17 Apr. 1898, FO78/4914. Nevertheless, just as some depredations had accompanied the short-lived Greek advance, so they did the ensuing Turkish invasion of Greece.

Hamid can have harboured little doubt that he would have to hand back conquered Greek territory eventually, but meanwhile Turkish opinion basked in the warm glow of unaccustomed triumphalism. Momentarily the political topography of the Near East was inverted. Sir Philip Currie, British Ambassador to the Porte, remarked how the Sultan was raised 'on a new pinnacle', and that Turkey was 'no longer a weak and rotten state'.[73] That the last phases of Ottoman power inside Crete evolved when the Sultan had won back a good deal of lost prestige is important in understanding the process—and its limits.

Part of the price Greece paid for Europe's grudging protection in its defeat was the withdrawal of its contingent from Crete. Athenian ministers pleaded that some Greek soldiers should remain as part of an international garrison. For Salisbury this was attractive. In some respects Greek precipitancy had eased his own situation. Meanwhile, by permitting a detachment of Hellenic troops to remain in Crete under European authority, a sop could be thrown to important elements in British opinion and smooth the way towards local autonomy. He was forced to retreat on the matter, however, before the Kaiser's insistence that Greece should have no 'bridge of gold' back to safety.[74] When Vassos and his men left on 27 May 1897, they were humiliated by being given hardly any time to escape through the blockade, leaving all their equipment behind. More lasting were the implications for the Greek population of Crete. Henceforth the best hope was that Turkish troops would also eventually have to leave, leaving the field clear for a genuinely autonomist solution. As a placation for the angry Concert, some insurgent leaders associated with extreme annexationist demands were hounded out of Crete by their Christian opponents, including a youthful and rising politician, Eleutherios Venizelos, allegedly stoned when taking ship for Athens.[75] It was a lesson Venizelos never forgot.

Of all Cretan towns, Candia, with its distressed Muslim refugees living on the Sultan's meagre flour dole, was bound to be most affected by Ottoman revival, and Colonel Chermside noticed a 'considerable efflorescence' amongst the population.[76]

A Conservative MP, who attached himself to Edhem Pasha's staff, not only observed the sacking of a Greek frontier town, but enthusiastically joined in. 'I collared as many portable things as I could', Sir Ellis Ashmead-Bartlett noted in his diary, 'in remembrance of my sojourn here.' See diary entries for 23–4 Apr. 1897, Ashmead-Bartlett Papers, Institute of Commnwealth Studies, University of London.

[73] Currie to Salisbury, 2 June 1897, FO78/4802. On being told of his enforced abdication in 1909, Abdul Hamid's immediate response was allegedly to say that he 'did not deserve to be deposed' because of his triumph in 1897. See Sir Edwin Pears, *The Life of Abdul Hamid* (London, 1917), 321.

[74] Buckle, (ed.), *Letters*, iii. 149–50.

[75] Chester Samuel Beach, *Life of Venizelos* (London, 1921), 53. Venizelos, in fact, had from the late 1880s been a leading 'moderate', but had taken up an 'extreme' position as the revolution in 1896/7 unfolded. Once in Athens after his hurried departure, his views again shifted, telling an Athenian editor in an interview that 'little states must adapt themselves to circumstances, and ... realize their national aspirations by degree. He alluded to Cavour and Italy.' Subsequently he always aspired to be the Cavour of Greece. See Doros Alastos, *Venizelos: Patriot, Statesman, Revolutionary* (London, 1942), 26.   [76] Chermside to Salisbury, 15 June 1897, FO78/4890.

Most tangible in Candia, too, were the reactionary currents flowing from Abdul Hamid's dispatch to the island of Djevaad Pasha, a distinguished Ottoman administrator and old friend of Biliotti, to take a closer grip on affairs. Through the summer a divergence now appeared between the political impulses in the British sector, and those of the other powers, especially France. In Sitia—from which most Muslims had been extruded—a Franco-Christian axis emerged. French soldiers helped rebuild Greek schools and hospitals, and on 14 July celebrated Bastille Day with local well-wishers to enthusiastic slogans of 'Long Live France and Crete', 'Down with Turkey', and, allegedly, 'Down with Germany'.[77] Biliotti detected a 'contagion of Turcophobia' amongst the other European forces in Crete flowing from the fact that their sectors overlapped with zones of Christian dominance. He described the situation in these latter areas:

The Christians are acquainted with European languages, in which they can hold conversations with [international] officers. They repeat in very moving terms their sufferings. The officers see their wrecked churches, and their desecrated tombs (an offence of which the Christians are not guilty). These officers are not in contact with Muslims, and when by chance they meet, they cannot speak together, nor do they see their ruined houses, which are far in the inland district.[78]

The British in Candia were inversely situated. Their interaction with the small Christian remnant was limited to throwing a thin line of protection around that quarter, especially the cathedral, at moments of tension, and guarding the Archaeological Museum, with its collections testifying to Crete's Hellenic legacy. To insurgents beyond the cordon and sympathizers in Europe, such a pattern made British troops seem little more than 'supports for the *bashi bazouks*'.[79] There was at least a grain of truth to this, although far from consorting with the locals as in other sectors, the British garrison in Candia remained largely confined to its encampments—an attitude which lent itself to much caricaturing, especially in French circles, as typical of British isolationist *hauteur.*[80]

Powerful feelings amongst Cretan Christians about British tendencies in Candia, recycled as they were through liberal-radical channels into British domestic politics, were accentuated by two main issues. The first concerned the pillage of Christian property. A Christian petition to the Council of Admirals pleaded that such looting was rampant, and there were indeed signs that Muslim beys were losing the ability to control their own community.[81] Chermside's retort to such statements was that there was actually less damage of this sort in Candia than elsewhere, despite the fact that Candia 'did not have a very distinct Christian quarter with Christian homes and shops scattered through a large Moslem city'.[82] Nevertheless, the impression

[77] Biliotti to Salisbury, 20 July 1897, FO78/4831.   [78] Ibid.

[79] Martinière, *La Marine française*, 101.

[80] Ibid. For a Cretan Christian complaint at the unwillingess of British troops to make direct contact with them see M. Korakes (General Chief of the Eastern Provinces) to Chermside, 6 July 1897, FO78/4890.   [81] Biliotti to Embassy, 17 Oct. 1897, FO78/4832.

[82] Chermside to Salisbury, 20 Nov. 1897, FO78/4890.

that British troops did little to secure Christian property was widespread, especially once a new rash of pillaging occurred as conditions deteriorated in early 1898. The second issue was even more sensitive: the profanation of graves. Chermside fiercely denied any such occurrences under British oversight, whereas there had been at least one such case in Russian-occupied Rethymno. A situation was developing, the British commander complained, whereby any faults in the European occupation 'are attributed to our blue jackets and soldiers, although their general conduct is far superior to that of the Italians, the French and the Russians'.[83] Chermside and Biliotti attributed this bias to the propaganda of 'foreign agents', but also to the machinations of the Archbishop of Crete, who now emerged in their eyes as a sinister influence in the island. The latter belief fitted into a growing pattern of alienation between the British presence and clerical Orthodoxy in the eastern Mediterranean.

What did these criticisms of English behaviour represent? Biliotti did not believe that they were 'a sign of hatred on the part of the Christian people' towards England.[84] Rather he thought they reflected how English influence in the island was becoming paramount. The Cretan Christians understood both that Greece was powerless to act on their behalf, and that the European powers were too divided to act unanimously together when it came to a final resolution. The sole hope of ending a permanent state of uncertainty and sporadic violence lay in one Great Power cutting through all the difficulties and imposing a solution of its own. That power might once have been Russia, but Russia had long since succumbed to Slavic, not Hellenic, sympathies. The only power capable of unilaterally effecting the fulfilment of Christian aspirations in Crete was Britain. The realities of Candia currently belied this expectation. But the severity, even the gross exaggeration, as Chermside and Biliotti thought, of the aspersions cast on British good faith nevertheless carried as their subtext a Christian plea for British help. The climax of the story was to afford credence to this psychological puzzle behind the Anglo-Hellenic conundrum within the island.

Meanwhile, Chermside was 'between the devil and the deep sea' amidst the sufferings of Candia.[85] If the town imploded under the external threat of Christian militia and internal distress—including divisions between better-off Muslims and their co-religionists whose future looked bleaker by the day—the British commander and his Seaforth Highlanders, Welsh Fusiliers, and naval marines could not avoid becoming embroiled. Chermside pressed for reinforcements, so that his troops could police the grazing areas of the refugees' starving flocks outside the town, and Turkish guards be withdrawn. Indeed, both Chermside and Biliotti had for some while shared Salisbury's conviction that the only way out of the impasse was a Turkish military evacuation from the whole island. As a *de facto* Christian administration began to appear in much of Crete, Candian realities appeared increasingly

[83] Biliotti to Sir Thomas Sanderson, 28 Jan. 1898, FO78/4939.
[84] Biliotti to Sanderson, 29 Jan. 1898, FO78/4933.   [85] Chester, *Venizelos*, 56.

anomalous. The possibility loomed of the British sector becoming an isolated and doomed rump of Muslim power. To manoeuvre out of this tight situation, Chermside sought from London a 'freer hand' to conduct an experiment in which bazaars along the cordon should encourage the revival of inter-communal commerce. Here was Biliotti's old ideal of rediscovering an identical interest between 'honest Christians and Muslims'. If it succeeded, the local British presence might yet spearhead a reconciliation between communities who for over a year, Biliotti told Salisbury, had 'only seen each other in fighting'.[86]

Salisbury needed persuasion to grant 'a freer hand' along these lines. He feared the obligations which more activity by British soldiers implied, especially since, the previous November, Germany had—in what became a famous contemporary metaphor—'laid down her flute' in Crete and increased its freedom of manoeuvre elsewhere.[87] The local risks were shown when Biliotti—gradually coming back to the fore—went to Candia to sound out Muslim civilians. He found them bitterly opposed to the reopening of internal communications, since 'they had nothing to sell nor money to buy anything, and that the markets would exclusively benefit the Christians'.[88] Salisbury nonetheless gave Chermside and Biliotti a tentative go-ahead, and on 6 April 1898 forty Muslim beys and about the same number of Greek chiefs met under British supervision in 'apparent cordiality', sharing a few sparse refreshments and 'deeply deprecating the situation' which they all agreed it was time to end.[89] Any reversal of present hatreds was bound to be a dangerous and patchy process, and there was a brief upsurge in the destruction of Muslim-owned plantations beyond the cordon. Yet by May a number of bazaars under British protection were operational, and in some locations Christian and Muslim villagers began to till the same fields for the first time since 1896.

With this apparent easing of tension, Colonel Chermside disappeared on leave on 24 June 1898. His departure conjured up the atmosphere in Candia. Turkish officials and notables accompanied him to the landing stage, whilst Chermside was 'preceded by men carrying huge bouquets and strewing flowers and rose-water in his path'.[90] Ordinary Muslims packed the streets and overhanging balconies. Christians were less effusive—a message was sent with 'a few words of acknowledgement for the assistance and protection he [Chermside] had afforded them at all times'. 'This is really remarkable and satisfactory,' it was noted in the Foreign Office,[91] for whom Anglophilia amongst Eastern Muslims was a rare phenomenon, and Chermside was made a major-general, and then knighted. Not all was harmony on his return, and critics in press and Parliament alleged he had done nothing in Candia 'beyond lending...support to the Turkish

---

[86] Biliotti to Salisbury, 11 Mar. 1898, FO78/4933.

[87] Austrian soldiers and sailors did not withdraw till Mar. 1898. The absence of what became the 'Central Powers' thereafter heightened British dominance of the Cretan Concert, but also made that entity a more fragile phenomenon.   [88] Biliotti to Salisbury, 8 Apr. 1898, FO78/4933.

[89] Ibid.   [90] Biliotti to Salisbury, 25 June 1898, ibid.

[91] Sanderson minute, 5 July 1898, ibid.

administration'.[92] Since Salisbury forbade any rebuttal of these allegations for fear of stoking controversy, Chermside's supporters could only ensure that a defence appeared in a friendly Athenian newspaper. In this account a Cretan deputy asserted that Chermside's instructions had only allowed him to observe Turkish troop movements, and pass warnings to Christians outside the town.[93] This he had certainly done, though the flourish that he 'had been the representative of the Christian insurgents in the town [of Candia]' went perhaps a bit far. More accurate was the conclusion that the British commander's conduct had always been 'very enigmatical'. Here was the enigma of international peacekeeping at the very outset of its modern history.

If the experiment of reconciliation was focused in and around Candia, however, so was a contradictory belief amongst Cretan Muslims in the 'staying power' of their government, and with it a conviction that this power would result 'in the retention by themselves of some measure of their old ascendancy'.[94] When Edhem Pasha,[95] the *kaimakam* or chief civil officer, requested that Muslim civilians be allowed to harvest crops and repair mosques outside the town under military protection, Biliotti warned Chermside's successor, Colonel Reid, that to allow this before Christians could do the same for their abandoned churches would only reignite conflict between the creeds. It was, however, the European Council of Admirals which lit the fuse under this powder keg. In early August it took the decision to set up a new Executive Committee to make contact with the Christian Assembly. This was clearly the precursor to a new administration. Such a 'shadow' government would need money; and money was something which Europe had always grudged. The quickest way to get cash was to seize control of the customs houses. At the very end of August the admirals, at Russian instigation, took the decision to occupy the Dimes, dismiss the Muslim staff, and replace them with Greek subordinates. This took place on 3 September in Canea and Rethymno. The local British authorities warned that 'that which is an easy task in Canea and Rethymno became a very dangerous undertaking in Candia', and stressed that there were not enough troops in the town to protect the Christians in the event of a violent backlash.[96] They were overruled. Afterwards it was Biliotti's view that this decision, by overfilling the cup of Muslim despair, was 'the final cause of our present troubles'.[97]

---

[92] The radical journalist H. N. Brailsford, himself just back from Crete, composed a diatribe against Chermside in the form of a report to the Grosvenor House Relief Committee. Chermside's detailed rebuttal is in FO78/4969. Another figure who took the opportunity to lash out at Chermside was the archaeologist Arthur Evans, who accused the colonel of having had his Christian servant thrown into jail for entering Candia. See J. Alexander MacGillivray, *Minotaur: Sir Arthur Evans and the Archaeology of the Minoan Myth* (London, 2000), 158–60.   [93] The article is in FO78/4933.
   [94] Chermside to Salisbury, 31 Mar. 1898, FO78/4969.
   [95] This Edhem Pasha is not to be confused with the Turkish commander-in-chief in Thessaly.
   [96] Biliotti to Salisbury, 30 Sept. 1898, FO78/4934.
   [97] Ibid. The Muslim grievances on the eve of the massacre are fully described in Dr Ittar to Chermside, 21 Sept. 1898, FO78/4934.

The events of 6 September in Candia can be briefly recounted.[98] At 1:30 p.m. a picket of Highland Light Infantry seized the Dime. A large and heated meeting of Muslims was meanwhile taking place in the centre of the town, which a group of beys had difficulty in controlling. According to an eyewitness, Edhem Pasha was seen in the harbour area giving out commands, and shortly afterwards 'an unarmed but unrestrained crowd of Muslims came pouring down the main street', only to be stopped at the main harbour gates by a British platoon.[99] Three of the soldiers were fatally stabbed to death. An account Biliotti believed to be accurate went on:

In about five or ten minutes fire was opened on the British soldiers by native Muslims and by one or two Turkish soldiers . . . stationed in front of the *Hotel de Crète* . . . The British soldiers who had not fallen retreated towards the harbour, and the gates leading to it having been closed, the native Muslims turned their fire against the Christians, while fire was set to their shops and storehouses.[100]

Whilst a wholesale massacre of Christians got under way, the British troops around the harbour were 'caught like rats in a trap'.[101] There were several fatalities on the small boats which HMS *Hazard* and HMS *Hazel* dispatched towards shore. The first the occupants of the main British camp on the western outskirts knew of the trouble was when they came under fire, surrounding houses having been loopholed for the purpose. Only when British warships began a blanket bombardment of the town after 3 p.m. did things gradually quieten down. Shortly after 5 p.m. Edhem Pasha re-entered the harbour, held his hands above his head, and the Muslim firing instantly ceased (leading to the assumption on the British side that the whole affair had been stage-managed). Regular Turkish troops then belatedly began restoring order. British deaths on the day were seventeen, with thirty-nine severely wounded; one Victoria Cross was posthumously awarded. Out of a Christian population recently swelled to around 1,000, up to 800 were killed; most survivors had crammed into the sanctuary of the Greek cathedral. Muslim fatalities were twenty-nine. Looking out at dawn from HMS *Camperdown* on 7 September, Biliotti could just make out the still burning shell of the home in which the British Vice-Consul Calymachus Calocherino and his family had perished.

The situation in Candia remained highly explosive. The principal danger was that, on hearing news of the massacre, the Christian militia would descend on the town, and trigger more fighting. Unless the remaining Christian women and children were taken out by ship, Biliotti told his military superiors, 'not one of them will be saved'.[102] British officers on the cordon were instructed to persuade

---

[98] A detailed chronology of the day's events from a British military perspective can be found in Ron Philips, 'Candia: 6 September, 1898', in Theocharis Detorakis and Alexis Kalokerinos (eds.), *I Teleftaia Fasi tou Kritikou Zitimatos* (The Last Phase of the Cretan Question) (Heraklion, 2001), 451–79.   [99] Biliotti to Salisbury, 30 Sept. 1898, FO78/4934.
[100] Ibid.   [101] Quoted in Chester, *Venizelos*, 64.   [102] Ibid.

the oncoming militia to halt, and to pass on news of any movements to the Turks—despite the fact that Turkish troops had just inflicted serious losses on Reid's command. 'No pretext can be left to the Muslims', Biliotti stated, 'for renewing the attack on British forces.'[103] The humiliation of the British position in Candia arose not only from the events of 6 September, but from their vulnerability during the following days when reinforcements had yet to arrive from Malta.

The sensitivity of British relations with the Christian leadership can easily be imagined. Only Biliotti had the linguistic facility and *savoir faire* to deflect the intense feelings at work. He travelled to the Christian headquarters at Patsides and explained that satisfaction might be had by shelling the Turks and hanging some Muslims, 'but that would not have been justice... We [the British] preferred doing things quietly but firmly, in order to arrive at a more satisfactory result without bloodshed.'[104] But Biliotti also held out to his Christian interlocutors, led by the Archbishop, the prospect of 'a prompt and radical solution of the Cretan question'. This was effective bait. Greek Christians had long hoped to secure the sympathy and patronage of the British. Now events had suddenly put it within their grasp. The Archbishop promised that he would try to keep the militia under control, and promised to guard the exposed British encampments. What he wanted most immediately from Biliotti was a list of Christian survivors in Candia. Flowing from these exchanges was the initial outline of a new configuration of power in the island. Suddenly all allegations of British conspiracy with the Turks were replaced by a rhetoric of 'powerful Albion', and the British Queen, not the Russian Tsar, emerged as the subject of gushing toasts.

British reprisals for Turkish actions were sure, but could not come immediately. Reinforcements had to be rushed to Crete from other Mediterranean stations. But proof was needed of the complicity of *regular* Ottoman troops in the killing of British soldiers. Chermside was packed off back to the island, not entirely willingly, by Salisbury to ascertain this central fact. Impending vengeance, meanwhile, had a narcotic effect on British opinion. Events in Candia coincided with the climax of the reconquest of the Sudan—seventeen years after the death of General Gordon. It was widely noted by London newspapers that British fatalities in Candia had been more than those suffered by General Kitchener's army at Omdurman just four days before.[105] Queen Victoria's taste for retribution latched onto the burning to death of Vice-Consul Calocherino's household. "Surely we cannot let our Vice-Consul be killed?' she asked Salisbury.[106] The latter had every intention of exacting his price. Over Armenia Abdul Hamid had ducked and weaved out of his reach. The shedding of British soldiers' blood brought the Sultan back within reach, and in exploiting the opportunity a strain

---

[103] Biliotti telegram to Constantinople Embassy, 7 Sept. 1898, FO78/4935.

[104] Biliotti to Constantinople Embassy, 21 Sept. 1898, ibid.

[105] The Ottoman press reported almost nothing about Candia from 6 Sept. onwards, and a great deal about the Sudan, where Christians were killing Muslims rather than vice versa.

[106] Buckle (ed.), *Letters*, iii. 180.

of hardness in the Prime Minister's character—and a strong distaste for Islam as a 'false religion'—plainly showed.[107]

With the arrival of more British troops, chastisement began on 13 September when Edhem Pasha was summoned aboard the British flagship, appropriately HMS *Revenge*. 'Full satisfaction' was demanded by Rear-Admiral Sir Gerard Noel: the initial requirement was the rounding up of all those suspected of complicity for attacks on British troops, the pulling down of loopholed houses, and the disarmament of Muslim civilians.[108] Given the fears of a violent Christian entry into the town, the Muslims' yielding of their arms was fiercely resisted, despite Noel's promise to keep the Christians on their side of the cordon 'as much as was possible'. The Pasha pressed for, and was provisionally given, a guarantee that in the event of disarmament the safety of his co-religionists would be assured. Here was the origin of what shortly became a European commitment to the Cretan minority, and the fact that it was made in a specifically *Anglo-Turkish* context was highly significant. For the moment Edham Pasha was left in no doubt of the duress that Turkish authority was under. Complaining that he had been accorded no salute on boarding the British warship, he was simply told, 'It was not the rule now in Crete.'[109]

There followed a succession of British blows to hammer home the new dispensation. When there was a delay in destroying loopholed buildings, Colonel Reid warned that they should be pulled down before sunset.[110] On 16 September, Admiral Noel decreed that civilian disarmament was to be completed within four days. Simultaneously Edhem Pasha was forced to leave the island, and Turkish troops were ordered out of their fortress 'with the exception of a few left to represent the flag', thereafter being confined to the grounds of their barracks. With disarmament secured, the rounding-up of Muslim suspects began, with over 140 taken aboard British ships pending trial. The gathering of evidence through interpreters was necessarily a rough and ready process, its dangers heightened by Salisbury's ruling that it be completed with the utmost promptness. The ensuing trials were to provide a notable precedent in the evolution of international law relating to war crimes.[111]

The fate of the Turkish flag—and therefore the Sultan's sovereignty as 'the real point of honour'—was the central question which had to be decided in the light of Chermside's assessment. On 21 September, Salisbury eagerly received the latter. First, Sir Herbert assured the premier that the Christian militia was 'fairly in hand', having responded to his appeals for patience and moderation.[112] With regard to recent killings, Chermside stated there was 'a strong case against Turkish

107 Steel, *Lord Salisbury*, 107.
108 Biliotti to Constantinople Embassy, 13 Sept. 1898, FO78/4935.
109 Biliotti to Constantinople Embassy, 13 Sept. 1898, FO78/4935.
110 Biliotti telegram to Constantinople Embassy, 14 Sept. 1898, ibid.
111 See unpublished work by R. John Pritchard, 'Essays Relating to the Cretan Troubles of 1896–1898: The Intervention of the Concert of Europe and the Genesis of Modern International Humanitarian Law', Institute of Commonwealth Studies Library, University of London.
112 Biliotti telegram to Constantinople Embassy, 21 Sept. 1898, FO78/4970.

administration and garrison on general grounds and details'. On this basis he recommended the eviction from the island of the Turkish Army except for their flag and a nominal garrison. Chermside reported that the town was firmly under British control, but that it was unlikely Turkish soldiers would voluntarily embark *without explicit instructions from the Sultan*. It was, as usual, left to Biliotti to tell Djevaad Pasha the essence of what was required. The Pasha gave an assurance that 'he thought that the departure of the [Turkish] troops is under consideration in the [Yildiz] Palace'.[113] Nobody with any experience of Ottoman government, however, could be under any illusion that 'consideration' by the Sultan was anything other than a process prone to calculated procrastination and possible reversal.

A power struggle was already under way in Constantinople. An influential faction contended that, as over Armenia, 'the Powers did not mean business' in Crete.[114] This assessment was held to be all the surer because 'England was in reality the only active partner in the affair [of Candia]'—that is, the other powers would not stand by it if Abdul Hamid rigidly maintained his rights to the full.[115] Yet such resistance to *force majeure* depended on the will of the Cretan Muslims themselves holding firm. The leaders of that community, however, now believed that their safety lay in pacification under European and, above all, *British* protection—and such pacification could only be prejudiced by the continued presence of Turkish soldiery. The first hangings under British military law on 29 September of those found guilty for acts of violence on 6 September crystallized this new Muslim dependency. A deputation of notables appealed to Biliotti that 'the only means for the Moslem population to save the little property still left to them was for the Sultan to agree to the evacuation of the fortified towns'.[116] Biliotti duly had this message passed on to the Yildiz Palace. That the Candian Muslims concurred in a transference of responsibility for their well-being from the Sultan to European authority underpinned the force of the explicit pledges which ensued.

Ottoman military power was now clearly doomed. What hung in the balance was the manner of its passing. Amongst the ambassadors in Constantinople managing the diplomatic aspects of the crisis, there was a delay in responding to British moves to expedite Turkish withdrawal. For the other powers, whose soldiers had not suffered any assaults, an opportunity arose to garner some credit with Abdul Hamid by seeming reluctance. Yet they had to be careful not to trigger a unilateral act by Britain—otherwise Crete might go the way of Egypt and Cyprus. On 5 October, Russia was the last to join in a collective note demanding that Turkey should agree within eight days to withdraw its troops from Crete. Silence ensued, but on 18 October, another seven condemned Muslims were

---

[113] Biliotti telegram to Constantinople Embassy, 29 Sept. 1898, FO78/4934.

[114] The debate in the Yildiz is fully described in Memorandum by Adam Block (Chief Dragoman, British Embassy), 19 Nov. 1898, FO78/4920.

[115] The aftermath of the massacre in Candia interacted with the overlapping Fashoda crisis on the Upper Nile, which brought Britain and France to the verge of war.

[116] Biliotti telegram to Constantinople Embassy, 19 Oct. 1898, FO78/4935.

hanged on the ramparts of Candia under British military law. Five days later Ottoman troops finally began to embark from Cretan ports. After a few days, however, this movement suddenly halted, with 800 troops remaining. The reason was clear. Kaiser Wilhelm was on a state visit to the Ottoman dominions, and the Sultan jibbed at any humiliation whilst the German Emperor was in his capital.[117] Whilst there, the Kaiser's own rising Anglophobia found ready expression— Britain, he allegedly told the Grand Vizier, was 'incontestably bent' on grabbing Crete for itself.[118]

For the Sultan, the key priority was the maintenance of his flag over the island as a symbol of suzerainty, to be guarded by at least 'a score or so of troops'.[119] The recently arrived British Ambassador in Constantinople, Sir Nicholas O'Conor, thought that such a residual token of Ottoman sovereignty should be granted, since otherwise any last shreds of British influence in the Turkish capital would disappear. When the Kaiser departed for Beirut[120]—where he was met by Djevaad Pasha, who had made a discreet escape from Crete himself—the outward flow of Turkish troops from the island still did not recommence. On 3 November, O'Conor told a Yildiz official that unless those troops left immediately, 'the Turkish flag [in Candia] would almost certainly be hauled down'.[121] It was obvious that, once down, it might not go up again. An assurance was therefore swiftly forthcoming that military transports were on their way. But what expedited the liquidation of the Ottoman military presence was a warning by the Greek Christian leadership—intensely uneasy at the interrupted evacuation—that, if the British did not act to bring it to fruition, they would do the job themselves. British troops swiftly occupied the main fortress and took over administrative buildings. The Ottoman Governor was informed that all Turkish military personnel were to be embarked by noon on 5 November. Just to leave no room for misunderstanding, the Ottoman flag in the town was lowered 'pending a decision on the Sultan's suzerainty and as a punitive measure for non-withdrawal of troops at a fixed date'.

Yet over two hundred years of Ottoman domination could not end without a last flourish of bitterness. It had always been assumed that the Ottoman troops themselves would never leave willingly unless an instruction came from their ruler. No such instruction was sent. When the appointed hour came, they simply stuck to their quarters. 'British soldiers occupied the barracks', Biliotti recorded the scene, 'and marched the Turkish troops to the harbour. They were then embarked without resistance to the last officer and man on board Turkish and British transports and left for Salonica.'[122] Five hundred women and children went with them, though not

---

[117] It was the Kaiser's second visit to Constantinople, the first having been in 1888.

[118] O'Conor to Salisbury, 26 Oct. 1898, FO78/4919.

[119] O'Conor to Salisbury, 14 Oct. 1898, FO78/4923.

[120] The Kaiser was on his way to Jerusalem, which he famously entered on a white horse.

[121] O'Conor to Salisbury, 3 Nov. 1898, FO78/4922.

[122] Biliotti telegram to Constantinople Embassy, 6 Nov. 1898, FO78/4935.

before every Turkish female was identified by the raising of the veil (it was feared the youngest daughter of Vice-Consul Calocherino had not perished in the family home, but had been taken into a harem—the girl was not found).[123] The bruised emotions here defy easy analysis. Some vestiges of past relations, however, survived. Just before the Turkish flagship departed, a delegation of British officers clambered aboard with presents as a mark of respect for their Ottoman counterparts. Even at such a moment the shared experience of the two armies in the Crimea was not forgotten.

In the following days the apparatus of Turkish civil and military authority was similarly disbanded in the other main Cretan towns. 'The whole process of exit', one description states,

suggested the workings of an eviction order on a grand scale. Here and there some soldier lingered; a General lagged behind; a minor official attempted to parley. But to no purpose.... [Turkish rule] was cast unceremoniously out of the island.[124]

De facto Turkish rule was dead. Yet the calculated lingerings of individual Ottoman soldiers and officials indicated that this was not a clean-cut exit—like some later West European decolonization.[125] The Sultan's sovereignty survived. Even in Candia, where the Turkish flag had been lowered, it was afterwards raised in a ceremony composed of both British and French troops. No Turkish soldiers remained to guard it. Their very absence, nevertheless, underlined the international protection the emblem was henceforth to enjoy. On 6 November, this protection was formally extended—both by local proclamation, and by a written promise to the Sultan—to the Cretan Muslims themselves. The centrality of these guarantees to the Ottoman departure from the island—and the model they might offer for similar, and for Europe potentially even more explosive, handovers elsewhere in the Balkans—was to be central to the continuing impasse in the island.

For the moment, the machinery of Turkish government could not be dismantled without putting something in its place. Biliotti had already suggested that Chermside might be made Governor. '[S]uch a measure', Salisbury firmly told Queen Victoria, 'is not exacting reparation, but taking possession. It would be looked upon by the other Powers as an act of bad faith, and as justifying the suspicion that we intend to annex the island.'[126] Nevertheless, after 5 November, British Army officers set off into the Candian interior to assume responsibilities as sub-commissioners and commandants of police.[127] This was how many British

---

[123] For Biliotti's later recall of this episode, and continuing rumours that Miss Calocherino had ended up in the household of an *effendi* in Salonica, where Biliotti had himself become consul-general, see Biliotti to Salisbury, 10 Nov. 1899 FO78/5005. In fact it seems certain that she had indeed been a victim of the massacre in Candia.   [124] Chester, *Venizelos*, 69.

[125] General Sir Garnet Wolseley had similarly complained about the tendency of Turkish Army officers to stay on after the British occupation of Cyprus in the summer of 1879. See Wolseley to Layard, 18 July 1878, MS Add. 39021, Layard Papers, BL.   [126] Buckle (ed.), *Letters*, iii. 282.

[127] For the experience in Crete of one of these young British officers with a distinguished career ahead of him see Ian Becket, *Johnny Gough, VC* (London, 1985).

regimes in different parts of the world had begun. The urgency with which the Russian government now pressed the appointment of Prince George of Greece as High Commissioner of an autonomous Crete headed off any such process. In fact, 'absolutely effective autonomy', as we have seen, had long been Salisbury's goal. Tensions in Athens surrounding Prince George's candidacy were temporarily submerged, since it promised to 'keep the spark of Unionism alive in the island' after the crushing military defeat in Thessaly.[128] On 30 November, the Sultan received a formal notification of the intention to make the appointment, which was duly confirmed. Prince George arrived in Canea, accompanied by European warships, two days before Christmas. Appearing at the window of the Konak he was ecstatically cheered by the Christian crowd, for whom a Greek prince was several steps up on a British governor. When the Prince visited the mosques next day even the cowed Muslims were respectful; though when he toured Candia shortly afterwards, the mood was inevitably more dour.[129]

In the tangled interplay of the British presence and Hellenic aspiration which is the setting of this book, played out in this case against the backdrop of failing Ottoman authority, the Cretan drama was full of unresolved contradictions. What did 'absolutely effective' Cretan autonomy really signify? Arthur Evans, whose archaeological excavations at Knossos got under way amidst these upheavals, predicted that all Prince George would bring to the island was 'Some smart *aides-de camp*, a few Court ladies, and a French cook'.[130] This was hardly fair. For one thing, the Prince had not been invested by the Sultan in a ceremony in Constantinople, as he would have been before 6 September. He was instead directly appointed by, and responsible to, the powers, symbolized by his arrival—designedly mimicking that of his father in the Ionian Islands in 1864—surrounded by a display of European naval authority. Yet although the new High Commissioner 'brought direct Greek influence into Crete',[131] he did not bring any tincture of Greek sovereignty. Indeed, on his arrival the Turkish flag still flew alongside that of the protecting powers above Government House, much to the puzzlement and irritation of Christians.[132] Crete might have been liberated from the presence of an Ottoman army at essentially British insistence, but the 'prompt radical solution' held out by Biliotti clearly remained unfulfilled. As long as this was so, the underlying tensions lamented by Kazantzakis' anxious Pasha of Megalokastro would not disappear, and might even intensify as the Cretan Question assumed new forms of intractability during a 'temporary rest' from disorder.

---

[128] Markopoulos, 'The Selection of Prince George of Greece as High Commissioner in Crete', 340.

[129] Biliotti to Salisbury, 24 Dec. 1898, FO78/4934. Biliotti's assessment was that the fears of Cretan Muslim civilians would have led them to emigrate *en masse* at this time had they been able to do so. As it was, about half the total left in the wake of the Turkish troops, the Muslim population stabilizing thereafter.   [130] Quoted in Chester, *Venizelos*, 61.

[131] Markopoulos, 'The Selection of Prince George of Greece as High Commissioner in Crete', 350.

[132] 'The Liberation of Crete', *The Times*, 22 Dec. 1898.

5

An Unfortunate Regime: The Experiment of Cretan Autonomy, 1898–1906

All the anomalies of the position here are coming out clearly under the pressure of the insurrection.

(Esme Howard, 15 May 1905)

No one really cared about Crete except as it reacted upon affairs in the Balkans.

(M. Zinoviev, 28 May 1906)

The years which followed the eviction of Ottoman power from Crete have a special significance for this study. We saw earlier how Gladstonian 'reform' failed to contain the dynamics of Hellenic nationalism in the Ionian Islands. Would a solution short of *enosis* in the form of autonomy under international supervision fare any better in Crete? The viability of such a transitional and inevitably ambiguous regime had a particular resonance for Great Britain, whose wider interests remained bound up with a steady but carefully *controlled* move towards a new, and as yet ill-defined, Eastern order. Yet the complexities surrounding the high commissionership of Prince George in the island posed an even broader question. Was it possible for the higher needs of general peace to be squared with fierce Balkan struggles of nationalism and ethnic identity which any alteration to the status quo seemed to generate? This conundrum was to lie at the heart of much European diplomacy before 1914. We shall therefore be dealing with a genre of interlocking internal and external questions in which the origins of modern international peacekeeping inevitably loom large.

High hopes were certainly invested in Prince George by the powers, and by Great Britain in particular. At the outset circumstances were not unfavourable. The vast majority of Cretans were sick of conflict. It was widely recognized that the immediate task lay in social and economic stabilization. The Cretan Concert, though tested by the crisis after 6 September 1898, had held together—just. The Turkish Sultan had reluctantly swallowed the new *de facto* reality in Crete. Although that reality fell short of union with Greece, following the war of 1897 the latter country was in a chastened mood. 'Agitation for foreign expansion', the British minister plenipotentiary in the Greek capital summed matters up, 'is at a discount now.'[1] Anglo-Greek relations blossomed as Greece was the only country to lend support to Britain in the war then raging in South Africa: the Royal Navy began to make increased use of Greek ports, where they were enthusiastically received.[2] British consular relations with the new Cretan regime, too, were eased when Sir Alfred Biliotti followed the departing Ottoman troops to Salonica, as Britain's consul-general (just in time to face the worsening situation in Macedonia). His successor, Robert Graves, had experience of the region, without being compromised by a long-standing involvement in local politics.[3]

Under the straitened circumstances, however, the local administration remained gimcrack at best. The admirals who had presided on the coasts since February 1897 did not wish to stay—they would only have hampered the Prince in his task of establishing autonomous government. They left on their various flagships on 28 December 1898. The powers were eager to withdraw some of the resources they had committed to Cretan duties. Thereafter only one *stationnaire* for each power was kept permanently in Cretan waters. The reduction of European troops proceeded more slowly. Initially Prince George was in fact little more than the special agent of the powers. But after the completion of a new con-stitution in June 1899 the situation was significantly altered. His administration became responsible for law and order. The European military commanders gave up most civil and judicial responsibilities, and the international garrisons were scaled down from the levels required by the preceding troubles. Yet each of the powers in the local Concert refused to give up their stake represented by the *secteurs* which had taken root after 1897. This indicated an uncertain faith in the new polity from the start—and significantly left British soldiers and marines as the ultimate guarantor for the safety of the great bulk of Cretan Muslims.

The ambiguity of the new dispensation was its strength, in that it could not otherwise have been accepted by all the interests involved. Yet ambiguity was also a weakness, since a degree of confusion was the inevitable result. After June 1899 it became common to speak of 'the government of Prince George'. But was it really *his* government, or that of the powers which had decreed its construction? Exploiting their own freedom from responsibility in the matter, German diplomats cast aspersions on the uneasy duality in the new arrangements.[4] Such dualism derived from Prince George's potentially clashing roles as 'Prince of Crete', as he had been officially dubbed when first coming to the island, and as High

[1] Memorandum by Sir Edwin Egerton on Greece, 6 Dec. 1900, Papers of 5th Marquis of Lansdowne, FO800/131, National Archives of the United Kingdom. Up until the First World War the British government representative in the capitals of the Christian Balkan states was styled a minis-ter plenipotentiary, not an ambassador. This preserved the superior status of the post of British Ambassador at the Porte, the prestige of which owed so much to the career of Stratford Canning.

[2] For the significance of Greek ports to the Royal Navy at this time see material in ADM 121/75, National Archives of the United Kingdom.

[3] With the establishment of Cretan autonomy, local European representatives were upgraded to consuls-general. For ease, the following text will stick to the more concise title of 'consul'.

[4] Jean-Stanislaw Dutkoswki, *L'Occupation de la Crète, 1897–1909* (Paris, 1953), 85. This book is a key text on the legal and juridical problems of Cretan autonomy.

Commissioner. In the first case, he had a primary obligation to the Cretan people; in the second case, he was obligated ultimately to the powers. None of this mattered for the initial eighteen months or so of the Prince's stay, taken up as he was in legislating the new constitution and putting together an administration. Ministries were established, a unified judicial system set up, and a central Bank of Crete inaugurated. Thereafter the fundamental contradictions were always likely to impose themselves.

Prince George's mandate as High Commissioner was limited to a term of three years (though in fact he was to be reappointed on two occasions). This limitation was the 'psychological error' which the Prince later identified as the stumbling block to his mission.[5] His reasoning was that as a result it was assumed by his Cretan charges that by the end of three years the status of the island would have attained its 'final solution'—that is, union with Greece. When this did not happen, the Prince recalled bitterly, the Cretans 'felt that they had been let down'— that feeling of disillusionment and ill usage which habitually ran through movements of Hellenic nationality. The Prince sought in retrospect to heap the blame on the powers, just as the powers ladled all the culpability for what followed on the Prince. Yet the time limit was simply a side effect of a more profound dilemma which it was not convenient for Prince George to recognize. Christian Cretan expectations had been fuelled by the disappearance of Ottoman troops. Yet that exit had been enforced, not by Christian militia, but by the powers. Any elation that autonomy was but a brief halting place on the way to union with Greece was therefore at odds with the real configuration of affairs. Here was the tap-root of a 'psychological error', but *whose* error was open to interpretation.

This instability built into the new Cretan polity, however, was related to another theme the significance of which also featured in Prince George's bitter recollections. This was his absolute determination to 'keep the Island free from inner political frictions'.[6] 'I want no political parties... in the coming three years', he remembered constantly impressing on the Cretan leadership he found *in situ*. This authoritarian attitude was often attributed to the prejudices acquired during Prince George's training at the Salamis Naval College. But the reasons for it were also embedded in the current dilemmas of the dynasty to which Prince George belonged, and which he 'represented' in Crete far more truly than he did the powers, or even the aspiration to union itself. Defeat at the hands of Turkey in 1897 had come close to destroying the Greek crown. The danger of emergent republicanism did not fully dissipate afterwards. Crete represented a continuing danger to Prince George's family either by allowing some Greeks to accuse it of 'treachery' to the national idea, or by compromising it in the eyes of European protectors without whose support it could not long survive. Either way, Prince George's unspoken task was to navigate between these forces. By 'no politics' in Crete, then, he meant no politics in which rumbustious Cretans might expose the fictions on which the new system was built.

---

[5] Prince George of Greece, *The Cretan Drama* (New York, 1959), 19.   [6] Ibid. 29.

Any idea that the Cretan politicians would 'retire' into private or professional pur-
suits, happy with whatever crumbs of patronage fell from the High Commissioner's
table, was, however, unlikely. Some of the older and more exhausted leaders, such
as the much-admired Sphakaniakis, whose own experiences stretched back to the
struggles of the 1860s, were prepared to disappear into contemplative privacy. But
this was not the case with the younger generation. Eleutherios Venizelos had,
through natural talent and vast energy, already emerged as a prominent leader, and
although temporarily forced out of Crete by opponents,[7] he had soon returned to
the fray. He was a lawyer by training, but a politician by every impulse he possessed. One can only wryly imagine his thoughts on being exhorted by a Greek
royal of Danish extraction to steer clear of politics as a forbidden zone; he certainly
shared a widespread resentment at the preferment accorded by the High
Commissioner to a clique of Athenians. At first Venizelos preoccupied himself
with the urgent tasks of his position as Minister of Justice. But it was inevitable
that before long he would take up the one issue which guaranteed public salience:
union with Greece. There were two parallel sets of dynamics in autonomous
Crete, each replete with psychological complexity—one between the Prince and
the powers, and the other between the Prince and the Venizelist faction unwilling
to accept the High Commissioner's claim to monopolize the *enosis* issue.

This is the background to the first major watershed in Prince George's Cretan
career—his trip to Europe in the summer of 1900, prompted by an invitation to
meet his relative, Tsar Nicholas II, at his Crimean retreat of Livadia. The 'Cretan
Concert' was certainly at pains to give the High Commissioner a sense of being
well loved. In August Queen Victoria had dispatched the Mediterranean Fleet
under its commander-in-chief, Sir John Fisher, to Crete where the Prince was
invested with the Grand Cross of the Order of the Bath. There was a danger that
he might thereby gain an exaggerated notion of his own credit with the powers.
On the eve of his journey to Europe, Graves warned Lord Salisbury that the
Prince's mind 'was full of the question of the ultimate annexation to Greece as the
only satisfactory and permanent solution of the Cretan difficulty'.[8] Yet the High
Commissioner was well aware that union *pur et simple* was not an immediate
prospect. What he needed was a payment on account which he could offer to
ordinary Cretans as resulting solely from his royal status. Prince George therefore
latched onto the precedent set by Bosnia-Herzegovina, which under the
Congress of Berlin in 1878 was occupied by Austria-Hungary, whilst remaining
under the theoretical suzerainty of Turkey. In this case, of course, the troops
would be Greek, not Austrian—and once Greek troops were back in Crete (this
time, unlike 1897, with the approval of Europe) the rest would surely follow.

The essence of the Prince's summer tour consisted of an exhilarating start
followed by unfolding disillusionment. At Livadia the Tsar gave assurances not

---

[7] See above, 96.
[8] Graves to Salisbury, 12 Sept. 1900, FO78/5068.

only that Russia accepted the Bosnian model for Crete, but that it would insist the Sultan did as well.[9] The High Commissioner proceeded to Western Europe confident of being able to make progress. Arriving in London he was ensconced in the familial warmth afforded by the Prince of Wales and his favourite aunt, Princess Alexandra. But this warmth was misleading. It was to be a hallmark of the handling in Whitehall of the Cretan Question that Prince George was always to be 'let down gently' because of the partiality of the Wales' household.[10] Lord Salisbury welcomed him on two occasions to the Foreign Office and conveyed in his deftest manner that British opinion would not risk offending Turkey further, or tinker needlessly with the delicate Balkan equilibrium. It was in Paris and Rome, however, that the Prince's optimism began to unravel. In the former, the Russian Ambassador afforded a broad hint that the Tsar's assurances did not necessarily commit his government; whilst in Rome the open opposition of the Italians surfaced. When the Prince heard that his proposal had been referred by the powers to a special conference in Rome, he knew that it was, in effect, being killed off. By the time he returned to Crete at the start of 1901, he was already disillusioned. On 22 February the European consuls called on him in his palace in Canea and communicated the decision that there could be no change in the foreseeable future in the status of the island. Afterwards the Prince told Consul Graves that 'he felt rather like a prisoner to whom his sentence had just been read out'.[11] The bile was never to leave him.

The Prince's 'sentence' was to continue to carry out his duties as the representative of the powers in Crete when the aspirations of most of the inhabitants for immediate *enosis* had evaporated, leaving him to deal with the politicians bent on exploiting the vacuum. The Prince threatened Graves—as he did the other consuls—with withdrawing from the scene altogether. Graves's retort was that not only would this thrust Crete back into the chaos from which it had just emerged, but that 'it would be regarded as an attempt to put pressure on the Powers, and would be rejected as such'—a rejection that could only embarrass crown and government in Athens.[12] The choreography of threat and counter-threat thereafter framed the relations between the Prince and Europe; and although at first he felt most 'shabbily treated' by Russia, gradually the emphasis of his resentment shifted towards Great Britain, if only because it was the British who increasingly drove Concert policy in the eastern Mediterranean.

The High Commissioner's fears for his position were not unjustified. After the rejection of his proposals in Europe, tensions emerged within the Cretan 'Government'. In putting forward his own model for Crete's immediate political

---

[9] Tsar Nicholas's sympathy for Prince George arose from a personal as well as a familial tie. On a tour of Japan in 1894 he had been attacked by a madman armed with a knife, and had only been saved by the intervention of the formidable Greek Prince then accompanying his entourage. See Martinière, *La Marine française*, 193.

[10] B. J. C. McKercher, *Esme Howard: A Diplomatic Biography* (Cambridge, 1989), 40–1.

[11] Graves to Lansdowne, 6 Mar. 1901, FO78/5133.

[12] Graves to Lansdowne, 6 Mar. 1901, FO78/5133.

future based on Eastern Roumelia, Venizelos implicitly challenged the Prince. Like Bosnia, Eastern Roumelia was only nominally under Ottoman suzerainty, but it differed in possessing a parliamentary and liberal constitution. Embedded in these contrasting benchmarks was an incipient factional and ideological conflict between Venizelism and royalism which was finally to link Crete organically to wider Hellenic contests.[13] On 18 March 1901, Venizelos (anyway about to resign) was dismissed, and although at first he kept a low profile, he was evidently preparing himself to act as an alternative focus for Cretan loyalties. 'Politics' had arrived, with a capacity to pitch some Cretans against the Glücksburg dynasty, against the Powers, and perhaps, yet again, against themselves.

The unravelling of Prince George's relations with the consuls ran alongside this process. The latter always resented being displaced by the admirals after February 1897, and after the bulk of the fleets had gone home, the consular body started arrogating some of their old privileges.[14] Such tendencies underlined the phoney quality of Cretan autonomy. Prince George tried the tactic of playing off one consul against another. He told Graves in June 1901, that 'he was the only one of whose conduct he had not reason to complain', but he said similar things to the Russian, French, and Italian representatives.[15] But when push came to shove it was most likely that the powers would unite against the High Commissioner, rather than splinter around him—the island was not worth the price of a broken Concert. Matters had not yet reached this state, but from mid-1901 onwards relations between the High Commissioner and the European consulates became strained and before long envenomed.

Such tensions were bound to feed into questions of law and order. The sequestration of arms was the most important concern of the international troops after November 1898, but nobody was under any illusion that the 'decommissioned' stock piles represented anything other than a small proportion of the firearms still circulating. Ideally a militia would have been set up with local officers who knew the terrain intimately. But Cretan society remained too riven by communal division to permit such an armed force to be established. Prince George had to make do with a European-officered gendarmerie. This institution was to win plaudits as 'the one satisfactory part of the Cretan administration'.[16] Yet it also became the lightning rod for shocks endemic to the system of autonomy. Its Italian officers were highly professional, and drawn from a Calabrian cadre experienced in dealing with the sort of lawlessness found in Crete. Their commander at first co-operated easily with the High Commissioner. Yet there was a fundamental dilemma. Who

---

[13] The origins and later course of the differences between Prince George and Venizelos are fully treated in Constantinos Svolopoulos, *O Eleutherios Venizelos ke I Politiki Krisis eis tin Autonomon Kritin 1901–1906* (Eleutherios Venizelos and the Political Crisis in Autonomous Crete, 1901–1906) (Athens, 1974).

[14] For a fuller treatment of the situation of the consular body see Dutkowski, *L' Occupation de la Crète*, 93–6.   [15] Graves to Lansdowne, 5 June 1901, FO78/5134.

[16] Howard to Lansdowne, 9 June 1905, FO78/5411.

had the right to control the gendarmerie in a crisis—Prince George, or the powers collectively through their local consulates? The more the High Commissioner tried to impose his own authority, the more resistance he met; the more, too, that the force itself became divided between an Italian officer cadre and the Cretan rank and file whose personal devotion to their Hellenic Prince was intense. Again, it took some while for such contests to take shape. Yet it was transparent that the Prince was menaced by 'une entière impuissance en cas de troubles, et puis une relative faiblesse en temps ordinaire'.[17]

The international troops therefore remained the ultimate guarantors of stability in the island. Prince George necessarily regarded them as 'a reserve force' that he could draw on in any emergency. Yet Graves and the other consuls never disguised their understanding that the European troops could only be used on direct instructions from their own governments.[18] The number of those troops was anyway vulnerable to cuts. If there was one attitude which the powers shared towards Crete, it was resentment at the financial burden. This was certainly the case with Britain, whose military deployments were skewed by events in South Africa. Graves fought a sustained battle against what he called the 'shabbiness' of the War Office, arguing that it contrasted painfully with what even the Italians ('poor as they are') were doing in Crete.[19] In early 1902 the plan of the Conservative Cabinet—still led by Salisbury, but now with Lord Lansdowne as Foreign Secretary—to reduce the garrison in Candia was only abandoned after a strong intervention by King Edward VII, who, having succeeded his mother in June, 1901, always kept a close eye on Cretan affairs.[20]

At least during the first phases of autonomy communal relations within the island stabilized, and in this Prince George played a constructive part. The *sharia* courts were allowed to operate without interference, as were Muslim schools. When occasionally Muslims were the victims of Christian malefactors, the Cretan authorities were quick to show 'solicitude' by apprehending the transgressor.[21] From early 1902, however, there were signs of renewed communal tension. This was not because of any increase in actual violence. As always in Crete, the process was more indirect and subtle. Having had his 'sentence' read out by the consuls, Prince George took his finger off the valve of annexationist feelings amongst Christians. Patronage was used to prop up his popularity, so that when any job held by a Muslim in the administration became vacant, it was given to a Christian loyalist of the Prince. As Muslim faith in the regime ebbed, rural emigration started up again. '[W]ith the exception of the villages where non-commissioned officers of the gendarmerie are stationed, the Muslim element will soon have entirely disappeared', the British consulate reported, 'and the land is rapidly being bought up by

17 Dutkowski, *L'Occupation de la Crète*, 90.
18 Graves to Lansdowne, 12 Jan. 1901, FO78/5133.
19 Graves to Sanderson, 18 Oct. 1900, FO78/5068.
20 Lansdowne minute, 2 Apr. 1902, FO78/2504.
21 Graves to Salisbury, 20 June 1900, FO78/5068.

the Christians.'[22] This was simply the renewal of a process that had gone on for several decades, but the recent European 'pledge' allowed the Porte to protest that it was not being met—protests which helped provide a screen behind which the Sultan could renege on his promises for reform in Macedonia.[23]

The Cretan and Macedonian questions, indeed, intersected with increasing frequency from this point. It was the advance of Greek interests in Crete represented by the eviction of Ottoman troops which encouraged Bulgarian elements to seek compensating advantages in Macedonia at Hellenic as well as Turkish expense.[24] Cretan volunteers began sporadically to flow northwards to assist their threatened kinsmen, and Prince George's failure to stop them provided an early dent in his reputation in Europe. These irregulars took their great hatred of Turks with them, and they often failed to grasp thereafter that under Macedonian conditions the local agencies of Ottoman power were frequently allies of Hellenic populations against revolutionary Bulgarian expansion. This imperfect 'fit' between the Cretan and Macedonian struggles was a reflection of growing tensions between rival prescriptions for meeting Hellenic imperatives and ideals.

Such tensions were significantly related to the chief emerging division within Cretan society—one not between Christians and Muslims, but between different Christian parties. It was not only Muslims who were excluded from the Prince's patronage. Christians who were even mildly critical of the regime had the same treatment. Many merchants felt they did not get a fair share of compensation for the damage of recent troubles, and grumbled at a continuing commercial stagnation which seemed to interest the Prince little. Here were the raw materials which Venizelos set about working into a political force, and his growing influence through 1902 was noticed in the British consulate.[25] Venizelos's re-emergence, however, was connected not only to his 'liberal' constitutional views, but to a particular slant on the modalities of the 'national' issue. He believed that when Crete eventually joined Greece, it had to do so with 'a coat on [its] back';[26] that is, it was not to be reduced to holding a begging bowl out to the powers, to Athens, and least of all to the Sultan. Such views differed fundamentally from those of the High Commissioner. 'It is I who have liberated you,' he once told a Cretan newspaper,[27] and such an assertion corresponded with his conviction that Cretan *enosis* should be brokered between the Greek dynasty and the protecting powers with everybody else (especially the Cretans themselves) looking passively on.[28]

[22] James MacGregor to Lansdowne, 30 Aug. 1902, FO78/2504.

[23] 'Le Musulman', Martinière states, 'ne s'accommode pas du régime chrétien et fuit le pays de gouvernement orthodoxe comme le lièvre fuit le lapin. Il se passe ici ce qui s'est produit en Grèce puis en Thessalie ... Ils étaient 70,000 à 80,000 en 1896; il en reste à peine 28,000 en 1910.' See *La Marine française*, 176.

[24] Douglas Dakin, *The Greek Struggle in Macedonia, 1897–1913* (Thessaloniki, 1966), 42.

[25] MacGregor to Lansdowne, 25 May 1902, FO78/2504.

[26] Esme Howard, *Theatre of Life, 1905–1936* (London, 1936), 31.

[27] *Neo Asty*, 17 May 1902, FO78/5349.　　　[28] Svolopoulos, *O Eleutherios Venizelos*, 32–47.

This attitude found expression in the 'electioneering' tour made by Prince George through the island in February and March 1903. Where he had once denounced 'politics' in Crete, he now meant to get his own politics in first. At tumultuous meetings he lambasted anybody disloyal to himself and the aspiration to dynastic *enosis* he represented. More politics carried the usual logic of more communal tension—a rash of clashes soon occurred, and the seepage of Muslims out of the island became more marked. Graves sought to lay the blame on the Prince's advisers rather than himself—they had, he told Lansdowne, 'not scrupled to drag his [Prince George's] popularity, prestige and Royal birth through the mud for the purposes of destroying the electoral chances of the Venizelist opposition party'.[29] But the mud began to stick to the High Commissioner as well. Of Prince George's continuing popularity in the eastern provinces there was little doubt. In the ensuing elections opposition candidates won few seats, and in the late summer of 1903 Venizelos was briefly incarcerated in Izzedin Prison and his newspaper *Kyrix* closed. Yet in the centre and west of the island—the classic breeding grounds of insurrection—the Venizelists appeared to be gaining ground, and by mid-1904 Graves's successor as British consul, Esme Howard,[30] warned in a private letter home that 'a sort of secret revolutionary movement' was emerging pitted against not just the Prince's Athenian entourage, but against the regime as a whole.[31]

In his memoirs Prince George depicted the new British consul as the principal author of his subsequent downfall. It is true that Esme Howard arrived just when the European representatives were starting to question whether Prince George was the right horse to back for their purpose—that of keeping Crete as tranquil as circumstances allowed. The appearance during July 1904 of armed men bearing Greek flags in the countryside—though quickly scotched by the gendarmerie and international troops—underlined the brittle atmosphere. For Prince George, this meant another dash to Europe—the instinctive Glücksburg response to looming trouble. It was to be, the High Commissioner insisted, his 'last effort'. Before going he impressed on Howard that he had struggled to keep the population quiet for nearly six years, and had sought to prevent friction between Christians and Muslims, but 'also what was perhaps more difficult, serious political dissensions amongst the Christian population'.[32] If the powers, he added, turned him down now, as they had before, it would be for them to maintain Cretan autonomy by force. There was, Howard confessed, 'much truth in Prince George's arguments'.[33]

Yet there was little chance of the Prince getting what he really sought from Europe: the entry into Crete of a detachment of Greek troops as a guarantee of future *enosis*. If anything, opinion in the British Foreign Office had hardened

[29] Graves to Lansdowne, 11 Mar. 1903, FO78/5281.

[30] Howard had just spent several years at the British Embassy in Rome. After 1899 the ambassadors in that capital temporarily discharged the 'supervisory' role over Crete previously carried out by their peers in Constantinople, and Howard had become closely acquainted with the island's affairs.   [31] Howard to Sanderson, 15 May 1904, FO78/5349.

[32] Howard to Lansdowne, 29 July 1904, ibid.   [33] Ibid.

against any such thing. When a sympathetic junior official in London remarked that 'although ... Crete is not entirely "split off" from Turkey ... she would appear for all administrative purposes to constitute a separate state', he was brusquely reminded that Crete 'is certainly not split off. The Powers are under engagements to the Sultan that it shall not be.'[34] Developments in Macedonia made the honouring of that engagement vital. The Austro-Russian Mürzsteg Programme for reform, reluctantly accepted by Constantinople in June 1903, had already proved abortive, as Lansdowne had expected from the first.[35] The latter pressed hard through 1904 for the institution of a full-blown 'concert' for Macedonia on Cretan lines, including enhanced European supervision. But Sultan Abdul Hamid was unlikely to accept such arrangements for Macedonia if promises recently made to him over Crete were shown to be hollow. Howard pleaded the urgency to 'get rid of the Cretan incubus', adding that if thereafter 'the Cretans should be uncomfortable on their Grecian bed ... that would be their affair',[36] but he made no headway in London. When the consul shortly afterwards received Lansdowne's rejection of the Prince's proposals, Howard recalled, 'how my heart sank when I read this document, the futility of which must have been as apparent to those who drafted it as it was to us in Crete'.[37] The Prince duly returned to the island in January 1905 as empty-handed as he had four years before.

This outcome left the High Commissioner acutely vulnerable to being outflanked by opponents veering towards the radical cry of 'pure and actual enosis'. Howard noted a 'conspiracy of silence' in the island,[38] and on 16 March he told the Foreign Office that the Venizelists were only awaiting a fresh arms consignment from supporters in Athens to start an outbreak.[39] Prince George's allegation that Howard was colluding with prospective insurrectionists is unsustainable.[40] In the enclosed world of Canea, he could hardly avoid knowing the leading Venizelists. But what enraged the High Commissioner was that, more than the other Europeans, it was the British consul who possessed the influence to deter troublemakers, but he did not do so. Indeed, Howard's advice to London that Prince George had 'burned his boats' with the powers marked a turning point.[41] The British consul began to look around for an alternative collaborator, and Venizelos was the obvious—in fact, the only—choice, providing that the latter did not tie himself irretrievably to intransigent unionism. All this remained inchoate, but the truth was that the Prince had exhausted his usefulness for the

[34] Note on the Position of Crete in Relation to the Ottoman Empire, 17 Feb. 1904, FO78/5349.

[35] For Lansdowne's growing anxiety that Macedonia would trigger a major European crisis and his desire to deflect this, as had been done in Crete, by a scheme for autonomy, see G. P. Gooch and Harold Temperley (eds), *British Documents on the Origins of the War, 1898–1914*, v: *The Near East: The Macedonian Problem and the Annexation of Bosnia, 1903–1908* (London, 1928), 49–67.

[36] Quoted in McKercher, *Esme Howard*, 38.

[37] Quoted in McKercher, *Esme Howard*, 49–50.

[38] Howard to Lansdowne, 21 Jan. 1905, FO78/5410.

[39] Howard to Lansdowne, 16 Mar. 1905, ibid.

[40] Prince George of Greece, *Cretan Drama*, 121.

[41] Lansdowne minute, 22 Aug. 1904, FO78/5439.

Concert. Howard and the other consuls were ready to cast him aside, like a used towel, *if they could do so safely*. To that extent the Prince's analysis of the roots of the Venizelist outbreak had a grain of truth.

The insurrection began on 23 March 1905 when around 300 armed men gathered at Therisso, a small village in the foothills of the White Mountains, the name of which was to be synonymous with the rebellion. The following day the insurrectionary leaders, Venizelos, Manos, and Fourmis, presided over a symbolic raising of the Greek flag. When a small force of gendarmerie approached, they were fired upon, one man being fatally shot by the side of the Italian commander. Such an attack on a European-led force was proof of the seriousness of the challenge. The rebels at Therisso rapidly came to number some 3,000. As Howard reported to London a few days later, under Venizelos' leadership they proceeded to dig entrenchments 'and are quietly awaiting the result of their appeal to the Powers'.[42] In the great tradition of Cretan insurrections, the goal was not to win a military victory, but to seduce, and if necessary extract by blackmail, the sympathy and political action of Europe—and especially of Great Britain.

From the start the Prince demanded that the consuls use international troops to squash the insurgents; and although in Athens King George at first hesitated nervously about any actions which might intensify 'a fratricidal war' *between* Greeks,[43] he soon added his pleas to those of his son. When the consuls met to discuss the High Commissioner's request, however, it was Howard who proved highly evasive. British troops remained penned into Candia town, with only a few outposts extended into the hinterland as a sop to exposed Muslims. When an international column was dispatched towards the rebels, it consisted of one Italian company, two French companies, a Russian detachment, and some gendarmes— but no British. The failure of this ramshackle force to quell the outbreak at the outset was critical.[44] Furthermore, the deduction generally derived that 'England would not act against the insurgents' was exactly the impression which Venizelos wished to disseminate since it boosted his credibility.[45] Although Salisbury's successor as Conservative Prime Minister, A. J. Balfour, agreed that extra British troops should be landed to show goodwill, he told Lansdowne firmly that they were not to participate in 'any wild goose chase in the mountains'. 'It does not matter much to us', he noted cynically, 'whether the whole mountains remain disturbed or not ... The [insurgent] movement will die of inanition if it is skilfully handled.'[46]

This attitude was in part merely the Cretan expression of isolationist currents in British policy which the recent Entente Cordiale with France had not expunged.

[42] Howard to Lansdowne, 26 Mar. 1905, FO78/5410.
[43] Lansdowne to King Edward VII, 5 Apr. 1905, FO32/758.
[44] Colonel Lubanski, commanding the force of European troops and gendarmerie, had two interviews with the insurgent leadership, including Venizelos, but failed to shift them from their demand for immediate annexation to Greece. See Martinière, *La Marine française*, 186.
[45] Howard to Lansdowne, 31 Mar. 1905, FO78/5410.
[46] Lansdowne note, 1 Apr. 1905, ibid.

This was little comfort to Prince George, whose authority was bound to crumble before any 'inanition' spread to the Cretan mountain tops. Rebel bands carrying the Greek flag were already circulating in the interior. The western provinces swiftly fell under insurgent control, and elsewhere real authority fell back into the hands of the consuls and international military officers.[47] Sooner or later the Concert was likely to lure the rebels to lay down their weapons. That meant a negotiation. Venizelos was already smuggling out interviews with Athenian newspapers signalling his interest in 'reform'.[48] Howard found 'nothing harmful or revolutionary' in his proposals for better Cretan government.[49] In reading Howard's dispatches on these themes, Lansdowne latched onto what he could already see were 'materials for a compromise'.[50] Whatever form compromise took, the Prince was likely to play a reduced part in it, which was why when Howard tentatively raised it with him he reacted so bitterly. His feeling of being 'abandoned by the Powers', not least by Britain, was almost complete.[51]

Yet the Prince could not easily be abandoned if it meant the implosion of the autonomous regime. The insurgent attack on the gendarmerie station at the village of Yukolies at the beginning of May, in which four policemen were killed, highlighted the risks. Howard provided Lansdowne with a moving depiction of the funeral of one of the Cretan policemen, with Prince George, European military officers, and the consuls present, the route lined by loyal gendarmes, and the long line of mourners headed by the wailing family.[52] In recording this scene, Howard conveyed a sense of the human reality of the situation. The incident also provided a peg on which to hang the advice that unless more forces were sent, the rebellion—far from petering out—would escape control.[53] Howard's pleas were countered by such views as those of Sir John Fisher, now elevated to First Sea Lord, that 'the life of one of our bluejackets is worth more than the lives of all the Cretan people put together'.[54] Such outpourings prefigured a gathering disenchantment towards Eastern Christians, and Balkan humanity in general. Nevertheless, Balfour and Lansdowne reluctantly concurred in the dispatch of 300 extra British troops. For this there was one principal reason: fear that a large-scale exodus of frightened Muslims from Crete might now suddenly unfold.

As in any Cretan disturbance, the Muslims were most exposed to danger. Their security necessarily lay in the international (especially British) troops and the gendarmerie. But few of the former were to be seen inland, and the latter began to withdraw from some of their stations in the countryside. The much-respected Italian head of the gendarmerie described the Muslims as 'seized with panic',[55]

[47] Dutkowski, *L'Occupation de la Crète*, 104–5.
[48] For interviews see material in Howard to Lansdowne, 14 Apr. 1905, FO78/5410.
[49] Howard to Lansdowne, 4 Apr. 1905, ibid.
[50] Lansdowne note, 25 Apr. 1905, ibid.   [51] Howard to Lansdowne, 27 Apr. 1905, ibid.
[52] Howard to Lansdowne, 8 May 1905, ibid.   [53] Howard to Lansdowne, 18 May 1905, ibid.
[54] Note by Sir John Fisher, 13 May 1905, ADM 116/999.
[55] Capt. Monaco to Howard, 13 Apr. 1905, FO78/5410.

and their fears were not assuaged by the proclamation in Venizelos' name that no harm was meant to their community. In these circumstances the pledge granted to the Sultan was put to an awkward test. Howard explained with frank sarcasm how both he and the senior British military commander, Colonel Panton,

feel pretty mean when, in reply to Deputations and telegrams from Mussulmans all over the island, we make our stereotyped answer that 'the Mussulmans have no cause for worry'. We cannot offer them any protection beyond the agreeable knowledge that a ship may be somewhere within five or ten miles of them.[56]

Here was the reality of the conundrum surrounding British power in Crete. Its naval preponderance meant that it could dominate the coastal regions and ports, and crucially influence the political fate of the island. But it could not affect what happened in the interior. The pledge to the Sultan was trapped in that contradiction. There was a line, however, beyond which indifference involved a high cost. From mid-May a spate of murders of Muslims occurred. 'We must keep a watchful eye upon the treatment of the Muslim population,' the Foreign Secretary stated. 'The situation will be considerably altered if an organized attempt was made by the [Christian] Cretans to wipe them out.'[57] This was the crux. The haphazard harassment of the minority—occasional sequestration of property, destruction of vines, or isolated loss of life—was not to be prevented in a society which offered inadequate protection to all. Indeed, insofar as such discriminations encouraged the very gradual disappearance of Muslims from Crete, there was an unspoken benefit, since the Cretan Question would quietly disappear with them. But a wipe-out was another matter. It would trigger Ottoman retribution in much of the Balkans and Asia Minor, and prove that the British could not help steer a steady course to pacification even in places where they enjoyed special advantages. So long as the Cretan Question survived, the British were not to be free from the spectre of extermination and its wider ramifications. Meanwhile it underpinned the necessity to bring the insurrection to a controlled end before the roof came down on everybody's head.

The Russians were equally eager to terminate the crisis. The year 1905 was one of revolution in the Tsar's backyard. Once Russia had wanted to subvert the Balkan status quo and Turkey with it. Now it sought to prop them up. Russian soldiers consequently cracked down hard in the Rethymno sector. Insurgent groups found themselves shot at by Russian patrols, and some villages had punitive fines slapped on them.[58] Howard advised against repression *à la russe* in the Candian sector, with its history of instability, since 'it may act as a match to light up the whole countryside'.[59] But British patrols became more active and their rules of engagement were loosened. Soon Candia showed signs of quietening down as well. The British Ambassador in Constantinople, Sir Nicholas O'Conor, was able

[56] Howard to Sanderson, 18 May 1905, ibid.   [57] Lansdowne note, 12 May 1905, ibid.
[58] Howard to Lansdowne, 9 June 1905, FO78/5411.
[59] Howard to Panton, 21 July 1905, ibid.

to assure the Sultan that his subjects in Crete were being more energetically protected, as evidenced by the recent deputation of Candian Muslims expressing their
'great gratitude' to Britain.[60] Such expressions were highly welcome in London,
increasingly desperate to conserve the shattered remnants of Britain's influence at
the Porte.

So long as the French and Italian sectors remained lawless, however, progress in
Crete was patchy, since the insurgency simply slid about within the island. From
the outset of trouble rumours had multiplied about divisions between the powers.
These were not unfounded. The representatives of France and Italy scarcely concealed their sympathy for the rebels, not so much because they favoured union
with Greece, but because they contended that the real goal of the Venizelists was
purely and simply to get rid of Prince George.[61] Howard himself was convinced
that the unionist demand by the insurgents was authentic. His information was
that Venizelos' life would be in danger if he tried to wriggle off the hook of his own
rhetoric.[62] 'It seems impossible', Howard lamented the unpredictable shifts
within the consular body, 'that any fixed or stable policy can come out of such
conflicting elements.'[63] The Concert, like Cretan autonomy, was becoming only
half-real—as it always did in a real crisis. Nevertheless, by midsummer there was
agreement to explore the scope for negotiation with the insurgents. In early July the
consuls drew up a 'surrender proposal', though the suspicions of Prince George
were not allayed by the haziness as to effective action if the proposal was rejected.
Armed with this document Howard as doyen led his consular colleagues by carriage and finally donkeys up to a meeting with the insurgent leaders at the remote
mountain monastery of Aghia Moni on the early morning of 15 July 1905.

This was a seminal moment in the process by which Venizelos inserted himself
into the exploding gap between Western power and the Hellenic national idea. He
had increasingly to straddle both roles: that of the rough insurrectionist, and its
natural opposite as the liberal, European-style politician. His subsequent oscilla-
tion between the two personas defined the essence of his strategy. This particular
occasion required him to dress in traditional peasant garb. Most of the insurgent
band stayed outside, but 100 armed men entered the monastery with him.
Howard reckoned they were there not so much to guard Venizelos, but to make
sure that he did not betray their ideals.[64] In fact, Venizelos' aim was not to negotiate—he could hardly do so thus surrounded—but to start rebuilding a bridge to
the consuls by justifying the resort to arms. After Howard had formally read out
the surrender proposal, Venizelos spoke eloquently of the autocratic methods of
the High Commissioner, his refusal to permit public meetings or press freedom,
and fixing of elections, and called for an International Commission of Inquiry to
put them right. Howard regarded these grievances as 'perfectly reasonable',

[60] Howard to Sir Nicholas O'Conor, 2 June 1905, ibid.
[61] Howard to Lansdowne, 9 June 1905, ibid.   [62] Ibid.
[63] Howard to Lansdowne, 6 July 1905, ibid.
[64] Howard to Lansdowne, 16 July 1905, ibid.

though he limited his immediate response to stating that all parties in the island had to forget the past. The implication, nevertheless, that the powers would forget—and forgive—the insurrection conceded to Venizelos his main point, and moderated the pressure on him.

On returning to Canea, however, Howard still believed that the leaders of the rebellion were the prisoners of the unyielding and radicalized movement for *enosis* they had created. His assessment was that they would have to be 'squeezed' further before they came to agreement. In Rethymno the Russians even began to pull down the family houses of leading insurgents. The British did not go that far in Candia, but by September the insurgency was more or less scotched in their sector; even the French sent reinforcements to their headquarters at Sitia.[65] With all of Venizelos' personal letters now being intercepted, the European consuls felt that he was reduced to clinging to the demand for union 'as a drowning man'.[66] The pilfered correspondence afforded the consuls a glimpse into the more complex structure of the insurrection. As Howard explained to Lansdowne, they

bring into the light of day a phase of this struggle, which may perhaps explain something of its origins. It is evident that the insurgent leaders are now openly allied to the anti-dynastic party in Greece and it is not impossible that the hostility of the High Commissioner may have been prompted from the first by a conviction that the latter entertained no friendly feelings towards him or his family.[67]

Under the pressure of the insurrection, not only were the anomalies of the autonomous regime more starkly revealed, but the Cretan Question started to fuse with party struggles in Greece itself. The stakes were commensurately increased. Venizelos knew that he needed the consuls as much as they needed him to terminate the crisis. More active repression by international forces had the advantage of bringing more pressure to bear on those 'intransigents' around Venizelos who cramped his room for negotiation. By 18 October, he felt able to address a letter to the consuls offering to lay down arms, in return for a reform of Cretan government guaranteed by the powers. A month later he met with Howard and his colleagues again at Aghia Moni. Here the basis of an understanding emerged, including municipal elections under international supervision, a Committee of Inquiry on recent events and their causes, and the revision of the constitution under European supervision.[68] As a signal of good intent by the insurrectionists, 700 weapons were given up.[69] At every stage of this rapprochement, Prince George felt isolated and let down. The bitterest cup of all was the amnesty shortly given to the insurgents, including Venizelos (the only exception being deserters from the gendarmerie). When the Prince opposed this, the consuls

---

[65] The more unified action of the European powers through the late summer and early autumn of 1905 in suppressing the Cretan insurrection also reflected closer co-operation in enforcing financial reforms in Macedonia.   [66] Howard to Lansdowne, 1 Sept. 1905, FO78/5412.
    [67] Ibid.   [68] Svolopoulos, *O Eleutherios Venizelos*, 214.
    [69] Martinière, *La Marine française*, 197.

went ahead anyway, and stuck the official notice on consular buildings and international barracks. Once Venizelos ventured back into Canea, Howard invited him into his own home, and found himself the object of Venizelos' considerable charm which hitherto had been largely directed at the representative of France. This was the real inauguration of an Anglo-Venizelist bond the significance of which was to extend well beyond the parochial Cretan Question.[70] As the last motley groups of rebels emerged from the mountains, what Howard called 'the tragi-comedy of this last grotesque insurrection' was over.

Although the powers had different slants on what reform in Crete might mean, the suitably vague Anglicism of 'fair play all round' emerged as the determining principle. When the British minister in Athens explained this personally to the High Commissioner, however, the Prince's sardonic retort was that the only person who never got fair play was himself.[71] The latter was inwardly bent on getting his revenge, and he saw a way to do it. The process by which the insurrection had been wound down involved a reimposition of *de facto* European control. Indeed, Venizelos's increasingly unveiled co-operation made him complicit in such regression, which explains why, whatever laurels he was to later to win in Greece itself, Venizelism remained for a long time a vulnerable phenomenon in Cretan politics. Prince George consequently set about putting himself at the head of a popular reaction against European interference and its local collaborators. His campaign was inaugurated in early January 1906 by an interview in the Athenian newspaper *Patris*, during which he railed that the island was once again 'governed by the Consuls, and through them by the enemies of Union'. This was potent stuff, and the Prince's government party won a clear majority in municipal elections towards the end of that month.

One event at the climax of those elections, however, had particular importance: at the village of Cambanú, an Italian soldier was beaten to death after a fracas with government partisans. The powers rallied together and extracted compensation from the Cretan authorities for the victim's family. But behind the distasteful incident lay a disturbing tendency whereby the opposed forces of order and insurrectionism as they had been defined by the events of 1905 were now rapidly exchanging roles. Prince George's frustration had occasionally led him to threaten to 'take to the mountains' himself. As a Greek prince, this was hard to take seriously; yet if he ever did so, he might cause more trouble than Venizelos. The only way to prevent such a scenario was to get the High Commissioner out of Crete altogether, and this was the logic which led Howard to advise the newly appointed British Foreign Secretary, Sir Edward Grey, in the Liberal government in London, that the time had come to consider a change at the head of the unstable Cretan experiment.[72]

[70] Venizelos' closest contact with the consular body had previously been with the French representative (and Sir Alfred Biliotti's son-in-law), Louis Blanc. The latter's departure in Oct. 1904 lubricated the process whereby Venizelos shifted his orientation towards the British. See Svolopoulos, *O Eleutherios Venizelos*, 37.   [71] Sir Francis Elliott to Grey, 28 Jan. 1906, FO371/47.
[72] Howard to Grey, 22 Jan. 1906, ibid.

Howard did not recommend such a leap in the Cretan dark without testing out some terra firma on which to land. He had extracted a promise from Venizelos that he would not 'under any circumstances join another insurrectionary movement'.[73] By this commitment Venizelos consigned much of his future into British hands. That did not mean any backtracking on union with Greece. Indeed, he explicitly denied to Howard all the allegations of his opponents that he was disloyal to Hellenism. But he accepted—as many Cretans and Greeks did not—the reality that 'the Powers would never agree to Union at once, but that it must come *par étapes*'. This was what the British consul wanted to hear. Nevertheless, establishing a framework whereby an approach to union could be safely charted—that is, one which did not trigger regional conflict, or undermine moderate and reliable forces within Greece itself—was not likely to be easy. Yet Howard expressed to Sir Edward Grey the opinion that sooner or later a move had to be made away from international occupation, thus 'arriving step by step, and without too sudden a shock, at that goal which is practically recognized on all sides as the only final solution of the Cretan Question, namely Union with Greece'.[74]

The arrival of an International Reform Commission in early February 1906 marked the preliminary exploration of such a framework. Since the very presence of this body testified to the continuing intrusiveness of the powers, the atmosphere remained tense. The Commissioners (whose British member was Sir Edward Law, well versed in Hellenic affairs) soon concluded not only that the Prince had no intention of doing anything conciliatory, but that the status quo had become unsustainable. Their report at the end of March stated emphatically that 'the only useful and real reform is annexation' to Greece. Yet because such a decision still seemed too radical a departure for the region as a whole, the report spelled out a series of measures to improve the present governance of Crete: the extension of customs surtaxes to service the loans required to kick-start the economy, the introduction of mixed tribunals to alleviate Muslim anxieties, the clarification of responsibilities exercised by the consuls and the High Commissioner, and the establishment of a militia *under Greek officers* which might eventually allow international troops to be withdrawn. The last of these was directed at the Prince's repeated emphasis on securing a Greek military stake in the island, so affording him a sliver of compensation. But the Commission also advised their respective governments that the Prince be made to accept a new set of political advisers. Given the High Commissioner's unyielding character, this was tantamount to forcing him out sooner rather than later.[75]

Indeed, leveraging the Prince out of the island now assumed a degree of urgency. Even Edward VII's sympathy for his nephew had cooled.[76] Yet the ties between the British and Greek royal houses meant that if Prince George was to be

[73] Howard to Grey, 12 Jan. 1906, ibid.   [74] Howard to Grey, 9 Mar. 1906, ibid.
[75] The first suggestion to force the Prince into resignation came from Sir Edward Law. See Svolopoulos, *O Eleutherios Venizelos*, 154.
[76] Sir Sidney Lee, *Edward VII: A Biography*, i (London, 1925), 495–6.

shunted aside, his exit had to retain some dignity. When the Greek monarch had visited London some months before, soothing assurances had been made, including a guarantee that there was no intention of keeping Crete 'in a condition of permanent tutelage'. Although Edward's VII's arrival in Athens with his consort aboard the royal yacht *Victoria and Albert* on 25 March 1906 was ostensibly in connection with the continued revival of the ancient Olympic Games, a subsidiary purpose (coinciding with the climax of the Reform Commission) was to discuss how Prince George might be 'enabled to escape from an intolerable position [in Crete] with the satisfaction that his mission had been practically fulfilled'.[77] Insofar as this pointed towards a wider Anglo-Greek accord—even some kind of *entente orientale*—it gelled with the British sovereign's continuing desire to be a 'foreign policy monarch', and one capable of making a contribution to the neutering of the Eastern diplomacy of his mercurial German relation, the Kaiser Wilhelm.

In fact, as the head of the British Foreign Office, Lord Hardinge, later recalled the visit, 'frankly speaking, none of us enjoyed it much, except perhaps the Queen'— Alexandra loving few things better than the company of her brother on the Hellenic throne.[78] For one thing, the British government had spent so little money on preparations that its athletes made a poor showing in the Olympic competition, except for the archery.[79] But on the business side there was the unpleasantness of having to endure Prince George's bitter complaints of his treatment. With Cretan elections looming on 20 May, the British were as keen as the Greeks to find a way of easing the tension. It was Hardinge who came up with the suggestion that the King of the Hellenes should have the right to nominate the next High Commissioner of autonomous Crete.[80] This would not mean that Crete became in any way part of Greece, but it was calculated to encourage the further permeation of the Hellenic spirit and institutions. Yet the fact of Turkish sovereignty was to remain undisturbed. Indeed the idea surfaced of embodying the Sultan's continuing rights by the daily ritual of raising his flag at the entrance of Canea harbour, if necessary by European hands. 'These are our obligations [to the Sultan]', Hardinge reiterated to Grey from Athens 'and they must be maintained.'[81]

These British proposals, however, failed to gain the approval of other powers. The Russian Foreign Minister, M. Izvolsky, rejected the proposed nomination of a Cretan High Commissioner by the Greek King as only likely to signal a stampede by other Balkan Christians to grab coveted slices of the Turkish Empire for themselves. Yet when Grey pressed Izvolsky for suggestions, all that emerged was a

[77] Hardinge to Grey, 26 Mar. 1906, FO371/50. The modern Olympic Games had been revived in Athens during Apr. 1896.

[78] For an account of the visit see Lord Hardinge, *Old Diplomacy* (London, 1947), 124–5. The *Victoria and Albert* had stopped at Corfu on the way, allowing some sightseeing of the remains of British rule in the island, which, Hardinge concluded, 'not even the want of care and slovenliness of the Greeks had been able to destroy'. So the old battles around the Ionian Protectorate enjoyed an afterglow into the twentieth century.

[79] Sir Francis Eliot to Sir Edward Grey, 3 May 1906, FO32/745.

[80] Hardinge, *Old Diplomacy*, 125.   [81] Hardinge to Grey, 26 Mar. 1906, FO371/50.

tarted-up version of the Reform Commission's report. At least the Cretan elections passed off without violence, assisted by an extra Royal Navy cruiser on patrol, whilst British troops undertook emergency policing in the fast disintegrating Italian sector.[82] The election results, however, presaged a worsening outlook— Prince George's government faction and the Venizelists were deadlocked, each entrenched in their respective heartlands, whilst the Muslims navigated carefully between them, fearful of being the chief losers should civil unrest be renewed. The prospect unfolded of a clash between the main Christian parties when the Assembly convened, and even a possible secession, leading to the scenario of two rival Assemblies making separate declarations of union with Greece. This possibility marked the *reductio ad absurdam* of Cretan politics, but in Crete the absurd often led to violence and a volatile cast of victims.

A breathing space was secured when the Assembly met on 13 July, and temporarily suspended itself after passing a resolution calling for annexation. A few days later the powers issued a Note which provided for a revision of the Cretan constitution, allied to a guarantee of non-discrimination against Muslims in the distribution of public offices. Greek officers would henceforth be recruited into the gendarmerie and into a newly established militia, though in both cases this cadre was restricted to the 'retired list' of the Greek Army to avoid divided loyalties. In addition, the withdrawal of international troops was for the first time officially broached, though subject to a complete assurance of safety on the part of the Muslims—a qualification with much potential for delay. To Greek opinion, however, all this was just more European prevarication to avoid the main issue, and the British minister in Athens reported 'universal consternation'.[83] Howard tried to bang home this feeling to London by telling his superiors that outsiders could not easily grasp the 'fanatically chauvinist' sentiments of Cretans, and that such diplomatic exercises as the Note only stirred up more instability in the future, which European troops would then have to suppress. 'The jam is not sweet enough,' he told Grey of the Note's bland contents,[84] to which the British Foreign Secretary—whose distaste for Balkan affairs was already becoming plain— testily retorted, 'One cannot spend one's days making jam for Cretans.'[85]

The ingredients of Balkan-style politics might be offputting to Grey, but his bitter experience was to be that they had nonetheless to be taken into account. So it proved here, as the mood in the island took a nasty turn through the summer of 1906. A tell-tale sign was the wobbling of Venizelos. Although he assured Howard that he was 'very pleased' with the Note, rumours quickly reached the consulates that outside European circles he was saying the complete opposite.[86] When

---

[82] Howard spent election day with British troops in the disturbed village of Cambanú ensuring that there was no repeat of the earlier bloody incident. Howard, *Theatre of Life*, 80–2.

[83] Young to Grey, 25 July 1906, FO371/50. For the text of the Collective Note of 23 June 1906, see 'Memorandum on the Affairs of Crete', July to Dec. 1906, FO421/257.

[84] Howard to Grey, 31 July 1906, FO371/51.   [85] Grey minute, 6 Aug. 1906, ibid.

[86] Howard to Hardinge, 25 July 1906, FO371/50.

confronted on the matter, and 'after some beating about the bush', he admitted that it was far too dangerous for him to speak favourably of the offer.[87] Such shufflings indicated why Howard repeatedly warned London that the situation looked set to become 'worse than an insurrection', because at least in an insurrection one could support one lot of Cretan insurgents against another. What beckoned was a real revolution, with the anger of Cretan Christians turned uniformly against Europe in general and Great Britain above all. In such a case the latter's only 'friends' were likely to be a rump of terrified Muslims rushing for whatever small boats the Royal Navy could provide.

A bit more 'jam' had therefore to be spooned out quickly. This took the form of returning to the idea of the Greek King's right to nominate the next High Commissioner, finally agreed to in St Petersburg with the proviso that the actual designation of the appointment should remain the preserve of the Concert. Although the Ottoman Porte protested strongly against any move to install a 'Greek Governor' in Crete,[88] a revised Note with this amendment was collectively presented to King George in Athens on 14 August on a take-it-or-leave-it basis. The King and his ministers knew that they had little choice but to take it—with the activities of Greek bands held responsible for the growing horrors in Macedonia, they were conscious that Hellenism was losing 'not only the official but the popular sympathies of Europe'.[89] But even after the Note had been accepted in Athens, the agreement could not be publicized, because Britain's partners in the Cretan Concert—driven by 'dread of Germany'—insisted that Kaiser Wilhelm first signify his approval.[90] Over Crete, as in the Balkans more widely, the ability of German power to dictate outcomes, even from the sidelines, began to frighten Grey and his colleagues in London.

For the European consuls, the delay was highly damaging. With no more 'jam' yet available to distribute, the local cycle of conflict intensified. Howard's relations with Prince George virtually collapsed, and the former's departure on extended leave was a discreet attempt to assist the Prince's own going. Howard's temporary replacement, Ronald Graham, and his European colleagues remained bent not only on forcing the High Commissioner out as swiftly as possible, but on making it *appear* that he went 'willingly and thoroughly satisfied with the agreement come to'.[91] Yet the Prince's disappearance under these auspices could only portend an abject humiliation. It was hardly likely that he would accept this meekly. The Prince was determined to return to Greece with his head held high, and his dynasty's prestige protected. Indeed, the degree to which the standing of the Glücksburg line in Greek hearts—'The Love of my People', according to the royal

---

[87] Howard to Grey, 31 July 1906, FO371/51.   [88] Grey to O'Conor, 26 July 1906, ibid.

[89] 'Extract from Annual Report for Greece, 1906', in Gooch and Temperley (eds.), *Origins of the War*, v. 119.   [90] Young to Grey, 11 Sept. 1906, FO371/52.

[91] Acting Consul Graham to Grey, 17 July 1906, ibid. Howard never returned to Crete. He subsequently enjoyed a glittering diplomatic career, becoming British Ambassador in Washington during the 1920s.

motto of 1863—had become entangled in Cretan developments was pregnant with significance for Hellenic political culture on a much larger plane. The first sign of serious trouble came with the descent of Prince George's peasant supporters on Canea, many armed with clubs and old rifles, and seemingly hell-bent on stopping their hero from leaving Crete. The Prince refused the urgings of the consuls to order his henchmen out of town. Yet it was Venizelos who was in the greatest danger. The latter had little recourse but to seek the protection of the Europeans, and to make sure of it he briefly linked his fate to that of the Muslims. Venizelos urged on Graham that if the imminent Assembly was convened, and proceeded to debate the Prince's future, the certain result would be a physical attack on both his own faction and representatives of the minority.[92] When on the evening of 7 September, news spread that the High Commissioner had called the Assembly into session for the next morning, Venizelos' career hung in the balance. If he was crushed, and Prince George emerged triumphant from the crisis, the powers would undoubtedly forfeit any leverage over what happened inside Crete thereafter. Not hesitating to seek the concurrence of their governments, the consular body ordered a mixed detachment of European troops to occupy the Assembly building at dawn and evict all members of the legislature. The bare veil over the Concert's rule in the island was ripped aside.

The closure of an elected chamber was an embarrassing event, and necessarily accompanied by a promise to reconvene it very shortly. Meanwhile tight control was imposed. Newspapers were censored, arms confiscated, and international patrols appeared in the streets of Canea. The fact that all this was presided over by Colonel Panton testified to how far responsibility was again falling into British hands. Security alone, however, was not enough. With the German Kaiser at last giving an imperious nod of approval, the European Note was published forthwith, and some show of Cretan co-operation extracted. On 13 September, thirty-six Venizelist deputies and their Muslim counterparts presented separate but simultaneous petitions deploring the recent agitation. 'It is particularly satisfactory', it was noted in Whitehall, where patience with Christian Cretans was now close to exhaustion, 'that the Muslims are satisfied.'[93] All that remained was for the Prince to leave, since until he did so there was no chance of the Assembly approving the Note itself. King George in Athens had already nominated a successor, Alexander Zaimis, an experienced politician not noted for superabundant energy (energy was the last thing the Powers wanted in Crete).[94] But the Prince knew, as did the consuls, that his own going would be 'the most dangerous moment', and he wanted to spin it out as long as possible to leave his mark.[95] Finally, on 22 September he announced that he would sail to Greece three days

[92] Howard to Grey, 6 Sept. 1906, ibid.

[93] Hardinge note, 14 Sept. 1906, FO371/53.

[94] Zaimis had been closely associated with King George's drive after the Graeco–Turkish war of 1897 to focus Greek affairs on domestic reforms. See Christmas, *Life*, 267.

[95] Graham to Grey, 11 Sept. 1906, FO371/52.

later. Struggling in Athens to deflect popular outrage away from Great Britain, the new British minister, Sir Frances Elliot, suggested to London that it would help if the powers issued an official expression of their gratitude to the Prince for all his hard labour in Crete. He received a curt reply that any such expression about the Prince could only be made 'when his unfortunate regime is at end'.[96]

To suppress a fresh outbreak in Crete, HMS *Barham* arrived off Canea on 24 September, and through the night its searchlights played on the town and surrounding heights. A force of British bluejackets was landed to stiffen Panton's patrols. With the agitation apparently cowed, the consuls prepared to accompany a sullen Prince George along the main road to Suda Bay guarded by international troops, from where the Prince would ceremoniously embark on a Greek royal yacht. The intended effect was to underline that the High Commissioner departed, as he had arrived in 1898, as no more than the subordinate instrument of the Powers. But when the European representatives arrived at the palace it became known that 3,000 armed demonstrators had cut the Suda highway. The only alternative was for Prince George to be hustled into an improvised exit from Canea, and rowed out to a waiting Greek warship, the *Psara*. More international forces were drawn from barracks to supervise the operation. By then insurgents were already entering the European suburb of Halepa. Firing became general in the town, and frightened Muslims crowded into the British consulate for safety. According to Graham's later report, at this critical moment the French and Italian troops 'disappeared into thin air'. Graham himself dashed off to see his Russian counterpart, Consul Bronowski. When he arrived, the Russian *cavasses* (or consular guards) were standing to arms to repel any attack. Graham's subsequent description went on:

I had just been pointing out to ... [Bronowski] some insurgents firing from behind an outhouse, when a heavy fire was suddenly and quite unexpectedly opened on the Russian consulate itself ... One of the first bullets ... struck the *cavass* at the window by which my Russian colleague and I were standing, blowing off the top of his head; he only lived a few minutes.[97]

It was assumed that the shot had been intended for the Russian consul himself.[98] In the Eastern world, of which Crete was *ipso facto* part, the shooting of consuls, or anybody connected with them, was extremely serious—more serious than heaps of local corpses. Nothing concentrated the consular mind more effectively, and no sooner had the news of the attack on the Russian compound spread, than the French and Italian consuls duly showed up to demonstrate belated solidarity. To prevent complete collapse, the representatives decided that Prince George had

[96] Sanderson minute, 22 Sept. 1906, FO371/53. For a portrait of Sir Francis Elliot, who later remained in this post amidst all the upsets of the 1914–18 war, see Mackenzie, *First Athenian Memories*, 8–9.   [97] Graham to Grey, 25 Sept. 1906, FO371/153.
[98] The fact that the Russian consul in the Macedonian province of Monastir had recently been shot dead gave this episode a particular edge.

to be hustled out without more ado. In the official rendering, it was 'respectfully suggested [to the High Commissioner] that ... he should have a boat sent from the *Psara* under the back of the Palace and leave immediately from the small landing there'.[99] On receiving this instruction, Prince George bitterly complained at being made to leave 'like a thief and a rascal', but he had little choice.[100] An unsympathetic French commentator later observed that Prince George's exit from Crete lacked even the dignity of that of Djevaad Pasha, the last Ottoman Governor of the island, just a few years before.[101] Yet in the Prince's calculations, even a rushed evacuation on a Greek warship was less damaging to his pride than going through the motions of a ceremony at Suda surrounded by emblems of European superiority. Things were different when he arrived in Piraeus two days later, met by hugely enthusiastic crowds. Sir Francis Elliott was present, and in an attempt to pour balm on the wound, stepped forward and 'conveyed to His Royal Highness, on behalf of the Powers, most sincere thanks for the continuous and indefatigable devotion applied to the task entrusted to him [in Crete]'.[102] Prince George replied with a sharp bow. The strained irony of this occasion captured in cameo the complex interaction of Greek royalty and European power politics as it was mediated through the Cretan Question.

In Crete, however, the crisis could not be truly ended until the Assembly formally endorsed the European Note, and it would not do that until High Commissioner Zaimis appeared on the scene, a bitter-sweet, if imprecise, augury of future union. Grey could not get him there fast enough. He was invested by King George in Athens on 29 September 1906, and quickly escorted to Crete by an international squadron. If the Prince's departure from the island, however, had been a dangerous moment, so it was feared would be Zaimis' arrival. Their nerves 'entirely gone', some of the consuls apprehended assassination when they joined Zaimis in the procession from the harbour to the old Ottoman Konak.[103] But they had little choice but to button on their tunics and hope for the best. Canea was illuminated the preceding night, and in fact the ensuing event passed off in festive spirit. Zaimis was cautious by temperament, but highly shrewd, and he shortly negotiated 'an honourable retreat' for the Assembly in which all those involved in the violent agitation—except for the killer of the Russian *cavass*—were amnestied, after which the Cretan legislature duly approved the new European dispensation. They did so, however, unaware that Sir Edward Grey, keen to mollify Anglo-Ottoman relations after a short but intense crisis over the Turco-Egyptian border in Sinaia, simultaneously sent a personal assurance to Sultan Abdul Hamid that union between Crete and Greece remained impossible.[104] The High

---

[99] Graham to Grey, 25 Sept. 1906, FO371/153.

[100] Howard, *Theatre of Life*, 96.   [101] Martinière, *La Marine française*, 203.

[102] Elliott to Grey, 29 Sept. 1906, FO371/53. The Prince left almost immediately afterwards for Copenhagen. His public career, and his usefulness to the dynasty, had been destroyed, and his life thereafter was largely spent in Europe—always more congenial to the Glücksburgs. See Hugo Vickers, *Alice: Princess Andrew of Greece* (London, 2000).   [103] Graham to Grey, 30 Sept. 1906, FO371/53.

[104] For the Sinai Boundary dispute which had continued through much of 1906 see Gooch and Temperley (eds), *Origins of the War*, v. 189–95.

1. King George I of Greece at the time of his election in 1863, aged seventeen

2. Cypriot villagers in 1878

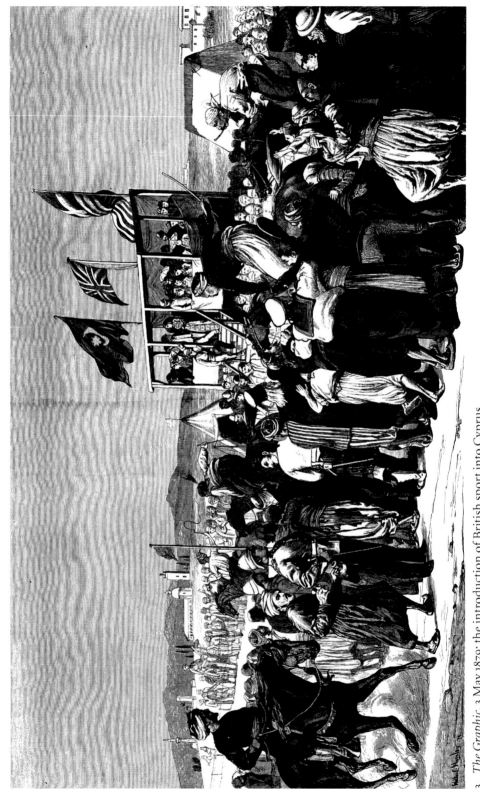

3. *The Graphic,* 3 May 1879: the introduction of British sport into Cyprus

4. Ottoman soldiers marching to Candia harbour during their eviction from Crete by British troops, 5 November 1898

5. High Commissioner Zaimis arrives in Rethymno, October 1906

6. British consular society in Canea, 1907

7. Cretan gendarmes guard the remnant of the Greek flag destroyed by International troops, Firka Fort, 28 July 1909

8. Muslim notables in Canea participating in the celebration of King Constantine's name day, 21 May 1913

9. View of Government House, Nicosia after its destruction by demonstrators, 21 October 1931

10. Governor Sir Herbert Richmond Palmer and Lady Palmer in the grounds of Government House, Nicosia in 1935. The new edifice (today the Presidential Palace) appears half-completed in the background

11. Winston Churchill at Government House, Nicosia, 1 February 1943. In foreground (left to right) Bishop Leontius, the Mufti, Churchill, Governor Sir Arthur Woolley

12. Archbishop Damaskinos and General Paget tour Rhodes Town on liberation, 14 May 1945

13. Colonel Acland meets representatives of the Greek, Italian, and Turkish communities in Rhodes after the declaration of British military administration in the Dodecanese

14. The Greek Sacred Regiment welcomes Archbishop Damaskinos to Rhodes

15. Scene in the Nicosia bazaar, c.1950

16. Trouble in Nicosia, 24 November 1958. An *enosis* demonstration is broken up by British soldiers

Commissioner, he stated, 'would be responsible to the Powers for continuing the protection of the Turkish flag, as had been done since the [European] occupation'.[105]

The most distinguished historian of the unification of the modern Greek state has written that by the end of 1906 Crete was 'earmarked for Greece'. It was certainly earmarked for nobody else, though suspicions that the various European naval powers (most notably, Great Britain) thirsted for possession of the great Suda anchorage were never to go away so long as Turkish sovereignty lasted. Yet as Grey's assurances dispatched to the Yildiz Palace indicated, there really remained nothing inevitable about the future. Crete might become more Hellenic in its cultural and political institutions, and yet get no nearer the apotheosis of Greek statehood. As for the Sultan's flag, its protection in Crete under European supervision might be, as a Russian diplomat scoffed, 'a comedy unworthy of a Great Power'. But so long as it continued there was no guarantee that the farce might not become serious—that some twist in the Balkan game might yet again transform Ottoman decline into revival, and with it alter the projected fate of the island. As one of Grey's advisers in the Foreign Office warned him, they, like everybody else, were still left 'waiting to see how the cat jumps in Crete'.[106]

But before tracing this further movement, it is important to note contemporary analogues to the 'unfortunate regime' we have just analysed. For the UN 'protectorates' imposed on Bosnia and Kosovo in the later 1990s share almost all these earlier hallmarks, even if the ethnic balances have differed.[107] In this recurring category, great powers look on in passive disapproval as Christians and Muslims slide into bloody fighting amidst a disintegrating status quo. They intervene only when the killing eventually impacts on the regional and international system. A complex and clearly provisional regime (in the case of Bosnia, under the Dayton arrangements negotiated in November 1995) is eventually imposed, locking in a tense and exhausted equilibrium, whilst peacekeepers patrol streets and villages. By buttressing quiescence with a flimsy constitution, external guarantors find a 'solution' for their own needs. But such solutions rarely address the essential issues which pitched these societies into fratricidal war. International diplomats speak of 'final' destinations, but in truth they want the journey to stop where it is, because otherwise they cannot be sure where it is heading. Yet inside these curious hybrid statelets created out of pressing necessity suspicions between competing groups habitually remain unassuaged, and even intensify.[108] The replications of an underlying deadlock are potentially endless—until, as we are about to see in Crete, some new *force majeure* finally intervenes to outflank the interventionists and imposes a less ambiguous dispensation.

[105] Grey to Barclay, 3 Oct. 1906, FO 371/54.

[106] Young to Grey, 3 Nov. 1906, FO371/51.

[107] Any student of the issues covered in this book, indeed, will find many echoes in Sumantra Bose, *Bosnia after Dayton: Nationalist Partition and International Intervention* (London, 2002).

[108] We should note also that the complexity of the phenomenon referred to is apparent in its occasional application even to independent states—as in Cyprus following the independence settlement of 1959–60 described below.

6

Britain, the Balkans and the Climax of Cretan Union, 1906–1913

In the Balkans . . . it is always the unexpected which happens.

(Sir George Buchanan, 3 Feb. 1909)

The Cretans are the Suffragettes of European politics.

(Sir Edward Grey, 28 Aug. 1912)

It will already be apparent that the question of Cretan *enosis* with Greece was bound up with wider international struggles. This was particularly the case in the final climax leading to union, achieved *de facto* amidst the dramatic events of the First Balkan War after 8 October 1912, and *de jure* under the terms of the treaties which brought the upheavals in the region—all too briefly—to a close. Events in Crete fed directly into the initial outbreak of hostilities between the Christian Balkan states and Turkey; and it was these hostilities which came to be acknowledged as the harbinger of the ensuing great European war after August 1914. Whilst tracing the resulting patterns, we are consequently dealing with scenarios on a plane far beyond the dimensions of the island itself. In a way this proved what Sir Edward Grey, who remained Foreign Secretary throughout this period, always contended about the contingent nature of the Cretan Question; his handling of it, however, casts a penetrating light on the limits and contradictions of his own diplomacy. Our principal theme will be the manner in which powerful regional and international currents first sucked Crete in one direction, and then another, before decisively settling its ultimate fate. It is the plasticity of the outcome, not its historical 'determinism', which stands out from a close reading of the process.

The intensity of these fluctuations could not have been predicted when Zaimis arrived as High Commissioner of Crete in September 1906. The facts of Cretan politics and demography seemingly presaged a further movement, however obliquely, *towards* the Hellenic kingdom. Alexander Zaimis' appointment as High Commissioner was a token that this movement was designed to unfold in a discreet manner calibrated to avoid complications elsewhere. The new High Commissioner played his part with the prudent competence that had recommended him. He quickly established a cordial relationship with the consular body, and especially with Esme Howard's successor, Arthur Peel. On this front matters were assisted by the departure of Baron Fasciotti, the Italian consul, whose anti-Hellenic attitudes had become plain—a sign of the expansionist impulses now emanating erratically from Rome. Amongst Zaimis' chief tasks was to preside over the introduction of a more liberal constitution, completed to the satisfaction of the powers by the end of 1906.[1] Some of the recent bile in Cretan politics consequently drained away. The elusive grail of Cretan tranquillity glimmered once more on the horizon.

Further progress hinged on holding elections without exciting divisions within Crete—either between Christians and Muslims, or amongst the Christians themselves. If the former cleavage was always to be the most profound, the latter remained the most volatile. Social differentiation between the rural traditionalism of Prince George's old faction, led now by Antonis Michelidakis, and the more urban and commercial complexion of the Venizelist grouping, was heightened by a trickle of refugees from Athens, who took up residence again in Cretan towns.[2] Suspicions in some quarters that Venizelos himself aimed, not at *enosis*, but at a permanent form of local autonomy, had not been dissipated by the crisis surrounding Prince George's abject departure. Yet the reassertion of the powers' authority meant that no Cretan Christian politician could risk rocking the boat on the new course set under Zaimis' careful pilotage. The elections held in June 1907 passed off without violence, government patronage helping to give Michelidakis' supporters a slim majority.[3] Yet the solid turnout of voters for Venizelist candidates helped to confirm that party's credibility in European eyes, aided by their leader's calls for Christians to fulfil their 'patriotic duty' by ensuring the safety of the Muslim community through the tense election campaign.[4]

A striking outcome of the elections was that the Muslim deputies held the balance of votes between the two main Christian parties in the chamber. This leverage helped the minority secure more government jobs. A Muslim deputy from Canea, Mehmet Bey Hamitzade, was soon appointed Councillor of Public Instruction and Worship, a portfolio carrying, ironically, some responsibility for Orthodox affairs. Another prominent Muslim became Prefect of Canea. The limited pool of patronage, and the scramble to secure positions by Christian factions, meant that Muslim applicants had nonetheless to make do with crumbs, and the old grievances concerning *Vakifs* (or Muslim foundations and their properties) continued. Consul Peel continued to press the new ministry to put more 'favours' in the way of the Muslims.[5] Yet here at least were the outlines of a revamped regime in which all parties and creeds could feel that they had a stake.

---

[1] For a summary of the constitution see Minutes of the Second Constituent Assembly, 1906–7, 39th Meeting, 29 Nov. 1906, printed in the *Epissimos Efimeris* (Cretan Gazette). The constitution was formally adopted on 8 Feb. 1907.   [2] Svolopoulos, *O Eleutherios Venizelos*, 472–3.

[3] The results of the elections on 11 June 1907 were Government Party 33, Venizelists 24, Muslim 8.

[4] Peel to Grey, 24 Apr. 1907, FO371/241.   [5] Peel to Grey, 21 June 1907, ibid.

In fact, the Cretan Assembly was not intended by the powers to enjoy anything but a restricted existence. On 23 July, Zaimis formally opened it, and immediately closed it down, permitting only the briefest display of Christian sentiment concerning *enosis* as 'but the expression of a pious wish'.[6] The High Commissioner, for his part, was interested above all in slotting into place more practical tokens of Greek participation in Cretan affairs. A precondition was the restoration of discipline within the gendarmerie, and the establishment of a militia. In the early autumn of 1907 a contingent of Greek Army officers, selected from the 'retired' list to avoid protest from Constantinople, had arrived under the command of the much-respected Colonel Monferatos to play their part in these tasks—this constituted, the British consulate reported, a 'landmark in the history of Crete'.[7] A few weeks later the Italian *carabinieri* left the island where they had seen arduous duty. The new Greek cadre were under the strictest instructions from their government to conduct themelves 'impeccably' within the limits set by Cretan autonomy, and they proceeded to do so. Under Monferatos' capable leadership, the newly formed militia not only brought enhanced physical security, but also a new integration to an island whose deep divisions took many forms over and beyond the communal fissure.[8]

Meanwhile the progressive relaxation and final abolition of martial law testified to the tranquillity descending on the island. Thereafter pressure from the Christians for the withdrawal of the international garrison mounted. The majority community had interpreted the new dispensation as a deal whereby in return for their passivity the protecting powers would allow the steady Hellenization of the island's political character to resume. This was indeed what Christian politicians had been led to believe by the spirit of the recent Note, as well as by the nods and winks of the consuls. The European governments, however, remained between the rock of mounting Hellenic expectation and the hard place of repeated obligations to maintain the Sultan's sovereignty. But Europe had learned already that the hardest place to be in Crete was confronted by widespread Christian militancy. In 1905 they had got away with it, but in any future breakdown it seemed likely that international troops would find themselves facing the hostility of the *entire* Christian Greek population—face to face, as the European policy code phrased it, with the Cretan Question. The surest way to avoid this fate was to evacuate international forces from the island. Sir Edward Grey's preoccupation with preserving the Concert's effectiveness for dealing with problems even more directly connected to European stability—for example, in Morocco, which had recently come close to triggering a major war between the powers—meant that he was keen to move as quickly towards an exit from Crete as circumstances permitted.

Such a prospect still remained shrouded in acute difficulties. There was the suspicion that one of the powers might exploit any transition to grab the prize of

[6] Peel to Grey, 25 July 1907, FO371/241.
[7] Acting Consul-General Wyldebore-Smith to Grey, 25 Oct. 1907, FO371/239.
[8] A.-J. Reinach, *La Question crétoise vue de Crète* (Paris, 1910), 14.

Suda Bay for themselves. Peel's suggestion in September 1907 for a staggered programme of troop reduction was as much to engender confidence between the powers themselves as amongst Cretans.[9] Data on alleged assaults on Cretan Muslims began to be assessed for any bearing on the practicality of European withdrawal. Peel admitted that whenever such a withdrawal came about, it was certain that the Cretan chamber would pass a resolution declaring Crete to be joined to Greece; but the consul passed on, approvingly, Zaimis' assurance that any such declaration would remain an 'empty gesture', since the Athenian authorities would do nothing to translate mere declaration into reality.[10] Balancing all these factors and considerations together, in November 1907 Grey and his cabinet colleagues authorized a promise to the High Commissioner that if tranquillity was successfully maintained during the next eight months, His Majesty's government would recommend to the other powers the commencement of evacuation by international forces.[11]

Cretan Christians were, as one Whitehall observer noted, 'not so foolish' as to indulge thereafter in actions against Muslim neighbours bound only to prolong a European occupation they were tired of.[12] Although the Porte tried to exploit the murder of a local Muslim in February, the island enjoyed a quiescence on all fronts it had not experienced for years. At the beginning of April 1908, in a carefully choreographed sequence, the High Commissioner took the salute of the refurbished local forces in front of his palace. Immediately afterwards he informed the Concert that the terms of the European Note had been met, and formally requested the withdrawal of international troops. In backing this request, the European consuls in Crete provided collective confirmation that, relative to population,

there is an equal distribution amongst Muslims and Christians of appointments in the public service, that crimes against Muslims are rare, that severe measures have been adopted for their repression and that such offences as have taken place have not been influenced by religious or political motives.[13]

In the light, therefore, of this assertion of both Cretan stability and the absence of discrimination, the British government persuaded the other protecting powers to join in an announcement on 12 May 1908 that the first European military detachments would leave the island during the coming July, and that the evacuation would be completed within one year.[14]

Just as Sir Edward Grey had lubricated the transition from Prince George by reiterated pledges to the Sultan, so he did, however, with regard to the decision to evacuate international troops. He told Rifaat Bey, the Porte's Ambassador in London, that the British government was firmly bent on a military departure from

[9] Peel Memorandum, 1 Oct. 1907, FO371/241.   [10] Ibid.
[11] Hardinge to Peel, 5 Nov. 1907, ibid.   [12] Alwyn Parker, 2 Apr. 1907, FO371/442.
[13] Peel to Grey, 7 Apr. 1907, FO421/426.
[14] Dutkowski, *L'Occupation de la Crète*, 118.

Crete, but 'only because their [European] Consuls were of the opinion that the step could now be taken without impairing the internal administration, without endangering the Muslims, and *without leading to a change in the status quo*'.[15] This did not convince Rifaat Bey, whose rejoinder was that evacuation was tantamount to annexation. Still, the Sultan's representative was able to pocket a fresh commitment, and for Grey a pattern was set whereby any transition in Crete was increasingly mortgaged to the fulfilment of written obligations to Abdul Hamid as the theoretic sovereign of the island.

What lay behind this pattern? The successive interweaving of Cretan, Macedonian, and Egyptian issues had recently provided a fund of opportunities for German diplomacy to exploit British unpopularity in Turkey. Alongside Grey's growing identification of Germany as the chief threat to European peace, there emerged a desire to claw back some of Berlin's gains at Constantinople. On most issues there was little scope to do so. Crete was one matter, however, where the British could show themselves punctilious with regard to Ottoman rights without compromising their interests. There was also something deeper at work. The British government's capacity to hold in place a wider European status quo was becoming more and more tenuous. In clinging to this goal Grey by 1908 was beginning to pin much of his faith on 'bits of paper'—that is, on previous written guarantees to respect existing frontiers. If such guarantees were shown to be worthless in the East, so, Grey was convinced, they would be in the West. In this way the pledges made in recent years to Abdul Hamid came to occupy a special niche in the peculiarly moral universe within which Grey conceived his aims and duty. Some came to regard Grey's world view as highly simplistic, but his defenders then and later saw in its simplicity a certain strength and transparency—in short, that it provided hope of a sheet anchor in a world being tugged into waters of unprecedented danger.[16] Grey's actions over Crete can only be interpreted adequately if they are related to powerful pyschological undercurrents— personal and national—which ran through this period, and indeed right up to August 1914.

Meanwhile evacuation from Crete without thinking through the implications was in some people's opinion courting disaster. Sir Francis Elliot pointed out from his Athenian post the likely ramifications. He told Grey that as soon as 'the last foreign soldier' left Cretan soil, the Greek flag would undoubtedly be unfurled over the island. In Elliot's view, before that happened, it would be sensible to bring the Sultan to accept the loss of the island to his empire.[17] Otherwise the British government would in the end have 'to recognize a fact being accomplished without their consent'—with all that this implied for Britain's prestige—or to face up to the highly disagreeable necessity to reintervene in Crete. The minister's forthrightness did not go down well in London, where his 'devout hopes' for *enosis* were swept aside.[18] Some of the other powers shared Elliot's instincts, not least as to the

---

[15] Grey to Barclay, 15 May 1908, FO371/442. Italics added.
[16] For a discussion see Keith Robbins, *Lord Grey of Falloden* (London, 1971).
[17] Elliot to Grey, 16 May 1908, FO371/442.   [18] Foreign Office minute, 18 May 1908, ibid.

wisdom of repeated assurances to Abdul Hamid. They jibbed at the British proposal that a small international force should remain in Crete as a token of those commitments.[19] An alternative resurfaced in which each of the four powers should contribute a *stationnaire* to take turns landing a party on the island in the middle of Suda Bay to lower the Turkish flag each evening, and to raise it in the mornings. As Grey rather forlornly admitted, Britain had little option but 'to fall in with this solution',[20] though its ephemeral character was obvious from the start.

A more immediate concern was that the first phase of departure by international forces would be marred by inter-communal disorder, especially in British-controlled Candia with its large Muslim population. To ensure there was no incentive for trouble, Peel impressed on Muslim opinion that the decision to withdraw troops was irrevocable. On 28 July 1908 a detachment of King's Royal Rifles marched down to the quayside in the town and embarked for Malta—each soldier being handed a laurel inscribed 'God Save Great Britain' by a cheering crowd of Christians. In the following weeks contingents from the other powers also left, without impairing the stability of the main Cretan towns. By the end of August 250 Russian troops had been shipped off to Odessa, without the last-minute equivocation in St Petersburg which had been anticipated. Overall, the international garrison was more than halved by the end of the summer of 1908.

Against this background, Peel was able to report the intense relief which swept through the Cretan body politic, and its beneficent impact on inter-communal relations. On the occasion of the Sultan's birthday in September portraits of Abdul Hamid and King George of Greece were carried side by side through the streets of Canea. 'No one with any experience of this country', the British consul informed Grey, 'can have failed to notice the steady and growing improvement in relations between the partisans of the two rival creeds, formerly separated by sentiments of such unmitigated hate and scorn.'[21] Peel's thrust was clear: a window of opportunity had come into existence to effect a definitive (that is, Hellenic) solution at a juncture when anxiety about Muslim safety and welfare was baseless. After so much Cretan heartache, some in the Foreign Office lapped it up. 'Crete', one senior official remarked, 'has never been so well governed since the first intervention by the Powers seventy years ago.'[22] The tranquillization of the island was seemingly complete at last.

It was not only Crete, but the entire Ottoman Empire which suddenly seemed to have good government within its grasp. At the outset of July officers of the Turkish Army in Macedonia—members of a shadowy organization, the Committee of Union and Progress (CUP)—defied government authority. Afterwards it came to be widely believed that the immediate trigger for the revolt was the rumour of an Anglo-Russian plan—discussed by Edward VII and Tsar Nicholas when they had met at Reval during June to review the new entente

[19] Peel to Grey, 28 May 1908, FO371/443. Also see the Venizelist newspaper *Kyrix*, 8 June 1908.
[20] Grey minute, 6 June 1908, FO371/442.   [21] Peel to Grey, 4 Sept. 1908, ibid.
[22] Parker minute, 10 Sept. 1908, ibid. The historical reference is to the insurrection of 1866–68.

between their countries[23]—to impose Cretan-style autonomy on Macedonia. This was to simplify the causes of the ensuing Turkish Revolution, but the fact that the coming to power of the Young Turks was coloured by a nationalist sensitivity to any suggestion that Madeconia should follow in the Cretan path was to prove significant. The first goal of the Young Turkish movement, however, was the restoration of the defunct Ottoman constitution of 1876, and on 23 July 1908, the Sultan reluctantly restored its provisions and ordered elections. The prospect of a constitutional and progressive Turkey produced waves of euphoria throughout the region. This was most remarkably the case in Constantinople. For religious minorities there seemed to be an end to the troubles of the recent past—all would be Ottomans 'equal under the same blue sky'.[24] Greeks, Turks, Armenians, Kurds, and Jews were caught up in a swirl of fraternity and reconciliation. The Greek Orthodox Patriarch and the *Sheikh-i-Islam* even shared a carriage along the Bosporus, fêted by an enthusiastic crowd. The flush of optimism concerning Crete was just part, then, of a wider regional efflorescence.

For Sir Edward Grey, the revolution in Turkey was an unexpected boon. As he recalled much later, Britain had long striven to 'keep its hands clean' in dealing with Abdul Hamid, but to watch Germany profit as a consequence had been 'a very barren and unsatisfactory result'.[25] An opportunity now arose to halt that process. A constitutional Turkey was by natural reflex pro-British, expressed in the appointment of the Cypriot-born, and Anglophile, Kiamil Pasha as Grand Vizier. The warm welcome extended to the new British minister, Sir Gerald Lowther, on his arrival in Constantinople on 31 July, was also an indicator of a transformed environment. 'As for us, we have the ball at our feet, to the great chagrin of our German friends,' George Fitzmaurice, the influential chief dragoman at the Embassy, crowed.[26] It was clear both that the 'new' Turkey looked to Britain to guarantee it against others, and that Grey was determined it 'should have every chance' of sinking deep roots under British patronage.[27] Much of the tragedy of Grey's peacetime diplomacy was to flow from the manner in which this chance was swiftly undercut by Balkan events in which Turkey's interests received short shrift indeed. '[October] 1908 held 1914 in its arms,' Grey's first biographer, G. M. Trevelyan, wrote of the larger effects of the crisis which followed.[28]

That crisis originated from the fact that others reacted impulsively and even with hostility to the advent of the Young Turks. The Austro-Hungarian government viewed nascent Turkish revival with deep concern, especially respecting their long-standing military occupation of Bosnia. At the same time, the proposed

---

[23] For the discussions at Reval, in which Crete also featured, see Gooch and Temperley (eds). *Origins of the War*, v. 232–45.

[24] Sir William Miller, *The Ottoman Empire and its Successors, 1801–1922* (London, 1923), 476.

[25] Viscount Grey, *Twenty-Five Years, 1892–1916* (London, 1925), 131–3.

[26] G. H. Fitzmaurice to Sir William Tyrrell, 25 Aug. 1908, in Gooch and Temperley (eds). *Origins of the War*, v. 268.   [27] Grey, *Twenty-Five Years*, 174.

[28] G. M. Trevelyan, *Grey of Falloden* (London, 1937), 225.

application to Eastern Roumelia of the new Turkish constitutional arrangements, however theoretically, threatened Bulgarian interests. Joint action was agreed when King Ferdinand of Bulgaria visited Vienna at the beginning of October. On returning home, the King declared the complete union of Bulgaria and Eastern Roumelia, its full independence from Turkey, and his new title of 'Tsar of all the Bulgars' (including, by implication, their Macedonian kin). Two days later, Vienna formally annexed Bosnia. Not only did the seeming 'under-handedness' of the Austrians horrify the liberal West (and even more, not-so-liberal Russia), stoking up the moral discourse of European diplomacy, but it was assumed in London and Paris that Vienna would not have acted as it had without the absolute certainty of support by Germany if war ensued. Henceforth, the odds could not be higher. Yet the sequence of events had a significant Cretan twist. As soon as the news regarding Bulgaria and Bosnia was confirmed in Canea on 12 October, the autonomous administration—minus Zaimis who, by happy accident or design, was away in Athens—declared union with Greece, as Rifaat Bey had always predicted to Grey. Taken together, these *faits accomplis* crucially modified the Balkan dispensation, though some of these facts were to prove more *accompli* than others.

Zaimis' absence from Crete—he was never, in fact, to return—was open to the interpretation of Greek collusion in the Cretan declaration of union. The Greek premier, Theotokis, strove to impress on Elliot that the action in Canea was entirely spontaneous, and pleaded that the British government should control its 'natural irritation with the Cretans' for being so precipitate.[29] In fact the evidence suggests that the Greek government did help to prompt the Cretan coup—the Austro-Bulgarian actions, after all, presented a heaven-sent chance to resolve the island's dilemmas.[30] Whatever the mix of spontaneity and calculation, on the day of the declaration Canea was festooned with Greek flags and surging Christian crowds.[31] There were no inter-communal incidents, and both the main party leaders and Orthodox clergy stressed the need to avoid any harassment of Muslims.[32] The chief focus was the oath of allegiance to the King of the Hellenes taken by the island's most prominent figures, with Venizelos at their head. There had in the past been many such declarations. This one, however, was different: it was followed by a real attempt on the part of the Cretans to govern the island *as if it were a province of Greece*, thereby affording a tincture of reality to the virtual union which had emerged in recent years. Furthermore, the fact that the foreign consuls remained in dialogue with the local authorities meant that they were compromised by a new revolutionary regime in the island, though they tactfully

[29] Elliot to Grey, 10 Oct. 1908, FO371/444.
[30] See papers from the Rangabé Archive cited in Eleni Gardikas-Katsiadakis, 'I Elliniki Kivernissi ke to Kritiko Zitima, 1908' (The Greek Government and the Cretan Question, 1908), in *Afieroma ston Panepistimiako Dhaskalo, Vas. Bl. Sfiroera* (Essays Dedicated to Professor Vas. Vl. Sfiroera) (Athens, 1992), 359–61.
[31] Spyros Melas, *I Epanastassi tou 1909* (The 1909 Revolution) (Athens, 1972), 126–9.
[32] Wyldebore-Smith to Grey, 11 Oct. 1908, FO371/444.

drew a line at receiving Cretan government documents headed 'King of the Hellenes'.

In Whitehall, however, ministers and officials were determined not to be compromised themselves, and scrambled to regain control of Cretan developments. A squadron of the British Mediterranean Fleet hurriedly assembled off Marmorice, on the Anatolian coast, ostensibly to intercept any 'sudden Greek descent' on the island;[33] but this was also widely interpreted as a warning to Austria in particular that the limits of the purloining of Ottoman territory had been reached.[34] In an internal minute which encapsulated the assumptions behind British actions in the next few years, the Foreign Secretary wrote:

It had been indicated to us from the beginning [of the crisis] that the Turks knew it was impossible for the Powers to send armies into Bulgaria and Bosnia in order to prevent what had been done, but that they felt the case with regard to Crete to be different, *as it was in our power to control the course of events there.*[35]

By 'our power', Grey meant British, rather than collective European, authority, because the Turks grasped that over Crete the British could dictate outcomes by virtue of their maritime preponderance—that it was one place, as Grey's senior adviser Louis Mallet expressed it, 'where we could put down a foot'.[36] Within the Foreign Office there lingered an uneasy awareness of the danger that, once the Turks realized the leverage over Crete they had fortuitously acquired, they would exploit it remorselessly, and use the local Muslims as pawns in so doing. But such a concern could not stand against the compelling logic driven by regional power politics. As the highly influential British Ambassador in Paris, Sir Francis Bertie, told his hosts, 'We [the British] do not intend to lose our influence at Constantinople to please the Greeks and the Cretans.'[37]

The Greeks and the Cretans had urgently to be pulled back from converting the declaration of union into reality. On 28 October, the powers issued a joint communiqué stating that they would 'view with benevolence a discussion of Cretan Union with Greece',[38] and it was the expectation of this concession which helped King George and his ministers in Athens to damp down popular feeling in the Greek capital. In truth, Grey viewed any such prospect with hostility. He set himself rigidly against any inscription of Crete on the agenda of the proposed international conference to rubber-stamp the altered status of Bulgaria and Bosnia, and he imposed this view on European partners. The French radical premier, Clemenceau, though concerned that the British were becoming 'more Turkish than the Turks', was not prepared to dispute this matter within the entente.[39]

---

[33] Foreign Office memorandum, 25 Nov. 1908, FO371/445.

[34] F. H. Hinsley, *British Foreign Policy under Sir Edward Grey* (Cambridge, 1977), 185.

[35] Grey minute, 23 Nov. 1908, FO371/445. Italics added.

[36] Louis Mallet minute, 19 Oct. 1908, FO371/444.

[37] Bertie to Grey, 25 Nov. 1908, FO371/445.   [38] Martinière, *La Marine française*, 23.

[39] Bertie to Grey, 25 Nov. 1908, FO421/247. For Clemenceau's willingness to see Crete annexed to Greece during the crisis, see Gooch and Temperley (eds), *Origins of the War*, v. 409.

Afterwards the belief was widely shared that the Turkish government *could* have been persuaded to swallow over Crete the final liquidation of a claim to sovereignty which it eventually did with regard to Bulgaria and Bosnia.[40] Crete was not mentioned, for instance, in the Sultan's speech when opening the newly elected Ottoman Parliament in December.[41] At the time Grey's defence was that to have pressed for a Cretan solution would 'have brought everybody to a standstill' in the attempt to hammer out a wider Balkan *modus vivendi*.[42] Such a justification, however, was widely held to conceal a preponderating concern with the survival in Constantinople of the 'antique Anglophile', Kiamil Pasha.

Meanwhile in Crete the declaration of union—disavowed though it now was by the Greek government—threatened to derail international evacuation.[43] The Cretan majority remained 'absolutely quiet' through the ensuing months, so as to avoid any pretext for delay. Although the Porte continued to play up those incidents where Muslims were victims, the information reaching London was that these allegations were 'purely fictitious'.[44] In general it was admitted in European circles that the Cretans were 'behaving rather well' in a Balkan crisis where this could not be said of many others.[45] But that did not stop Grey ordering a temporary halt to any further reduction of British troops in the island. His action meant that it was the British who now found themselves under the spotlight for ulterior motives in prevaricating over departure; it was widely noticed in January 1909 that, just as another Russian contingent left, more British Army reliefs arrived. Grey's hesitations arose from what now became a basic British assumption: sooner or later the Cretans would realize that, far from recent events carrying the island *towards* union with Greece, the possibility was in fact *receding*. Once this knowledge dawned, serious trouble was certain.[46] There was already an inkling of it. When in February the Greek Ambassador in London sought assurances from Sir Charles Hardinge, and got none, he drew the blunt deduction 'that things had changed in the last two months'.[47]

That change was only deepened by a fresh coup in Constantinople. Tensions between palace conservatives, old Ottoman liberals, and radicalized Young Turks escalated. In mid-February Kiamil Pasha was toppled, an event warmly greeted in Berlin and Vienna.[48] On 14 April 1909 Sultan Abdul Hamid caved in to European pressure and announced his readiness to recognize an independent Bulgaria. This crystallized a ramshackle counter-revolution of religious traditionalists and army

[40] This was certainly the assessment in the British Embassy in Constantinople. See Lowther to Grey, 14 Mar. 1909, FO421/255.

[41] Feroz Ahmad, *The Young Turks: The Committee of Union and Progress in Turkish Politics* (Oxford, 1969), 30. [42] Grey minute, 20 Nov. 1908, FO371/445.

[43] Helen Gardikas-Katsiadakis, *Greece and the Balkan Imbroglio: Greek Foreign Policy, 1911–13* (Thessaloniki, 1992), 36–40. [44] FO memorandum, 13 Feb. 1909, FO371/647.

[45] Kilmarnock minute, 19 Oct. 1908, FO371/444.

[46] Hardinge note, 11 Jan. 1909, FO371/647. [47] Grey to Elliot, 12 Feb. 1909, ibid.

[48] Philip Graves, *Briton and Turk* (London, 1941), 126. Kiamil Pasha briefly became Grand Vizier again in Dec. 1912, before fleeing to Cairo, where he sought the patronage of the British High Commmission. He died in Cyprus during 1916.

dissidents.[49] In the ensuing disturbances, the Young Turk primacy was only saved by General Shefket Pasha, who marched his Salonica corps to the capital. Amidst the confusion, Fitzmaurice from the British Embassy made several visits to the Yildiz, and afterwards this was said to have begun 'an anti-British whispering campaign' for allegedly clinging to the previous leadership.[50] Shefket Pasha carried out a purge, and the despised Sultan's reign finally ended, being replaced by a figurehead, Mehmed V.[51] What emerged was a new revolutionary cadre dedicated to the salvation of the Ottoman Empire by military assertion and crude Turkification. Its binding quality was chauvinism. Lowther warned London that the reformulated regime intended to pound 'the non-Turkish elements in a Turkish mortar', and his distaste for those coming to the fore was plain.[52] Grey shared some of the aversion, but not the implications for British policy. That policy, he stressed, should not 'be driven by dislike of the Committee [of Union and Progress] into an anti-Turkish attitude'.[53] Indeed, the even more prominent role taken by the Turkish Army was, in Grey's view, entirely to be welcomed in putting more backbone into the regime.[54]

The coup of April 1909 thereafter rooted into place an edgy process whereby Crete emerged as the flagship of a policy whose overblown rhetoric, as a British newspaper correspondent observed, hinged on 'the progressive recapture of all the lands over which the "Star and Crescent" had once floated'.[55] Furthermore, with Italy already lodging an aggressive claim to Tripolitania, a tangible fear existed that liquidation of a residual stake in Crete would be swiftly replicated in North Africa.[56] Young Turkish radicals especially feared that without the support of the army their domestic reform agenda would fizzle out, and it was above all young army officers who resented any sign of weakness in any matters connected to Greek ambition.[57] An astute contemporary French observer noted:

sentiment national, nécessités de l'empire, intérêts de parti, enthousiasme de l'armée, tout semble donc conseiller au gouvernement ottomane de pousser jusqu' à la guerre sa résistance à toute modification à l'état de choses reconnu par lui en Crète.[58]

[49] For a full account of the failed 'counter-revolution' as viewed from the British Embassy, see Gooch and Temperley (eds), *Origins of the War*, v. 313–19.   [50] Graves, *Briton and Turk*, 136.

[51] Abdul Hamid was thereafter held captive at the Villa Allatini in Salonica. To prevent the indignity of the ex-Sultan falling into Greek hands during the Balkan war of 1912, he was taken by a German frigate back to Constantinople. He died in 1918.

[52] Cited in Alan Cunningham (ed.), *Eastern Questions in the Nineteenth Century: Collected Essays* (London, 1993), 239.

[53] Grey minute, 9 May 1909, FO371/647. Despite Grey's injunction, Lowther subsequently kept his distance from the revamped Young Turkish regime, a stance sometimes held reponsible for gradually pushing the latter back once more into the Austro-German camp. See Graves, *Briton and Turk*, 152.

[54] Grey to Lowther, 30 Apr. 1909, Gooch and Temperley (eds), *Origins of the War*, v. 319.

[55] W. H. Crawfurd Price, *The Balkan Cockpit: The Political and Military Story of the Balkan War in Macedonia* (London, 1915), 5.   [56] Reinach, *La Question crètoise*, 57–9.

[57] A notable exception to this, however, was a young army officer, Kemal Atatürk, who opposed any Turkish concessions to Bulgaria, but advocated the cession of Crete as the price of an understanding with Greece. Graves, *Briton and Turk*, 170.   [58] Reinach, *La Question crètoise*, 70.

Indeed, in Young Turk circles an opportunity was glimpsed not only to put a stop to any further slide in the island, but to reverse the elements of Hellenization which had already occurred. After all, the Ottoman case in international law seemed strong—the Sultan had not signified his direct agreement to any change in the status quo since the European occupation started in February 1897. Porte officials began to talk of a 'final solution' which simply put Crete on the same basis as Samos, with a Christian Ottoman subject as governor—a step *backwards* which the British Cabinet, for all its heightened Ottoman sensibilities, considered inadmissible.[59] In the Foreign Office it was clearly understood that faced with any such regression the mass of the Cretan population would 'rise like a man', and probably murder the Muslims in the process.[60] Yet there could be no assurance that the Young Turks would bear such dire consequences in mind, especially as the mess created would have to be cleared up, not by themselves, but by the powers.

If the Cretan Question touched on volatile currents in Turkish politics, however, so it did in Greece. Under repeated British threats that they would be held responsible for any further trouble in Crete, the Greek government had sought to be 'purer than Caesar's wife' on the matter. There was a domestic price to pay for this impeccability by Premier Theotokis and his ministry, and even more for the dynasty, which had always striven to associate itself with a Cretan fulfilment. Radical and republican stirrings—a certain mimicry of Constantinople—showed themselves in Athens through the spring of 1909. King George's natural reaction was to emit another distress call to Europe. The King told Elliot in late June 1909 that he might soon abdicate over Crete—'just go and never come back'.[61] Grey was not impressed. 'A revolution in Greece', he noted crisply, 'would be less serious than the alternative in Turkey. I do not see why our hands should be forced.'[62]

Such priorities clarified during the run-up to the departure of all international troops from Crete. Ottoman diplomats in London pressed for its cancellation, and the Turkish Ambassador ominously stated that it would only prove 'the beginning of a more serious question'.[63] This was what the British feared, and for some while Grey still hankered to maintain a token international force in the island. But in the end his hand was forced by the other powers, each of which was straining to depart, and unwilling to provide the British with an excuse for staying. In London, too, much of the pressure emanating from Constantinople appeared German instigated, and it was feared that any reversal of the original decision would reveal the degree to which British policy was now open to manipulation by Berlin. Grey therefore reluctantly decided that the safest course was to go through with withdrawal.[64] But in doing so Grey once again assured Rifaat Bey—now Grand Vizier—that no change to Cretan status was implied, and, crucially, that obligations to Turkey would be fulfilled even if that involved reoccupation. 'This

---

[59] Cabinet Conclusions, 30 June 1909, CAB41/256.
[60] FO memorandum, 7 Jan. 1909, FO371/647.   [61] Grey to Elliot, 17 June 1909, FO421/255.
[62] Grey minute, 28 June 1909, FO371/648.   [63] Hardinge to Grey, 2 June 1909, ibid.
[64] Grey minute, 12 June 1909, ibid.

would be a very disagreeable thing', Grey stated, 'but it might become necessary.'[65] The fact that reoccupation was mooted even before the *existing* occupation ended was a telling indication of the true grain of developments.

With these tendencies at work, the argument that it was vital to settle the Cretan Question quickly and permanently whilst the European troops were still present to control the transition was essentially stillborn. This was despite the growing inclination of the French government for Cretan *enosis* and criticism of British actions on the matter for 'doing tomorrow what should have been done today'[66]—views which reflected resentment in Paris of the displacement of traditional French influence in Constantinople.[67] Clemenceau was scathing of the projected compromise designed to sustain Turkish sovereignty by European naval protection of the Ottoman flag on Suda island. He prophesied:

> The Cretans being hotheaded some one or more of them would haul down the [Turkish] flag; the crew of the *stationnaires* would rehoist it and the Cretans would pull it down again, but that sort of thing could not continue. It would become ridiculous.[68]

Grey sought to deflect such criticism by raising the stakes of the debate. He pointed to information that Turkish Army divisions were already mobilizing, and asserted that if some sign of annexation occurred—most dramatically, by Cretan deputies travelling to Athens to take up seats in the Greek Parliament—then war would result.[69] In the end it came down to this: were the Turks bluffing? Clemenceau was not alone in thinking so. Consul Peel recalled that in relation to Crete the Turks had not resorted to force since 1897, despite provocations.[70] None of this washed in the British Foreign Office. The French and others, in their view, failed to grasp that 'things had changed' in Constantinople since the April coup, and that it was all too likely that the Young Turks 'may regard war as a way out of their internal difficulties'.[71] When the Greek government privately claimed that its armed forces would be able to give a better account of themselves than before, one British official simply stated that the Greeks were drifting towards 'a terrible awakening'.[72]

Meanwhile the international evacuation could hardly take place without an accompanying statement by the powers, and the Note published at Grey's prompting on 1 July 1909 formally unveiled the ritual that was in future to surround the Turkish flag at Suda. 'The present [dispensation] could not be considered a definitive solution,' the Note further stated, 'and the governments of the four Powers would at a more opportune moment negotiate with the Sublime Porte on the future administration of the island.'[73] Yet 'opportune' did not sound

---

[65] Grey to Lowther, 3 June 1909, ibid.   [66] *The Times*, 15 June 1909.
[67] Hinsley, *British Foreign Policy*, 257.
[68] Bertie to Clemenceau, 12 June 1909, FO371/638.
[69] Grey to Bertie, 8 June 1909, FO371/648.   [70] Peel to Grey, 8 June 1909, ibid.
[71] FO memorandum, 16 July 1909, FO371/649.
[72] Parker minute, 17 June 1909, ibid.   [73] Dutkowski, *L'Occupation de la Crète*, 203.

like any time soon, and the substitution of 'supreme rights' for 'sovereignty' did nothing to correct misunderstandings. Greek opinion was shocked, and Theotokis resigned rather than face opposition riots in Athens. By contrast, Crete remained quiet, though it was the passivity of a population which feared the European retribution any outburst might bring. In fact, as in the Ionian Islands in 1864, so in Crete during 1909, the local population did not actually believe the occupiers would leave right up to the end.[74] When reality dawned, inter-communal relations came under pressure. The British Army chaplain in Candia told Peel of a casual conversation with a Turkish photographer, who stated that

both parties were armed, that the long strain of the crisis was telling on everyone's nerves, that 'the question' [of final status] was the sole topic of conversation ... morning, noon, and night, and that he felt that some slight struggle might so act on excited nerves as to produce very serious results.[75]

At this juncture, both creeds did their utmost to prevent a bloody outcome. Christians overwhelmingly responded to the injunction of their own civil and religious leaders: 'at all costs don't attack Muslims.'[76] The minority kept silent, though the British Foreign Office suspected that its leaders were merely awaiting a *mot d'ordre* from Constantinople to begin agitation.[77] In the event, the climax of 28 July was carefully stage-managed, and no fatal 'scuffle' took place. Many Greek flags were displayed by the crowds which watched European contingents depart from various ports, but there was no hint of disorder.[78] Venizelos addressed the mixed international force gathered on the quay in Canea in his fluent French. In a measured and discreet farewell he spoke of gratitude to the protecting powers, referring to their garrisons as 'an army of liberation'. Yet it had always been considered likely that when the last European soldier left, some more tangible action testifying to the aspiration for *enosis* would ensue. So it was that when the flags of the protecting powers were lowered at Firka Fort overlooking the harbour of the capital, it was the Hellenic colours which, Peel reported, were raised on the main harbour flagpole 'in deference to [the] public wish'.[79]

Superficially, this act was innocuous enough. A Greek flag had been raised at Rethymno harbour when the Russians left there, and the Porte said nothing. As the Greek Ambassador later protested, there were not only Greek flags all over Crete, but they also flew in 'British' Cyprus and even Constantinople, without any fuss resulting.[80] The Cretans had, after all, not pulled down an Ottoman flag, only raised a Greek one in what was overwhelmingly an Hellenic island. Furthermore, on the eve of evacuation, Venizelos had told the consuls that 'he would be lacking in candour' if he had not warned them of a Greek flag to be flown on the capital's harbour front, and although the European representatives

---

[74] Reverend Fleming to Peel, 2 July 1909, FO371/650.   [75] ibid.
[76] Fleming to Peel, 9 July 1909, ibid.   [77] Mallet minute, 23 July 1909, ibid.
[78] For a Greek eyewitness account see Melas, *I Epanastassi*, 221–4.
[79] Peel to Grey, 30 July 1909, FO421/256.   [80] Grey to Elliot, 11 Aug. 1909, FO371/651.

had warned him of the consequences, they had not expressly forbidden it.[81] Peel's considered advice to Grey on 30 July was that it would be an error to precipitate a crisis 'merely because one more Greek flag had been raised', especially since the Muslims were simply looking for a pretext to put down a marker of their own.[82]

Yet from Grey's vantage point, such advice was distorted because it considered disorders in Crete 'as the greatest evil to be faced, whereas they are in fact the lesser'.[83] For Grey the big picture—the one that mattered—was defined by the recent Turkish threat that evacuation would merely provide the beginning of a more serious question, one, that is, prejudicing international stability. The newly raised flag at Canea signalled such a commencement, however unintended by those who had put it up. This, indeed, was the danger with flags in such contexts: people could take exception to them as and when it suited their interests to do so. On 3 August, the new Grand Vizier, Hilmi Pasha, told Lowther that Turkish public opinion was aroused, and that the Ottoman fleet was being readied to enter Cretan waters.[84] It was to stuff the genie of this 'more serious question' back into its bottle that Grey became absolutely determined 'that the Greek flag shall cease to fly in Crete'.[85]

The ensuing events provide an insight into Grey's conduct at the Foreign Office. He did not forbid the expression of dissident views.[86] One official, Lord Kilmarnock, voiced the opinion that it had become important to take a firm line with the Turks,[87] whilst others pointed out that the latter's threat to launch military action in Crete was simply not credible.[88] Grey took consideration of such views, and did not refrain from putting pressure on Constantinople, warning Hilmi Pasha that if an unprovoked attack were launched on Greece, Turkey would forfeit all the goodwill earned since the crisis over Bulgaria and Bosnia.[89] Yet when Grey made his mind up, it was implacable, and in this case it was made in favour of Turkey. At bottom, when the Ottoman minister in Athens boasted that the opportunity had arrived 'to teach the Greeks a lesson',[90] he was expressing a view which Grey shared. The pulling down of the Hellenic flag in Crete was to check once and for all the dream of annexation which in the British Foreign Secretary's opinion the broader requirements of European security ruled out of court for as far ahead as one could see.

The Turkish government set about teaching the Greeks a lesson with aplomb: on 6 August an ultimatum was sent to Theotokis' successor as premier, Demetrios Rhallys, insisting on an explicit disavowal of annexation. With Turkish forces arriving on the Macedonian frontier, Rhallys had little choice but to submit

---

[81] Peel to Grey, 26 July 1909, FO371/650.   [82] Peel to Grey, 30 July 1909, ibid.
[83] Grey minute, 31 July 1909, ibid.   [84] Lowther to Grey, 4 Aug. 1909, ibid.
[85] Grey to Bertie, 5 Aug. 1909, ibid.   [86] Trevelyan, *Grey of Falloden*, 112–13.
[87] Kilmarnock minute, 13 Aug. 1909, FO371/651.
[88] Mallet minute, 9 Aug. 1909, FO371/650.
[89] Grey to Lowther, 16 Aug. 1909, FO371/652.
[90] Elliot to Grey, 7 Aug. 1909, FO371/651.

in the form of a statement that Greece would accept whatever the powers decided on the future of Crete. This submission was to trigger fundamental changes in Greek politics. Meanwhile, there was the problem of who would actually pull down the flag still fluttering on Canea harbour. The Cretans refused to do it themselves—the local executive resigned *en masse* at the prospect. That left the Europeans to bear the odium. Yet here there was a difficulty: the other powers showed themselves more hesitant than ever in the face of Grey's Cretan diplomacy. At one point it seemed the British might have to act only with Russia, and even the latter was 'inconceivably dilatory' at rushing an additional warship to the eastern Mediterranean.[91] Grey, convinced that the regime in Constantinople might take some action with uncontrollable consequences, watched the European naval build-up in Cretan waters with impatience, ordering on 15 August that as soon as an adequate force was in place the Greek flag should come down 'without further delay'.[92] He was greatly relieved when by 18 August enough warships were on hand to execute an intervention which for the naval officers involved promised no glory, and some embarrassment.

The prospect of a clash between European bluejackets and local people was certainly unpleasant. Bands of armed peasants had again descended on Canea. It was therefore essential that the harbour be 'swept clean of Cretans' to avoid bloodshed.[93] The ad hoc Cretan authorities co-operated sufficiently to ensure that the gendarmerie kept local people out of the area. A party of 200 European marines under the command of Captain Thursby from HMS *Swiftsure* then went ashore at the break of dawn.[94] Thursby apologized for the task ahead to a Greek commander of the militia, who glumly accompanied the marines to Firka Fort. The ensuing ritual was described in a Cretan newspaper:

Having formed a square around the flagstaff, four sailors (one each from the International forces) were ordered to take up positions around the flagstaff, holding axes. The commands to the conscripted woodcutters were given in their national languages.... After many ... orders and blows, the flagstaff was cut and fell to the ground. Then ... the attacks ... on the flagstaff divided it into four equal parts ... Each contingent took a piece to their warship in Suda Bay.[95]

The martyrology of this account, with its evocations of crucifixion, conjures up elements in Cretan Orthodox mentality. The fact that these blows—spears thrust into the Hellenic side—were inflicted by Europeans, under British leadership and at the behest of Constantinople, profoundly affected relationships. The symbolic

---

[91] Parker minute, 17 Aug. 1909, FO371/652. In fact the Russians had only accepted the scheme to protect the Ottoman flag at Suda under British insistence—see Gooch and Temperley (eds), *Origins of the War*, v. 242.   [92] Grey to Peel, 15 Aug. 1909, FO371/651.

[93] FO memorandum, 16 Aug. 1909, ibid.

[94] For a full description see Capt. Thursby to Admiralty, 21 Aug. 1909, ADM116/1078.

[95] Costa E. Padouva, *Kriti 1897–1913: Poliethnikes Enobles Dhinamis Katochi-Autonomia-Enosi me tin Elladha* (Crete 1897–1913: International Occupation and Autonomy-Union with Greece) (Athens, 1997), 205.

fact that the very flagpole had been destroyed drove a wedge between consuls and Cretans which was to widen over time.[96] The British presence was most prejudiced as a result, and it was logical that the other powers tried to deflect any odium by signalling that they had acted largely at the instigation of London. Most ominous of all was the fact that the choreography of the flag destruction signified the looming threat of a resurrected Turkish influence *within* the island.

One effect immediately became clear when on 28 August 1909, a mutiny in the Greek Army, organized in a 'Military League', forced the Rhallys ministry to resign—in the description of Thanos Veremis, 'the first autonomous political action by the Greek military'.[97] The basic causes of the rupture lay in an underlying crisis of Greek modernization, linked to a significant weakening of the Hellenic position in Macedonia—under European pressure, the Greek government had recently slackened its patronage to paramilitary bands. A matching failure to assert primacy *even* over Crete served as a convenient advertisement for the grievances of the dissidents. The reality of Greek politics was that its traditional components were now deadlocked, and incapable of charting a course through the kingdom's internal and external constraints. Coincidentally, however, Crete provided an escape, since Venizelos, whose father was a Greek citizen, emerged as the only figure who could mediate a fresh equilibrium. In January 1910 the Military League invited him to Athens as their political adviser, and it was an index of King George's diminished role that he entered into dialogue with his family's old Cretan adversary.[98] Venizelos played down his own anti-dynastic past. Greek and Cretan politics had always overlapped at the margins; but henceforth their flows were to converge, overwhelming old barriers and markers in a way that neither European diplomacy nor stalled attempts at Ottoman regeneration could eventually handle.

Venizelos had long yearned for a role on the larger Greek stage. The opportunity arose when his own thinking about the Cretan Question had been transformed. Previously he had believed that the Cretans themselves should have the prime role in manoeuvring their path into union. Now he grasped that the key to that outcome lay not in the island, but in Greece itself (though still, of course, under his own transplanted aegis). He remained convinced that Crete and Greece could only be successfully joined under the protection of the Western maritime powers, especially Britain. But the humiliation of the flag crisis underlined for him that in future, when seeking Western help, Greece must do so from a position of

---

[96] A. C. Wratislaw, *A Consul in the East* (London, 1924), 269. On the damage to the local position of the consuls, see Rangabé to Dragoumis, 2 Apr. 1910, cited in Eleni Gardikas-Katsiadakis, 'O Stephanos Dragoumis Ke I Oristiki Lisi tou Kritikou Zitimatos' (Stephanos Dragoumis and the Final Settlement of the Cretan Question), in Detorakis and Kalokerinos (eds), *I Teleftaia Fasi*, 71.

[97] Thanos Veremis, *The Military in Greek Politics: From Independence to Democracy* (London, 1997), 45.

[98] During the crisis of the 'mutiny' in the Greek Army, Edward VII had—as his mother had always done at moments of crisis in Greece—ensured that a Royal Navy squadron was sent to patrol Phaleron Bay, ready to take off Greek royals if their safety demanded it.

enhanced leverage, not traditional 'supplication'. Such a reversal could only come about through military reform and co-operation with other Christian Balkan countries. Thus Venizelos began to advocate a Graeco-Bulgarian entente, a connection surrounded with complications, but which a violent Turkish drive to disarm *all* Macedonian Christians helped to effect.[99] These alterations in Greek strategy needed time, and in the interval it was essential that the Cretan Question did not keep exploding at inconvenient moments. Throughout the ensuing events, therefore, Venizelos exhorted his fellow Cretans to keep quiet until other Greeks acted on their behalf.[100]

Keeping quiet, however, was not very likely when a sense of grievance amongst most Cretans was deepening. Esme Howard, still interested in Cretan affairs from his new consular post in Budapest, captured this discontent when complaining to London that the apparently covert retrocession of the island to Turkish oversight was an 'outrage on the conscience of Europe', and criticizing 'the shabby way the Cretans have been treated'.[101] That the Cretans felt more shabbily treated than ever compounded a determination to regain the ground that was being lost. Without any formal government of their own, and having only an informal executive headed by 'two lawyers and a doctor',[102] it was decided to hold elections to fend off disintegration. After these polls it was mooted that the successful deputies should at last assert *de facto* union by going to Athens and taking their seats in the Greek legislature. Yet to Venizelos this was just the sort of hasty action which played into the hands of the enemies of Hellenism. During the political debates in Crete which culminated in voting on 21 March 1910, the dominant issue was whether elected Muslims would submit to an oath to the 'King of the Hellenes' when taking their seats in the Assembly. The dispatch of Christian deputies to the Athenian Parliament remained as yet too risky a gamble, but the administration of the oath provided a placebo around which the political Hellenization of the island could be fought out.

Although the electoral majority now secured by Venizelos was slender, it allowed him to form a government not dependent on the support of Muslim deputies. The latter, he hoped, would take the consuls' advice and simply absent themselves from the ceremonial oath. This was how matters had been finessed ever since 1908.[103] It might have continued to be so had not attitudes in Constantinople hardened. The fact that the Turkish regime was currently facing an Albanian rebellion helped to explain this, and the tendency to foster a more

[99] Graves, *Briton and Turk*, 155–6. Venizelos used J. D. Bourchier, the Balkan correspondent of *The Times*, and frequent advocate of Bulgarian interests, as a conduit for his approaches to Sofia. Bourchier had a long association with Cretan affairs dating back to a close friendship with Sir Alfred Biliotti. See Lady Grogan, *The Life of J. D. Bourchier* (London, 1926), 56–7.

[100] Gardikas-Katsiadakis, *Greek Foreign Policy*, 45–6.

[101] Memorandum by Esme Howard, 8 Nov. 1909, FO371/654.

[102] Mallet minute, 3 Jan. 1910, FO371/880.

[103] Cretan Christians were, in fact, taken aback by the Muslims' insistence on a different course on this occasion. See the Rethymno newspaper *Dhrasis* (Action), 9 May 1910.

intense Ottoman patriotism.[104] Being drawn into this process made the Cretan Muslims (their population now standing at 33,000, or just over 9 per cent of the total[105]) little more than pawns of Young Turk tacticians. They had long resisted this process, but after the European military evacuation their confidence sagged, and with it their capacity to act independently.

When the Assembly met on 9 May the Muslims did not, then, stay away. Furthermore, as the oath was proceeding, one of their representatives began reading out two statements, the second of which—in the opinion of Peel's successor as British consul, Alfred Wratislaw, clearly composed in Constantinople[106]— refused to recognize the validity of any change in the status of Crete since February 1897.[107] An irate Christian held his hand over the speaker's mouth, and the Assembly was suspended amidst confusion, though not before the majority voted that no members should be readmitted unless an oath was taken to the Greek monarch. In Venizelos' view, it was the Cretan Muslims who had over-stepped the mark. 'They had done the bidding of the Porte', he said, 'and drawn an abrupt dividing line between the two elements of the population.'[108] But to European observers although the fact that the Muslims had been bent on making trouble was transparent, their expulsion was equally seen as crossing a critical line.[109] 'I think that we shall have to do something over Crete', was Grey's testy conclusion.[110]

On 12 May 1910, the protecting powers therefore afforded yet another assurance regarding the 'sovereign rights' of the Sultan, and Grey shortly stated in the House of Commons that it was precisely because a new constitutional regime existed in Constantinople that the powers intended to show 'increased regard for the susceptibilities of Turkey in any settlement … not less regard, but more. Now that is what governs the situation.'[111] The Foreign Secretary was already impatient to foreclose the risk to wider stability by reoccupying Crete, but found the road to it obstructed by French and Russian opposition. According to an older pattern, external blockage helped to polarize inter-communal relations inside Crete, with a spate of attacks beginning on Muslims, followed by the rape (almost certainly orchestrated) of eight young Christian females in Rethymno. Although a complete implosion of Crete was not yet considered imminent by Whitehall, the feeling grew that the possibility of a large-scale massacre of Muslims was

---

[104] Gardikas-Katsiadakis, *Greek Foreign Policy*, 103. The Albanians were crucial to the status quo in European Turkey, and the rebellion in that province was a major blow to the regime. See Ahmad, *The Young Turks*, 156.

[105] The 1911 Census appeared in the official publication suggestively entitled *Parartima tis Efimeridos tis Kiverniseos en Kriti* (Gazette of the Royal Hellenic Government in Crete) on 6 Oct. 1911. The Muslim population is given as 27,852 and the Christian population as 307,812. See Stephanos Dragoumis Archive, File, 25.2 *Apografi Kritis 4-5 Iouniou 1911* (Cretan Census 4–5 June 1911).

[106] Wratislaw, *A Consul*, 273–4. Wratislaw's previous consular posting had been in Persia.

[107] Wratislaw to Grey, 13 May 1910. Also see the two texts of the Muslim declaration in enclosures in FO41/267.   [108] *Kyrix* (Herald), 16 May 1910.

[109] Wratislaw, *A Consul*, 274.   [110] Grey minute, 11 May 1910, FO371/880.

[111] *Hansard Parliamentary Debates* (5th series), vol. xvii (Commons), 15 June 1910, col. 1381.

growing—and might even be welcomed in Constantinople for the possibilities of exploitation it contained.[112] In the event King George in Athens helped to pull everybody back from the brink, appealing to the Cretans to cease their opposition to the Muslims entering the Assembly.[113] In Wratislaw's view, the vital role, however, was played by Venizelos in scraping together a majority in the Cretan chamber allowing the Muslims on 22 July to absent themselves from the oath, before sidling unopposed onto their benches.[114] It was an indication of a growing British dependence on Venizelos to exert a leverage slipping beyond their own reach.

For this reason, Wratislaw, instructed by London, tried hard but unavailingly to persuade Venizelos not to forsake his Cretan duties for a beckoning political destiny in Greece.[115] On 24 July 1910, the latter left the island once more, ostensibly for a medical consultation in Europe, but en route being successfully elected as deputy for Attica Boetia in the Greek national elections, before returning to Canea. Considerable uncertainty still attached to whether he would take his place in the Athenian Parliament. On 17 September, he again sailed from Canea in a specially chartered steamer, covered in Greek flags and ablaze with red lights. It was a refutation of the persistent allegations that union was not one of his ideals. Before leaving Venizelos told Wratislaw only that his future programme was geared to 'the general scheme of regenerating Greece'.[116] The tentative and ambiguous relationship between that regeneration and Cretan union went to the heart of the complex phenomenon of Venizelism during the critical phase ahead.

Venizelos was clearly not going to be a mere Athenian deputy for long. Shortly after his arrival, a Cabinet break-up allowed King George to appoint him as premier at the head of a liberal-radical block. Confirmed in power by further elections during November, he set about an intensive programme reshaping the constitution, improving the civil and financial administration, and updating the armed forces with Western advisers (the gendarmerie was accorded to Italy, the army to France, and the navy to Great Britain).[117] Henceforth, the powers had to consider in relation to Crete not only the need to nurture Turkish constitutionalism, but also the danger of derailing the Venizelist modernization of Greece. Venizelos's calculations included two critical preconditions. First, that war between Turkey and the Christian Balkan states—whose own emerging combination remained fragile—should not take place before the spring of 1913; and secondly, that no sudden Cretan impulse should interrupt the smooth unfolding of his plans.[118] The essential requirement was to prevent Cretan deputies from setting off a major crisis prematurely by transferring themselves to the Greek Parliament as a 'one-stop' act of union. During the autumn of 1910 Venizelos

[112] Wratislaw to Grey, 9 Aug. 1910, FO421/270.
[113] Wratislaw to Grey, 11 July 1910, FO421/268.
[114] Wratislaw, *A Consul*, 274.   [115] Wratislaw to Grey, 28 July 1910, FO371/884.
[116] Wratislaw to Grey, 18 Sept. 1910, FO371/885.
[117] John S. Koliopoulos and Thanos Veremis, *Greece: The Modern Sequel* (London, 2002), 53–4.
[118] See I. Gennadios to I. Gryparis, 31 Dec. 1910, KY69/5. AYE (Greek Foreign Ministry Archive).

succeeded in imposing restraint, but, with his own 'moderate' followers in Crete weakened by his absence, there was no guarantee than this line could be held for long.

In fact, with the growing paralysis of the Cretan executive, including its judicial machinery, the island's interior slid into chaos. Venizelos sought to stop the rot by sending Zaimis back as High Commissioner, but there was no stomach in London for pressing this on the Turks.[119] The latter, indeed, were already agitating for the withdrawal of Greek officers from the Cretan militia, and the apprehension of Cretan Christians that the ground had radically shifted in favour of Constantinople— not least with British connivance—became intense.[120] This was the prospect which became real in early May 1911 when rumours began to circulate that the Porte was about to announce the appointment by the *Sheikh-i-Islam* of three *cadis* (religious judges) and their dispatch to the island for the first time since November 1898.

The entry of such officials under the cover of European naval protection, would be, as Cretans fully grasped, the 'thin end of the wedge' of renewed Turkish rights.[121] With tension escalating on all sides, angry meetings of Christians took place in Crete; the one in Canea on 7 June was the largest Wratislaw had witnessed since his arrival.[122] In the circumstances Europe could do little except to act as an emergency buffer—between Christians and Muslims inside Crete, and between Greece and Turkey outside. The powers sought to deflect the Turkish government by firmly insisting that religious appointments could only be made at the request of the Cretan Muslim community itself. No such request was made as yet, but there could be no certainty that one would not ensue at a juncture which suited the fulfillment of Constantinople's wider purposes.

The immediate crisis passed without the *cadis* making their appearance, yet the effect had been to bring certain features into high relief. One was the fear of Christian Cretans that their privileges were being rapidly reversed. Another was the basic inclination of Sir Edward Grey when conceiving of the future of Crete. He harboured, in truth, no ambition of physically letting the Turks back into the island. For one thing, it had long been understood that British public opinion would never tolerate such a retrocession— and Grey was, after all, a member of a Liberal Cabinet. Instead, as he explained to his Italian counterpart, he looked forward to a Cretan state emerging as 'a practically autonomous one, subject to the control of the four Protecting Powers'.[123] It was true that such a polity might one day opt for union with Greece, but it was equally likely, given the countervailing

---

[119] The Greek Ambassador in Vienna reported that the powers blocked the return of Zaimis to Crete because 'they could not ... give Turkey a blow at that time', George Streit to Greek Foreign Ministry, 15 Dec. 1911, KY69/1, AYE.

[120] This critical mood was encapsulated in much contemporary Greek satire, especially that of George Souris. See Athina Blazoudaki-Stavroudaki, *O Souris ke I Kriti* (Souris and Crete) (Canea, 1998), 116–18.   [121] Wratislaw to Grey, 12 May 1911, FO371/1103.

[122] Ibid.   [123] Grey to Marquis Imperiale, 14 Aug. 1911, FO371/1104.

pressures, to harden into a kind of permanent and 'guaranteed'—that is, enforced—independence. One Whitehall official conveniently (and half-facetiously) found a precedent for such Cretan 'independence' in the era of King Minos.[124] This was the outcome which in the summer of 1911 was seemingly the most likely given the realities of European power politics.

These realities, nevertheless, were shifting all the time. In European perspective, the struggle over Cretan oaths—whatever its implications for Balkan stability—paled besides the simultaneous explosion over the fate of Morocco triggered by the appearance of a German gunboat at Agadir during July. For some weeks the Great Power blocks hovered on the brink of war. That crisis appeared temporarily to fade away, but on 28 September 1911, Italy—sensing that a North African partition was imminent—got its blow in first by seizing Tripoli.[125] So began—almost in slow motion, since these new Roman conquerors of an African province got bogged down along the coasts—the final, if ultimately very prolonged, liquidation of the Ottoman Empire. Meanwhile, the fact that the warships of Britain, France, and Russia did not insist that the Cretan lighthouses dim their lights according to the norms of belligerency, as Constantinople insistently requested, was a telling sign that the 'shadow' of Turkish sovereignty over the island was in the end simply that—a shadow, and nothing more. From the outset of the Italo–Turkish war, Christian Cretans were seized by a strong emotion that 'the Turkish difficulties may be Crete's opportunity'.[126]

At first, Wratislaw was optimistic that Cretans would not try to seize that opportunity until they saw how the wider picture unfolded. The fact that the fighting between Italians and Turks did not spread beyond North Africa helped. But by the end of October the consul gloomily warned that 'matters are moving towards a *coup d'etat*'.[127] There was no doubt what this meant—a rush by Cretan deputies to take their seats as Greek citizens in the Athenian Parliament. Such a scenario was what the Cretan Assembly now approved in principle, and there was not much likelihood that Wratislaw's urgent warnings to Cretan politicians that they would 'bring about the ruin of themselves and of Greece' would deter them.[128] The British consul had become an acute observer of Cretan psychology, and it was in the Christian majority's sense of being 'sheep without a shepherd', of sinking into a state of complete disintegration unless salvation quickly intervened, that he found the main clue to their sudden preparedness to go for broke.

The Cretan deputies naturally could not legitimately enter Parliament in Athens without the consent of the Greek government, and Venizelos had no intention of permitting anything which constrained his own room for manoeuvre at such a crucial time. He declared flatly in the Greek chamber on 24 November

[124] Foreign Office note, 18 Sept. 1910, FO371/886.
[125] For the general context see R. J. B. Bosworth, 'Italy and the End of the Ottoman Empire', in Marian Kent (ed.), *The Great Powers and the End of the Ottoman Empire* (London, 1984), 57–63.
[126] Wratislaw to Grey, 29 Sept. 1911, FO371/1105.
[127] Wratislaw to Grey, 28 Oct. 1911, ibid.   [128] Ibid.

that so long as his government lasted 'it would take all the measures indicated by circumstances to prevent the intentions of anybody in Crete to drag us into war and to sit beside us in this House'. Yet Venizelos also frankly warned Elliot that he might not be able to survive the reaction in Greek politics which the physical barring of Cretan deputies would arouse. There was, however, one way to forestall the plans of the Cretan deputies which was less explosive—their prevention from actually leaving the island in the first place. At the end of November, HMS *Diana* arrived off Crete to assist such an operation, and British pressure to ensure additional French and Russian vessels was increased. With a Revolutionary Assembly meeting in Canea from early December to select deputies to go to Athens, the three powers (Italy, of course, no longer having normal relations with the Porte) gave an assurance to Turkey that Cretan legislators seeking to leave their native island would be intercepted.

Intercepting Cretans determined on going to Greece was, however, easier said than done. Wratislaw told his bosses that the plan for the execution of it was not so straightforward as they supposed. Individuals would leave 'in ones and twos', and not on regular steamers. Still, when a party of twenty-four tried to leave in early December they were seized 'internationally' by a mixed European naval party so that the ill will could, as usual, be parcelled out amongst the powers. The prime responsibility, nevertheless, was British, and when the intention to send the detainees to Malta foundered because the Governor of that colony refused to take them, they had to be kept on board ship until the danger had passed with the closure of the Greek parliamentary session. On 3 January 1912, they were dumped—according to Captain Parker of HMS *Minerva*, a 'rather forlorn and depressed company'—back on Cretan soil, though not before having been charged two shillings *per diem* for their upkeep. British parsimony was another trait to which the Cretans had become used. The senior naval officers' conclusion was that the difficulties of apprehending Cretans at sea would be 'hardly worth the candle' next time round. More worrying still was Parker's report that amongst Cretans there was circulating a belief—harking back to vivid memories as to the real reason why the Ottoman Army had been evicted in 1898—that 'if an English [naval] officer was done to death, the Cretan Question would be solved'.[129]

Murder was already escalating in Crete. Wratislaw reported a significant deterioration in the security of the minority.[130] The Royal Navy increased its patrols at a time of rising tension, but the 'moral effect' had long since drained from such displays.[131] The mood darkened still further with the formation of a 'provisional revolutionary government' by the Christians, and its subsequent decision that voting would be held on 24 March alongside the elections scheduled for Greece.[132]

---

[129] Captain Edmund Poe (HMS *Exmouth*) to Admiralty, 20 Jan. 1912, ADM116/1188.
[130] Wratislaw, *A Consul*, 294.
[131] Capt. Hyde Parker (Senior Naval Officer, Crete) to C-in-C Med. Fleet, 16 Feb. 1912, FO371/1352.   [132] *The Times*, 4 Jan. 1912.

If there was a moment for the powers to reoccupy the island, this was it. But both France and Russia were more opposed to such action than ever—testimony to the limits of the ententes. Even inside the British Foreign Office fissures were appearing. The contention by some officials that it was vital to prevent an 'extermination' of Cretan Muslims was met enigmatically, but suggestively, by such tart retorts as 'How do the Turks treat Christians in Macedonia?'[133] Here were the tell-tale signs of a policy machine at odds with itself.

All that could be done against this background was to hope that Venizelos would emerge strengthened from the Greek elections, and to make another 'naval demonstration' off Crete in the hope that the revolutionary government would be deterred. Yet when the British Foreign Office approached the Admiralty, a senior official in the latter said that he 'had no definite ideas as to what a naval demonstration consists of'—witness to the Admiralty's irritation with Cretan tasks, and to the more profound fact that the *Pax Britannica* was not what it had been in the days of Palmerston.[134] In practice a few more British warships simply hovered offshore. The Cretans were scarcely intimidated. On 24 March, they duly selected sixty-nine deputies, all of whom began to pack their bags for Athens. Venizelos won a thumping majority in Greece, but that did not stop the first Cretan representatives escaping under cover of night on 18 April, and soon thirty had got away. Under strong criticism for alleged passivity, the European consuls and naval commanders arrested twenty deputies who attempted to depart with what was described as 'a certain degree of demonstrativeness'. But paradoxically, this group turned out to be loyal Venizelists, leaving the Greek premier to plead for the release of his supporters. 'We must think of the Turks, not of the Greeks' was Louis Mallet's blunt response as the request was rejected.[135]

Venizelos was duly left with the unedifying task of barring those Cretan deputies who got to Athens from entering the Greek Parliament when it opened on 1 June. This was a task Venizelos could do without. He was preoccupied with securing an agreement with Bulgaria, without which any outbreak of hostilities with Turkey held great risks for Greece. On 30 May a document was signed secretly in Sofia. But this was not yet a military agreement, and Venizelos had failed to persuade the Bulgarians to discuss who would get what in a Macedonian carve-up. Venizelos' strategy still required time, and he sought to buy more of it. When the Cretan deputies arrived at the doors of the Parliament building, they found it guarded by troops with fixed bayonets. A scuffle ensued and one of the Cretans succeeded in making a fleeting appearance in the chamber itself, which was then promptly dissolved. But it was doubtful whether Venizelos' fragile position could bear a repeat, and even in London, once the news of a Graeco-Bulgarian 'understanding' broke in *The Times* on 1 August, it began to dawn that

---

[133] Foreign Office minute, 14 Apr. 1912, FO371/1351.
[134] FO minute, 24 Mar. 1912, FO371/1353.
[135] Mallet minute, 25 Mar. 1912, FO371/1354.

'a regular flare up in the Balkans' might shake the kaleidoscope in wholly unpredictable ways.[136] The ultimate paradox began to take shape: whilst Britain and its fellow powers for many years had striven to prevent the Cretan Question becoming the cause of a major war, in the end it was only through the instrumentality of war that a solution might be found. That was to be the measure of the moral and practical failure of the European Concert in its Cretan guise.

There was a further paradox: through the high summer of 1912 the noisy Christian Cretans suddenly went dead quiet. So did the Muslims, if only because the Young Turk regime was now too distracted to manufacture Cretan incidents.[137] In fact everybody on the island anticipated that the fate of Crete would now be settled elsewhere, and waited for larger events to unfold. Yet for Venizelos it was vital that they should not do so too quickly—or at least not before he had agreed with his Balkan partners on a distribution of spoils. He could not be oblivious to the possibility that if Greece used its fleet to bottle up Turkish troops in Asia, the only result might be to let the Serbs and Bulgarians grab the lion's share in Macedonia. But from mid-September the Greek government came under pressure from both Sofia and Belgrade to trigger the move to war *before an Italo-Turkish armistice made things easier for the Turkish Army*.[138] In seeking to avoid being dragged along, Venizelos exercised extreme care that the potential *casus belli* offered by the admission of the Cretan deputies remained under his strict control. The Cretans might be quiet, but embedded in their pregnant silence was the 'accident' that the island had emerged as one of the pegs on which a new Balkan age was seemingly suspended.

For a moment, indeed, further developments seemed to hinge on the success of the Cretan deputies in entering the Athenian legislature. 'Nothing is of any use except reoccupation,' Grey lamented the dramatic decline in the Concert's leverage, but with the island stuffed with arms to resist any renewed intervention, even he accepted that this option was fast disappearing.[139] The foundations of British policy began to crack open. One Greek historian has written that Venizelos 'misread the intentions of his Balkan partners' and in the end had to rush to catch up with them; certainly the proximity of an Italo-Turkish peace treaty indicated that if the decisive moment to partition Macedonia was to be seized, there could be no more hesitation.[140] On 1 October, Greece mobilized following a Balkan agreement that Montenegro would start border 'provocations' one week later. Crete mobilized in unison, and three days later volunteers started leaving for Greece—'the Union of Crete and Greece', Grey despairingly summed up the reality thus unfolding, 'is being made effective at this moment'.[141] Although a

[136] Parker minute, 28 Aug. 1912, FO371/1356.

[137] The solidarity of the Muslim community had now begun to crack, with some holders of public offices amongst them taking an oath to the Greek King.

[138] For a full treatment of the context see Gardikas-Katsiadakis, *Greek Foreign Policy*, 110–30.

[139] Grey minute, 11 Sept. 1912, FO371/1356.

[140] Gardikas-Katsiadakis, *Greek Foreign Policy*, 110.

[141] Grey minute, 5 Oct. 1912, FO371/1358.

European blockade of the island was declared, the exercise was purely formal—Winston Churchill, the First Lord of the Admiralty, insisting that the instructions to the British naval commanders rule out any use of force.[142] As hundreds of militia gathered at Cretan ports waiting for Greek steamers, Wratislaw advised with scarcely concealed sarcasm, 'I do not think it is safe to rely entirely on bluff.'[143] All along bluff had been a principal weapon in the policy presided over by Grey, and when it was called, the junction of Crete and Greece was sealed.

On 14 October, Venizelos duly welcomed the Cretan deputies into the Greek Parliament, though this was done with little fuss so as not to offend European sensibilities. The British Embassy had long anticipated this action as 'the preconcerted signal for the outbreak of hostilities' in the Balkans.[144] Yet it was a signal which when it came Turkey struggled not to recognize. Not only did the Porte omit to declare war on Greece when doing so against Bulgaria and Serbia on 17 October, but it scrambled to keep Greece out of the fighting by offering to yield its claim to Crete.[145] A couple of years before such an offer might have crystallized a Graeco–Turkish rapprochement. But it was too late, and meanwhile 1500 Cretan militia had already left in Greek troopships—'the more ... the better', Grey now concluded, since the number of arms in the island was thereby reduced.[146] His chief preoccupation was of a massacre of Cretan Muslims behind the screen of a wider conflict, and the counter-atrocities this would entail in Asia Minor. For the last time his mind turned to reoccupation, if necessary without Concert partners, and despite Elliot's information that 'any ... [European] troops or seamen landed now, especially British', would be attacked.[147] Yet no such massacre of Muslims occurred. Ethnic and religious clashes in Crete had always been driven by political uncertainty, and when a final resolution at last loomed, the coiled spring of intercommunal relations did not, in fact, snap. One daily ritual continued to be carried out under the vestigial patronage of the Concert. The Sultan, Wratislaw sardonically remarked, whatever his other worries, at least 'had the consolation of knowing that the Turkish flag is still flying in Suda island' under the protection of British marines.[148]

That lonely ensign was still flying when Venizelos' appointee, Stephanos Dragoumis, arrived on 25 October 1912 as 'Governor of Crete'.[149] This was a discreet choice—Dragoumis had no track record over Crete to offend European sensitivities.[150] His first public action was to issue a manifesto stating that his task

142 Churchill minute, 11 Oct. 1912, ADM116/1200.
143 Wratislaw to Grey, 13 Oct. 1912, FO371/1358.
144 R. Beaumont (British Embassy, Athens) to Grey, 4 Oct. 1912, ibid.
145 There were signs that the Turkish government would gladly now have forfeited any claim on Crete in return for Greek non-belligerence in Macedonia, had Venizelos been prepared to strike such a deal. See Crawfurd Price, *The Balkan Cockpit*, 39–40.
146 Grey minute, 20 Oct. 1912, FO371/1358.   147 Grey to Bertie, 17 Oct. 1912, ibid.
148 Wratislaw to Grey, 24 Oct. 1912, ibid.
149 See Eleni Gardikas-Katsiadakis, 'Stephanos Dragoumis'.
150 In fact Dragoumis had been the first of two men proposed by Venizelos to the consuls for the position of High Commissioner in 1906. The second had been Zaimis. Svolopoulos, *O Eleutherios Venizelos*, 269.

was to execute the existing laws, and guarantee equality of races.[151] For those British officials long associated with Grey's Cretan policy all this was nonetheless hard to take—'a most insolent measure' was one description in Whitehall of Dragoumis's effective annexation.[152] The triumphant entry on 8 November of a Greek Army led by Prince Constantine into Salonica gave a sharper edge to feelings of angst at such a surprising Hellenic apotheosis. But there were other figures in London who grasped at the opportunity to seal a new orientation in British policy in the eastern Mediterranean, and who saw in Cretan developments a way of firming things up. The most prominent of these was the Chancellor of the Exchequer, Lloyd George. 'You may consider Crete as your's,' he told John Stavridi, a key *interlocuteur* with Venizelos, when they dined in 11 Downing Street on 10 November, stressing how the memories of the defeat of 1897 had now been erased. 'The only power that could prevent you from having it is England, and England will not fire a shot or move a ship to prevent you from doing so.'[153]

Like many 'Questions' which at one time or another rock nations and even entire regions, the matter of Crete was fated to end in a whimper. The European warships slipped away one by one to more pressing duties elsewhere—first the French and Russian vessels, followed by the departure of HMS *Hampshire* to Salonica, where the local European community was caught up in the tension of the occupied city.[154] Europe's involvement in Cretan affairs simply imploded. By February 1913 HMS *Yarmouth* was left on its own, going through the motions of protecting the emblem of the Sultan on Suda island. At this point even Grey's preoccupation with the husk of paper pledges was displaced by concern at being 'in the position of the sole guardian of the Turkish flag in Crete'.[155] The *Yarmouth* was hastily ordered to Milos, but before departure on 13 February some of its crew presided over a ceremony in which the flag, instead of being hoisted in the bleak dawn, was packed up and taken to Wratislaw as the doyen of an essentially defunct consular corps. 'It was agreed', the consul recorded succinctly, 'that, for the present,

---

[151] During his short tenure as Governor, Dragoumis made a point of ensuring the preservation of mosques, including those which had at some point in their history been Christian churches. See correspondence in File 94.3, Archive of Stephanos Dragoumis, Gennadion Library.

[152] Nicholson minute, 26 Oct. 1912, FO371/1358.

[153] Michael Llewellyn Smith, *Ionian Vision: Greece in Asia Minor, 1919–22* (London, 1973), 13. Yet even at this late stage suspicions that the British government was angling to grab Suda Bay for itself had not disappeared—the British Ambassador in Berlin was shocked when the German Chancellor, Bethman-Hollweg, made this hoary old accusation to him at a dinner on 17 Oct. See G. P. Gooch and H. Temperley (eds), *British Documents on the Origins of the War*, ix: *The Balkan Wars*, part 2: *The League and Turkey* (London, 1934), 40.

[154] The Cretan gendarmerie previously dispatched to Macedonia was used by Prince Constantine to patrol the streets of Salonica, since it had considerable experience of coping with communal tension. The last task of HMS *Hampshire* in eastern Mediterranean waters was to help escort the body of King George back to Salamis after his assassination. *Hampshire* later became famous as the ship which foundered with Viscount Kitchener aboard after hitting a mine off the Orkneys on 5 June 1916. [155] Wratislaw to Grey, 3 Feb. 1913, ADM116/1200.

the flag should remain in my custody.'[156] Although the British had been largely instrumental in evicting the Ottoman Army from Crete in 1898, fifteen years later they were responsible for ensuring that the sign of the Sultan departed with a vestige of honour—though this sop was unlikely to save the wreck of Anglo-Ottoman relations. Immediately the *Yarmouth* left, under Dragoumis' orders the Greek flag was raised amid much enthusiasm, and guarded by Greek bluejackets whose own arrival provided the most visual proof that Crete was now a part of Greece.

Inevitably, this denouement could not pass without a temptation on various sides to recriminate. When Elliot and Venizelos discussed the momentous events of the last few months in mid-February 1913, the Greek premier asserted that 'the Cretan question had undoubtedly been the proximate cause of the [Balkan] war', and added that 'if annexation [of the island] had been permitted earlier, war might have been postponed for four or five years'.[157] This may simply have been Venizelos' way of deflecting some of the responsibility for the wider breakdown onto Great Britain, since Grey himself had been a principal barrier to such a pre-emptive annexation. Given the accelerating drift in Balkan alliances, it is doubtful whether a regional conflict could have been so easily postponed, or that Greece could have remained aloof once other powers in the area had taken up arms in Macedonia. Still, Venizelos's comment reinforces a sense, inherent in our analysis, that the various elements in Balkan regional diplomacy during the run-up to the interlocking wars of 1912–14 need to be unpacked anew, and not simply renarrated as a predetermined prologue to European Armageddon.

Meanwhile, however, Turkish resistance to Cretan *enosis* had effectively disintegrated by the end of 1912. At the conference convened in London the following January to shape a Balkan peace, the Porte signalled its willingness to accept any decision about the island recommended by the powers. The matter was soon overshadowed by the future of the Dodecanese islands, which Grey, horrified at the potential for 'a number of new Cretes', wished to see quickly hived off to Greece whilst the opportunity existed.[158] He was blocked by Italy, whose troops were already entrenched, creating a new Roman *imperium* in the East. In this way a good deal of trouble for the future was indeed stored up. Meanwhile Crete itself sank into the peaceful banality of a mere province, and in this obscurity the Muslims temporarily found a safety which European protection had rarely provided. The fact that Muslims participated in the Cretan mourning following the assassination of King George in Salonica on 18 March 1913 signalled the intention to accept with grace the union with Greece which was duly confirmed under Article IV of the Treaty of London (30 May 1913). Realism, however reluctant and resigned, had usually prevailed amongst that community's leadership in times of greatest crisis.

[156] Wratislaw to Grey, 15 Feb. 1913, ibid.
[157] Quoted in Gooch and Temperley (eds), *Origins of the War*, ix. 496.
[158] Hinsley, *British Foreign Policy*, 266–7.

Paradoxically, then, although the Muslims of Crete were one of the most exposed minorities in the process of Ottoman liquidation, they were never subjected to that extermination which had caused British policy makers such nightmares. This afforded retrospective legitimacy to those—mostly, but by no means exclusively Greeks—who had contended that a clean-cut solution through union, and not the mere freezing of a problem under European authority, offered *all* Cretans the best hope for the future. There was no significant emigration of Muslims after the consummation of Greek sovereignty (as there had been after the inauguration of autonomy in December 1898), and with the ensuing stability some returned to rural homes.[159] Yet given the underlying structures of local society and regional politics, the minority remained vulnerable to sudden external shocks. During 1921, the new war in Asia Minor was to take its toll in Crete. Armed men roamed the hills, evading conscription and harassing country people. As ever, Muslims bore the brunt of lawlessness.[160] It was, moreover, never likely that their community could be the exception that proved the rule in the mass population exchange prescribed by the Treaty of Lausanne in July 1923. The first boatload of a total of 25,500 deportees left Rethymno for Turkey, a place most had never seen and whose language they did not speak, during January 1924. A young Greek boy watched them go. He later recalled:

When the ships came to take them away, a kind of madness possessed them; they tore the shutters from their houses, ripped the doors and woodwork, intending to take with them these scraps of their former life... It was not until midday that the steamers hooted, the anchors were weighed and... a great cry arose from thousands of Turkish mouths, wild and full of entreaty... carried by the wind in great surges to the shore.[161]

Subsequently dispersed along the southern Anatolian coast, Cretan Turks found themselves regarded with suspicion, and even referred to as *yarim gaours* ('semi-infidels'). They survived, as many had tried to survive in autonomous Crete, by blending into the background, with the result that today the cultural traces of a Turco-Cretan community are hard to find.[162]

In treating so fully the prolonged crises surrounding the union of Crete with Greece we have necessarily tapped into many themes: amongst them, international

[159] It has been suggested that it was this aspect of Cretan experience which later led Venizelos to believe that large Muslim populations in Anatolia would acquiesce in Greek sovereignty. Suggestively, in 1919 the Greek premier was to send a Cretan politician, Mavroyakis, to Smyrna to make contact with local Turco-Cretans as potential co-operators. 'The mission was a success,' a historian of the ensuing Anatolian disaster states. 'Little groups of Turcocretans were to be seen sitting in village squares... and recalling nostalgically with Mavroyakis the old life in Crete.' See Smith, *Ionian Vision*, 86.

[160] See consular reports from Rethymno and Heraklion (the old Candia), Dec. 1921, in FO 286/898.

[161] Pantelis Prevelakis, *To Chroniko mias Politias* (Chronicle of a City) (Athens, 1938), 86.

[162] An investigator of this ruptured legacy has been told by a Turkish informant with a Cretan background that 'the first [Turco-Cretan] generation after Lausanne had a strong sense of Cretan identity... the second rejected this in favour of strict Kemalism, and ... the third is rediscovering its Cretan roots in a less turbulent cultural environment'. See Chris Williams, 'The Cretan Muslims and the Music of Crete', in Tziovas (ed.), *Greece and the Balkans*, 208–19.

peacekeeping, ethnic discord, Concert diplomacy, and eventually the Balkan origins of what became the Great War of 1914. Indeed, unless questions of irredentism and mastery are closely related to the multiple phenomena cutting across them, there can be no real understanding of the problems faced by those caught in their wake. From the perspective of this book, however, the Cretan climax rooted into place a paradigm of long and sacrificial struggle which afterwards flowed powerfully into Hellenic political culture. One subsidiary element in that paradigm was that, whereas in the Ionian case union had been secured under the patronage of Great Britain, in Crete *enosis* succeeded in the teeth of growing British hostility. Embedded in this logic was an enhanced sense of the primacy of internal Hellenic forces capable of imposing themselves against all the odds, at least in island societies with a dominant Greek imprint. The Cretan experience now fed into the movement for Cypriot *enosis* just as the latter was assuming a mature form. It is to the long Cypriot struggle, and ultimately to its much more ambiguous and even distorted outcome, that we must now turn.

7

The Peculiarity of Cyprus, 1878–1931

We are hampered on all sides by the peculiar position of Cyprus.

(Colonial Office minute, 28 Nov. 1901)

The Union Jack was flown at Government House when the Governor was in residence, over the Court and over the Commissioners' offices and houses in the Districts. Apart from that, a British flag was rarely visible.

(Sir Ronald Storrs, *Orientations*, 1937)

Both the territorial expansions of the Greek state we have dealt with so far—the integration of the Ionian Islands achieved in 1864, and the absorption of Crete in 1913—created paradigms within the wider ideological and emotional world of Hellenic *enosis*. Both paradigms were defined in terms of 'struggle'. These struggles were not identical. The first was conducted directly against British occupiers. The latter was first and foremost against the Ottoman Porte, and in its final phases against the collective constraints imposed by the protecting powers. In the latter case, as we have seen, Great Britain was along the way the immediate instrument of redemption, and later the principal agency for sustaining an impossible status quo. Yet, whatever the differences, Ionian and Cretan experiences were held to validate the ultimate triumph of a 'steady and persistent will' within Hellenic society. The complex international and regional factors which triggered the climaxes of 1863–64 and 1912–13 subsequently tended to be airbrushed away.

The next in the quartet of cases defined by a politics of *enosis* with which this book will be concerned is that of Cyprus. In this instance the outcome proved significantly different. That island did not pass into the constitutional fabric of Greece. It eventually became an independent republic whose freedom of action had imposed on it unusual limitations in the age of decolonization. The option of independence once loosely contemplated for Crete became the ultimate reality for Cyprus. The travails of the resulting republic will not concern us. Our underlying focus will be on why the Cypriot outcome differed, and on the British involvement in that process. In the present chapter we shall trace the roots of this 'peculiarity' between the British occupation of 1878 and the first violent demonstration on the part of Greek Cypriots against colonial authority in 1931. In doing so, we shall find that the island was always surrounded by externalities, uncertainties, and ambiguities intense even by the standards of the volatile *enosis* phenomenon.

An outlying fragment of the Aegean archipelago, clinging to the edge of what Western strategic cartography successively defined as the 'Near' and 'Middle' East, the fate of Cyprus always seemed to be that of an exception to other people's rules. Histories of the island were usually content to catalogue the long list of invaders and foreign rulers. In 1571 it had passed under Ottoman domination. By the mid-nineteenth century the population was roughly composed of nearly 80 per cent Greek-speaking Orthodox Christians, just under 20 per cent Muslims, and a smattering of Maronites, Jews, 'Latins', and others. Unlike Crete, the Christian population had not fought against their Turkish rulers after 1821—a passivity secured in part by the execution of the Orthodox Archbishop, other senior clergy, and some 500 members of the Greek intelligentsia in 1821.[1] Although Cyprus was sometimes included in definitions of the 'ideal' territorial frontiers of a new Greek state, it was usually towards the rear of such lists, and of its separation from Ottoman authority there was no real prospect. Nor thereafter was the island much coveted by European powers. The British, for example, from the 1840s onwards were suspected of designs on Crete far more often than of harbouring any desire to add Cyprus to their empire.[2]

A compulsion on the part of the Conservative ministry led by Lord Beaconsfield to acquire somewhere—a 'new Gibraltar' in the eastern Mediterranean[3]—as a potential sop to British pride should Russia break into Constantinople became compelling during the course of the Russo–Turkish war after April 1877. It became even more so once Russian influence flooded through the Balkans with the signature of the Treaty of San Stefano on 3 March 1878. Two decades before British public opinion had been prepared to counter such an advance on the battlefield. This was no longer the case. Yet because of that very reluctance Beaconsfield needed some territorial compensation to offset Russian gains which, though eventually baulked by Ottoman arms before Constantinople, had enjoyed success in Asia Minor. This was the immediate context for the secret signature of the Cyprus Convention in the Ottoman capital on 4 June 1878, by which Cyprus passed under British control, even though the Sultan's juridical right to sovereignty remained theoretically unimpaired.

Although news of this English coup leaked out as soon as the Congress of Berlin—convened by the German Chancellor, Count Otto von Bismarck, to revise the terms of San Stefano—assembled, for some weeks Sultan Abdul Hamid dragged his feet in issuing the necessary imperial *firman*. The British Ambassador to the Porte, Sir Austen Layard, resorted to a variety of threats, including one that further delay would lead Great Britain to support the reiterated Greek claim to Crete.[4] Finally, on 8 July the British government was able to confirm its forthcoming occupation of Cyprus. This Disraelian flourish in Eastern gamesmanship

---

[1] See generally John Koumoulides, *Cyprus and the Greek War of Independence* (London, 1974).

[2] Dwight E. Lee, *Great Britain and the Cyprus Convention Policy of 1878* (Cambridge, Mass., 1934), 5.   [3] Steel, *Lord Salisbury*, 133.

[4] Lee, *Great Britain*, 98.

allowed Beaconsfield to claim to have retrieved 'Peace with Honour' for Britain.[5] As the passage of the premier's carriage from Charing Cross Station to Downing Street on his return was strewn with flowers, the crowd dubbed him 'the Duke of Cyprus'; the very term 'jingo' was invented to convey the superheated patriotism which had come to prevail during the diplomatic crisis, and which this exotic and highly calculated subterfuge helped to deflect. In the following decades the island was to be a backwater in Britain's overseas *imperium*. Yet at crucial junctures its talismanic characteristics in British politics made themselves felt.

At the time the British move into Cyprus caused widespread surprise. Even in Berlin the French delegates had expected them to demand Mytilene, so much closer to the Dardanelles.[6] The British War Office gave serious consideration to Crete as an alternative, but the size and 'troublesome' nature of that island proved forbidding.[7] Yet if Cyprus was not an obvious choice, it possessed, as the closest study of this process long ago concluded, all the 'requisite characteristics' for British purposes.[8] Above all, Beaconsfield claimed that the island, together with Alexandretta on the adjacent coast of Asia Minor, afforded 'the keys to Asia', enjoying a commanding naval position in the eastern Mediterranean from which power might be projected in several directions.[9] The most essential direction was down through the Euphrates River, securing a land route to India should passage through the Suez Canal be threatened. The subcontinent loomed large in the British consciousness, and Beaconsfield touched this nerve when arguing that 'in taking Cyprus, the movement is not Mediterranean, it is Indian'.[10] Not surprisingly, given these makeshift origins, the value attached to the new British possession was nonetheless questioned. Lord Granville, for the opposition, said he did not know any British naval officer who accepted the Prime Minister's military theories about Cyprus.[11] The island did not even have a decent port. Certainly it could not be of any immediate use. As Lord Salisbury admitted, it had to be made healthy first, malaria being a major impediment to any troop presence.[12] Then, in September 1882 the British pulled off a coup in the eastern Mediterranean which put Cyprus in the shade—they took Egypt. The Nile, not the Euphrates, was to provide the main axis of British expansion thereafter. The problematical character of the strategic stake in the island sapped the porous foundations on which British control was always to stand.

But strategy was not the only motive in the acquisition of Cyprus. That occupation was also trumpeted as the harbinger of a larger regional development—the beneficent reform of Asia Minor under English guidance and patronage. In truth, Beaconsfield did not take Ottoman reform at all seriously. Salisbury at this stage still did. But it was because Turkey-in-Europe was already written off by him that it

[5] For Disraeli and the Congress of Berlin see Robert Blake, *Disraeli* (London, 1966), 629–54.
[6] Medlicott, *Congress of Berlin*, 111–12.   [7] Lee, *Great Britain*, 78–9.
[8] Lee, *Great Britain*, 78–9.   [9] Ibid. 133.   [10] Ibid. 113.   [11] Ibid. 116–17.
[12] Salisbury to Major-General Sir R. Biddulph, 4 July 1879, FO421/32.

was felt all the more vital to consolidate Asiatic Turkey as a barrier to Russia. It could only be so if economic development, improved government, and social peace transformed the Ottoman polity. Cyprus after July 1878 was briefly conceived as a distinctively British Mediterranean model of such a transformation—a model which was to be implemented in Asia Minor proper with the help of a cadre of British officials ostensibly in the service of a modernizing Sultan. If ever foreign rule is established in Asia', one correspondent wrote to Sir Austen Layard, 'and the condition of those unhappy people ameliorated and their country developed ... it will date from the period when this Treaty [the Cyprus Convention] is put in place.'[13]

In fact Layard himself was sceptical about this vision. In his view Beaconsfield's grab at Cyprus had only served to intensify the suspicions which the Sultan Abdul Hamid and his ministers already felt towards the British. This development was therefore not likely to anticipate an Anglo-Ottoman reforming alliance. Nor did it. The 'pacific invasion of Englishmen into Turkey' which Salisbury envisaged never occurred.[14] A group of British military consuls was dispatched to the Asiatic provinces of the Ottoman Empire. But these officials did not prove to be the spearhead of a wider British presence, and they spent much of their time uselessly attached to the staffs of provincial *valis*.[15] The much talked of Alexandretta-to-Baghdad Railway built by British capital and engineers remained a pipe-dream. Such plans for British-led reform in Asia Minor dissipated after Gladstone became Prime Minister in May 1880. In that election campaign he had castigated the taking of Cyprus as 'an insane covenant'.[16] In essence, then, Cyprus was taken as the linchpin of an ambitious policy which was soon shipwrecked both in Turkey and in Britain. Consequently, there was always to be a lingering quality of being bereft, verging on pointlessness, which British rule there could never quite shake off. The island was an imperial possession in search of a role which remained tantalizingly beyond reach.

These wavering qualities impressed themselves from the moment that General Sir Garnet Wolseley was appointed the first British High Commissioner in Cyprus. Even before leaving London, he found that leading public figures opposed the new venture. Lord Northbrook, recently retired Viceroy of India, for example, confessed that he 'hated the whole arrangement'.[17] Wolseley's own opinion was that taking Cyprus was 'a rather poor half-measure', a lodgement nearer the Persian Gulf being preferable.[18] His impressions did not improve on reaching the island. Landing with his troops at Larnaca on 28 July 1878, and

[13] J. T. Compton to Layard, 11 July 1878, MS Add. 39021, Layard Papers, BL.

[14] For Salisbury's initial confidence about this experiment, based on the welcome British troops had received in Cyprus, see Roberts, *Salisbury*, 209.

[15] In fact the only new appointment amongst this consular cadre reckoned to have had any real impact was Colonel Allix in Crete, attributed to the fact that that island 'had already been to a great extent removed from the influence of the Porte'. See Medlicott, *Congress of Berlin*, 340.

[16] Lee, *Great Britain*, 117.

[17] Maj.-Gen. Sir F. Maurice and Sir George Arthur, *The Life of Lord Wolseley* (London, 1924), 92.

[18] Ibid.

welcomed officially by a 'Moolah with a rather dejected air' and a bevy of Greek clergy, Wolseley soon moved on to the capital, Nicosia, which he found to be 'a filthy hole'.[19] He arranged for his own residence to be built a few miles from the walled city, and Wolseley spent very little time in the capital during his brief sojourn. In this way began a physical and psychological distance between British occupiers and local society which never disappeared.

Wolseley took few pains to conceal his contempt for any larger scheme of Ottoman revitalization, but on assuming his post he hoped at least to bring Cypriot institutions 'into something like British shape'.[20] He soon found himself hemmed in by his instructions from Lord Salisbury not to 'dislocate the existing [Ottoman] machinery'.[21] British officials therefore stepped straight into the shoes of the dismissed Muslim *kaimakans*. Within a few weeks, Wolseley was complaining that his own position as High Commissioner was 'little better than a Turkish Pasha without the arbitrary power the Turkish law gave him'.[22] This was not to say that the new British administration did not have much to get on with. Wolseley found himself taken up with 'currency, constructions, customs, *cadis*, cantonments, consuls, religious properties, harvests and finance'.[23] Raising taxes and judicial reform, including the imposition of English procedures and legal principles on a moribund Ottoman court system, were to be the principal preoccupations of British administration in its first few years. The failure at the very outset to introduce sweeping change, and in particular the tendency for the administration to settle into existing Ottoman grooves, reflected instincts which shaped policy making in the years ahead.

Clearly, this had implications for relations between British authority and the Greek majority. Wolseley was instantly impressed by 'the danger of an Hellenic propaganda' encouraging annexation to Greece.[24] 'It is an apprehension', Salisbury told his successor, Sir Robert Biddulph, after Wolseley had been called home in April 1879 for more pressing duties in South Africa, 'which the history of the Ionian Islands naturally fosters.'[25] Here was that deeply laid suspicion of incorrigible Hellenic nationality which Ionian experience branded into British official mentality. Wolseley had brusquely rejected the suggestion—made by the first deputation he received from the Christian Greeks—to make Greek the official language.[26] This was, indeed, to be English, with Turkish and Greek translations of all government business, whilst all three languages were to be used in the small (and wholly nominated) Legislative Council which replaced the old Ottoman *Medjli Idare*. Between the two indigenous languages, Turkish was

[19] Sir George Arthur (ed.), *The Letters of Lord and Lady Wolseley, 1870–1911* (London, 1922), 127.
[20] Maurice and Arthur, *Life of Wolseley*, 101.   [21] Ibid. 93.
[22] Anne Cavendish (ed.), *Cyprus 1878: The Journal of Sir Garnet Wolseley* (Nicosia, 1991), 56.
[23] Maurice and Arthur, *Life of Wolseley*, 93.
[24] Salisbury to Biddulph, 4 July 1879, FO421/32.   [25] Ibid.
[26] Wolseley 'shuddered' at the prospect of stimulating an indigenous language question similar to that which had caused much friction in Malta. See Maurice and Arthur, *Life of Wolseley*, 94.

accorded precedence. Even as Christian translators of Greek material the British administration chose for some while to employ Armenians rather than Greeks. In the initial period of British occupation the Greek community was naturally quiescent as it adapted to new masters, but it was not long before its representatives began to express discontents, amongst which the imperfections of the judiciary and discriminatory treatment over official employment were prominent.

There was one institution within Christian Greek society, however, which was rapidly at odds with the British. This was the Orthodox Church of Cyprus. Wolseley did not like monks or monasteries, especially with an Eastern flavour.[27] He was instinctively on the alert when being welcomed on behalf of Cypriot Greeks by the Bishop of Kitium at Larnaca. According to the 'legend' of *enosis* politics, on that occasion the Bishop hailed the British appearance as a gratifying replacement for the Ottomans, but also looked forward to the British government repeating its liberal generosity when it had ceded the Ionians to 'Mother Greece' in 1864. Recent historical research has thrown doubt on the Bishop's precise use of words.[28] Certainly it was not in the interest of the Greek ecclesiastical hierarchy to start off on the wrong foot with the British, but that some gliding reference was made to the 'national aspiration' seems fairly certain—if not at Larnaca, then when Wolsleley first met the Archbishop, Sofronious, in Nicosia.

The British difficulty with the Church had profound roots. Under the *Millet* system of Ottoman imperial administration, the Archbishop of Cyprus enjoyed the role of civil and religious leader of the Orthodox community.[29] Such privilege had included the right to tax its own faithful, and to receive the assistance of law and order agencies to ensure that levies were paid. The British by contrast brought with them ideas of a strict separation of Church and State. Latent misunderstanding was illustrated early on when a priest was arrested under British direction for a minor felony, imprisoned in Famagusta jail, and, most notoriously, had his head shaved. When the Archbishop protested against this infraction of clerical immunity, he was told that according to British notions all were treated alike in the face of the law. Nor did the Archbishop obtain satisfaction when he complained that, in contrast to the late Turkish regime, *zaptiehs* (police) were not being made available to help the clergy secure monies from recalcitrant members of their community.[30] As time went on, the Church and the British official machine found ways of cohabiting, since they had a shared interest in guarding social stability in a poor and fractured island. But their mutual relations were always uneasy and, given the gulf of culture and sympathy, probably doomed to rupture.

[27] Ibid. 101.
[28] Rolandos Katsiaounis, *Labour, Society and Politics in Cyprus during the Second Half of the Nineteenth Century* (Nicosia, 1996), 25–8.
[29] For treatments of relations between the Church and British administration see Sir George Hill, *A History of Cyprus*, iv: *The Ottoman Province. The British Colony, 1571–1948* (London, 1953), 569–607, Panayiotis K. Persianis, *Church and State in Cyprus Education* (Nicosia, 1978) and Benedict Englezakis, *Studies in the History of the Church of Cyprus 4th–20th Centuries* (Aldershot, 1995), 421–51.
[30] Biddulph to Lord Kimberley, 19 Mar. 1878, FO78/3374.

Very swiftly under the new dispensation responsibility for Cyprus was transferred within Whitehall from the Foreign to the Colonial Office. It was therefore Lord Kimberley, as Colonial Secretary under Gladstone's premiership, who introduced a new liberal constitution under an Order-in-Council on 30 November 1882. Under these arrangements, the Legislative Council consisted of eighteen members, six being British officials appointed by the High Commissioner, nine elected by Greeks, and three by Turks.[31] These elections on a popular franchise were to be on separate communal roles, encouraging, it was often alleged, differences between the Christian majority and Muslim minority. Nevertheless, the mere fact that the allocation of elected places in the chamber recognized a Greek plurality—not the mere equality of the *Medjli Idare*—represented a significant alteration within island society.

The impact of constitutional life in Cyprus was part and parcel of a social and to some extent economic effervescence compounded by what were generally accepted as the improvements of British administration. Whether measured by imports and exports, revenue raised, newspapers read, or by other criteria, Cyprus emerged as an expanding society with a new sense of civic space.[32] But this growth and prosperity was differentially spread between Christians and Muslims, who, although they intermingled easily enough, still belonged to different traditions and cultures. Furthermore, a shift in landownership towards Greek predominance—a phenomenon which had transformed Cretan society through the nineteenth century[33]—got under way in Cyprus. The Greek elected members brought the resulting vitality into the Legislative Council. In doing so they increasingly came up against the real powerlessness of their position, since a combination of British and Muslim representatives could still push government legislation through. True, occasionally one or more Muslims in the chamber sided with the Greeks, if only to remind the British that they could not be taken for granted. But on the most vital issues the elected Greeks found themselves stymied, and the feeling grew that politically they were no better off than they had been under the Ottomans. This was the understanding which made the worm turn within Anglo-Greek discourse under Cypriot conditions.

To such an outcome one question made a significant contribution—for a long while more so even than the matter of *enosis*. This was the annual tribute payable under the Cyprus Convention to the Porte, and fixed thereafter at £92,000. This sum did not go to the Sultan, because shortly before his government had defaulted on servicing the 1855 Crimean War Loan. The tribute from Cyprus was thenceforth siphoned off by the British to their own bondholders and those of France—one

---

[31] For an astute discussion of the 1882 constitution see Evanthis Hatzivassiliou, *The Cyprus Question, 1878–1960: The Constitutional Aspect* (Minneapolis, 2002), 25–8.

[32] For the growth of 'print activity' in Cyprus, spreading after a lag from the Greek to the Turkish communities, and which in both cases occurred in 'high' literary rather than demotic forms, see Rebecca Bryant, *Imagining the Modern: The Cultures of Nationalism in Cyprus* (London, 2004), 33–4.

[33] For changes in landed property see Katsiaounis, *Labour, Society and Politics*, 99–118.

supplementary benefit being the appeasement of French feelings, bruised first by the British coup over Cyprus, and then even more hurt by the subsequent move into Egypt. The Treasury regarded the flow of Cypriot tribute through London as a 'heaven-sent relief', and clung to it tenaciously. Many English Liberals thought this disreputable, and the ruse underpinned a moral uneasiness which attached itself to British administration of the island. Sir William Harcourt told the House of Commons in 1886 that Cyprus 'was the only Dependency I know of from which you take money and devote it to other purposes'.[34] Had the speaker looked more closely around the British Empire, he might have found more examples. Yet the appropriate parallels were not imperial but Balkan. Cyprus was the only territory freed from *de facto* Turkish rule from which a tribute continued to be exacted in practice as well as theory.[35] Consciousness of this fiscal peculiarity—adding as it did to the burdens of a population struggling with heavy taxation—proved more irksome than any other public question.[36]

The question of the tribute was nonetheless looked upon differently by Christian and Muslim Cypriots. The Muslims approved of the tribute itself as a sign of the Sultan's continuing legal rights in the island; what they disliked was that the money was taken from their titular sovereign and given to Europeans. The Greeks detested the tribute precisely because it testified to a Turkish stake in the island which they considered defunct. Both communities, however, resented the drain of money from the island. That detestation intensified as the tribute settled down as a permanent element in British arrangements. By November 1901 the High Commissioner, Sir William Haynes-Smith, by no means a natural philhellene, impressed on the Colonial Secretary, Joseph Chamberlain, that the tribute was 'the constant thought of all [Greek] classes. They speak of it on every occasion; they dream of it; and I believe never refer to it without a curse in their hearts.'[37] As long as both Greek and Turkish elected members to the legislature concentrated simply on securing relief from the Treasury's parsimony, their mutual relations were not prejudiced. But the growing attacks of the Christian Greek elite, inside and outside the Council, on the *principle* of the tribute began to bring into focus the matter of fundamental loyalties. This was where the preoccupation with the tribute met the veiled passion for *enosis* amongst Cypriot Greeks, and its counter-feeling amongst both Turks and English officials.

The idea of *enosis* had certainly never dissipated from the onset of the British occupation. The susceptibility of that phenomenon to rumours of sudden fulfilment

---

[34] Quoted in Hill, *Cyprus*, iv. 468.

[35] Under the Treaty of Berlin, both Bulgaria and Eastern Roumelia were liable to continue paying tribute to the Sultan as a mark of the latter's sovereignty. In practice, the former never paid a penny, and the latter only occasional sums. Cyprus was therefore unique in the regular outflow of funds connected with an obligation under direct Ottoman rule which no longer existed in practice.

[36] In 1889 taxation per head of population in Cyprus was 16s., compared to 14s. 3d. in Samos, and 8s. in Crete. This difference in a still largely peasant society was considerable. For further comparison, see Sir William White (Ambassador, Constantinople) to Salisbury, 14 Sept. 1889, in *State Papers*, lxxxii (1890), 25.   [37] Sir W. F. Haynes-Smith to Joseph Chamberlain, 28 Nov. 1901, CO883/6.

which had so marked the Ionian and Cretan movements was evident here too. Gladstone's entry to Downing Street in May 1880 fuelled strong expectations, especially when news circulated that a resolution favouring *enosis* for Cyprus had been carried in the Reform Club.[38] Gladstone proceeded to 'undeceive' Cypriots as he had once tried to undeceive Ionians, replying to some petitioners from Larnaca in the following April that the British held Cyprus under a convention with the Porte, 'and that proposals which would be a violation of that convention cannot be discussed'.[39] This mantra was to be endlessly repeated. Indeed, there was a dangerous corollary: that if Britain ever did cede Cyprus, it could only be retroactively to the Sultan. With Near Eastern crises following upon each other from the mid-1880s onwards, Christian Greeks had to consider the possibility that should the British ever leave, the next formal welcome on Larnaca seafront might be to a returning pasha. Under these conditions, although *enosis* remained a staple element in Greek Cypriot culture, it led a curiously submerged life, whilst public politics focused on the tribute and such matters (always crucial to Greek public culture) as the funding of education.

The distinctiveness of Cypriot circumstances was underscored by the sustained crisis in the Near East between 1896 and 1898. Considering the tension throughout much of the Graeco-Turkish world, the respective communities in Cyprus remained relatively quiet. In part this reflected a general predisposition to communal coexistence. But it also indicated the tendency of Cypriots to react hesitantly to grave external crises, waiting to see how the various communities would be affected by events. At the outbreak of the war between Greece and Turkey in April 1897, the British kept the police in readiness should Greeks and Turks come to blows. They did not do so, though a more pronounced communal separation showed itself, the menfolk sticking more rigidly to their designated coffee shops.[40] Suggestively, however, Christians began to volunteer for service in the Greek Army. In the run-up to hostilities, about 1,000 young men were shipped off to Greece having been addressed at the quayside by the Greek consul.[41] Although the British administration took the necessary measures to intervene against such movements should the Porte demand it, no such request was made, if only because the war proved so short. Certainly there was an echo in Cyprus of that check to Greek hopefulness which the sweeping Turkish victory in Thessaly during 1897 effected throughout the region.[42]

[38] Biddulph to Kimberley, 12 Apr. 1881, FO78/3374.
[39] Gladstone to Biddulph, 19 Apr. 1881, ibid.
[40] Walter Sendall (High Commissioner) to Joseph Chamberlain, 23 Apr. 1897, CO67/105.
[41] For a study of the phenomenon of Cypriot volunteers in *enosis* struggles, see Petros Papapolyviou, *Fainon Simeion Atichous Polemou: I Simmetochi tis Kiprou ston Ellinotourkiko Polemo tou 1897* (A Bright Point in an Unfortunate War: The Participation of Cyprus in the 1897 War) (Nicosia, 2002) and *I Kipros kai I Valkaniki Polemi: Simvoli stin Istoria tou Kipriakou Ethelontismou* (Cyprus and the Balkan Wars: A Contribution to the History of the Cyprus Volunteers) (Nicosia, 1997).   [42] Colonial Office minute, 21 Aug. 1899, CO67/119.

Yet the outcome of the war and its aftermath did have significant consequences for Cypriot affairs. Crucially, despite the Sultan's victory over Greece, he had, as we saw earlier, been forced by Europe to disgorge his gains in Thessaly. After that—and especially after the massacre of British troops in Candia on 6 September 1898—it was scarcely credible that the British could ever hand Cyprus back to the bloodied Hamidian regime. This did not stop British ministers repeating stale threats for want of anything better. In November 1902 Joseph Chamberlain advised Haynes-Smith, for example, to respond to any raising of *enosis* in the Legislative Council with the warning that the only way Cyprus could be disengaged from the 1878 Convention was by being returned to the *de facto* control of Turkey. But thereafter, against the background of often bloody chaos in Macedonia, such studied warnings trailed away, and the looming shadow of retrocession lifted. As it did so, Cypriot Greeks gained a greater freedom—politically and psychologically—to debate, and agitate for, their ideal of *enosis*.

This stimulation to Christian political energy within the island gained encouragement from the example set by the emergence of an autonomous Cretan state headed by a Greek prince. This was a model which Greek Cypriots envied, and although, as we have seen, the government of Prince George attracted much British opprobrium, many Cypriots considered—by some natural reflex—that the Cretans were better off than themselves. Figures on educational spending were often trotted out to prove the point.[43] Recent Cretan events helped shape the atmosphere surrounding an exhibition in Athens during 1901 organized by members of the Cypriot intelligentsia, which displayed costumes and handicrafts testifying to the Hellenic character of their own island.[44] Although King George tactfully avoided the opening ceremony, he visited the event soon after; and when it ended, a party of organizers and participants from Cyprus stopped off in Canea on the way home to join a Hellenic demonstration in front of Prince George's official residence. 'Crete is not a pleasant neighbour for Cyprus,' Haynes-Smith complained to Chamberlain in London,[45] and particularly so, he felt, because that island provided a model of approaching *enosis* through violent methods which more extreme elements in Cyprus, alarmingly, were also beginning to advocate.[46]

Over the previous two decades the British rulers in the island evolved a special survival instinct under Cypriot conditions. They habitually sought to remain as neutral as possible in disputes between and within the communities, keeping at a distance from the often bitter rivalries within the Muslim *evkaf* (or religious foundations), and from the equivalent disputes between Christian parties. British officials sought to keep their heads down, concentrate on administration, and

[43] See, for example, *Phoni tis Kiprou* (Voice of Cyprus), 12 Oct. 1901 and *Alithia* (Truth), 8 May 1908.
[44] For the 1901 exhibition, testifying to a growing interaction between Athens and Greek Cypriot society, see Ioannis K. Mazarakis-Ainian, 'The Cypriot Exhibition of 1901', in *Cypriot Costumes in the National Historical Museum: The World of Cyprus at the Dawn of the Twentieth Century* (Athens, 1999), 31–47.   [45] Haynes-Smith to Chamberlain, 30 Aug. 1902, CO883/6.
[46] Ibid.

identify by trial and error a working equilibrium between 'British', 'Greek', and 'Turkish' identities and loyalties. At the Anglo-Hellenic end of this complex spectrum a prescribed decorum became established. At a ball during 1895 held in Larnaca for youth drawn from the professional classes, this phenomenon was neatly encapsulated:

The Consul of Greece, M. Philemon, who sat at the head of the table, raised a toast for Queen Victoria, which was answered by the hurrahs of those present and the orchestra, as if by a signal, played the English anthem. Mr. E. Hoare ... raised, in English, a toast for the King of Greece, the sounds of hurrah filled the room and general enthusiasm was raised by the Greek national anthem.[47]

Such descriptions were rather arch, but they summed up an accommodation between all those involved. Yet such polite improvisations flaked apart during the *fin de siècle*. M. Philemon was subsequently recalled to Athens following protests from the British Embassy, when he was prominent in an Olympic sports display at Limassol in which there was much waving of the Greek flag and, this time, a striking absence of cheers for Queen Victoria.[48] Tension built up within the Legislative Council, since the overtness of *enosis* sympathies outside that body had a kind of placebo in the fierce battles over the tribute within it. The British administration began to panic, since it only needed one Muslim deputy to desert for government to become impossible. In his last few years as High Commissioner Haynes-Smith uttered a series of *cris de cœur* to his superiors that action might have to be taken against the Greek opponents of British rule. In May 1903 he reported an 'aggressive extension' of the *enosis* movement;[49] a year later he noted that it was 'more emboldened' still.[50] On the eve of his departure from Cyprus he finally advised that the small British military garrison be increased and the constitution of 1882 radically altered, and possibly even abandoned.[51] In so doing he crudely defined the central dilemma which, one way or another, was to bedevil British rule in the island through to its ultimate demise in 1960.

In the Colonial Office Hayne-Smith's repeated requests for more troops were ignored. The reaction to his parting diagnosis as High Commissioner echoed an earlier pattern frequently repeated in the Ionian Islands. A new, mildly philhellenic replacement, Sir Charles King-Harman, was dispatched from London, charged with wooing local politicians into co-operation, and avoiding an embarrassing breakdown. The new High Commissioner rather conveniently concluded that the basic problem was financial, and secured a special grant-in-aid of £50,000 to ease the pressure. He succeeded for a while, assisted by the fierce divisions amongst Greek Cypriots aroused by the contest to elect a new

[47] Katsiaounis, *Labour, Politics and Society*, 80.
[48] Egerton (British Ambassador, Athens) to Salisbury, 24 Jan. 1900, CO883/6.
[49] Haynes-Smith to Chamberlain, 22 May 1903, ibid.
[50] Haynes-Smith to Lyttelton, 4 Apr. 1904, ibid.
[51] C. A. King-Harman to Secretary of State for Colonies, 21 Apr. 1910, CO883/7.

archbishop.[52] As Evanthis Hatzivassiliou has pointed out, the archiepiscopal question which commenced in 1900 was not simply ecclesiastical, but 'reflected two different ideological approaches as well as two patterns of attitudes towards colonial rule'.[53] It followed from this that, although the diversion held tactical advantages for British administration, *enosis* sentiment by no means disappeared. When Winston Churchill visited the island in 1907 he stated in a speech that union with Greece was regarded by the Greek community 'as an ideal to be earnestly, devoutly, and fervently cherished'.[54] Whilst King-Harman comforted himself, and London, therefore, as to the 'steady effacement of the bitter ill feeling between the people and the government', the underlying problem was becoming more, not less, acute.[55]

Churchill's visit, which assumed a folkloric status in Greek memories, had one practical effect: it boosted Christian expectations, not initially of *enosis*, but of further financial generosity by Britain which the rising British politician went out of his way to advocate. During 1909 there was a recrudescence of discontent at first focused on the tribute, but which now became increasingly linked to a demand for an increase in the number of Greek-elected members in the Legislative Council. By the spring of 1910 King-Harman was sending warnings home that unless relief from the tribute was made permanent 'a serious constitutional crisis ...will be brought about', in which Greek elected members would desert the Council, and present the ugly choice long feared: that of having to govern through a legislature dependent exclusively on Muslim votes, or of doing without a representative institution at all. 'I know the temper of the Greek Cypriots,' King-Harman warned, '[and] I do not underrate their capacity for agitation and disturbance.'[56]

The High Commissioner did secure some extra relief from Whitehall, but it was grudgingly given,[57] and he was shortly sent off with the doubtful promotion of governing British Guiana. Before leaving, however, he provided the unwelcome

---

[52] Suggestively, the Turkish Cypriot community also witnessed a sharp division in the early years of the new century, between factions of the chief *cadi* and the *Mufti*. These controversies in the two main communities were both coloured by confrontation between self-consciously 'popular' and 'elite' forces, the latter linked to a national-ethnic project. See Bryant, *Imagining the Modern*, 103–4.

[53] Hatzivassiliou, *The Cyprus Question*, 30. For the classic process in which an expatriate administration, whilst wishing to remain uncompromised, was nonetheless drawn into local conflict, see 'Notes on the Archbishopric of Cyprus' in CO67/220/13.

[54] Such honeyed words, however, were by no means reflected in Churchill's private assessment to British ministers that, whilst it had become incredible that Cyprus could revert to Turkey, cession to Greece also remained unacceptable because the 'loyal' Muslim community would suffer the same fate of eviction that had occurred to many of their co-religionists elsewhere in the Balkans. See 'Condition of Cyprus: Memorandum by Mr. Churchill', CO883/7. For a latter-day account, see G. S. Georghallides, 'Cyprus and Winston Churchill's 1907 Visit', *Thetis*, 3 (Mannheim, 1996).

[55] C. A. King-Harman to Secretary of State, 21 Apr. 1910, CO883/7. [56] Ibid.

[57] King-Harman was firmly reprimanded at this time by the Colonial Office for striving to maintain Christian-Muslim co-operation rather than preoccupying himself with repelling attacks on the British presence. See Secretary of State to King-Harman, 19 May 1910, CO883/7.

advice that some elements of the radical measures mooted back in 1904 could no longer be avoided.[58] His successor, Sir Hamilton Goold-Adams, was imbued with a strong bias against Greek politicians, increasingly stereotyped by British official-dom as the sole cause of instability in a territory which, whilst theoretically still Ottoman, was treated more and more like a plain crown colony. Early on during his stay Goold-Adams formed the conviction that the vast majority of Cypriots 'do not wish for annexation to Greece, and are content with British rule if outside rule has to exist'.[59] A psychology of denial in relation to feelings of Hellenic nationality, frequently stigmatized as irrational and artificial, had impregnated the old British Ionian Protectorate, but never so persistently, or to such calculated effect, as eventually underpinned the same syndrome in 'British' Cyprus. This discourse was seemingly oblivious to the heightened bonding between Greek Cypriot civic society and the cosmopolitan world of contemporary Hellenism, so that Greek Cypriot lawyers were more and more officially registered as advocates in Athens, whilst their commercial peers cultivated links with, for example, Greek entrepreneurs in Alexandria.[60]

But whatever the truth of Goold-Adams's assessment of Greek-Cypriot atti-tudes to union, did his crucial rider ('if outside rule has to exist') still apply? The tremor that ran through the status quo in the region after Italy and Turkey went to war in September 1911, and the news that Cretan deputies were intending to take their places in the Athenian Parliament, had Cypriot after effects. Christian Greek leaders continued to avoid a head-on clash with British authority by limiting the focus of their activity to the tribute and reform of the legislature. But, as King-Harman had once stressed, they paid a price in not 'magnifying themselves' within their own community by failing to express the *enosis* demand more aggressively.[61] Once the archiepiscopal question was resolved with the elevation of the radically inclined Bishop of Kitium, and amidst growing tensions in the area, there was a tendency to close ranks firmly against the British presence. On 17 April 1912, the Greek-elected members resigned *en masse* from the Council, and large demonstra-tions followed. 'A little local excitement but all quiet,' Goold-Adams telegraphed Sir Lewis Harcourt, the British Colonial Secretary, but given the uneasiness always underlying British rule this was not wholly reassuring.[62]

The evidence Goold-Adams provided for this tranquillity, despite appearances, conveys something of the complexity behind popular *enosis* in the island. According to his account of a tour through the remote north-eastern region of Karpass, the absence of Hellenic flags in the villages he visited was so striking that the Greek leadership in Nicosia had to send orders that they were to be raised

---

[58] King-Harman to Secretary of State, 25 Feb. 1911, ibid.

[59] Goold-Adams to Sir Lewis Harcourt, 22 Feb. 1912, CO67/165.

[60] From 1903, for example, a new weekly ferry between Cyprus and Athens, replacing a monthly schedule, meant greater accessibility across a wide front of activities.

[61] King-Harman to Secretary of State for Colonies, 20 May 1910, CO883/7.

[62] Goold-Adams telegram to Harcourt, 18 Apr. 1912, CO67/166.

wherever the High Commissioner ventured. For the rest of his perambulation, many such flags were to be seen whenever his itinerary was publicized, but otherwise it remained the case that no flags or 'signs of great love for Greece' were allegedly observable.[63] Goold-Adams assumed the latter to be the truth. But what the flying of the Greek colours 'up close and personal' to the High Commissioner signified above all was a tendency for the majority community to define its aspiration *against the British themselves*. Hence, when the High Commissioner did not appear—or was not anticipated—then *ipso facto* the tendency was suspended. As always in the Graeco-Turkish world, the psychology surrounding flags was highly complex, and their distribution through space and time, as in this case, was usually open to totally contradictory interpretations.

Greek flags might irritate a British governor, but they could also frighten Muslims and trigger reactions in Constantinople. As the 'little local excitement' took shape, constitutional issues and inter-communal relations began to bump up against each other more frequently. The occasions when Christian- and Muslim-elected members in the Legislative Council voted together grew fewer. By extension, the degree to which the Greeks felt that the Turks were an obstruction in their path increased. The crisis unleashed by the Greek resignations from the Council was especially bound to impact on communal relations. These sensitivities were compounded by the Turco-Italian war. Goold-Adams wrote to a senior official in the Colonial Office that some Greeks were insulting the Muslims, calling them ' "dogs of Turks" ... and generally gloating over the Italian successes in the Aegean Sea'. The Turks, he stated, clung all the more closely to the administration, 'sullenly depressed' at what was happening, and fearful that the British might eventually betray them within the island. 'The upshot', the High Commissioner concluded, 'is that the air is full of electricity.'[64] A developing sense of Greek power in the surrounding region therefore shortly penetrated Cypriot affairs, prompting the Porte to begin a series of *démarches* to London seeking to breathe life into the old Cyprus Convention, just as they had sought, as we saw earlier, to revive a battered but still theoretically sovereign claim to Crete.[65]

The political electricity produced in May 1912 the most extensive disturbances in Cyprus since 1878—indeed, in their communal complexion, they were not to be exceeded till the last stormy years of British rule. The trouble broke out on the 26th in a village outside Nicosia, though the more serious event occurred in Limassol the following day.[66] There were five fatalities, and seventeen seriously hurt. The subsequent Commission of Inquiry (including an Englishman, a Greek, and a Turk) was unable to agree as to responsibility, though common concern was expressed at the reliability of the police (still composed, as it had been throughout

[63] Goold-Adams to Harcourt, 25 Apr. 1912, ibid.

[64] Goold-Adams to G. Fiddes, 30 May 1912, ibid.

[65] For various Turkish *démarches*, see Foreign Office to Colonial Office, 4 May 1912, CO67/128.

[66] For the protest lodged by the Porte on behalf of their co-religionists, see Tewfik Pasha to Sir Edward Grey, 10 July 1912, CO67/168.

British occupation, largely of Muslims) in controlling disturbances.[67] In London the most disquieting factor was held to be the occurrence of riots in several places simultaneously.[68] The atmosphere in the island soon lifted. Both Christian and Muslim leaders were quick to bear down on their communities—in fact, the Orthodox Archbishop had for some while tried to guide Greek political activity away from any collision course with the minority. But, as so often with communal rivalries, a residue remained, intensified by the powerful dynamics of Greek Cypriot volunteering for the Hellenic armies in the Balkan wars.

The Muslim leaders in Cyprus had reason for fearing that their leverage over the British was at risk. The more value the British attached to securing the strategic co-operation of the Greek kingdom in the eastern Mediterranean, the more threatened it was. With British naval resources stretched in that theatre as warships were recalled to northern waters, ministers and officials in London— most notably Lloyd George at the Treasury, and Churchill now ensconced at the Admiralty—began to calculate the advantage of transforming Greece into an active proxy.[69] On 28 October 1912, the British chiefs of staff noted that 'the sole use of Cyprus is its possible value as an asset wherewith to negotiate [with the Greeks] for more important requirements elsewhere'.[70] At the London conference on a Balkan settlement, Lloyd George and Churchill floated before Prime Minister Venizelos—his prestige flushed with Greek military success—the idea that Cyprus might be traded for British access to a port on Cephalonia. This proposal soon receded, but rumours of such a deal abounded, and in Cyprus senior Muslims, such as the mufti and chief *cadi*, began to seek from the High Commissioner a guarantee of their welfare should the island ever be ceded to Greece.

The administration in Cyprus remained opposed to any concessions to Greek Cypriot demands. 'The Greeks are to be given nothing [on the constitution] because they are agitating,' Lewis Harcourt commented cryptically. 'When they cease agitating, we shall be told that they obviously want nothing. The old story.' Greek Cypriot tactics continued to be caught in this classic bind through much of 1914, when accumulating rumours of a war in which Britain and Turkey would be on opposite sides put all public questions into limbo.[71] In early October 1914 a martial law edict was drawn up, ready for an emergency, the Muslim preponderance in the police now being a special cause for anxiety. The High Commissioner need not have worried. With war imminent on 2 November 1914, Goold-Adams summoned the chief *cadi*, the Mufti, and other leading Muslims and read them a

    [67] In 1912 there were 464 Turkish *zaptiehs* (9 of whom could not speak Greek) and 276 Greek *Zaptiehs* (of whom 48 could not speak Turkish). The greater propensity of Turks to speak Greek was central to the rationale for maintaining a largely Muslim police force.
    [68] Harcourt to Fiddes, 29 June 1911, CO67/166.
    [69] Llewellyn Smith, *Ionian Vision*, 12–15.
    [70] Chiefs of Staffs Paper on the Mediterranean, 28 Oct. 1912, ADM 116/3098.
    [71] Colonial Office minute, 20 May 1914, CO67/170.

statement on the breakdown in Anglo-Turkish relations. '[T]hey expressed', he reported, 'the view that Great Britain was now fully justified in taking any action against Turkey as was thought fit, and ... added that Cyprus should be annexed by England and her inhabitants ... released from the intrigues of Constantinople.'[72] The interests of the Cypriot Muslims as a community hinged in future on clinging as tightly as possible to their new status as *British* subjects.

Indeed, a wider tendency towards Anglo-Hellenic rapprochement showed signs of penetrating Cyprus. The local Greek leadership had followed, if grudgingly, the advice pressed on them by the consul of Greece to moderate their agitation whilst so much was at stake elsewhere, principally enforcing Greek claims in the Aegean during the various Balkan conferences of 1912–13.[73] By way of response, Goold-Adams formed a particular tie with Theophanis Theodotou, an ardent Venizelist member of the legislature; later he sent a British official to attend the memorial service for Christodoulos Sozos, an ex-mayor of Limassol and Legislative Council member, who had died fighting in the Hellenic Army near Ioanina in December 1912. Amidst the crisis of early November 1914, the Greeks were not to be outdone by Muslims in expressing their loyalty, though in their case it was more an expression of shared democratic principles which they expected to see fulfilled in Cyprus as elsewhere. Thus the Archbishop and Greek-elected members of the Legislative Council sent an address to the Colonial Secretary on 8 November—three days after the declaration of war between Britain and Turkey—expressing the 'sympathy and honour' of the Greek people and Church in Cyprus for the noble struggle which Great Britain and its Allies were undertaking 'on behalf of the supreme moral principle' of liberty in international relations.[74]

The prompt British annexation of Cyprus under Order-in-Council did not, in fact, signify any fundamental decision on the island's ultimate status. It merely simplified for purposes of the war the juridical position, with a specific application to shipping. Annexation, indeed, was conceivably only a brief halting place on the way to *enosis*, and in 1915 that possibility suddenly loomed large. Inducing Greece to join the Entente emerged as a matter of extreme urgency, since it provided the most efficient means of stabilizing the Balkan front, and getting aid to Serbia (threatened by Bulgaria) in the form of Greek troops. It was to achieve this end that the British government resorted to using Cyprus as bait. This time there was nothing tentative about it: the offer was crudely dangled before the Greek government in mid-October 1915.[75] News of the offer only gradually filtered

---

[72] Goold-Adams telegram to Harcourt, 2 Nov. 1914, CO67/174. At the declaration of war, the British official sent to inform the Muslim notables that they were now British citizens found that his news was accepted with 'dignified resignation'. See Sir Harry Luke, *Cities and Men: An Autobiography*, ii (London, 1953), 3.

[73] King George to Venizelos, 1 Mar. 1913 and Report of Greek Consul Adamides to Foreign Ministry, Athens, cited in Papapoiyviou, *I Kipros kai I Valkaniki Polemi*, 271.

[74] See the address in CO67/174.

[75] For this episode see M. Woodhouse, 'The Offer of Cyprus, October 1915', in Constantinos Svolopoulos (ed.), *Greece and Great Britain during World War I* (Thessaloniki, 1985), 82–6.

through to the island. When it did, a Muslim deputation quickly waited on the High Commissioner to express extreme concern. They cannot have been calmed by the imprecise assurance of Sir John Clauson (who had recently succeeded Goold-Adams) that whatever happened the British government would safeguard their 'spiritual and material interests'.

Yet the British offer was rejected by King Constantine and his Prime Minister, Alexander Zaimis (once so prominent in Crete's troubled autonomy). Vilifying the King's pro-German leanings later became the central feature in Allied propaganda in the Balkans.[76] In fact, Constantine had no desire to join the Central Powers, but he was equally determined not to be seduced by the Western Entente, and end up prejudicing all that Greece had recently gained by giving Bulgaria the chance of revenge. On 22 October, the Greek Ambassador in London handed Lord Grey at the Foreign Office the message that 'military assistance to Serbia would involve the defeat of the Greek nation'.[77] Measured against that risk, the compensation of Cypriot *enosis* was marginal at best. News of the refusal first reached the island via Athenian newspapers a few days later. To the High Commissioner this was 'an inconceivable refusal'. It must have been equally hard to digest by the Greek population. 'Perplexed and passive' was how Clauson described their response,[78] the Archbishop merely sending a memorial to London expressing his 'gratitude' for the offer that had been made.

Both the perplexity and the passiveness were comprehensible. Greek Cypriot agitation had always sought to elevate the island's future to a level where the Greek government could 'solve' the matter directly with London. What they discovered was that elevation to the international plane entailed a process in which Cypriot *enosis*, far from being advanced up the Hellenic agenda, found itself being assessed, weighed, and occasionally relegated amongst the territorial priorities facing hard-pressed Athenian ministers. As for passiveness, Christian Greeks knew that on their own, and with a war raging, there was little they could do. After all, Greece might well join the Entente sooner or later, and still be awarded Cyprus in doing so. Meanwhile they consoled themselves with what became their stock theory about the historic 'offer' of late 1915—that by making it the British admitted the illegitimacy of their presence in the island. Neither the British administration there nor the Colonial Office were under any illusion that they were 'off the hook'. 'It would be very satisfactory', one official in Whitehall noted, 'if we could say that Cyprus is now indissolubly united to the British Empire. But I am afraid we cannot do that.'[79]

Cyprus did become 'indissolubly united' to the British imperial connection during the following war, but only gradually, and in subterranean ways. From 1916 onwards there was a growing emphasis within the British war machine on establishing

[76] For an analysis by a British commentator sympathetic to the dilemmas of King Constantine see Abbott, *Greece and the Allies, 1914–22*.   [77] Quoted in Trevelyan, *Grey of Fallodon*, 287.

[78] Clauson to Colonial Secretary, 11 Nov. 1915, CO67/177.

[79] Colonial Office minute, 3 Nov. 1915, ibid.

the spoils to be gained at the peace.[80] Those territorial ambitions were principally in and around the Fertile Crescent of the Arab lands, and once in late 1917 Field Marshal Allenby's long-awaited advance began from Gaza up through the Levant, rich prizes—Jerusalem, Baghdad, Damascus—fell into Britain's lap. Indeed, the mobility of the British Army depended not least on the mass purchasing of Cypriot mules by a new army supply centre at Famagusta, giving a sharp boost to the prosperity of rural Cyprus. But behind the logistics lay a more profound fact: the British stake in the island, which in 1878 had been defined in relation to Asia Minor, had now become reoriented towards a new strategic zone marked out by Allenby's triumphant advance. To echo Lord Beaconsfield's original dictum, the movement in which the fate of Cyprus was freshly bound up was not so much Mediterranean, and not Indian, but Middle Eastern, and British possessions in this region— whether old or new—were not given up thereafter except under considerable duress.

So long as the war lasted, at least, Greek Cypriot agitation for *enosis* was in abeyance; instead, the majority community rather divided on 'Venizelist' and 'Constantinist' lines.[81] It was testimony to their irreversible self-definition as Greeks that they quarrelled the way most other Greeks did. After the flight of King Constantine from Athens in June 1917, the Venizelists were on top everywhere. With Greece's belated entry into the war alongside the Entente powers, and its army prominent in the final push into eastern Thrace leading to the Mudros Armistice in the East (30 October 1918),[82] there seemed a good chance that the claim to Cypriot *enosis*, blocked amidst the tangled war diplomacy of 1915, might be made good by the peacemaking of 1919. Everything hinged on Venizelos's leverage with the Allied leaders, and above all over Lloyd George, on whom Venizelos turned the entire battery of his charm. This was not a time for any group with political claims on the future to be passive. On 4 December an *enosis* deputa- tion led by Archbishop Kyrillos III was seen off at Nicosia railway station en route to Paris and London by an enthusiastic crowd of 6,000 well-wishers.[83] The Colonial Office, rattled by rumours that Venizelos was about to take up the Cyprus Question, ordered the administrative secretariat in Nicosia to supply it with a full panoply of arguments to fend off the impending demand.

The Greek premier did include Cyprus in the list of Greek territorial desiderata presented to the Allied Supreme Council in early February 1919. But he did so more in the spirit of a reminder that it was an island with a largely Greek identity than as a concrete demand. Venizelos' treatment of the issue thereafter was reflected in his oblique relations with the archiepiscopal delegation. 'At the Peace

---

[80] The 'Sykes–Picot Agreement' of Jan. 1916 sought to demarcate British and French gains in the area. It stipulated that Great Britain would not give up Cyprus without prior consultation with France, since to do so would have repercussions for French control in and around Alexandretta.

[81] Paradoxically, given King Constantine's allegedly pro-German bias in the war, the Cyprus gov- ernment was alleged to favour the 'Constantinists' within the island. See material in CO67/188.

[82] See J. M. Wagstaff, *Greece: Ethnicity and Sovereignty, 1820–1994. Atlas and Documents* (London, 2002), 87–9.

[83] Kyrillos III had been elected to his post on the death of his predecessor in 1916.

Conference', the leading historian of Cyprus in this period, George Georghallides, has written, 'the main task of Greece was to liberate the bulk of the long-suffering Greek communities living near the Asia Minor coast and in Thrace and to consolidate the Greek occupation of the Aegean islands.'[84] Since Greece's war record had several blemishes in Allied terms—including the death of Allied soldiers in Athens during 1916—Venizelos had his work cut out to secure these goals.[85] Ever since he had made the transition to Greek metropolitan politics in 1909/10, his priority had been to secure the kingdom's vulnerable northern frontiers. If Crete had been a subsidiary matter then, Cyprus was even more subordinate a decade later. This was the reality he impressed on the Cypriot deputation on the few occasions they met, and he did not hesitate to be rough when necessary. Thus on one occasion he instructed the representatives of Cyprus that, just as the Greek Cypriots had accepted the necessity for the British 'offer' of *enosis* in 1915 to be refused by Greece on the grounds of more pressing needs, so in present conditions 'they should not appear ... intransigent to the advice of the National Centre'.[86]

One diplomatic historian has remarked on Venizelos's 'monumental blunder' in failing to secure Cypriot *enosis* in Paris.[87] His charisma made him seem to contemporaries, and sometimes to latter-day commentators, almost an equal of the greatest Allied statesmen—a classic case of a national leader able to punch above their weight.[88] Yet charisma cannot reverse the natural currents of power. Venizelos's guiding principle was to associate Britain with his main goals, and to this end, one diplomat in Paris remarked, he was willing to make Greece into 'an almost vassal state in the eastern Mediterranean'.[89] At no point did Venizelos raise Cyprus in any of his exchanges with Lloyd George. The price he wished to extract from the Western Allies for Greek assistance in stemming a Turkish resurgence towards the Straits was *not* Cyprus, but continuing political and financial support for the Greek forces which had entered Smyrna and its hinterland during May 1919. With the Treaty of Sèvres (10 August 1920) the Greek premier attained the apogee of his own tempestuous career, framed by a greater Greece of 'two continents and five seas'. Cyprus, however, along with Northern Epirus and the Italian-ruled Dodecanese, was not included in this climax.

Against that background, the task facing the Cyprus delegation was Herculean. Early on Venizelos persuaded the Archbishop and his colleagues to go to London, where in effect they had to kick their heels and beg access to relevant departments. In the Foreign Office there was some preparedness to consider a discussion of

[84] G. S. Georghallides, *A Political and Administrative History of Cyprus, 1918–1926* (Nicosia, 1979), 106.

[85] In 1916 British and French troops occupied the Piraeus and parts of Athens, incurring a number of fatalities in clashes with Greek royalist forces.

[86] Quoted in Georghallides, *Political and Administrative History of Cyprus*, 124.

[87] John Fisher, 'Lord Curzon and Cyprus in British Imperial Strategy, 1914–23', *Journal of Byzantine and Modern Greek Studies*, 23 (1999), 161.

[88] W. S. Churchill, *The World Crisis: The Aftermath*, v. (London, 1919), 383.

[89] Harold Nicolson, *Curzon: The Last Phase, 1919–25* (London, 1934), 55.

Cypriot *enosis,* though even this support ebbed once Lord Curzon, allegedly harbouring a 'bias against the Greeks', became Foreign Secretary in October 1919.[90] The Colonial Office cobbled together a powerful inter-departmental consensus against cession. The individual merits of the arguments that went into this process were not the point. What mattered was their collective weight. Here the advice tendered by the Admiralty to retain Cyprus at all costs was critical, fleshed out by references to the impact of air strategy in the Middle East—the first mention of a factor to loom large in future. 'I am glad that we have got [all] this on record,' a senior Colonial Office official stated when collating the material.[91] By the time the Cyprus delegation got to see the new Colonial Secretary, Leopold Amery, on 26 October 1920, the tide against *enosis* was in full flood. When one of the Cypriot delegates, referring to the recent treaty on a Turkish peace, said that Britain was 'handing over far more Turks to Greek rule elsewhere than we should be handing over in the case of Cyprus', Amery hit back that, unlike the Muslims who had been 'handed over' at Sèvres, those in Cyprus 'had behaved well in the past and were accustomed to British government'.[92] As usual, when the British and the Greeks got frustrated with each other, they argued about the Turks.

Whilst there appeared to be some prospect of *enosis* being secured at the conference table, the curb on Greek agitation in the island nonetheless remained firmly in place.[93] Amery's rebuff to the deputation, and Venizelos' crushing election defeat in Greece on 14 November 1920, however, rapidly curtailed any such hopes. Thereafter *enosis* agitation resurfaced on a scale not witnessed since the eve of war. One form this took was an 'opposition policy' of rigid abstentionism from participation in British administrative organs, most notably the Legislative Council, a policy confirmed by the National Council of December 1921. The latter was simply one proof of a developing organizational sophistication in the political world of *enosis,* coupled with a distinctive sense of 'Cyprus alone'— that is, an awareness that Greek Cypriots had *if necessary* to seek their national redemption independently of Athens. Certain implications arose from such an insight. 'The danger of the adoption by the Greek Cypriots of "Sinn Fein" methods', the High Commissioner, Sir Michael Stevenson, warned Winston Churchill, newly appointed Colonial Secretary, 'is for the moment remote...but in all seriousness the essential possibility must not be lost sight of.'[94]

If Greek Cypriot politics turned in on itself, so did local British administration. After so much upheaval since 1914, expatriate officialdom exhibited an instinct to isolate itself anew from external complications. Resentment at having to make a contribution to the housing of Russian and Armenian refugees pouring out of

---

[90] Georghallides, *Political and Administrative History of Cyprus,* 114.
[91] CO memorandum, 10 Aug. 1920, CO67/189.
[92] Amery minute, 26 Oct. 1920, CO67/201.
[93] Sir Michael Stevenson to Lord Milner, 15 Apr. 1920, CO67/197.
[94] Stevenson to Churchill, 25 Dec. 1921, CO67/204.

Constantinople was just one example.[95] There was a desire to impose a tighter control over the island, and in particular to curb the 'Hellenizing' activities of Greek schools. This had to be approached in a roundabout manner—initially through legislation during 1920 which conferred financial benefits (and closer control) on non-Greek schools, but which Greek tax-payers largely paid for, and subsequently by an education law touching the Greek establishments directly.[96] Then there was a temptation to lash out at hardened advocates of *enosis*. The ultimate weapon here was deportation. Although Sir Garnet Wolseley had introduced enabling legislation, later high commissioners had always hesitated. The veteran agitator Nikolaos Katalanos had come close to being targeted in 1912, but the government had finally accepted that such action simply gave the movement for *enosis* the oxygen which it needed to survive.[97] In April 1921, however, High Commissioner Sir Michael Stevenson deported Katalanos, along with the Mayor of Larnaca, Philios Zannettos. Deportation remained thereafter the touchstone of *ultra* sentiment which ran more deeply in 'British' Cyprus than in more conventional overseas possessions.

'The Catastrophe' of the Greek Army's defeat in Asia Minor during the high summer of 1922, the burning of Smyrna (13–14 September 1922), and the Graeco-Turkish settlement enshrined in the Treaty of Lausanne (24 July 1923) could not but have powerful, if largely indirect, effects on Cyprus. In sum, a Greek historian has noted of the logic behind the massive population transfers involved, Hellenism was contracting within the confines of the territorial Greek state.[98] Greece became ethnologically homogeneous, and the incoming refugees from Asia Minor were so distributed as to effectively stabilize at last the frontiers of Greek Macedonia and Western Thrace.[99] Since Turkey, by recognizing under the new treaty the British annexation of Cyprus in November 1914 had explicitly forfeited its own claims, Greek governments and Greek Cypriots more generally were henceforth able to treat the island's future status as exclusively an Anglo-Greek, not a Graeco-Turkish, question. But what really stands out is that, after decades of turmoil in the Near East, long-standing animosities between Greece and Turkey had been resolved *without any account being taken of Cypriot enosis*. In a structural sense, therefore, Hellenic aspirations within the island were the orphan of the Lausanne process and its aftermath.

By this very token, the opportunity opened to convert Cyprus formally into a crown colony. As one Colonial Office official remarked, this was not likely to be

---

[95] In the case of a boatload of Armenian orphans in early 1920, for example, Lord Milner (then Colonial Secretary) had to insist that the reluctant Cyprus administration afford sanctuary.

[96] For a survey of Cypriot education see Persianis, *Church and State*.

[97] 'An expelled Katalanos', one official in Whitehall had sagely advised, 'is likely to be much more useful to the Union with Greece agitation than any amount of rhetoric.' See Colonial Office minute, 8 May 1912, CO67/166. For Katalanos's role in local Hellenic nationalism see Katsiaounis, *Labour, Politics and Society*, 215–25.

[98] Dimitri Penzopoulos, *The Balkan Exchange of Minorities and its Impact on Greece* (Paris, 1962), 126–7.   [99] Eastern Thrace was returned to Turkey under the Lausanne Treaty.

welcomed by Cypriot Greeks but 'we do not intend to cede Cyprus to Greece and
nothing is to be gained by pretending that we do'.[100] An Order-in-Council in
early February 1925 introduced a constitution increasing the number of members
of the Legislative Council, but keeping the ratio of Greeks, Turks, and British
nominees the same; and on 1 May the dawning of British colonial status was
ushered in with appropriate pomp in Nicosia. Such moves necessarily posed a tactical
dilemma in the world of Greek Cypriot politics. Some protagonists stuck rigidly
by a stance of 'unqualified enosis'. Others tended to the opinion that Greek
interests were no longer served by abstaining from the Legislative Council 'as a
source of political life'.[101] The latter proponents have been described as *enosis-
autonomists*, whose immediate goal became a large measure of self-government
along the lines recently achieved by Malta.[102] Inevitably there was a broad
spectrum at play here, but embedded within it was a potential splintering of the
Greek Cypriot community, a possibility underlined by the emergence of the
Communist Party of Cyprus (KKK) focusing on social issues and with a distinctly
fuzzy attitude to the 'National Question'.[103]

Here was an opportunity for the British to perform the classic gambit of locat-
ing a wedge between 'moderate' and 'extremist' opponents. Yet it was consciously
spurned. The immediate nightmare for British administration in Cyprus was not
violence Sinn Fein style, but slipping into ungovernability through legislative
deadlock. Any measure of self-government would only hasten that prospect. Such
fears were no mere chimera. Under Cypriot conditions, any dilution of government control would undoubtedly have ushered in a relentless harrying of official
business, with the spectre of *enosis* in the background. But the British failure to
respond to Greek moderation only validated the case of their radical opponents
that restraint did not pay. Meanwhile in Cyprus government circles there was a
temptation to hit hard when the chance arose. '[A] straight talk would do His
Beatitude good,' the second highest official in the government commented when
the mild-mannered and by no means highly political Archbishop Kyrillos III
dispatched yet another memorial to London seeking recognition of the claims of
the Hellenic majority.[104]

Here, then, were two forces set on a collision course: Greek Cypriot nationality,
spurned and resentful, and British colonial reaction Mediterranean style. The
dangers were obvious. Seeking to reduce the risks, the British government once
more resorted to a new governor with some claim to being 'Hellenic'. This was
Sir Ronald Storrs, who had considerable experience of dealing with prickly Greek
prelates in Alexandria and Jerusalem, extensive (if rather ostentatiously displayed)

[100] Colonial Office memorandum, 14 Jan. 1923, CO67/210.
[101] G. S. Georghallides, *Cyprus and the Governorship of Sir Ronald Storrs: The Causes of the 1931
Crisis* (Nicosia, 1979), 360.   [102] Ibid.
[103] A member of the Executive Committee of the Communist Party, writing to the International
Department of the British TUC, stated that the National Question left him and his colleagues 'partly
indifferent'. See D. A. Chrysostomides to TUC (London), 12 Mar. 1924, CO67/213.
[104] C. D. Fenn (Cyprus Colonial Secretary) to Leopold Amery, 28 Aug. 1925, CO67/215.

classical learning, and a natural bent for supple political behaviour. After arriving in the island during November 1926, Storrs sought to encourage a distinctive 'Cypriot' patriotism, to deflect Greek identity away from *enosis* and towards 'a more innocuous feeling of educational and cultural pride', and to increase social contacts between British officialdom and the local population, not least in the villages.[105] 'A man is of the race that he passionately feels himself to be,' Storrs later summed up his approach as Governor on the critical issue of emotional affiliation. 'No sensible person will deny that the Cypriot is Greek-speaking, Greek-thinking, Greek-feeling, Greek, just as the French Canadian is French-speaking, French-thinking, French-feeling and French.'[106]

Storrs' reaching out to Greeks was not merely rhetorical. With Churchill now heading the Exchequer in London, the Governor was able to use the memory of his diatribe against the Cyprus tribute in 1907 to good effect, and obtained the wherewithal to secure its demise.[107] Nonetheless, by the end of Storrs' first year in post his 'honeymoon with the Greeks' was already over, and by the end of his second a new deadlock had come into being.[108] Greek politicians were not seduced by airy compliments, and soon resented Storrs' too-artful habit of wearing blue and white in his lapel one day when dealing with them, and red and white the next when dealing with Muslims. The abolition of the tribute was sullenly received, since there was no question of the British government returning the sums which had been mulcted from the Cypriot purse over many years. Beneath such reactions lay a fear that behind Storrs' benevolence there was a hard-nosed intent to 'dehellenize' the island. Faced with challenges all the more deadly for their insidiousness, the Greek Cypriot political class was stung into sinking its differences in a fresh campaign against British autocracy. The focus of their attacks in the legislature was successive annual estimates of government expenditure as public revenues began to fall in the wake of commercial depression.

Driven increasingly to rely on the frequent use of prerogative machinery through Orders-in-Council, British officialdom arrived at the conviction that its authority in Cyprus could only survive by breaking with a constitution which remained essentially the Gladstonian invention of 1882. Proposals for 'reform' were sketched which sought to ditch elective elements in favour of an official and wholly nominated body based on the *Medjli Idare* as 'a survival of old Turkish times'.[109] When it was suggested by the Nicosia secretariat that the abolition of the tribute provided convenient 'cover' for such an imposition, the Colonial

---

[105] Georghallides, *Governorship of Sir Ronald Storrs*, 12.

[106] Ronald Storrs, *Orientations* (London, 1937), 550. Storrs' common-sense view remains today the only valid basis for defining Greekness. Veremis and Dragoumis, *Historical Dictionary of Greece*, state, 'Today's Greeks are those who think of themselves as Greeks ... thus making Greekness a largely subjective, chosen attribute ... Their identity is not racial, or religious, but cultural.'

[107] In theory the tribute proper had lapsed with annexation from Turkey in Nov. 1914, but the requisite funds continued to be appropriated from the island's public coffers.

[108] Georghallides, *Political and Administrative History of Cyprus*, 67, 116.

[109] Colonial Office memorandum, 13 Apr. 1929, CO67/227/4.

Office bulked at associating a keenly desired goal with an issue on which virtually everybody realized justice had long lain with the Greek Cypriots.[110] Nevertheless, the scrapping of the present constitution was admitted to be only a matter of time, though for the moment doubt remained 'whether we have reached the psychological moment for performing the operation'.[111] It became axiomatic that such a juncture would come when the Greek-elected members of the Legislative Council finally put themselves 'in the wrong' in such a way that the operation could be sold to international, and especially British, opinion.

The survival of British authority was all the more problematical because its relationship to the Turkish Cypriot community had also become compromised.[112] Given the delicate situation in the legislature, this was highly destabilizing. Under the Lausanne Treaty, Cypriot Muslims were made to choose whether to remain in the island and accept British subject status, or to go to Turkey. Only about 5,000 departed, in part because the Cyprus government made sure it did nothing to encourage them. Yet the consolidation of a secular, 'modern' republic in Atatürk's Turkey affected Muslim society in Cyprus as well. A younger generation felt at odds with the old-fashioned, religious, and fez-wearing Cypriot Turks whom the British traditionally patronized as interlocutors. Turks, just like the Greeks, often found Storrs' tactics too subtle by half. His recognition of the Greeks as the majority element in Cyprus—for example, by giving the Orthodox Archbishop precedence over the mufti—was resented.[113] The tendency for the Turkish-elected deputies in the legislature to withhold their support from British officials, and even to flirt with the Greeks as they had in former days, was, Storrs anxiously reported to the Colonial Office in January 1931, a disturbing weakness in the new situation.[114] It was a weakness which made it all the more imperative to dispense with elected representatives as swiftly as circumstances allowed.

To this parlous situation there was another development potentially fatal to the viability of British colonialism: the definitive emergence of the Orthodox Church as the 'real leader' of the *enosis* movement.[115] Although the elderly Archbishop Kyrillos abided by an older, if tepid, cohabitation with foreign rulers, younger and more hostile bishops—such as Nicodemus Mylonas of Kition—manoeuvred for position, seeking above all to ensure that the Church itself was not outflanked by more secular elements jostling for leadership of their energetic community.[116] It was Kition who played a leading role in the conference called at Saittas, near Limassol, on

110 Dawe minute, 2 Aug. 1929, CO67/220/12.
111 Dawe minute, 19 Dec. 1928, CO67/227/4.
112 For an overview see James A. McHenry, *The Uneasy Partnership, 1919–1939: The Political and Diplomatic Interaction between Great Britain, Turkey and the Turkish-Cypriot Community* (New York, 1987). 113 Georghallides, *Governorship of Sir Ronald Storrs*, 8.
114 Storrs to Passfield, 4 Jan. 1931, CO67/239/14.
115 Nicholson to Sidney Webb, 12 June 1929, CO67/221/5.
116 For an interesting interpretation of this phenomenon, see Sia Anagnostopoulou, 'I Eklissia tis Kiprou kai o Ethnarchikos tis Rolos [The Church of Cyprus and its Ethnarchic Role] 1878–1960', *Sichrona Themata* (Current Affairs), 68–70 (1998–9), 210–11.

12 September 1931 at which Greek deputies and senior ecclesiastics met to discuss the fresh crisis sparked by an unpopular hike in customs taxes. The climax of this gathering was the unveiling of what was instinctively interpreted in the colonial secretariat as a 'revolutionary manifesto'.

It was the appearance of this manifesto, confirmed by a meeting of the Greek Cypriot National Organization on 3 October, which prompted Storrs to announce his intention to return to London immediately for emergency talks. Governors rushing off to Whitehall for consultations always raised the temperature of Cypriot politics, conjuring up the most basic of Greek objections—that their future was being determined without their participation. On the evening of 21 October, the eve of Storrs' departure, and with the public atmosphere heightened by the resignation of two Greek deputies, a crowd of 5,000 set out to heckle the Governor. Gathered in front of the rambling wooden structure of Government House, some of the demonstrators—according to the inevitable description in *The Times,* egged on by several priests—suddenly escaped the control of the police.[117] A lighted torch was tossed through a window; before long the edifice was ablaze; and within a few minutes it had burned comprehensively to the ground (though not before Storrs had made a hasty exit through the rear).[118] In the island-wide outbreak that followed British authority hovered on a brink for the first time since 1878; villages as well as towns were affected, with Famagusta the epicentre of unrest. Order was only restored by British troops and warships rushed to the scene from Egypt and Malta, and—at a time when the experiment of 'air policing' was spreading through much of the 'British' Middle East—by RAF Vickers Victorias overflying trouble spots, intimidating those beneath with a novel display of power. When all was over, there had been seven Greek fatalities.

The rupture of October 1931 was to define the polarities of colonial Cyprus for a long time ahead. On 24 October, Storrs threw a military road block around the archbishopric, so much a centre of Nicosia life. When the mild Kyrillos sought to pass through, the Governor seized the opportunity to give him the good 'talking to' his officials had long pressed for.[119] This was, symbolically, the moment when the wobbly British *modus vivendi* with the Church snapped, confirmed by the deportation to Malta of the bishops of Kition and Kyrenia, hauled from their residences in the middle of the night, and accompanied into exile by five Greek Cypriot politicians.[120] Although the most informed Colonial Office 'expert' on Cyprus insisted that the whole affair 'was not part of a carefully worked out plan, but ... more of a spontaneous outbreak,'[121] the more critical view prevailed that the outbreak had been 'elaborately organized' by the Church and the Greek

[117] *The Times,* 23 Oct. 1931.
[118] Cmd. 4045, *Disturbances in Cyprus in October 1931* (London: HMSO, 1932).
[119] Governor to Colonial Office (telegram), 8 Nov. 1931, CO67/240/11.
[120] For the deportations see G. S. Georghallides, 'The Cyprus Revolt and the British Deportation Policy, October 1931–December 1932', *Journal of the Society of Cypriot Studies* (Nicosia, 1995), 37–114.   [121] Dawe minute, 3 Nov. 1931, CO67/240/13.

legislative deputies.[122] 'This was a purely Greek rebellion,' Storrs asserted, able to point to the tranquillity and loyalty displayed by the Muslim minority.[123] It was therefore the Greeks who had to pay the price, in the first instance in the form of a suspension of the constitution which, though purporting to be temporary, always had about it a whiff of permanence.

The British Ambassador in Athens, Patrick Ramsay, following these accumulating tensions in Cyprus, had been struck by their resemblance to the deadlock in the Ionian Islands which had led to the Extraordinary Mission of 1858—testimony, again, to how deeply that earlier episode had permeated British memories. Gladstone's famous mission, Ramsay recalled, had failed, with the result that the Ionian Islands had been ceded to Greece as the only alternative 'to the abolition of [the Ionian] parliament . . . by arbitrary measures unworthy of Her Majesty's Government'.[124] What was 'unworthy', or ideologically unacceptable, in the 1850s had clearly become much less so by the end of the 1920s, with the result that Cyprus became entangled in a wave of British colonial reaction. Ramsay's concern that Great Britain's standing in Greece itself could not remain unaffected did not take long for confirmation. Two weeks after the burning of Storrs's residence, students in the University of Athens, notably replacing 'Armistice Day' with a new Hellenic celebration of 'Cyprus Day', demonstrated, not forgetting, however, to hang garlands on the bust of Gladstone prominently placed in the elegant nineteenth-century avenue of the Athenian Academy. The crowd was broken up by police acting under the direction of Venizelos, in office for the last time as Prime Minister. 'The maintenance of friendly relations with Great Britain', read the stern statement issued by Venizelos, 'has been the policy of Greece since independence, and those who jeopardized this were insane.'[125] The days of the rebel of Therissos were long gone.

Wherein, then, lay the peculiarity of Cyprus? The answer must be found at a number of levels. It can be located partially in the ambiguity of the island's status and constituent identities which ran parallel with each other, without ever blending into a common Cypriot consciousness. Greek Cypriot *enosis* was distinctive in its vulnerability to marginalization and the spectre of defeat. Ionian and Cretan Greeks prior to their own unions, for all their difficulties, had enjoyed more 'room to breathe', more scope to develop the dominance of their political culture, than Greek Cypriots possessed later on. Yet although the latter did not develop a Cretan-style insurrectionism to overcome obstacles in their path, they evolved a remarkably tenacious and corporate form of political expression, in which the Church assumed a critical role. The peculiarity of Cyprus was compounded by a strong sense amongst Greek Cypriots, born of bitter experience, that they had to look to themselves, and not to Athens, to secure their Hellenic goals; and by the

[122] Colonial Office minute, 13 Nov. 1931, ibid.
[123] Storrs' telegram to Colonial Office, 8 Nov. 1931, CO67/240/11.
[124] Quoted in Georghallides, *Governorship of Sir Ronald Storrs*, 365.
[125] *The Times*, 24 Oct. 1931.

fact that amongst our case studies Cyprus was unique in being transformed into a fully fledged British crown colony, with all its rigidifying effects. These complex circumstances were to have profound consequences. Meanwhile, whether the British and the Cypriots after October 1931 could find a way of digging themselves out of the hole which repression always creates for both rulers and ruled remained to be seen.

8

The Dodecanese Experience, 1939–1948

It is clear that the key to the strategic situation in the Mediterranean...is expressed in two words: 'Storm Rhodes.'

(Winston Churchill, 9 Oct. 1943)

This island is lovely. Fruit and blueness and grey olive-crowned promontories. Only I wish we'd leave. I am sick of our policy and our faces in Greece.

(Lawrence Durrell to T. S. Eliot, 7 Nov. 1945)

Beset with the chronic political problems traced in the preceding chapter, Sir Ronald Storrs had long cast an envious eye towards Italian administration in the Dodecanese, an island chain off the western coast of Anatolia covering approximately 44,400 square miles.[1] It offered precisely the model which British officialdom in Nicosia would have liked to emulate. Storrs even entertained the aristocratic Italian governor, Mario Lago, in the appropriately Venetian location of Famagusta, seeking tips on the awkward matter of administering an overwhelmingly Greek community.[2] When Storrs was invited back to Rhodes, the principal island in the Dodecanesian archipelago, he was struck that the only Greek flag on the island flew over the consulate of the Hellenic kingdom. Storrs subsequently advised the Colonial Office that they they should 'take a few leaves' out of the Italian book in the eastern Mediterranean.[3] The many millions of lire lavished on the construction of a new fascist-colonial architecture in Rhodes town itself, alongside the prevailing political quiescence,[4] impressed many impartial visitors in the later 1920s and 1930s.

[1] The islands known as the Dodecanese, or sometimes Southern Sporades, are Rhodes, Patmos, Leros, Calymnos, Cos, Astypia, Nisyros, Telos, Chalki, Symi, Cassos, Castellorizo, and Lipso. See map 6.7 in Wagstaff (ed.), *Greece*. For a description see Royal Institute of International Affairs, 'The Italian Colonial Empire: The Dodecanese', Information Department Papers No. 27 (1940), 54–8.

[2] According to a census taken in 1936, the total population was 140,848, of which approximately 80% was Greek, 8% Turkish, and 8% Italian, with approximately 5,000 Jews. Of Dodecanesian Turks, around 1,500 had a Cretan provenance. In the Jewish community some 2,000 remained when the Germans took full control in early 1944. These were taken *en masse* to Auschwitz, only 303 surviving. For the latter, see *The Times,* 31 Mar. 1947. [3] Storrs, *Orientations*, 500–1.

[4] Although the harsh methods of Lago's successor, De Vecchi, were unpopular, the Dodecanesian intelligentsia *in situ* were broadly acquiescent in Italian rule. The Dodecanesian diaspora, however, was deeply anti-Italian. For an analysis, severely limited by reliance on oral sources, see Nicholas Doumanis, *Myth and Memory in the Mediterranean: Remembering Fascism's Empire* (London, 1997).

Against this background, it is ironic that on 31 March 1947, in a brief and unostentatious ceremony, it was a British military administration which handed the Dodecanesian islands over to Greek control. The intervening drama of a new world war inevitably provided the context for such an unanticipated outcome (the Dodecanese constituted the first Italian overseas possession to be formally redistributed in the post-1945 era). The Dodecanese thus offers a further instance where the British found themselves presiding, albeit with sometimes doubtful enthusiasm, over an expansion of the Greek state. Compared with all the exertions and sacrifices once made by Ionians and Cretans to attach themselves to the Hellenic motherland, and the continuing frustrations of Greek Cypriots to strike out towards the same goal, the Dodecanesians seemingly slipped into Greece in a relatively unproblematical fashion. Although, as we shall see, the realities on the ground were somewhat messier than such a characterization allows, our task is to explain why this was so.

As in the other cases we have studied, the historical background must be sketched. Greek Orthodox Dodecanesians had taken part in the Greek Revolt after 1821, and thereafter the islands had been held by rebel forces. They were nonetheless returned to the Sultan in compensation for the incorporation of Euboea, so close to the Peloponnese mainland, into independent Greece. In 1912 Italy seized the islands during its war with Turkey, and although it did so allegedly on a purely provisional basis, the Italian presence insidiously took root before becoming entrenched under the terms of the Treaty of Lausanne in 1923.[5] Thereafter the islands never became an Italian colony proper, but rather a *possedimento Egee*, firmly under the jurisdiction of the Ministry of Foreign Affairs in Rome. As such the Dodecanese offered a showpiece for those Italian dreams of expansion in the Near East which had recently received a setback with the failure to retain a slice of south-western Anatolia,[6] but which had by no means expired. This role of a 'model' possession distinct from a plain unvarnished colony was reminiscent of that which Lord Beaconsfield had once entertained for 'British' Cyprus, and in both cases an air of ambiguity—for all the tinsel-grandeur of Italian Rhodes—was the result.

The Mediterranean theatre thereafter became increasingly salient in British perspectives as the diplomatic crisis of the 1930s unfolded.[7] The demands on British resources became intense, and at the Imperial Conference of 1937 the Australian and New Zealand governments sought and obtained renewed promises from Britain that the Royal Navy would go immediately to their aid in a crisis, and not be detained in Mediterranean waters. Clearly, a Mediterranean proxy would

---

[5] For the early phase of the Italian presence see Philip Carabott, 'Italy's "Temporary" Acquisition of the Dodecanese: A Prelude to Permanency', *Diplomacy and Statecraft*, 4-2 (1993), 285–312.

[6] Italy's claims to the Ottoman province of Adalia went back to the secret Treaty of London in Apr. 1915. Under the Treaty of Sèvres in 1920 Italy was accorded a narrow but deep zone in south-western Anatolia. Italian troops were quietly evacuated at the end of 1922 before suffering the catastrophe which overcame the Greek Army. See Smith, *Ionian Vision*, 68–71, 75–83, 108–9, 241.

[7] See Lawrence R. Pratt, *East of Malta, West of Suez: Britain's Mediterranean Crisis, 1936–39* (London, 1975).

be needed to help bridge the gap between continuing British interests and the military assets available in a war. Lloyd George had once looked to Greece—and above all to Venizelos—to play this prospective role. But Greek military capacity had lost its sheen in 1922, and Anglophile Venizelists had no place in the ruling dictatorship of Ionnis Metaxas. By contrast, Turkey, modernized under the aegis of Kemal Atatürk, appeared a more credible partner, if only its co-operation could be secured. That the Dodecanese was the price anticipated by the regime in Ankara led by Atatürk's successor, Ismet Inönü, emerged clearly at the meeting of British, French, and Turkish negotiators in Aleppo during March 1939.[8] Accordingly when a military convention was agreed in the following October it was stipulated that if an attack on Thrace led to Turkish entry into the war, its forces would occupy the Dodecanese 'as far as possible' assisted by Anglo-French naval and air action.

Not only, however, did Turkey remain inactive when Italy joined Germany in war in June 1940, but to the surprise of some it held aloof from affording any aid to Greece when the latter was assaulted by Mussolini's forces the following October.[9] The degree to which Turkey cleaved to neutrality was to shape the eventual destiny of the Dodecanese. In part this policy arose from the fact that Ismet Inönü's generation of Turkish politicians had all shared in the experience of Ottoman involvement during the war of 1914–18, and the price that had then been paid. Overlying the Turkish consensus that there should be no repeat was the not unrelated belief—itself the sole remaining legacy of Hamidian statecraft—that the nation was best served by playing off one avaricious European power against another. An evasive neutrality was the plainest expression of this conviction after 1939–40. Nor were the authorities in Ankara at all likely to be shifted by such marginal temptations as being allowed to occupy the Dodecanese. What evidence there is suggests that the temptation which really whetted Turkish territorial appetites was Syria, having already succeeded in gaining a significant frontier rectification in that direction during 1938.[10] The chances of 'Free France' under General de Gaulle giving up a scintilla of control over its slippery Syrian stake, however, was always nil.

Meanwhile, as we noted earlier, the valiant Greek effort which had first held, and then reversed, the Italian incursion in October 1940 underpinned a burst of philhellenic sympathy in London, and nobody gave warmer expression to this feeling than Churchill. This did not mean that His Majesty's government was likely to reward Greece by helping it occupy the Dodecanese. It remained vital to cause no offence to the Turks. But it did mean that for a while Hellenic aspirations

---

[8] Minutes of Aleppo Conference, 19 Mar. 1939, WO106/2049.

[9] When the US Ambassador raised the subject of Turkey with the dictator Ionnis Metaxas in Aug. 1940, the latter 'spoke of [Turkish] sympathy for Greece ... and stated that should Bulgaria join Italy in a war on Greece, Turkey will attack her'. King Boris III's commitment to Bulgarian neutrality through the autumn of 1940 explains why Turkey was not drawn in at such a vital point. See John O. Iatrides (ed.), *Ambassador MacVeagh Reports: Greece, 1933–1947* (Princeton, 1980), 219.

[10] Frank Weber, *The Evasive Neutral: Germany, Britain and the Quest for a Turkish Alliance in the Second World War* (Columbia, Mo., 1979), 65.

assumed a heightened profile in British assessments. Insofar as strategists in London gave thought to occupying the Dodecanese, the inclination was to capture them piecemeal in a 'nibbling policy'. But after the debacle of the Greek campaign during April 1941, Britain was in no position to occupy anywhere in the Aegean. Putative redistribution of the Dodecanese was a source of potential embarrassment, since on the one hand the British did not wish to rub Greek faces in the mire of defeat, and yet means had to be found to keep Turkey from converting its Treaty of Friendship with Germany (May 1941) into active alliance. The British attempt in the autumn of 1941 to steer the Greek government in exile, now relocated to Cairo, and Turkey towards bilateral talks on the Dodecanese—allied to ideas in the Foreign Office of an 'autonomous regime under Greek-Turkish protection'[11]—was a classic instance of how the British sometimes sought to 'square the circle' of their own clashing priorities, but the exercise got nowhere.

All this remained purely speculative so long as military realities remained unchanged. In May 1943, however, British and Allied forces at last extruded the enemy presence completely from North Africa, and on 8 September, Italy surrendered. Whereas the minds of most of his high-level colleagues, including the Americans, started to concentrate on an Allied re-entry into Europe, Churchill exhibited a *heightened* propensity to direct his attention towards the eastern Mediterranean. He looked for some new toehold, and the Dodecanese offered the most obvious possibility. On the very day of Italy's surrender, a British officer was parachuted into Rhodes in the hope of persuading the Italian garrison to round up the smaller German forces; and when instead the latter imposed their own control, the British commander-in-chief, Middle East Forces, General Maitland Wilson, dispersed 4,000 British troops through the archipelago and the Greek island of Samos. For Churchill, this rapidly developing engagement became an obsession. 'Winston was in good form,' Harold Macmillan, himself back briefly from the Mediterranean, remarked of a meeting, 'but he would not talk about any of my problems. He was only interested... in Cos, Leros, Rhodes and the other islands of the Dodecanese.'[12]

For the first time decision makers in London found themselves having to contemplate hard practical choices as a prospective need to establish British military administrations in the area loomed. Implications about the long-term future could not be avoided. As the head of the Foreign Office, Sir Alexander Cadogan, commented on 24 September 1943, a distinction had perforce to be made between liberated Greek islands, like Samos, whose return to Hellenic sovereignty could not be in doubt, and the Dodecanese, whose post-war status remained undecided.[13] Cadogan was keenly aware that, in using Italian troops to re-establish order under

---

[11] Lord Halifax to Knatchbull-Hugesson, 4 Oct. 1941, FO371/33233.

[12] Harold Macmillan, *War Diaries: The Mediterranean, 1943–1945* (London, 1984), 250. As British minister resident in the Mediterranean, Macmillan came to be deeply involved in Greek affairs.

[13] Sir Alexander Cadogan to Sir Frederick Bovenden (War Office), 26 Sept. 1943, WO32/12270.

Allied authority, intense Greek resentments were likely to be stirred, and he felt that the case for giving Greece at least a share in an incipient occupation of the Dodecanese was strong. In registering this view, however, Cadogan was conscious that any consideration of Greek claims might all too easily be swept aside by Churchill's determination to persuade the Turks to co-operate with Britain in shaping a new post-war regional dispensation. 'Can we offer them Rhodes?' Churchill had indeed mused some time earlier in discussing the prize of Turkish co-operation, and in what followed the British premier's eagerness to gain control over the Dodecanese as a future bargaining chip with Ankara, and thereby pre-empt any German-Italian surrender directly to the Turks, was a critical factor.[14]

The British attempt to break into the Dodecanese in the autumn of 1943, however, proved, in the words of the only English war correspondent on the spot, 'a disaster as big as Dieppe'.[15] Far from retreating from the scene, the Germans set themselves to retake the strategically important island of Leros and repel any attack on Rhodes, should Churchill succeed in his frantic attempt to persuade the Americans to provide the necessary air cover.[16] The issues posed went right to the heart of Allied dilemmas. For the Chief of the Imperial General Staff, General Sir Alan Brooke, it marked a high point of his acute frustration with Churchill's war leadership. He groaned:

I can control him no longer. He has worked himself into a frenzy of excitement about the Rhodes attack, had magnified its importance so that he can no longer see anything else, and has set his heart on capturing this one island even at the expense of endangering his relations with the President and the Americans on the future of the Italian campaign.[17]

If Brooke could not control Churchill, the Allied Supreme Commander in the Mediterranean, General Eisenhower, was better placed to do so. 'We must... choose between Rhodes and Rome,' Eisenhower laid down at a meeting of top-level commanders in Tunis. 'To us it is clear that we must concentrate on the Italian campaign.'[18] Any prospect of an attack on Rhodes dissipated. What followed was in many ways the worst of all worlds. The British did not gain any air cover, either from the Americans or the Turks, and yet Churchill insisted that 'Operation Accolade' to save Leros went ahead. When the tide of the fighting turned in the wrong direction, he exhorted the British forces on the spot to cling on as long as possible—just as he had once so catastrophically done over Singapore. But on

[14] Martin Gilbert, *Road to Victory: Winston S. Churchill, 1941–45* (London, 1986), 373. One historian has found a root cause of today's continuing Graeco-Turkish tensions in the Aegean in the uncertainties created by wartime British policy. See Alexis Alexandris, 'Turkish Policy towards Greece during the Second World War and its Impact on Greek-Turkish Détente', *Balkan Studies*, 23-1 (1982), 185–7.

[15] Quoted in Dear (ed.), *The Oxford Companion to the Second World War*, 308. For a full treatment of the campaign see Jeffrey Holland, *The Aegean Mission: Allied Operations in the Dodecanese, 1943* (London, 1988).

[16] Leros had been decribed in 1940 as an 'eastern Mediterranean Malta'. See Royal Institute of International Affairs, 'The Italian Colonial Empire', 57.　　　[17] Gilbert, *Road to Victory*, 521.

[18] Ibid. 526.

12 November, the British garrison was overwhelmed following a German landing. 'Leros lost last night,' Cadogan agonized, 'First German success for more than a year.'[19] What remained of the British expedition was now rapidly withdrawn, except for the little island of Castellorizo.[20] Losses were high: 4,800 men and six destroyers sunk, several of which belonged to the Greek Navy.

From that point onwards the significance (however contested) of the Dodecanese in Allied strategy sharply declined. As the German Army unexpectedly dug in south of Rome, all attention was directed elsewhere. Yet there was another shift in the higher balance of the war the rippling effects of which were to be felt in the distant Dodecanese: following the relief of Stalingrad, the long counter-offensive of the Russians began. For Turkey, this brought acute anxiety, since as Soviet forces advanced across the Caucasus, Stalin was likely to turn at some point to imposing a penalty for Turkish neutrality. Here lies the key to that Turkish pliability over the Dodecanese issue which marked the following period, since Ankara was not likely to pick a quarrel with Western powers over such a trinket when their help might be required in relation to its own security. When, in the summer of 1944, British forces (including units of the Indian Army's Bhopal Regiment) finally began 'nibbling away' successfully at the Dodecanese, taking one island after another, no Turkish claim to the area surfaced. In March 1945, the Turkish government began to feel the full weight of Russian pressure when Stalin lodged a claim for joint control of the Straits, topped up with the traditional territorial demand for Kars and Ardahan.[21] If such bullying was designed to keep the Turks nervously subdued whilst large-scale issues were decided elsewhere, it certainly succeeded.

Turkey's own belated declaration of war on Germany in the previous February must be understood, then, in this context of protecting itself against retribution for perceived wartime evasions. Yet if this can be appreciated in retrospect, at the time there were fears—especially in Athenian circles—that the Turks were positioning themselves to take whatever slim opportunities might open up for them when international conditions appeared so fragile. On the whole the British did not think that Turkey would seek to pre-empt their own operations in the Aegean by intervening in the Dodecanese,[22] though Turkey's stake in Castellorizo was felt to

---

[19] David Dilks (ed.), *The Diaries of Sir Alexander Cadogan, 1938–45* (London, 1971), 576. For the severe effect on Churchill's spirits of this defeat, see Gilbert, *Road to Victory*, 555–6.

[20] This easternmost island of the Dodecanese tucked up against the Turkish coast had suffered prolonged bombings and a devastating fire. The entire population was subsequently evacuated. In the following period Castellorizo was frequently touted as potential compensation for Turkey when formal cession of the Dodecanese to Greece should take place. For an eyewitness account, see *Dodekanissi Epitheorissi* (Dodecanese Review), 5 (May 1947), 222.

[21] David H. Close, *Greece since 1945: Politics, Economy and Society* (London, 2002), 32.

[22] In fact the Greek Ambassador in Ankara held the same opinion, telling his superiors that the Turks were totally preoccupied with their own national security, and that there were no Turkish troop movements in relation to the Dodecanese, 'except … small units which the competent British authorities have asked for in order to guard more effectively the Turkish coastline opposite to islands still in German hands'. Quoted in Lena Divani and Photini Constantinopolou (eds), *The Dodecanese. The Long Road to Union with Greece: Diplomatic Documents from the Historical Archive of the Ministry of Foreign Affairs* (Athens, 1997), 108–9.

be legitimate. Still, it was considered better to be safe than sorry, and when the British Embassy lobbied hard that Ankara should be told plainly that they were 'not in the running' where the Dodecanese were concerned, Anthony Eden agreed to send the necessary communication.[23]

Given the varied experiences traced in this book, it is hardly surprising that there was another suspicion lodged in some Greek minds: that the British, once ensconced in the Dodecanese, would end up keeping it for themselves. Amongst Greek left-wing circles, and also in the American press, it was occasionally mooted that British support (and above all, that of Churchill himself) for the restoration of King George II in Athens would at some point be bargained against the allocation of the Dodecanese and Crete as post-war British bases. After the British liberation of Athens during September 1944 descended the following December into bloody fighting between the republican and royalist right and the communist-dominated EAM (National Workers' Liberation Front) such allegations became inextricably caught up in wider factional and ideological rivalries. Churchill strove to defend the controversial British intervention, stating that 'we take nothing—no territory, nor airfields, nor naval bases'.[24] But as British forces subsequently mopped up the Dodecanesian islands, some officials soon began querying whether Greece would ever be in a position to provide an efficient administration in the archipelago. If the answer to that question should ever appear to be negative, or if the Greek mainland seemed to be slipping inexorably out of British control, then the British premier's self-denying ordinance in the islands might not last long.

Here was the subtext (rather than simply the text) of Anglo-Hellenic relations refracted through the Dodecanese question. Meanwhile there was the more immediate and practical matter for the British of how to acknowledge a Greek stake in the future of the islands, without making an irrevocable promise. One way was to allow Greek troops to participate in the new occupation. Indeed, the Greek Sacred Regiment led by Colonel Christodoulos Tsigantes, under the full control of the British Commander-in-Chief, Middle East Forces, was already playing a part alongside British units,[25] and the presence of Greek soldiers in that capacity gave a special flavour to the delirious welcome which the local population afforded the Allied liberation of Rhodes. 'There were other great and joyful days,' one Rhodian noted of this occasion, 'but 9 May, 1945 was the birthday of all others.'[26] The trouble was that a Greek military presence, under whatever auspices,

[23] Leeper telegram to Eden, 5 Apr. 1945, FO371/48342.

[24] Quoted in Richard Clogg, *Anglo-Greek Attitudes: Studies in History* (London, 2000), 115–16.

[25] The Greek Sacred Regiment, named after a formation active in the Greek War of Liberation in the 1820s, was a 'commando' organization formed out of elements of the Royal Hellenic Army in Egypt during 1942. In addition to participation in covert opertions in the Aegean, it had been used by the British in quelling the rising by the leftist forces of ELAS in Athens during Dec. 1944. For a first hand account see I. K. Manetas, *Iepos Lochos, 1942–1945* (Sacred Regiment, 1942–45) (Athens, 1977).

[26] Apostolos, Bishop of Carpathos and Cassos, *To Chronikon tis Italokratias tis Rodhou* (The Chronicle of Rhodes under Italian Rule) (Athens, 1973), 165–9.

was prone to misinterpretation elsewhere. It was reported in some Allied newspapers as implying an imminent Greek annexation.[27] Churchill cracked down hard. 'This . . . must be stopped,' he minuted urgently. 'There is no question of handing these Islands over to Greece at present, and it is not for us to take such a decision without our Allies.'[28] Very shortly the Greek Sacred Regiment (though not, as we shall see, Colonel Tsigantes) was dispatched back to Egypt, and disbanded. This summary treatment of a force some of whom had fought gallantly alongside British regular and special forces in the Aegean theatre was deeply resented.

If the presence of Greek troops was too sensitive to permit, then there was the possibility of the British government issuing a short statement on the future *intention* to transfer the islands to Greece. Desperate for any means to give legitimacy to the British role in Greek affairs, the Embassy in Athens reiterated how essential such a move was. Eden was in favour, chiefly because it would 'make things so much easier for our occupying forces in the Dodecanese islands'.[29] The Foreign Secretary, like military headquarters in Cairo, was determined to avoid British soldiers becoming embroiled in all the boiling emotions of frustrated *enosis* which had proved so compromising elsewhere. Again, Churchill was the stumbling block. He was adamant that His Majesty's government would not depart from the principle that all territorial adjustments 'should be settled or confirmed as the case may be at the Peace or Armistice Treaty' with Italy that was bound to ensue.[30] No formal statement was made, and so long as this was the case, Greek suspicions were not likely to be assuaged by nods and winks as to the ultimate certainty of Dodecanesian union with the Hellenic kingdom.

Churchill's bar on British complicity in premature territorial adjustments set the critical parameters within which Dodecanesian union subsequently unfolded. As so often, a question of Hellenic nationality became covertly mortgaged to developments elsewhere—developments which were themselves full of pitfalls. In this case, just as the Dodecanesian occupation neared completion, Yugoslav partisan forces had taken over the disputed province of Venezia Giulia, including Trieste. They were strongly backed by the Russians, now entrenched in Austria. Western allies were bent on outlawing such land grabs. The British Ambassador in Athens, Reginald Leeper, might contend that 'other people were taking what they want' whilst opportunity offered, assisted by their Great Power patrons, so that there was no reason why Greece, helped by Britain, should not do the same in the Dodecanese.[31] For Churchill, however, the vital consideration was to abide by the repeated American emphasis on the need to continue to treat the Dodecanese as Italian national territory until such time as a new dispensation was formally agreed. Yet again where Greek aspirations and interests were involved, British

[27] The *Daily Herald*, 14 May 1945, reported Dodecanesian events under the heading 'Ex-Italian Islands Given to Greece'.　　[28] Churchill minute, 13 May 1945, FO371/48342.
[29] John Colville minute, 27 Apr. 1945, ibid.　　[30] Churchill minute, 26 Apr. 1945, ibid.
[31] Leeper telegram to Eden, 9 May 1945, ibid.

policy at the highest level was conducted with more than one eye fixed firmly in other directions.

A more immediate preoccupation was the war-ravaged condition of the islands. Rhodes town was severely bomb damaged. Famine had been a constant threat ever since 1940, and the livestock population was gone completely.[32] An official survey of post-war relief in the islands later summarized the situation:

Both the occupying Germans and the inhabitants were forced to eat dogs, cats and weeds, whilst the death penalty was imposed for stealing wheat or bread ... When the Allied forces arrived they found the German troops seriously undernourished, whilst the condition of the Islanders was considerably worse.[33]

Even before British troops stepped ashore on Rhodes, emergency supplies were organized by the British commander on Symi, Brigadier Peter Acland, with the co-operation of the Red Cross. Yet malnutrition cases were still appearing in Rhodes at the rate of six per day in the early phase of British military administration (BMA), and the situation of the smaller islands was particularly dire. 'There is no work, [and] nothing to sell or buy,' it was reported to London, 'and an air of shiftless indetermination hangs over everybody.'[34] The grim atmosphere did not disappear quickly. Although the British quickly set 1,850 calories per day as a benchmark for each person, the essential supply line from Egypt on which it hinged proved highly erratic. Despite subsequent efforts to revive local animal husbandry (including a new pig population imported from Cyprus), the average calorific intake soon slipped back to around 1,000. One year on the United Nations Relief and Rehabilitation Mission to the Dodecanese was still having to report that they could 'only ensure that the population lives above the starvation level'.[35] The fact that almost everybody in the islands remained hungry in some degree or another must inevitably colour our account.

These straitened circumstances did not mean, however, that the great majority of Dodecanesians were oblivious to the political, as well as merely material, prospects that liberation opened up. 'The Greeks', it was noted in a summary which also highlighted the prevalent unemployment and deprivation, 'are impatient for some sign that the island will become their property.'[36] Such a sign Churchill was prepared to give, since the very vagueness of the gesture did not create undue hostages to fortune. Thus the Regent of Greece, Archbishop

[32] *The Times*, 31 Mar. 1947.

[33] Richard Ford, *UNRRA Assistance to the Dodecanese*, Operational Analysis Papers, No. 15 (London, 1947), 7–8.

[34] Ministry of Information memorandum, 'Long Term Propaganda in the Dodecanese', May 1945, FO930/276.

[35] Ford, *UNRRA Assistance*, 20–1. Given the difficulties, it is not surprising that relations between the BMA and the UNRRA mission were brittle, with the former accusing the latter of importing 'a lot of junk', including fur coats and roller skates. See Patrick Reilly, 'Report on the Dodecanese', June 1946, FO371/58825. The UNRRA mission departed at the end of 1946, by which time the goal of 1,850 calories per day per person had still not been met.

[36] 'Long Term Propaganda in the Dodecanese', FO930/276.

Damaskinos, whom Churchill himself had selected for that role, was not allowed his request to send representatives to all twelve of the islands, but he was permitted to make a one-day visit to Rhodes on 14 May. It proved a highly emotional occasion. The Archbishop arrived on HMS *Averoff* and was greeted by an enthusiastic crowd of 5,000 people waving the Hellenic colours, some Union Jacks, and even a few Stars and Stripes.[37] Although the British had expected the Regent to bring with him no more than a small suite, over 100 disembarked from the warship, including a contingent of Evzone guards.[38] As Damaskinos made his way to the cathedral to participate in a Te Deum, a flight of Royal Air Force planes flew over the town dropping leaflets each inscribed with the Greek flag and the word 'FREEDOM'.

Seeking to convey the 'local colour' of this charged event to people back in Whitehall, and also to deflect the sourness towards expressions of Hellenism which he knew sometimes to exist there, a British diplomat present wrote that

First, there is no gainsaying the depth of the feeling for Union with Greece ... In every village that we passed a Greek flag was flying from the Church steeple and innumerable Greek flags had been painted on the walls of the houses.[39]

Reginald Leeper reinforced this account from Athens by assuring Anthony Eden that the visit of the Regent-Archbishop had been 'truly national in character', with no sign of bitterly conflicting monarchist, republican, or communist allegiances. In doing so the Ambassador was no doubt conscious that such a picture gelled nicely with the 'moderate', non-party, and pro-Western polity which the British were struggling to cultivate on the Hellenic mainland. Damaskinos, for his part, remained highly judicious. He declared his own presence as a 'public affirmation of the strength of desire for Union [with Greece]', thus making it easier for Dodecanesians 'to wait patiently for the final decision of the peace conference' to be achieved.[40] Admittedly, the impressions created on the day were marred by bruised feelings over the looming disbandment of the Greek Sacred Regiment, whose banner was presented by Colonel Tsigantes to the Archbishop. The crowd which witnessed the latter's evening departure had shrunk somewhat, a fact explained in the official British account by the undernourishment of the people, who by then had been busy for two days in their preparations, and perhaps also because Damaskinos had not announced immediate *enosis*, as some locals expected.[41] Nevertheless, the reality remained that once Damaskinos had been allowed to touch Dodecanesian soil in this manner, there could be no easy going back on the implication of union with Greece in the foreseeable future.

---

[37] There were many hundreds of Dodecanesians who had relatives in the United States, or claimed American nationality for themselves.

[38] 'Visit to Rhodes by the Regent of Greece', 14 May 1945, WO106/3260.

[39] Harold Caccia to Sir Orme Sargent, 19 May 1945, FO371/48342. The Greek colours had to be painted on houses because in the circumstances available fabric was being used for clothes, not flags.   [40] Leeper telegram to Eden, 19 May 1945, CAB 121/574.

[41] 'Visit to Rhodes by the Regent of Greece', 14 May 1945, WO106/3260.

For the moment, however, the BMA had to be set properly into motion. There was a strong apprehension that what was inevitably a very improvised machine— one which came under the aegis of the civil affairs branch, military headquarters in Cairo—should not have its task complicated by any surrounding political furore. With this in mind Greek flags were kept off all official buildings, and, once the euphoria of liberation passed, there were occasional arrests of individuals found by British patrols painting the ubiquitous 'Long Live Greece' on walls.[42] The Greek government's wish to nominate its own officials to BMA departments was firmly rebuffed. Instead there was a rump Greek military liaison mission, headed by Colonel Tsigantes. Even pending a peace conference, certain things nevertheless could be done to meet the grievances of the population, so that a Greek-language education system refused under Italian rule was started up.[43] The BMA's determination to retain control of the appointment of teachers, however, came to be resented, as was the appointment of an Englishman to oversee the initiative.[44] Since propaganda was considered crucial where Greeks were concerned, a Press and Information Office was speedily established, with the writer (and Greek speaker) Lawrence Durrell at its head. Durrell proceeded to edit a Greek-language daily newspaper, *Chronos*, which tapped into popular sentiments. News coverage from Greece covered much of the front page and there was no attempt to fudge the Greek identity of the Dodecanesians.[45] Publications with a more overtly *enosis* line, however, such as a new weekly periodical, *Patris* (Fatherland), were closed down. Not least importantly, a new police force was instituted, trained in Cyprus, and manned to a large extent by Cypriot and Dodecanesian Egyptian NCOs, plus a handful of British officers.[46]

Devoid of political self-interest though it might claim to be, the BMA suffered from inherent weaknesses. Its main practical difficulty was that under the relevant clauses of the Hague Convention of 1907 it had only a very limited right as an occupying authority to amend the existing system of laws and institutions. In present circumstances this meant that the BMA had to keep essentially within the tramlines set by the old Italian set-up. Such limitations could be adjusted, so that in July 1945 Italian judges were replaced by Greeks in civil cases, with Greek as the official language, whilst British military courts dealt with criminal cases.

[42] C. Tsigantes to Greek General Staff, 16 Apr.1946, quoted in Divani and Constantinopolou, *The Dodecanese*, 92.

[43] Significantly, the British found the signs of Italian influence everywhere in the islands, not least in education, so that 'a very great number of Greek children seem unable to read or write Greek'. See 'Long Term Propaganda in the Dodecanese', FO930/276.

[44] The BMA had originally sought to appoint an experienced British education officer from Cyprus, but the latter had turned the job down on the grounds that his appointment could only give credence to allegations, however spurious, that Britain intended to keep the islands. See material in the Cyprus State Archive, SA1/746/1945.

[45] See *O Chronos* (Time), 25 Mar. 1946, and more generally issues of the paper held in Rhodes Municipal Library.

[46] Under Italian rule there had been a flow of Dodecanese migrants to Egypt, who blended with the pro-Venizelist Greek community in Alexandria and Cairo.

Nevertheless, a major BMA staffing problem arose from the dearth of Greek Dodecanesians with the necessary skills, the refusal of the authorities to employ Dodecanesians of Greek nationality, and the resulting appointment of some Italian settlers.[47] This move was much resented. Over time 6,000 Italian settlers and 7,000 prisoners of war were repatriated, and as this evacuation proceeded the acuteness of anti-Italian feeling subsided.[48] By the same token, the apparatus of the *possedimento Egee* became wholly arcane, and the fact that the BMA was responsible for keeping its forms alive could only prejudice its own relations with local Greeks. This was especially the case since few of the latter found employment in the administration. All senior British officials observing affairs closely were therefore unanimous that the sooner the BMA handed over to Greek authority, the better it would be for everybody.

Nor was this assessment controverted in London, where a Labour government had come to office in July 1945 with Clement Attlee as Prime Minister and Ernest Bevin as Foreign Secretary. Getting the 'boys in uniform' home to their families and jobs was one of their top priorities. There seemed no good reason for keeping scarce British manpower in the Dodecanese. An opportunity to liquidate this commitment began to take shape when the 'Big Three' (United States, Great Britain, and the Soviet Union) agreed at Potsdam to press ahead with the conclusion of separate peace treaties with the defeated states in Europe, orchestrated by a Council of Foreign Ministers. Any treaty with Italy clearly had to deal with the complex question of that country's overseas possessions. Although in the hierarchy of Greek territorial claims those requiring rectification on the Albanian and Bulgarian borders were the most important, it was soon clear that the latter met with little sympathy in the Council of Foreign Ministers. Unwillingness—or inability—to assist Greece on its exposed nothern frontiers was especially unfortunate when Britain was trying to prop up successive ministries essentially of its own making in Athens. When Bevin therefore recommended to Cabinet during September 1945 that the Dodecanese be speedily transferred to Greece, he was not only motivated by pressures of British troop demobilization, but also by the necessity to do as much politically for Greece at the international level as Britain's own constrained leverage permitted.[49]

The chief barrier to such a move, Bevin told ministerial colleagues, lay in a 'process of blackmail' by the Soviets. As early as 1942, indeed, the British had begun to worry yet again about Russia's age-old dream of acquiring unhindered access to the Mediterranean, a potential means being through the acquisition of some lodgement in the Dodecanese.[50] Such concerns became acute during the peace negotiations from the late summer of 1945, as the Soviet Foreign Minister,

    [47] Harold Caccia to Orme Sargent, 19 May 1945, FO371/48342.

    [48] For population changes over this period see K. A. Doxatis (ed.), *Dodekanissos: Meleti tou Ipourghiou Anikodomisis* (The Dodecanese: A Report by the Ministry of Reconstruction) (Athens, 1947), 253–7.   [49] Bevin Memorandum, 'The Dodecanese', 19 Sept. 1945, FO371/48342.

    [50] See material in WO106/3260.

V. I. Molotov, started to send out signals regarding a Russian stake in the various ex-Italian possessions around the Mediterranean shore, including Tripolitania.[51] It seemed all too likely that Molotov would block the resolution of any of the issues regarding Italy until the Soviets got what they wanted. When no progress was made at a meeting of the Council of Foreign Ministers in London, Bevin in frustration told Cabinet on 26 October that the time had come to act unilaterally, not on the matter of sovereignty, which necessarily required Allied agreement, but by transferring the Dodecanese islands from British to Greek military administration. In giving Bevin discretion to go ahead, the Cabinet welcomed a 'valuable political stimulant' which would reinforce the impression of robust British support for Archbishop Damaskinos in Greece, and deflect the recent blow to Greek pride delivered by international recognition of the Albanian government led by the partisan general Enver Hoxha.[52]

At first, Bevin held back in the hope that the Soviets might soon prove more accommodating, and allow a move directly to Greek annexation. Yet even when this failed to occur, he did not exploit the discretion he had been given. The reason was that during Attlee's current visit to Washington, the United States Secretary of State, William Byrnes, injected into their conversation the danger of any rash decision about the Dodecanese. Greek elections were due some time in the New Year, and if an 'unreliable' government emerged in Greece, Byrnes argued, there was a real prospect that it might grant Russia strategic facilities in the islands. He told Attlee

that if the Russians get into the Dodecanese either directly or by securing control of the Greek government, then the the whole British position in the Mediterranean would be jeopardized and the fight which had been put up against the Russian advance into Tripolitania would have been of no avail.[53]

For Attlee, this can only have been somewhat wryly received, given that American policy over Palestine at that very time was itself jeopardizing British interests in the region. But it was a warning signal not to make a move over the Dodecanese that could earn his government a black mark with the Americans. Although Bevin still raised the issue at the Council of Foreign Ministers in Moscow during December, Stalin repeated the standard Soviet line that no transfer of the islands should take place before a full peace treaty was concluded. Boxed in on all sides, it was clear at the British Foreign Office that 'no hope could be held out to Greece'.[54] Here were the traces of a familiar pattern in which the British government seemingly made up its mind to move in the direction of *enosis*, only when it

[51] The British were particularly exercised about Tripolitania because from that position the Russians could further pressurize the British base in Egypt. See Wm. Roger Louis, *The British Empire in the Middle East, 1945–51: Arab Nationalism, the United States and Postwar Imperialism* (Oxford, 1984), 29, 270.   [52] CP (45) 182, Cabinet Conclusions, 30 Oct. 1945, CAB121/574.
[53] Halifax (Washington Embassy) to Bevin, 14 Nov. 1945, FO371/48342.
[54] D. S. Laskey, 2 Feb. 1946 FO371/58825.

came to the vital moment to backtrack in the face of the destabilization of which it might prove to be the harbinger.

In the following few months, the focus on Greek affairs centred unremittingly on the first post-war elections. These were boycotted by EAM, and the voting at the end of March 1946 did not as a consequence reflect their strength in the country, especially in rural districts. A populist-royalist government led by Constantine Tsaldaris emerged victorious, and although the British—like most outsiders—had little respect for the old pre-war political class which Tsaldaris represented, they had little choice but to continue to provide financial and military assistance. Immediately the hounding of the left intensified, and by May communist bands were taking to the hills. The number of communist fighters was to grow thereafter, reaching a peak of around 26,000 in March 1948. One of the unique aspects of Dodecanesian union in the history of Greek expansion was that it was to occur during a war *between* Greeks (one, indeed, that did not end effectively till the close of 1949), rather than a war against an external foe.

Although the future of the Dodecanese paled in comparative significance with mainland events, that matter was bound to be affected by the larger flux—though in ways that were mostly indirect, and as such obscure both to contemporaries and historians. Most importantly, the suddenness with which fighting inside Greece had been renewed faced Stalin with an extremely awkward decision: whether to support the Greek communists, at the risk of incurring Western responses that might impede Soviet goals in other places, or to leave them to their own devices. He did the latter. Stalin, in the famous 'percentages' agreement with Churchill in October 1944, had already accepted that Greece was 90 per cent British—that is, it lay fairly and squarely in the British sphere of influence in the Balkans and eastern Mediterranean.[55] By the spring of 1946, however, Stalin's eye was undoubtedly fixed on American, not British, reactions—and American interest in Greece was escalating. Stalin's wish to send a discreet signal that Russia was not going to meddle in Greek troubles helps explain why right at the end of April the Soviet delegation to the Council of Foreign Ministers at the Palais de Luxembourg in Paris moved significantly towards acceptance of a transfer of the Dodecanese to Greece, though on conditions that as yet remained unspecified, but in which demilitarization began to feature.[56]

When the Foreign Ministers renewed their discussion in Paris during May, no further progress, however, was made. The Soviets remained impervious to Bevin's repeated pleas that, since the Dodecanese had not been a formal Italian colony like Libya, its status could be resolved entirely separately. But after a further delay things unexpectedly came to a head on 28 June. As soon as Secretary of State Byrnes raised the topic afresh in an exchange with Molotov, the latter was quick to

---

[55] Holland, *Pursuit of Greatness*, 191.
[56] See record of 4th meeting of the Council of Foreign Ministers, Paris, 29 Apr. 1946. FO371/58825.

convey the news that the Soviet Union withdrew its objection to the draft Article 12 of the Italian Peace Treaty. This Article stated: 'Italy hereby cedes to Greece in full sovereignty the Dodecanese Islands. These Islands shall be and shall remain demilitarized'.[57] The British embarrassment at failing for so long to secure a peacetime trophy for a country clearly under its own charge was reflected in the manner in which they sought to extract profit from this breakthrough. The Greek Foreign Minister was immediately told the good news through the United Kingdom delegation, but under Bevin's instruction he was *not* informed 'that it was Mr. Byrnes who had raised the [Dodecanese] question' with Molotov.[58] Here was a telling psychological insight into the British sense of failing power, in small matters as in large, and the instinctive desire to conceal it—especially from satellites such as Greece, amongst whom a need for alternative patrons was already becoming tangible.

The announcement in Parliament by the Greek Prime Minister of this removal of Soviet objections was warmly greeted, though not without some disappointment that the country's other territorial claims had so far proved unrequited, whilst several deputies 'expressed the hope that Britain would soon take a similar decision about Cyprus'.[59] The Tsaldaris government meanwhile set up a committee of seven Cabinet ministers to preside over the Greek side of the prospective transfer arrangements. In the wider context of this book, however, it is the Turkish reaction which stands out. The government in Ankara lodged no protest about the decision of the 'Big Four' (now including France) with respect to the Dodecanese, and no claim to any of the islands involved, including even Castellorizo, surfaced. Indeed, the Turkish newspaper *Haber* went so far as to state on 1 July that Turks shared in the Greek pleasure about developments. Remarking that a matching decision over the Bulgarian frontier was keenly awaited, the editorial went on:

If the award of the Dodecanese to Greece had been discussed twenty-five years ago, a storm would have broken out in Turkey. But today, instead, satisfaction is generated. We feel now that a part of our coasts in the Mediterranean is more secure.[60]

Despite this Turkish amenability, however, any hope that a Greek *annexation* of the islands would follow swiftly was soon disappointed. Bevin firmly told his Greek counterpart in Paris on 2 July that there were 'serious objections' to the formal completion of the transfer before the conclusion of the Italian peace treaty.[61] Clearly such completion remained in hock to those arguments—over Trieste and ex-Italian North Africa, for example—which continued to delay comprehensive agreement. Bevin meanwhile conceded to his Greek counterpart the urgency of instituting the 'necessary skeleton' for a transfer of responsibility

---

57 United Kingdom delegation telegram to Foreign Office, 28 June 1946, FO371/ 58826.
58 Ibid.   59 Norton to Bevin, 1 July 1946, ibid.
60 Quoted in Divani and Constantinopolou, *The Dodecanese*, 110.
61 United Kingdom Delegation to Foreign Office, 2 July 1946, FO371/58826.

into Greek hands, and—given the civil war in progress—'in order to enable them [the Greek authorities] to watch the internal situation more closely'.[62] Again, just as in the Ionian Islands many years before, the climax of *enosis* overlapped with a crisis of the Greek state itself, generating uncertainties which underpinned a persistent scepticism of the Greek population most closely affected that its hopes were indeed on the cusp of fulfilment.

A conference of civil and military British officials was nonetheless convened in Rhodes on 19 July 1946 to map the complicated tasks to ensure a smooth transfer. Its first decision was that the initial transition should be from British hands to a Greek military administration. On the assumption that the handover would take place in two months, the Greek government was permitted to expand its Military Liaison Committee in the islands with a cadre ready to move into BMA departments. An invited team of experts from Athenian ministries spent August and September in the islands drawing up a plan for future administrative development. Yet this progress thereafter ground to a halt as rumours of imminent departure were swiftly 'followed by counter-rumours to the opposite effect'.[63] The reasons for the blockage were not transparent to British officials most immediately concerned with the Dodecanese, let alone the Dodecanesians themselves. Yet through the later summer and autumn of 1946 the very survival of the regime in Greece became problematical. Although the Soviet Union stood on the sidelines, an open invasion by Yugoslavia and Bulgaria (both of whom were supplying EAM and its hard-core communist equivalent, KKE, across their frontiers) for a while seemed quite possible. A moment when in Whitehall civil servants and ministers were beginning to confront 'what effect the overthrow of the Greek Government would have on British strategic requirements in the eastern Mediterranean' was not one for rushing to yield a long chain of islands in the Aegean.[64]

In such circumstances, relations between the BMA and the Dodecanesian islanders were bound to deteriorate. As we saw, the British had been warmly welcomed as liberators. But they were not meant to stay, and the longer they did, the more the cracks in the situation showed. It was galling to local people that BMA expenditure was increasingly propped up by selling off movable legacies of Italian rule, leading to accusations of racketeering.[65] But there was also a clash of styles. Lawrence Durrell was attuned to a growing irritation amongst his Greek friends with the 'crude and phoney' ways of British officers (a phenomenon which he had anyway observed very closely in wartime Egypt).[66] Yet Durrell perhaps was part

[62] 'Arrangements for the transfer of the Dodecanese', 4 July 1946, ibid.

[63] 'A Note on the Transfer of the Dodecanese from British to Greek Military Administration', Apr. 1947, FO31/67026.   [64] Foreign Office memorandum 10 October 1946 FO800/468.

[65] A salient example being the hotel Albergo delle Rose, the pride and joy of the Rhodian tourist industry, which was stripped bare of carpets, furniture, crockery, and cutlery. Hoyland to Reilly, 21 Jan. 1947, FO371/58832.

[66] Gordon Bowker, *Through the Dark Labyrinth: A Biography of Lawrence Durrell* (London, 1998), 168.

of the problem himself, careering around Rhodes in a commandeered German Army staff car on tours of antiquities and deserted beaches which form a staple part of his *Reflections on a Marine Venus*. The departure of Brigadier Acland—popular not least as an emergency supplier of provisions—from his post as chief administrator in January 1946 had not helped. He was succeeded by Brigadier Gormley, seconded from war duties in Cairo, but whose principal experience was as an official in Kenya colony. Durrell depicts Gormley in his atmospheric portrayal as a blimpish character, and if precise exactitude was never the real point about the writer's evocation of Greek islands, there were indeed traces in the post-war Dodecanese of an instinctive 'Africanization' ingrained in British official culture in the region. Since the BMA itself came under the wing of 'British' Cairo, this was not altogether surprising. Nevertheless, an apprehension amongst local people that expatriate officialdom was settling into a comfortable niche grew over time.[67] It provided a handy argument for dissidents on the left beginning to raise their head gingerly above the parapet.[68]

Differing evaluations as to the potential danger posed by the left in the Dodecanese was one source of tension in the relationship between Colonel Tsigantes at the head of the Greek Military Liaison Committee and Brigadier Gormley. The British generally downplayed the local communist presence. An estimate sent to the Foreign Office by the Embassy in Athens put the figure at 900 individuals, largely made up of anti-British returnees compromised by the recent Greek Army mutiny in Egypt, and local sponge fishermen whose working conditions were often atrocious. Yet the Greek government, whose representative Tsigantes was, could not be so nonchalant. They, not the British, would ultimately have to bear responsibility, and the threat that KKE activists were penetrating other Greek islands was real (the communists, for example, were strongly entrenched on Samos). Athenian ministers therefore wanted elections in the Dodecanese delayed until they were able to control the outcome. Tsigantes opposed the holding of municipal elections in August 1946, and when the BMA insisted that they go ahead with referenda to circumvent the lack of a proper legal framework, the Greek colonel clashed with Gormley over the procedures for appointing successful candidates as town mayors. Ironically, then, it was the British, more than the Greeks, who first introduced post-war democracy to the Dodecanese—one mayor commented that the regular discussions between the BMA and the previously appointed representatives of the various islands was the first time the Dodecanese had been consulted for hundreds of years.[69] But

---

[67] C. Tsigantes to Greek Army Chief of Staff, 29 May 1946, quoted in Divani and Constantinopolou, *The Deodecanese*, 53.

[68] The left-wing underground organization EMPA (National Front of Pan-Dodecanesian Fighters) made a shadowy appearance in Oct. 1946. Its name belied relatively benign activity such as daubing slogans on walls. See 'Dodecanese: Monthly Report', 15 Nov. 1946, FO371/58832. For a left-wing Dodecanesian account, see Photis Kypriotis, *Dodekanisiaki Ethniki Antistasi sta Chronia tis Italo-Yermano-Anglokratias, 1912–1948* (Dodecanesian National Resistance during the Years of Italian, German, and British Rule) (Rhodes, 1988), 459–63.   [69] BMA Monthly Report, 17 Sept. 1946, WO106/3261.

what 'democracy' meant in Greek-speaking societies during this period was a very slippery thing indeed.

In fact politics in the Dodecanese remained for the most part as yet essentially parochial and personal. The most lively controversy surrounded the Metropolitan of Rhodes, Bishop Apostolos, for his long-standing attempts to form an autocephalous Church (that is, one free from the supervision of the Ecumenical Patriarch), and for his more recent collaboration with the Germans. Colonel Tsigante's association with the campaign against the Metropolitan did not help his dealings with the BMA, since the latter continued to throw a blanket over any divisions likely to complicate its work. Gormley disallowed Durrell from publishing material hostile to the Metropolitan in his official newspaper, *Chronos*, although the civil affairs branch in Cairo at the same time discreetly lobbied the Patriarch in Istanbul to persuade Bishop Apostolos to stand down.[70] As ever, British authorities in the eastern Mediterranean sought to remain publicly aloof from sometimes internecine and always complex Orthodox rivalries, but found themselves ineluctably drawn into the contest.[71] Even in its short life, the BMA was no exception.

The biggest risk, however, was that the British presence might end up being seen as a barrier, rather than a bridgehead, to union with Greece. Patrick Reilly, First Secretary in the British Embassy in Athens, deputed to oversee Dodecanesian affairs, impressed on the Foreign Office in late July that the desire for *enosis* was fast 'becoming a neurosis' amongst the population.[72] As we have seen, this did not have the desired effect at the highest levels of hurrying on the actual transfer into Greek hands. But at a lower level—in London, Athens, Cairo, and Rhodes— British officials conscientiously continued to work on preparations for the BMA's future liquidation. A Greek government delegation was welcomed to Rhodes in August 1946 to refine these further.[73] British military officials sought 'the most lenient interpretation' of the stipulated demilitarization,[74] especially once the Ukrainian delegation to the resumed peace conference demanded that this be 'complete', conjuring up disturbing images of widespread demolition. Finally, in early December a British delegation went to Athens to clarify the remaining details, after which 'the stage was set as completely as was possible so that the [transfer] ... could begin as soon as higher authority gave the sign to ring up the curtain'.[75] Indeed, by then the bulk of the British garrison in the Dodecanese had already been withdrawn, much to the War Office's relief.

---

[70] See BMA Annual Report, 1946, FO371/67024. For opposing local views of the dispute, see Apostolos, *To Chronikon*, 189 and Bishop of Rhodes, *Apomnimonevmata ... 1912–1947* (Memoirs, 1912–47) (Athens, 1947), 67–9.

[71] An analogy in the context of this book is the battle over the archiepiscopal vacancy in Cyprus after 1900. See above, 173.   [72] D. P. Reilly minute, 26 July 1946, FO371/58828.

[73] They included technical experts whose report, compiled in co-operation with the BMA, formed the basis for future development in the island.

[74] 'Chiefs of Staffs Commmittee. Demilitarisation of the Dodecanese', 30 July 1946, FO371/58828.

[75] 'A Note on the Transfer of the Dodecanese Islands from British to Greek Military Administration', FO371/670.

Yet *still* no sign came to ring up the official British curtain in the Dodecanese. The Greeks were now chafing at the bit both in Athens and in the islands. When the acting Greek premier, seeking to deflect attention from rumours that Greece's hopes of a border adjustment with Bulgaria were about to be scotched, publicly stated that the British would be out of the archipelago entirely by the end of the month, the new British Ambassador, Sir Charles Norton, told him that there could be no handover of executive authority until explicit instructions were received. Meanwhile in Rhodes one observer noted that 'relations between the BMA and Tsigantes [had] reached breaking point'.[76] The deadlock was understandable on both sides. Gormley's replacement as chief administrator, Stanley Parker, could not induct Greek civil servants into Dodecanesian departments until the transition was properly authorized—but meanwhile Tsigantes had to keep the reins over a cohort of officials bottled up in the confines of the Greek Military Liaison Committee.[77] As always, the reason why a situation which had about it the classic traits of Anglo-Hellenic political comedy could not be brought to a neat conclusion was buried obscurely in the stratosphere of high diplomacy. When Bevin was in Washington at the start of December he received news of the successes of communist bands in Greece and a crisis surrounding the drachma. On the 4th the Foreign Office informed him from home that at Cabinet level 'the whole grounds of our policy towards Greece . . . is [sic] in the melting pot'.[78] Bevin was angry and dismayed that a commitment which went so deep in recent British experience suddenly seemed about to be ditched, but there was little he could do to stop the rot.[79]

In fact the decision on Dodecanesian transfer to Greece, small scale and largely predetermined though it may have been, had become entangled in one of the great crisis points of post-war British strategy. A final go-ahead on the Dodecanese could only come after, not before, the impending British statement on Greece; and that latter statement had itself to be calibrated with the announcement of fundamental decisions on Palestine and India. Meanwhile in early January Bevin reiterated the convenient principle that the Aegean handover must wait till the very final procedures had been exhausted, even though the latter remained 'highly problematical'.[80] Yet however secondary the Dodecanese issue might be, it had its own rhythms, and it was becoming uncertain whether these could be held in check. For one thing, the Athenian authorities, at a time of acute pressure on its security organs, had assembled a force of 400 gendarmes ready to ensure order in the islands.[81] They could not be kept hanging about much longer. Nor was it

---

[76] Eve Durrell to Tom French in McNiven, *Lawrence Durrell*, 318.

[77] Brigadier Gormley had disappeared on sick leave. Parker was promoted from the civil affairs branch, British military headquarters in Cairo.

[78] Minister of State (Foreign Office) to Bevin, 4 Dec. 1946, FO800/468.

[79] Bevin had been the only senior Labour figure in the wartime British coalition government to support Churchill over reintervention in Greece.

[80] D. J. McCarthy, 7 Jan. 1947, FO371/67023.   [81] McCarthy minute, 18 Jan. 1947, ibid.

clear that the BMA, having been gradually drained of expatriate staff over the preceding months, was *capable* of carrying on for anything but a brief period.[82] Indeed, for the first time a state of suspense prevailed in the archipelago itself.[83] Although British officials involved in the planning could not state the case plainly, the frustration they showed reflected the reality that either the process of transfer in the Dodecanese went forward, or it risked falling off the rails in some unforeseeable way.

During the course of February, however, the blockages were progressively removed. On 10 February, the Italian peace treaty was at last signed, including its provision for Dodecanese cession.[84] What followed had much more more radical implications in, and indeed well beyond, the eastern Mediterranean. On 15 February, it was announced in Parliament that Britain would be submitting its dilemmas in the Palestine Mandate to the United Nations; on 20 February came a historic declaration that Britain would be leaving India; and on 21 February, the British Ambassador in Washington informed the Under-Secretary of State at the State Department, Dean Acheson, that Britain could no longer provide the substantial aid required to ensure the survival of the democratically elected government in Greece. When a few days later this latter news was communicated to the Westminster Parliament, it was—following emergency Notes exchanged between London and Washington—coupled with an assurance that the United States would fill the gap (though the British police mission to Greece was not fully withdrawn till 1950). The policy which later became famous as the Truman Doctrine was enunciated by the President, with specific reference to both Greece and Turkey, in the United States Congress on 12 March.[85] In the lee of these critical world events, the relevant British authorities during the last week of February at last received the signal to 'bring down the curtain' on British military administration in the Dodecanese.

With the final plans for implementation in place, the British Embassy in Athens was therefore able to inform the government in Athens that transfer to Greek military administration would take place on 31 March.[86] It had previously been

---

[82] McCarthy minute, 18 Jan. 1947, Ibid.   [83] H. Hoyland to Reilly, 10 Jan. 1947, ibid.

[84] For its wording, see Wagstaff (ed.), *Greece* Document 48. Continuing tensions between Greece and Turkey in the Aegean stem from a lack of precision in the treaty's original wording with regard to the area that was to be ceded to Greece. Although the fourteen bigger islands were listed in Feb. 1947, no map was attached to the treaty clarifying the situation with regard to adjacent islets. The Greek government on the day of the treaty's signature stated in its observations that the islets mentioned in the text were those which had been under Italian sovereignty when Italy entered the war, and which had, in fact, been fully listed in the Treaty of Lausanne when Turkey had ceded the Dodecanese to Italy in 1923. This has not precluded Graeco-Turkish arguments thereafter.

[85] President Truman in his speech gave a clear warning to the Soviet Union that in future the United States 'would support free people who are resisting subjugation by armed minorities or by outside pressure'.

[86] It should be noted that Greek military administration was to remain in theory responsible not to Athens, but to the British Commander-in-Chief, Middle East Land Forces in Cairo. Thus the system of Allied oversight put into place at the Italian surrender necessarily continued until the fact of sovereignty was itself altered. Practice, of course, was something else.

axiomatic that a full month was required for 'understudies' patiently waiting in the Greek Military Liaison Committee to slot into their positions in the Dodecanesian bureaucracy. Now it was decided that it could be done more quickly. In fact the meticulously planned arrangements went well until Colonel Tsigantes, who, despite previous frictions, the British were quite happy to see take over as chief administrator, was suddenly dismissed on 28 March. He was replaced by a Greek admiral, Pericles Ionnides. As a staunch Venizelist republican, Tsigantes had long been the target of royalist critics in Athens, and their move against him on the very eve of transfer was finely calculated. Behind the motive of mere faction, however, was another recurrent theme: the desire to associate the Hellenic crown with expansions of the Greek state, just as the young King George I had toured the Ionian Islands in June 1864. Here there was a difficulty in that any ceremonial visit by the monarch to the Dodecanese had to await the final induction of Greek sovereignty.[87] Meanwhile it at least sufficed to replace Tsigantes with Ionnides, whose wife's blood relationship to the Greek dynasty through the Russian line afforded him the nickname in Athens of 'Grand Duke'.

There were faint echoes of the long-distant British departure from Corfu in other ways, too: a grinding of financial screws and the necessary implementation of demilitarization. Although the original plans for transfer had emphasized the need to hand the islands over as 'a going concern',[88] when it came to the crunch other temptations kicked in. One was for the remnant of British forces to take away with them whatever fragments of the BMA infrastructure they could. Even more notable was the desire of the British Treasury to extract from Greece the full 'occupation costs' incurred in the Dodecanese since May 1945. Perhaps the latter is less remarkable when it is remembered that Britain was shortly to be rocked by the most dramatic sterling crisis in its history, only to be saved—like Greece—by American assistance.[89] Nevertheless, as Patrick Reilly warned an old friend in the Foreign Office, the effect of any such meanness would be 'to remove what is left of the gingerbread for the Greeks' in receiving their new acquisition.[90] A compromise emerged in which the Greek contribution to signing off the BMA accounts was purely notional.[91] As for demilitarization, the pedestrian task of scrapping machine-gun emplacements and anti-aircraft facilities—if only as a symbolic reassurance for Turkey—was spread out over the final months of 1946, so that little was left to do at the end. The residents of Rhodes in 1947, unlike those of Corfu town in 1864, were saved at the climax from the unseemly spectacle of British Army engineers dynamiting parts of the historic fabric as they prepared to leave.

[87] Norton to Bevin, 12 Mar. 1947, FO371/67024.
[88] Director of Civil Affairs (GHQ, Cairo) to the War Office, July 1946, FO371/58828.
[89] This was the convertibility crisis of Sept. 1947.
[90] Reilly to Sir John Colville, 5 Feb. 1947, FO371/67023. As Churchill's wartime private secretary, Colville had considerable prestige, and in writing to him on the matter Reilly was doubtless seeking a way of outflanking the Treasury.   [91] For details, see material in F371/67024.

On 31 March 1947 the British Ambassador and Greek premier were able to initial the formal documents authorizing transfer, whilst in Rhodes the outgoing chief administrator and Admiral Ionnides presided over a brief ceremony conducted amidst the mock-medievalism of the old Italian government buildings.[92] Similar formalities took place in the other islands of the archipelago, and British and Greek military officers bade mutual and good-natured farewells. After all, whatever the uncertainties which had dogged Dodecanesian *enosis*, deep divisions had not fundamentally affected Anglo-Greek relations, nor was union in this case the climax of a bitter internal struggle. The final monthly report of the BMA was able to state that throughout 'there was complete harmony; not a single "incident" of any sort took place'.[93] Whilst the Greek population welcomed union with profound satisfaction, politics was not, after all, the only major subject of concern in the public sphere; the recent failure of the monthly shipment of civilian rations to arrive from Egypt was a source of immediate anxiety, especially in the less fertile islands.[94] When Admiral Ionnides stepped from his shiny new limousine, imported to afford some glamour to his post, in Rhodes town a few days after the transition ceremony, he was greeted by a waiting crowd with shouts of 'Freedom and jobs, Freedom and bread'. His reply, allegedly was 'just Greece, Greece—not jobs and bread'.[95] Greece, at least, had arrived.

It was nearly one year, in fact, before Greek military administration itself gave way to the complete integration of the Dodecanese into the Hellenic state. This interregnum in part arose from the sudden death of George II on 1 April 1947.[96] At the beginning of March 1948, however, George's successor Paul I, his consort Queen Frederika, and two of their children, Crown Prince Constantine and Princess Sophia, were escorted to Rhodes on a Greek cruiser to take their part in the occasion.[97] American and British destroyers also brought official representatives of their respective countries. What—in the ritual comings and goings associated with seminal days in the growth of Greek statehood—had once involved the presence of a veritable panoply of protecting powers, including the French, German,

[92] For a Greek view of events on each island, including Admiral Ionnides' address to the people of the Dodecanese, see *Dodecanisi Epitheorisis* (Dodecanese Review), 5 (Mar. 1947). For coverage in the British press see 'Today's Transfer of the Dodecanese: A British Task Ended', *The Times*, 31 Mar. 1947.

[93] Monthly Political Report, BMA, Mar. 1947, FO371/67026. The same report stated that the president of the Turkish Community and the Mufti called on the chief administrator three days before handover 'to thank him for the B.M.A.'s treatment of the Turks and to ask that a good word for the Turkish community should be said to Admiral Ionnides. Asked their views about the future, the Turkish spokesman said they did not fear persecution and discrimination; the good relations between the Turkish and Greek Governments, and the fact that both were in the same defensive position towards slav expansionism, should be a guarantee in that connection.' There were then 8,550 Turks remaining on Rhodes and Cos.

[94] Ibid. The islands most at risk were Leros, Symi, Castellorizo, and Casos.

[95] Kypriotis, *Dodekanisiaki Ethniki Antistasi*, 461.

[96] The King's sudden and unexpected death occurred only eight months after he had returned to Greece following a plebiscite on the restoration of monarchy.

[97] See the report in *The Times*, 8 Mar. 1948. The 5-year-old Princess Irene was left at home. Princess Sophia later became Queen of Spain.

Austrian, Italian, and Russian navies, was now down to the sober Anglo-American couple. This symbolized the disappearance of a traditional European (or 'Great Power') hegemony in the eastern Mediterranean which, if only through dynastic sympathy, had for so long provided the Greek throne itself with a layer of protection.

Largely isolated from the upheavals then afflicting so many of their compatriots on the mainland, Dodecanesians did, in fact, shortly acquire more bread and jobs to go with the satisfactory fulfilment of *enosis*. When Sir Charles Norton visited Rhodes in November 1949 he reported on progress since the British departure twenty months before. He told Bevin:

> The Greek Administration has made a good start. What it lacks in resources is made up in the goodwill of the inhabitants. Greek methods are different from Italian and the 'colonial splendour' of Rhodes may not be...maintained...[but] given a continuing effort economic conditions in the Dodecanese may be appreciably improved.[98]

In providing Whitehall with this positive if condescending evaluation of Greek rule in a territory bequeathed under the auspices of Great Britain, the British Embassy in Athens was not blind to one very logical deduction: that what had proved good for the Dodecanese, might also be good for Cyprus. The parallel had, in fact, already been sympathetically noted by at least one senior figure in the British Foreign Office.[99] Greek Cypriot protagonists of *enosis* were equally beginning to utilize the argument that if Britain could so happily yield one lot of Hellenic islands to Greece, it could do the same for their own.[100] Something of the Anglo-Greek comradeship of the recent war years, for all its ups and downs, still survived to make this sound deceptively straight forward. Wandering around Rhodes town in the years immediately after 1947, a new generation of British tourists would have come across seemingly familiar street names: a Churchill Street, and other streets named after such fading BMA figures as Acland, Gormley, and the old British Army garrison commander, General Paget. By 1956 these thoroughfares boasted new Greek names associated, one way or another, with a struggle in Cyprus which pitted Britons and Greeks more directly against each other than in any of the situations with which we have so far been concerned. Our next chapter will deal with that much grimmer experience.

Before doing so, however, we should reflect on the essential paradox of the unification of the Dodecanese with Greece: that a group of islands where the aspiration to *enosis*, whilst powerfully felt once the pressure of Italian rule lifted, was relatively unformed and lacking in political organization, should have come to fruition so *relatively* smoothly. A rather different outcome was by no means inconceivable. Had Turkey not stuck to its neutralist course after 1939–40—had Churchill

---

[98] 'Report of a Visit to Rhodes', 4 Nov. 1949, FO371/78464.

[99] Louis, *British Empire*, 208–9.

[100] In fact a self-styled Greek Cypriot 'representative' visited Rhodes at the time of the hand over in Mar. 1947, and at one municipal celebration had been presented by the mayor with a Greek flag. See Athens to Foreign Office, 7 May 1947, FO371/67027.

succeeded at his meeting with Ismet Inönü at Adana during January 1943 in his aim of 'fitting them [the Turks] up...with arms and...trust to the march of events to bring them in at the climax of the Mediterranean campaign'—then the future of the Dodecanese might well have been compromised in the territorial bartering bound to follow.[101] But already by the time of the Adana conference the Turks were overwhelmingly fearful of the Soviet Union, and crucially that anxiety did not abate for the rest of the decade. Thus, a barrier to Greek unification in an adjacent area, which had sometimes been so formidable in other places, was here disabled for the duration.

Meanwhile, the convergence of the growing fragility of British military administration after May 1945, combined with a much wider crisis in Britain's external engagements by the end of 1946, helped create a window of opportunity for the Dodecanese to fall under *de facto* Greek authority. Yet it was perhaps as well that the preparations were fully ready for the rapid implementation of transfer in March 1947. Through the ensuing summer the civil war in Greece took a turn for the worse. That October, indeed, Norton warned Bevin that unless American aid was stepped up 'a Communist regime in this country by Christmas, 1948 is a racing certainty'.[102] Had the Dodecanese question not *already* been effectively foreclosed, those 'second thoughts' to which the process of *enosis* was, as we have charted in earlier chapters, always intensely vulnerable might have intervened once more. We have seen that the accidents of timing and context invariably shaped the outcomes of the island struggles covered by this book. In these respects the Greeks of the Dodecanese, whatever their wartime sufferings, had ultimately proved fortunate. Whether their Cypriot brethren could be as lucky was about to be tested.

---

[101] For the Anglo-Turkish conference at Adana, see Gilbert, *Road to Victory*, 316–27. On leaving Turkey, Churchill made his second and last visit to Cyprus en route to Cairo, staying overnight at Government House in Nicosia.   [102] G. W. Wallinger minute, 24 Oct. 1947, FO371/67084.

9

Mastery and Despair: Cyprus, 1931–1960

It seems to me inconceivable that the Cypriots could become vicious like the Egyptians.

(Richard Brooman-White, Conservative MP, 1954)

I have a feeling ... that few people feel a sense of obligation to the Greeks or the Turks in the island.

(Sir Hugh Foot, 26 Apr. 1958)

The 'peculiarity' of Cyprus as a British colonial territory has previously been explored in Chapter 7. That distinctiveness, however, was most powerfully revealed in the trajectory of its eventual decolonization from British sovereignty. The creation, after a bitter late colonial struggle, of an independent island republic in August 1960 eventually marked Cyprus off in Hellenic experience from that of the Ionian Islands, Crete, and, indeed, the Dodecanese archipelago. Equally, it was the legislative and international limitations of Cypriot statehood—or, as we shall see, 'quasi-statehood'—which distinguished that process within the rather different historical category represented by the ending of the British Empire. Considered, then, either as a largely Hellenic society, or as a colonial polity, something funny happened to Cyprus on the way to self-rule. This chapter will attempt to draw together the threads of a uniqueness which made the Cyprus Problem one of the most intractable questions in contemporary international relations.[1]

After October 1931 the island fell into constitutional limbo. Critics of Sir Ronald Storrs's 'liberalism' amongst his own compatriots closed on their wounded prey, and Storrs soon found himself relegated to what he found the highly uncongenial post of Governor of Northern Rhodesia. Although the suspension of the 1882 constitution was intended to be temporary, the practice soon hardened into something more lasting. In mid-1933 consideration was given in London to the

---

[1] For full treatments of the troubled genesis of the republic of Cyprus see François Crouzet, *Le Conflit de Chypre, 1945–59*, 2 vols. (Brussels, 1973); Evanthis Hatzivassiliou, *Britain and the International Status of Cyprus, 1955–59* (Minneapolis, 1997); Robert Holland, *Britain and the Revolt in Cyprus, 1954–59* (Oxford, 1998); Diana Markides, *Cyprus, 1957–63: From Colonial Conflict to Constitutional Crisis. The Key Role of the Municipal Issue* (Minneapolis, 2001); and Stefanidis, *Isle of Discord*.

restoration of the Legislative Council, but this was abandoned when the
Governor, Sir Reginald Stubbs, advised that Cypriots respected strong government but were always ready 'to take advantage of a weak one'.[2] Stubbs' successor,
Sir Herbert Richmond Palmer, refined a system which passed into Greek folklore
as 'the Palmerist Dictatorship', but which a recent historian has given the more
sober but accurate description of 'colonial government by decree'.[3] These laws
limited the holding of public meetings and press freedom, and specially targeted
the Church.[4] Even the ringing of church bells was made subject to regulation, and
after the death of Kyrillos III in November 1933, the election of a new archbishop
was banned. During a decade of widespread depression a tendency to retreat
behind a screen of petty absolutism characterized many British administrations
overseas, but the Cypriot case had a special Mediterranean twist.[5] As an official
in the Colonial Office observed in 1938, 'the [Cyprus] Government is becoming
imbued with the political philosophy of Mussolini, and . . . [is] thoroughly afraid
of criticism in any form'.[6]

Opposition to British rule in Cyprus did not disappear, but it went underground, especially on the left, where stalwarts of the Cyprus Communist Party
focused on organizing strikes among poorer urban workers. This at least afforded
an incipient role in society. On the political right, the absence of a Legislative
Council meant that older divisions between co-operators and abstainers faded;
but, equally, it meant that the right lacked an integrating issue around which to
cohere. The British located enough local collaborators, both Greek and Turkish, to
man an Advisory Council, whilst a policy of 'Cypriotization' of the lower and middle reaches of the administration was introduced, albeit somewhat half-heartedly,
and severely curtailed by fear of diluting control from above. It has been
contended that this juncture—and not those so frequently identified later on—
constituted the critical 'missed opportunity' when the British might have
exploited their advantage by reintroducing a 'moderate' constitution tolerable to
themselves.[7] But the vogue for authoritarianism, for which the perceived Italian
achievement in Rhodes provided inspiration, militated against any such experiment. Consequently in Greek Cypriot society a moral and political vacuum
prevailed, filled only by the Church in its traditional ethnarchic role, embodying
the strong feeling in its surrounding community that the receding prospect
of *enosis* only heightened the necessity to preserve the Hellenic cultural heritage.

[2] Quoted in Hatzivassiliou, *The Cyprus Question*, 40.   [3] Ibid. 39.
    [4] See G. S. Georghallides, 'Church and State in Cyprus, October 1931 to November 1932: "A
Systematic Humiliation of the Autocephalous Church of Cyprus"', *Epeteris* (Nicosia), 19 (1992),
361–448.
    [5] Similar tendencies were to the forefront in British colonial Malta during the 1920s and 1930s.
See Henry Frendo, *Party Politics in a Fortress Colony: The Maltese experience* (Valetta, 1992).
    [6] Quoted in Yiorgos Leventis, *Cyprus: The Struggle for Self-Determination in the 1940s* (Frankfurt,
2002), 157.
    [7] G. S. Georghallides and Diana Markides, 'British Attitudes to Constitution-Making in Post-
1931 Cyprus', *Journal of Modern Greek Studies*, 13-1 (1995), 58–72.

A rearguard action was therefore fought during these years against sporadic British attempts to influence school curricula and to appropriate the power to appoint teachers.[8]

The Second World War after September 1939 had profound effects on conditions in Cyprus, even if it was not the scene of fighting like many other Mediterranean islands. First, it put the *enosis* ideal back into the frame of public consciousness. In the previous decade this had been obscured, though not eradicated, internally by repression, and externally by the manner in which Greece had retreated into the dictatorship of General Metaxas (Metaxas' political testament was one in which any hint of foreign 'adventurism' was explicitly excluded).[9] As we have already noted, Greek success in repelling the subsequent Italian invasion breathed new life into Anglo-Hellenism. When the Greek Prime Minister, Alexander Korizis, requested that, as a token of Anglo-Greek alliance, Cyprus should be ceded by Britain, Anthony Eden considered that the matter might at least be identified as a subject to be taken up once hostilities ended.[10] The issue faded—like much else—with the debacle on the Greek mainland and Crete in the spring of 1941. Nevertheless, a certain residual inclination towards Cypriot *enosis* for a while remained discernible in the Foreign Office. Meanwhile continuing Greek resistance inevitably generated expressions of Hellenic solidarity within Cyprus. The colonial government itself recruited for the Cyprus Regiment under the slogan 'For Greece and Freedom'. Behind the rhetoric of unity Governor Sir Charles Woolley still felt convinced that a new 'trial of strength' between the British and Greek Cypriot nationalists would follow before too long.[11] When a senior Colonial Office official, Sir Cosmo Parkinson, visited the island during 1944, the British authorities felt it necessary to limit his movements—as it often did with visiting dignitaries—to prevent him providing a focus for excessive manifestations of Hellenic unionism.[12]

The 1939–45 war thus sapped the British position in Cyprus, and began to radicalize competition in the Cypriot political marketplace. Even in a strategic backwater it was simply not possible to deny all outlets for political activity in a war predicated on a fight for democracy. Increasingly chivvied from London, the Cyprus government allowed more scope for political parties to operate, and in 1941 communists and centre-left elements combined to form AKEL (Progressive Party for the Working People). From the start AKEL was one of the few political institutions to which both Cypriot Greeks and Turks belonged. Some sort of election could hardly be avoided, and in March 1943 one was permitted at the

---

[8] See Persianis, *Church and State*, 101–9.

[9] For the relationship between the Metaxas dictatorship in Greece and *enosis* ideals see John Koliopoulos, *Greece and the British Connection* (Oxford, 1977), 52.

[10] In rejecting Eden's suggestion, Churchill, recurring to his views enunciated after his visit to Cyprus in 1907, alluded to the 'substantial Moslem population ... who would much resent being handed over to the Greeks'. See C. Svolopoulos, 'Anglo-Hellenic Talks during the Axis Campaign against Greece', *Balkan Studies*, 23-1 (1982).   [11] Quoted in Leventis, *Cyprus*, 72.

[12] Percy Arnold, *Cyprus Challenge: A Colonial Island and its Aspirations* (London, 1956), 45.

municipal level, with AKEL mayors victorious in two principal towns. The liveliness of the contest, and the immediate continuity displayed with previous debates surrounding co-operation with colonial institutions, however, only heightened British reluctance to ease restrictions on political activity any further. So long as the war lasted, there seemed little chance of any wider programme of reform being implemented.

For one thing, suspicion of the Church, far from ebbing, assumed a more intense form. As is often the case, a minor anecdocte may best conjure up the flavour. In 1944 a young journalist, Percy Arnold, was dispatched by the Ministry of Information to liven up the *Cyprus Times* and hopefully break down some of the barriers between the British and the Cypriots. Soon after arrival he sought and obtained an interview with the *locum tenens* as archbishop (the ban on any election to that position still being in place). During their discussion, Bishop Leontios assured Arnold that he wished to co-operate with the colonial administration. 'Back at my desk,' Arnold recalled, having returned from the archbishopric inside the old walled city, 'I realized I had been away little more than an hour, but in that time I had peeped into another world.'[13] In this passing observation was encapsulated the cultural and emotional gulf between 'British' Nicosia, and the heartland of the Cyprus Church, separated as these two spheres were by only a few streets. A few days later Arnold went to see Governor Woolley and, he recalled,

gave him the message I had received from Bishop Leontios that during the war the Church of Cyprus would do nothing to oppose the Government. Sir Charles' only comment was to say a little cynically, 'He said that, did he?'[14]

Whatever the painful experience on which Woolley based his somewhat arch scepticism, embedded in such an enigmatic response was a negation which ultimately defined—on all sides—a still inchoate tragedy.

If old divisions remained, new ones were also in the making. The fragility of the right, its lack of a clear focus, and its vulnerability to allegations of being compromised in regard to colonial authority, meant that sensitivity to any challenge from the left was acute. Governor Woolley identified a dialectic which was significantly to affect events. He reported to the Colonial Office:

The labour movement holds the key to the political situation ... there is a cry for 'political liberties' ... [and] for representative institutions in which labour is confident of ruling the roost ... In reply, somewhat plaintively, the Greek nationalists re-echo the time-honoured cry—'*enosis* or nothing'; for they foresee their eclipse in elected institutions.[15]

War conditions therefore conjured an incipient political dynamic in which effervescence on the left frightened, disoriented, and energized the right in self-protection. Simultaneously, if the right foresaw its eclipse in electoral institutions, so did the British colonial regime. In order to strengthen their own position in an

---

[13] Percy Arnold, *Cyprus Challenge*, 38.
[14] Ibid. 43.   [15] 'Political Situation in Cyprus during November 1942', CO67/314/12.

emerging contest, the British had two logical choices: they could link up with the right in common hostility to the secular progressive left, or join with the left to crush the clerical nationalist right. They did neither, still wedded to the ideal of being 'masters in their own house'. Whereas in some British colonies during the war years there was a real engagement with issues of future political planning, the expatriate administration in Cyprus emerged with its traditional immobility more or less intact.

There remained a scenario, however, in which local obstacles to Cypriot *enosis* might have been swept aside by imperatives essentially external to the island (just as had happened under Ionian conditions during the 1860s). Amidst the British reintervention in Greece after September 1944, Churchill had personally selected Archbishop Damaskinos to serve as Regent of Greece, charged with spanning the acute differences between royalists and old Venizelist republicans. Propping up Damaskinos as the only person capable of holding together a common front against the communists thus became the essence of Britain's new Greek adventure.[16] We saw in the last chapter how this concern led Churchill to authorize a brief but emotional visit by the Archbishop to Rhodes in May 1945. The following September Damaskinos was invited to London, by which time Britain had a Labour government. On the eve of the Archbishop's arrival in London, Sir Orme Sargent, Under-Secretary in the Foreign Office's Southern Department, composing a memorandum dealing with the communist threat in Greece, noted that

The demand for Cyprus is one of the principal lines of attack against our position in Greece. Its cession would deprive them [the communists] of this useful weapon and would strengthen the position of the Regent and other elements favourable to us . . . We shall probably be obliged to disappoint all other Greek claims for territorial gains (apart from the Dodecanese). The acquisition of Cyprus would be a powerful consolation for such disappointments.[17]

During the discussions in London Damaskinos pressed the cession of Cyprus to Greece, and argued that it was better to resolve that issue quickly than wait for it to evolve under unpredictable post-war circumstances.[18] Yet for both the British and the Greeks the real focus of talks was the planned referendum on the return of George II to his throne in Greece, and the matter of Cyprus received fitful attention at best. What consideration it had was swiftly blocked by the manner in which British policy makers began to assess Cyprus policy exclusively in the context of Britain's need to protect its position in the wider Middle East. The chiefs of staff intervened, not for the last time, to assert the strategic indispensability of the

[16] For this remarkable escapade in Churchill's wartime career see Macmillan, *War Diaries*, 614–30. George II had been in exile since 1941. After the debacle in Crete, the Greek monarch sought permission from the British government to take up residence in Cyprus, but was refused as a result of the complications which a Greek royal presence within the island would have presented. He went to London instead.

[17] Orme Sargent memorandum, 'The Future of Cyprus', 5 Sept. 1945, FO371/48344.

[18] For the Regent's visit, see Leventis, *Cyprus*, 124–31.

island, and the Foreign Secretary, Ernest Bevin, was increasingly disposed to take their word as final. This was where any analogy between Ionian cession in 1864 and the fate of Cyprus after 1945—an analogy which Greek Cypriot nationalists were perennially fond of making, along with the current Dodecanesian parallel—broke down; for whereas in the Ionian case the value placed on 'saving Greece' for British interests had been high, by the time the Cyprus issue acquired a new salience a considerable discount prevailed as Greece slid into a brutal civil war.

Although the question of the future of Cyprus had therefore not been resolved as an aspect of post-war Anglo-Greek relations, it might have been so in the lee of two phenomena accentuated by mounting pressures in the metropole: a putative British withdrawal from the Middle East, and a retreat from the burdensome obligations of empire. As pressures built up around his administration, Labour Prime Minister Clement Attlee made a serious bid during 1946 to disengage British forces from much of the Arab hinterland, establishing what he called 'a wide *glacis* of desert and Arabs between ourselves and the Russians'.[19] But although the British did indeed cut themselves loose from a number of burdensome obligations, military and bureaucratic interests in Whitehall blocked any further British evacuation from the Middle East. Similarly, any possibility that the independence of India in August 1947 would open the floodgates to a larger imperial meltdown was closed off. Had decisions in London on these strategic planes gone in another direction, then the micro-context of policy making towards Cyprus (linked as it had always been to Britain's Eastern policies) could not have remained immune. As it was, the Labour government during the second half of the 1940s was increasingly defensive and resistant to any challenge to the status quo. It had taken one great decision—that over India—and was in no mood to take others if they were at all avoidable. It is against this background that the evolution of a constitutional impasse over Cyprus must be assessed.

It was precisely because of an intention to retain sovereign control over Cyprus that the British were keen to reintroduce a degree of local representation and 'responsibility'—a cautious return, that is, to the legislative system which had foundered in 1931. In October 1946 the Colonial Secretary, Arthur Creech-Jones, suggested in Cabinet the holding of a local Consultative Assembly to discuss constitutional development in the island. The following March the Dodecanese islands passed from British to Greek military administration, leaving Cyprus the only large island in the eastern Mediterranean not in Greek hands, a fact not lost on the Cypriots themselves.[20] It was a timely moment for a new governor to replace the stern Sir Charles Woolley. His replacement, Lord Winster, as a

---

[19] Raymond Smith and John Zametica, 'The Cold Warrior: Clement Attlee Reconsidered, 1945–7', *International Affairs*, 61-2 (Spring 1985), 237–52.

[20] When newsreel of the transfer of the Dodecanese to Greek military administration was shown in Nicosia, there was much enthusiasm amongst cinema-goers. See George H. Kelling, *Countdown to Rebellion: British Policy in Cyprus, 1935–55* (New York, 1990), 103.

trade unionist, did not come from the narrowly drawn cadre of his predecessors. Winster's instructions included the possible inauguration of 'a standard medium grade constitution'.[21] This suggested pedestrian limitations, and his tenure got off to a bad start when—with the British withdrawing that very weekend from the Dodecanese—four Greek Cypriot members of the Advisory Council failed to attend the formal dinner on his arrival, and were dismissed from their posts.[22] The two Turkish Cypriot members remained *in situ*.

Lord Winster did have one means of quickly getting relations with the Greeks back on track: the authorization of a proper election for Archbishop. This was an important departure, a sign that the Governor was determined to close the page on 1931. The subsequent elevation of the *locum tenens*, Leontios, marked a further advance by AKEL, building on their successes in municipal elections the previous year. Winster's subsequent invitations to organizations within local society to participate in the Consultative Assembly interacted with Cypriot politics in highly combustible ways. Leontios' sudden death not long after his election served to heighten the effect, since the right set about ensuring the elevation of their own candidate. They succeeded with the election of Archbishop Makarios II (not to be confused with his more famous successor and namesake) who, as Bishop of Kyrenia, had been one of those exiled in 1931, but recently allowed to return. The newly entrenched influence of the once exiled cadre did not bode well for relations between the Cypriot right and the British. But it boded even less well for harmony between left and right, since Makarios II's highly equivocal attitude to the colonial administration was eclipsed by his bitter anti-communism. From the start Makarios II riveted into place a church policy of '*enosis* and only *enosis*' the principal aim of which was to sabotage the emergence of an electoral politics in which the left seemed destined to be clear winners, since only they had a programme and methods with a mass social base.

These cleavages were now defined by the issue of participation in the Governor's consultative exercise.[23] Although there were some Greek Cypriot conservatives who believed that a boycott would dangerously foreclose their future options,[24] church discipline alone ensured that the decision of AKEL to take part was met by a fierce onslaught. These attacks could not prevent the convening of the Assembly on 1 November 1947 with ten Greek Cypriots (all with AKEL connections), seven Turkish Cypriots, and one Maronite under the chairmanship of the Chief Justice of Cyprus, Sir Edward Jackson. Pressure from the right, however, meant that their opponents' ability to negotiate with the British thereafter was very confined, since any hint of 'phoney' arrangements— arrangements, that is, which left the British with a clear monopoly of decision-making and administering powers—was bound to prove deeply compromising.

[21] Quoted in ibid. 78.   [22] *The Times*, 1 Apr. 1947.
[23] Full treatments of the ensuing Consultative Assembly in Cyprus can be found in Rolandos Katsiaounis, *H Diaskepiki, 1946–8* (Nicosia, 2000) and Leventis, *Cyprus*.
[24] Leventis, *Cyprus*, 198.

The recent granting by the British government of a new constitution for Malta provided a convenient measure amongst Cypriots for conceiving an acceptable form of self-rule. The analogy appeared to be especially appropriate since Malta was also an island deemed to be of highly strategical significance; indeed its constitution had been suspended in 1928 for reasons very similar to those which operated in Cyprus three years later. The new Maltese constitution of 1947 provided for a large degree of self-government, with elected politicians in control of functional ministries except for foreign affairs and defence. For both left and right in Cyprus the control of elected representatives over ministerial departments became a 'mercury test' for a workable constitution of their own. What seemed to Cypriots of various persuasions a perfectly sensible Maltese model, however, by no means fitted into British perspectives. Any Maltese inclination towards union with a foreign power—in their case, with Catholic Italy—had disappeared during the Second World War. After 1943 Malta basked in warm British approval as the 'George Cross Island' which had withstood enemy siege so bravely; and whilst the local Roman Church, like the Orthodox Church of Cyprus, was scared of a secular and organized left, in Malta the effect was to soften traditional tensions between the clerical hierarchy and British authority rather than the opposite. As so often, internal Cypriot logic and British colonial assumptions ran along different grooves from those prevailing elsewhere.

From the start of this renewed debate on Cypriot constitutionalism, British officialdom was itself divided. The Colonial Office was not prepared to envisage full self-government, but inclined towards a transitory scheme moving gradually towards Cypriot-controlled ministries. Attlee, ever the instinctive radical on colonial issues, felt that this would only encourage 'irresponsibility' amongst Greek Cypriot politicians—far better to go the whole hog now. But others in Whitehall, now including the Foreign Office, were unsympathetic to any but the most restricted regime of Cypriot participation in the government of a strategically situated 'fortress colony'.[25] During January 1948 the Cabinet accepted an amended version of the Colonial Office proposals, and during the following weeks discussion revolved around whether this scheme needed to be pepped up with elements of an embryonic ministerial system to elicit co-operation from Greek Cypriots. On 7 May 1948, the British government's formal offer was transmitted to the Consultative Assembly, and although it made no clear provision for Cypriot ministers, it did incorporate a Greek Cypriot elected majority in the reconstituted legislature. The latter concession, however, was offset by a clause forbidding any future discussion of *enosis* in the chamber. The latter provision met the need of the Cyprus government not to be pushed back into the slough of despond it had, according to its own received wisdom, so happily escaped in 1931.

[25] For the 'fortress colony' concept in Cypriot context, see Diana Weston Markides, 'Britain's "New Look" Policy for Cyprus and the Harding–Makarios Talks, January 1955–March 1956', *Journal of Imperial and Commonwealth History*, 23-3 (1995), 480.

The clerical ethnarchy lost no time rejecting what had been put forward as 'phoney'. 'The ways are from now on entirely separate,' the right-wing newspaper *Ethnos* declared, stating its strong conviction that the history of Ionian cession was being repeated. '[L]et the faint-hearted progress towards Autonomy and we towards *Enosis*. And we shall see who will reach the finishing line first.'[26] Indeed, Greek Cypriot moderates and leftists could no more afford being left high and dry should union with Greece suddenly arrive than the narrow band of Ionian 'friends' of the Protection in 1863–64. They scrambled to protect themselves, which in the first instance meant walking out of Winster's carefully constructed Assembly. Thereafter AKEL fell into line under the ethnarchy's goading, and urgently revised party strategy. Under contemporary Cypriot conditions, any possibility of a progressive secular politics hinged on the forging of a British–AKEL understanding. Instead, the manner in which the British now turned against AKEL was fundamentally to constrain their own tactical possibilities. The British government's offer was not withdrawn, but it hung in limp suspension, whilst the Governor's advice that momentum should be regained by simply imposing the May 1948 proposals was rejected in Whitehall. Winster resigned the following October, and although in doing so he told the Colonial Secretary that there was no immediate prospect of violence sullying the Cypriot scene, he added darkly that it was 'not out of the question'.[27]

The limitations of the British government's scheme put to the abortive Assembly have not prevented one Greek historian from characterizing it as 'a remarkable constitutional offer'.[28] Its rejection, Evanthis Hatzivassiliou concludes, meant that the future was 'mortgaged in many different ways'.[29] Central to this assessment was the acceptance by Britain of a Greek-elected majority, something which they were not to contemplate again for several years, by which time positions had hardened all round. It is at this juncture that the conception of a 'lost opportunity' has become grafted into conventional understandings of the dilemmas of late colonial Cyprus.[30] All historical wisdom is, of course, *ipso facto* retrospective. The relevant question here surely is: what were the basic forces underpinning decisions which to many came to appear fatally injudicious? The reason must be found in the role of fear: fear of making a false move, of yielding some entrenched tactical position, of allowing an advantage to be grabbed by seemingly inveterate opponents. To strip out the distortion of crippling anxieties is to take from the narrative the motor which drove it forward. Those anxieties gripped the British just as much as they confined the judgements and prejudices of other parties. Most societies in the later 1940s were fearful of what lay ahead—this was why civil wars, cold wars, and acute social tensions were so prevalent. Yet the colonial, ideological, and inter-communal circumstances of Cyprus meant that fear and suspicion played with a rare intensity on the judgements of individuals and groups.

[26] Quoted in Katsiaounis, *H Diaskeptiki*, 328.   [27] Quoted in Leventis, *Cyprus*, 16.
[28] Hatzivassiliou, *The Cyprus Question*, 48.   [29] Ibid.
[30] A classic example is Evangelos Averoff, *Lost Opportunities: The Cyprus Question, 1950–63* (New York, 1986).

Winster's successor in Cyprus, Sir Andrew Wright, was not new to the island, having been a senior official at the time of the burning down of Government House in October 1931—indeed, the shade thrown by that conflagration always retained a curious knack of reconstituting itself over Cypriot affairs. Wright's instructions from London, whilst not ignoring the desirability of restoring a local constitution, were distinctly vague as to how that might be done, and given his views—an American observer rather tartly remarked that he 'looked upon the Cypriots as children who needed a firm hand [and] ... and an occasional spanking'[31]—it was not surprising that the real agenda of his administration was to rebuild the defences of British administration. This involved a closer link with the Turkish Cypriot community, buoyed by the fact that the representatives of the latter had accepted the May 1948 proposals, and thereby reaffirmed their opposition to self-government as an unwelcome precursor to *enosis*. An official committee on Turkish Cypriot affairs was established with a remit to enquire into grievances concerning the administration of the *evkaf* (which looked after religious properties) and the relatively sparse provision for Turkish Cypriot education.

Turkish Cyprus as yet remained, however, on the sidelines of the island's political struggles, manipulated by others rather than an actor in its own right. At the heart of these struggles lay divisions between Greek Cypriot left and right, embittered still further by currents flowing from the civil war raging in Greece. Elements of Khi, the fanatically anti-communist Greek organization led by Colonel George Grivas, had established a toehold in the island.[32] Meanwhile AKEL abandoned its traditional distance from the Communist Party of Greece (KKE) and, after 1948, increasingly sought its cue from the mainland. Against this background, including a bitter and ultimately unsuccessful strike in the rich Cypriot copper mines,[33] AKEL suffered setbacks at the municipal elections of 1949. Desperate to maintain the advantage it had enjoyed in 1946–47, it sought to protect its flank by becoming more national than the nationalists, and in October 1949 the party declared a willingness to join a 'national embassy' to raise the question of *enosis* at the United Nations. Here was the root of an internationalization of the conflict inside the island the effects of which were to prove dangerously unpredictable.[34] What had already come into being was a highly unstable trilateral dynamic in which the clerical right, the secular left, and the colonial British were each engaged on an offensive to gain leverage over the uncertain future.

It was from the belief in Cypriot public life that the main protagonists were fighting for survival that its elemental quality derived. Of none was this more true than the Church. Custom and accident had grafted onto its religious agency a leading socio-political status now under threat. Its hierarchy felt driven to enter the fray

---

[31] Quoted in Holland, *Revolt in Cyprus*, 16.

[32] For the activities of Khi in Cyprus see Kelling, *Countdown to Rebellion*, 85 and Katsiaounis, *H Diaskeptiki*, 328.

[33] The American-owned copper mines at Amiandos were the largest-scale economic enterprise on the island.   [34] Stefanidis, *Isle of Discord*, 5–7.

more decisively than ever to protect its stake. Exclusive control of the *enosis*
demand and the anathematizing of secular constitutionalism under colonial auspices were its principal methods. The Holy Synod therefore trumped AKEL's call
for a 'national assembly' to New York by declaring on 1 December 1949 that a
plebiscite would be held on the question of *enosis*, and when the Governor
responded that the issue of sovereignty was closed, the Archbishop decided to go
ahead unilaterally. Greek Orthodox congregations throughout the island were
called upon to sign a resolution after Sunday mass. Of the votes cast in this way
between 15 and 22 January 1950, 96.5 per cent favoured *enosis*, the Turkish
Cypriot community naturally being sidelined from such an exercise.[35] On the eve
of the event, Governor Wright advised the Colonial Office that the exercise was
proof that Cyprus was not ready for self-government, let alone self-determination,
and asked for repressive powers described by one sceptic in that department as 'far
and away the most extreme demand put forward by any [colonial] territory so far
as my experience...extends'.[36] This was the point at which the reactive cycle of
enosis mobilization on a new mass basis and instinctive coercion by local British
administration threatened to become irreversible.

This cycle was driven by the dialectic between an intensification of the *enosis* ideal
in Greek Cyprus on the one hand, and the consolidation of the British conception of
the island as an irreplaceable asset on the other.[37] Once Britain was evicted from
Palestine in June 1948, and its Suez base increasingly harassed by *fedeyeen* fighters, a
slide rule began to be passed over alternative 'homes' in the region for British forces.
Cyprus did not immediately loom largest in such a beauty contest. Yet there was one
variable at work which steadily told in its favour. For decades British access to key
Middle Eastern bases had hinged on negotiated leases or treaties with foreign countries. Post-war events showed how tenuous such rights were. The fact that Cyprus
was *sovereign* British territory thus underscored its attractions. This factor influenced
the Chiefs of Staff's assessment requested by the Cabinet during early 1950, and
which soon resulted in an unambiguous statement as to the indispensability of
Cyprus as base, not merely a base on Cyprus.[38] Experience in Egypt and Iran during
the next couple of years highlighted the merits of access based on unvarnished own-
ership. By early 1954 the need to clarify a fall-back position from Suez was urgent,
and led to the definition of Cyprus as a 'Commonwealth Fortress' the retention of
which justified whatever costs were involved.[39] The following July the move of the
headquarters of British land and sea forces to the island was confirmed. Although
this headquarters was meant just to have a 'planning' role, it became apparent that
British military chiefs intended to replicate as much of the old Suez set-up as they

[35] There was, however, a very small number of Turkish Cypriot signatures appended to the resolution.
[36] Minute by John Bennett, 21 Jan. 1950, CO537/6228.
[37] An indispensable survey of the strategic factor is Klearchos A. Kyriakides, 'British Cold War
Strategy and the Struggle to Maintain Military Bases in Cyprus, 1951–60' (doctoral dissertation,
University of Cambridge, 1996).
[38] Chiefs of Staff memorandum, 'The Strategic Importance of Retaining Full Sovereignty in
Cyprus', June 1948, CO537/6244.   [39] Holland, *Revolt in Cyprus*, 35.

could, and not even an intervention by Prime Minister Churchill could halt an expensive new enterprise.[40]

One of the unfortunate but acceptable costs of keeping Cyprus as an imperial fortress by early 1954 was presumed to be good relations with Greece. In the later 1940s the old Venizelist principle that the Cyprus question could not be allowed to prejudice the 'traditional framework of Anglo-Hellenic friendship' still held sway in Athens. But that principle was predicated on an assumption of British maritime power in the eastern Mediterranean which was losing credibility fast. During the later phases of the civil war American power (and money) progressively replaced the British in stabilizing Greece on pro-Western lines. One indirect consequence was to afford Cypriot advocates of *enosis* more scope to work on natural Greek feelings. The first real sign of this came in the summer of 1950 when the young and dynamic Bishop of Kitium, Makarios, went on an *enosis* mission to Greece, taking the many leather volumes of the recent church plebiscite with him for pictorial effect. The British Ambassador in Athens reported how the effect of the Bishop's campaign was to 'make all Greeks Cyprus-conscious', adding that the 'daily rubbing-in of Greek expectations, and the identification of every kind of national and local organization ... with these hopes [of *enosis*] is a fact'.[41] In some profound way this 'Cyprus-consciousness' represented just one means by which a society emerging from a savage civil war sought to restore its own values and self-respect.

The latter process was too submerged to be visible to British policy makers. Foremost in the consciousness of Whitehall was instead the 'ingratitude' of the Greeks in demanding Cyprus despite the debt they allegedly owed to Britain for 'saving' them during and after the Second World War. Who owed what to whom was an old tripwire in the Anglo-Hellenic tie, and in this context the problematic became especially marked. Anthony Eden, as British Foreign Secretary after October 1951, felt acutely on this point if only because he had been so closely involved in wartime Greek affairs. In his own way he tried hard to defuse the Cyprus device threatening to explode Anglo-Greek harmony. His method was to declare with unmistakable force that Cyprus was a 'closed question' for Britain. Having tried this on various Greek diplomats who crossed his path, however, he proceeded to do the same with the Greek Prime Minister, and distinguished military hero, Field Marshal Papagos, when visiting Athens during September 1953. In telling Papagos that Cyprus was non-discussable he added gratuitously that 'there was a considerable Greek population in New York, but he did not suppose that the Greek Government was demanding *Enosis* for them'.[42] The Field Marshal

---

[40] The last document handled by Churchill in 10 Downing Street as British Prime Minister concerned the inquiry he had set up to examine what he regarded as the inflated size of the new Cyprus base. See Anthony Montagu-Browne, *Long Sunset: Memoirs of Winston Churchill's Last Private Secretary* (London, 1985), 183.   [41] Norton to A. Rumbold, 16 June 1950, FO371/87720.

[42] Record of Conversation between the Secretary of State and Field-Marshall Papagos, 22 Sept. 1953, FO371/107499.

did not forgive the slight, and the characteristic expressions of Anglo-Hellenism started to dissipate. An exhibition in Athens on British philhellenes and the Greek War of Independence was cancelled. A Rubicon was crossed when, on 23 February 1954, the Greek government announced that it would take the Cyprus issue to the United Nations if a solution was not shortly found. Within a few weeks an inter-departmental meeting of ministers and officials in Whitehall concluded that friendship with Greece was dispensable should the evolution of the Cyprus matter require such a sacrifice.[43] This critical deduction locked in British intransigence over the island, and reverberated through events thereafter.

Meanwhile the Cyprus government's repeated requests to London for new repressive powers from early 1950 onwards had been refused by the Labour government. Governor Wright's expectations that the Conservative ministry elected in October 1951 would prove more responsive were disappointed. The new Colonial Secretary, Oliver Lyttelton, had enough problems elsewhere—the British High Commissioner in Malaya had just been assassinated—and instead warned Wright not to 'drive the disease [of *enosis*] inward by suppressing the symptoms' the growth of which the Governor constantly bemoaned in his dispatches.[44] So long as there remained a residual hope of awakening the sleeping beauty of Cypriot 'moderation' such an injunction carried considerable weight. But the growth of *enosis* feeling in Cyprus associated with Archbishop Makarios III following his elevation from the see of Kitium in November 1950 eroded any such calculation. By the time that Sir Robert Armitage replaced Wright as Governor in January 1954 the premium attached to Greek 'moderates' in British decision making was ebbing fast—as the new Governor later put it, this elusive faction had 'no organization, no party, no funds, no agents, and they will win nothing'.[45] It followed that the way was open to a blunt statement of British intentions with regard to the island, assuaged only by the 'offer' (really designed as a genuflection towards United States opinion) of a new constitution which involved even fewer concessions than in 1948. This offer now excluding a Greek-elected majority in a restored legislature was attached to a statement in the House of Commons on 28 July 1954 in which a junior Colonial Office minister used the word 'never' when discussing the prospect of self-determination in Cyprus.[46] Whilst this infelicity did not bear the load of responsibility for the subsequent breakdown which some later asserted, it did mark the juncture at which the mirror image of British and Greek Cypriot *immoderation* became fixed for contemporary purposes.

The resulting tangles of policy and emotion might have been less fatally entwined had they not been played upon by the contemporary crisis in right-wing Tory politics in Britain. That crisis was above all mediated through Egyptian issues. But in British perspectives Cyprus and Egypt had always been linked one

---

[43] See notes of meeting held by the Minister of State, 29 June 1954, FO371/111848.
[44] Note of meeting at the Colonial Office, 2 Apr. 1952, CO926/12.
[45] Armitage to Thomas Lloyd, 13 Sept. 1954, CO926/500.
[46] *Hansard Parliamentary Debates*, 3rd Series, vol. dxxxi (Commons), 28 July 1954, cols. 504–7.

way or another, and over the first half of the 1950s that linkage assumed very specific forms. The 'Suez Group' of Conservative MPs which after 1952–53 sought to fight a rearguard action against a British military withdrawal from Egypt maintained a supplementary focus on the retention of Cyprus. Eden therefore followed a natural logic in offsetting the risks he continued to run in seeking an agreement with Gamul Abdul Nasser over Suez by ensuring that the dangerous tag of being an 'appeaser' in the Middle East was not validated by Cypriot developments. In this vein the 'never' statement on the future of the island in the British Parliament had been judiciously placed in the wake of Eden's statement that same afternoon on a settlement with Nasser.[47] Through the autumn of 1954, and coming to a head at the beginning of 1955, Eden's bitter struggle with Tory enemies in London to ensure his long-awaited succession to the premiership continued to be refracted through a Cypriot prism. Insofar as Greek Cypriots miscalculated the obstacles to the fulfilment of their own aspirations, they did so not least with respect to the complicated and veiled manner in which those aspirations got caught up in purely British power struggles beyond their own angle of vision.

This was another reason, indeed, why the Ionian precedent of 'spontaneous' British cession to Greece often cited by Greek Cypriots was misleading. That earlier decision had been shaped by British self-interest, but a self-interest defined by the liberal mid-Victorianism epitomized by Lord Palmerston. The British political class nearly a century later was much less sure of itself, and fearful of the future. The Greek Cypriot leadership was too bound up with its own fears—fears of being excluded from constitutional advancement being progressively granted to other colonial peoples—to notice that the Britain they were dealing with was not the one enshrined in modern Hellenic memory. This gap between historicized images and current reality underpinned that 'crisis of mistrust' which, in the judgement of a Conservative MP visiting the island in early February 1955, essentially defined the problem.[48] Once mistrust reaches a certain pitch, only direct personal contact can dispel it. In mid-March, Governor Armitage and Archbishop Makarios, both nervous of an impending physical struggle, agreed through their intermediaries to meet together in secret at the remote monastery of Kykko. The initiative was curtly dismissed by Eden because it would permit a 'shout of triumph' to the Greeks which could be used against him by opponents at home.[49] No meeting occurred, and on 1 April, the explosion of a number of bombs in Nicosia signified the start of an insurgency by a shadowy organization calling itself EOKA (National Organization of Greek Cypriot Fighters). Four days later Anthony Eden succeeded Churchill at No. 10 Downing Street.

Neither the British nor the Cyprus governments had anticipated the *kind* of violence which now supervened, and which took a turn for the worse the following

[47] For the 'never' statement and its consequences see R. F. Holland, 'Never, Never Land: British Colonial Policy and the Roots of Violence in Cyprus, 1950–54', *Journal of Imperial and Commonwealth History*, 21-3 (1993).   [48] Patrick Maitland to Eden, 3 Feb. 1951, FO371/117624.
[49] Holland, *Revolt in Cyprus*, 51.

June when EOKA began to assassinate members of the Cyprus police. It had always been expected that violence might erupt haphazardly as an incidental outgrowth of the political 'demonstrations' so much a part of *enosis* culture. Such disorder—like that of 1931—would surely splutter to a halt almost as spontaneously as it had occurred. What had not been contemplated was the emergence in Cyprus of a carefully calibrated and precisely targeted use of force reminiscent of the deadly Zionist campaign which had brought the British Mandate in Palestine to its knees in the later 1940s. The full extent of the physical challenge posed to British rule in Cyprus only gradually became clear (indeed, the fact that EOKA was headed by Colonel George Grivas, now in somewhat sullen retirement from the Greek Army, was not known for some while). As the scope of that challenge became discernible, however, the higher echelons of the British Army became commensurately determined not to be made to fight terrorism with 'with one hand tied behind the back', to which had been attributed the sorry mess in Palestine. From the British viewpoint, a Palestinian shadow always hovered over what eventually became the Cyprus Emergency.

Significantly, EOKA's targets at the outset were British personnel and Greek Cypriot 'traitors', *not* Turkish Cypriots. Leaflets circulated on 1 April 1955 simply instructed the latter to stand to one side whilst the future of the island was determined. The mistake of the protagonists of *enosis* during these years was not one of gratuitous victimization of the Muslim minority (the first killing of a Turkish Cypriot policeman did not occur till January 1956). Rather the mistake lay in the assumption that both the chief minority, and Turkey as its 'motherland', could be kept on the margins. This error was understandable. Turkish Cypriot sensitivities had deepened alongside an intensifying *enosis* movement after early 1950, but for a long while there was little overt 'nationalism'. Similarly, Turkey had left the running in UN debates during 1954 to the British, and had to be prodded by London into stepping up their own anti-*enosis* rhetoric.[50] There was also a fatal tendency to assume that the British government would always be willing and able to impose its views on Ankara when it was urgent to do so. For a long time after April 1955, the conflict still remained a colonial confrontation between the British and the Greek Cypriots, not a communal struggle between Greeks and Turks. Only as the security apparatus established by the British impacted on the main communities were the dividing lines between them soldered into place. Communal alienation and hatred, in short, were far from being inherent in the basic structure of events, and only became so as a secondary function of the tactics and ploys which unfolded as the logical accompaniment of an essentially Anglo-Greek struggle.

A watershed was passed during the summer of 1955 when management of the Cyprus issue was temporarily grasped in Whitehall by the Foreign Office, headed by Harold Macmillan. Macmillan was little interested in the colonial empire as such and its petty local politics of which Cyprus offered for him but one very

---

[50] Holland, *Revolt in Cyprus*, 41–4.

trying version. As a biographer has noted, he was much more drawn to securing a 'broker's commission in diplomatic advantage'.[51] His natural instinct was to seek international solutions—or fixes—to colonial problems. As Britain's 'Viceroy of the Mediterranean' during the recent war he also reckoned he knew the Greeks, and that the best way to check their ambition was to set them up against the Turks. His method in this case was to hold an international conference into which at some appropriate moment might be tossed a plan in which Cyprus remained a British colony, but in whose governance both Greece and—more especially— Turkey would be accorded a role. Macmillan called this a plan for tri-dominion, though one of its opponents in Whitehall thought it far more likely to produce pan-demonium.[52] Even Macmillan himself was surprised when his reluctant Cabinet colleagues agreed to let him go forward with the proposal.[53] The Tripartite London Conference of 29 August–7 September 1955, however, fell apart in disarray, as many had predicted, though the fallout represented by fierce anti-Greek riots in Istanbul was even worse even than critics had foretold.[54] Once the internationalization of the struggle for Cyprus had thus been made a reality, its logic could not easily be reversed.

Macmillan made one other contribution to Cypriot affairs at this stage: he pressed Eden to sack Governor Armitage for weakness and incompetence.[55] In late September Eden gave in, and the current Chief of the Imperial General Staff, Field Marshal Sir John Harding, was appointed in his stead. Harding's instructions were to defeat EOKA, and to 'get moving on the road to self-government if possible', in that order of priority. The complex relationship between security goals and political progress were always to bedevil his governorship. Throughout his tenure, however, Harding cleaved to one crystalline belief about the problem he faced: there could be 'no middle way' between speedy agreement on the immediate constitutional future, and the strict exercise of coercion.[56] Before the application of the latter, however, it was necessary at least to try to secure a peaceful settlement. The so-called 'Harding–Makarios negotiations' which commenced with the first meeting of the two principals on 4 October 1955 constituted one of the most intensive and subtle episodes in the political history of British decolonization.

Left to themselves, the Field Marshal and the Archbishop, for all their differences, might have found a solution, since both realized (if in different ways) the drastic

---

[51] John Turner, *Macmillan* (London, 1994), 137.

[52] H. Bourdillon to John Martin, 23 July 1955, CO926/259.

[53] Peter Catterall (ed.), *The Macmillan Diaries: The Cabinet Years, 1950–57* (London, 2003), 443–4.

[54] For the riots see the comprehensive account in Spyron Veronis, *The Mechanism of Catastrophe: The Pogrom of September 6–7, 1955 and the Destruction of the Greek Community of Istanbul* (New York, 2005) and Robert Holland, 'Greek–Turkish Relations, Istanbul and British Rule in Cyprus, 1954–59', *Deltio: Bulletin of the Centre for Asia Minor Studies* (Athens, 1994).

[55] Catterall (ed.), *Macmillan Diaries*, 467, 481.

[56] Quoted in Holland, *Revolt in Cyprus*, 91.

implications of failure. Harding soon discovered the truth asserted by his predecessor: that self-determination, not narrow self-government, was 'the one real, vital, all-absorbing point',[57] and that any solution had to take account of it. He was able to insist, as Armitage could not, that Her Majesty's government began to face this awkward reality. A search was on for 'golden words' capable of glossing Anglo-Cypriot differences, and by mid-January 1956 the elements were sufficiently established for the two sides to turn to the arrangements which would prevail before ultimate self-determination arrived. It was on this matter—and above all the old stumbling block of a Greek-elected majority—that the talks irretrievably broke down on 29 February 1956. In essence, even when Harding and Makarios could just about agree on a somewhat fuzzy definition of the final goal, they could not do so on the *transitional* mechanisms. Many were puzzled at the time and since as to why the negotiations stalled at the last hurdle,[58] but what Harding called 'the struggle for mastery' in Cyprus was always defined more by control over the *journey* towards self-determination, than by the arrival at it.[59] This was entirely congruent with the general imperatives in British decolonization, accentuated by the fact that in Cyprus the British were dealing with a population simply not prepared to be *led* towards the future as their counterparts elsewhere, especially in Africa, so often were. This was the difference made by the irredentist, rather than simply colonial, nature of the fight for mastery over the island.

In this regard, an official in the Colonial Office once acutely observed that in a curiously inverse manner the British came to worship the 'cult of Makarios' almost as much as the Greek Cypriots themselves.[60] That it was so reflected the Archbishop's success in confirming *enosis* as 'the only legitimate anti-colonial policy of the Cypriots', and in stamping that policy with the indelible mark of church authority.[61] There was certainly a kind of cultic obsession in the reasoning on the British side for the breakdown: that Makarios was so tricky and unreliable a partner that any settlement with him would prove more dangerous than the alternative. By this time Field Marshal Harding was itching to act decisively to take the Archbishop 'out of the picture', and the British government was in no position to deny him. On Friday, 9 March, Makarios was arrested in his palace, bundled onto a Royal Air Force transporter, and taken off to a simple but by no means harsh captivity in the Seychelles. 'Operation Apollo', as this was officially designated, struck even the Colonial Office, however, as 'reminiscent of Henry VIII' in its draconian character.[62] Any hope of scrubbing the Archbishop out of Cypriot minds was delusory, as senior figures in Whitehall appreciated in their calmer moments. Mistake

[57] Armitage to Martin, 26 June 1955, CO926/265.

[58] The well-informed United States consul Raymond Courtney blamed the breakdown partly on Makarios's failure to encourage a 'moderate' faction in Cypriot politics, but equally on the slow and tentative evolution of British policy which allowed the basic mistrust between the parties to escalate. See Holland, *Revolt in Cyprus*, 115.   [59] Harding to Lennox-Boyd, 31 Jan. 1956, FO371/123867.

[60] Aldridge minute, 5 Sept. 1958, CO926/592.

[61] Anagnostopoulou, '*I Eklissia tis Kiprou*', 77.

[62] D. Smith minute, 15 Mar. 1956, CO1035/6.

or not, the action against the Archbishop revealed the reality inside the island of a fight which both the British and the Greeks had come to feel was too important to lose.

All of Harding's previous 'offers' to the Archbishop had been allied to a threat that failure to agree a settlement would lead to 'a most unpleasant time'. What followed was certainly that. Detention camps filled up with suspects whom even the Colonial Office in London recognized were 'man-in-the-streetish' rather than hardened malefactors.[63] Curfews were swiftly imposed on villages and suburbs following even minor pretexts, and the fierce heat of the summer made the lot of the inhabitants distinctly miserable. Martial law was never proclaimed during the Emergency in Cyprus, but the system of Special Courts largely manned by British judges possessed summary characteristics—though, significantly, the judiciary was one institution in which most Cypriots retained confidence throughout the Emergency. The British Army combed its way through the rugged Cypriot countryside, increasingly preoccupied with one objective: finding and eliminating Colonel Grivas. Their methods were inevitably often rough and arbitrary, house searches being especially resented. The Governor's actions in the security sphere were widely alleged to be counterproductive in terms of winning the 'hearts and minds' of Cypriots. That was not how Harding saw it. In his view, only by bringing home to the majority the costs of straying from the path of 'moderation' would they be impelled to cut loose from the *enosis* idea and the men of violence who had recently appropriated it.

Two particular forms of 'unpleasantness' had particularly grave consequences for Anglo-Greek discourses inside and outside Cyprus. The first concerned allegations of ill treatment and even brutality to EOKA suspects caught in the security force's net. What seems incontrovertible is that the British Army, cut off from any reliable sources amongst the Greek population, became so dependent on obtaining scraps of information that the process of interrogation became subject to precisely those pressures likely to give rise to claims—and occasionally the reality—of 'roughing-up' or 'torture'.[64] The second form of unpleasantness was the execution of those found guilty of terrorist crimes under Emergency laws. Nine young Greek Cypriots went to the gallows during Harding's governorship (though, it should be noted, not before there had been seventy EOKA-related fatalities). Again, in Harding's judgement the preparedness of Her Majesty's government in London to accept his decision as Governor not to extend clemency was the absolutely critical test that policy was not slipping into the fatal 'middle way' he despised. But the resulting costs in international (especially American) and indeed United Kingdom opinion became harder to sustain as time went on—and especially once

[63] H. White minute, 29 Apr. 1957, CO926/81.

[64] Interrogations involving Turkish Cypriot special police were especially liable to infringe legal proeecdures. See Tom Hickman, *The Call-Up: A History of National Service* (London, 2004), 272 for the 'psychological scars' left on some British military personnel by such involvements.

the outcome of the Suez crisis in the last months of 1956 transformed the moral climate of colonial questions more generally.[65]

By extension, relations between Britain and Greece were now poisoned over Cyprus as they had not been by any previous issue of *enosis*. Not even an indirect warning of Makarios' sudden arrest had been directed from London to Athenian ministers, despite the fact that the act was bound to transmit shock waves through Greek society. Arguably even more controversial than the exiling of the Archbishop were the confirmations of the first two capital punishments of convicted EOKA 'terrorists' in May 1956 (though in one of these the original offence had not involved an actual fatality, whilst in the other the prosecution case was widely seen as flawed).[66] The British Ambassador in Athens, Sir Charles Peake, now received death threats—not something to which any of his predecessors had been exposed, despite their occcasional unpopularity; and although Peake was embarrassed to proffer a recommendation to his superiors which 'might seem even unconsciously to be biased by a desire to preserve my own skin', he told the Foreign Office that hanging Greek Cypriots would 'set us back a long way for a long time' so far as any restoration of friendship with Greece was concerned.[67] They went ahead anyway, in line with the decision already taken as to the dispensability of Anglo-Hellenic accord.

These Anglo-Greek polarities were filtered through the distortions of the major international crisis triggered by Egyptian nationalization of the Suez Canal. It was skilled Egyptian-Greek pilots who kept the ships moving through the Suez waterway when their British and French counterparts were withdrawn at the behest of their governments. At this stage one British Foreign Office official premissed a despairing call for a more sympathetic appreciation of current Greek dilemmas on the tentative assumption 'that we do not wish to destroy Greece altogether'.[68] Not even amidst the war crises of 1897 or 1916 had the imponderable of 'destroying' Greece—whatever that might mean in practice—been floated in Whitehall. The British traditionally had one final resort in the Greek political sphere: drawing on their fluctuating investment in Greek royalty. When an attempt was made, however, to influence the new ministry of Constantine Karamanlis in December 1956 via King Paul, the ruse failed, marking, it was concluded in Whitehall, the end of the Glücksbürg dynasty's 'power for stabilization' in Greek affairs.[69] There was a certain irony in the fact that, whereas that dynasty's original elevation under British patronage had provided the trigger for Ionian cession, it was the struggle pivoting around *enosis* for Cyprus which helped to break the link between stabilization and dynasticism in modern Greek history.

---

[65] For an acute comment on shifts in the moral climate of British public culture and decolonization which has considerable relevance for events in Cyprus, see John Darwin, *The End of the British Empire: The Historical Debate* (Oxford, 1991), 18–19.   [66] Holland, *Revolt in Cyprus*, 90–1, 128.
[67] Peake to Selwyn Lloyd, 19 Apr. 1956, FO371/123884.
[68] Ward minute, 25 July 1956, FO371/117865.   [69] Holland, *Revolt in Cyprus*, 165.

Such developments went well beyond the perspective of Governor Harding. Yet the latter was not just the unimaginative soldier of EOKA propaganda. He understood that to combat *enosis* in Cyprus, repression was not enough. He told Lennox-Boyd firmly that it was vital that the British government should have 'fixed a visible light at the end of the tunnel for the Greek Cypriot people' if the latter were to be guided away from violence.[70] At all the critical stages of his governorship, he pressed the British Cabinet to make a clear and unequivocal statement committing the United Kingdom to ultimate self-determination for the island. By 'ultimate' Harding came to mean after an interval of some three to five years, ideally under the auspices of NATO as a non-British, and therefore impartial, arbiter. Such pleas were consistently rebutted in London. Although Prime Minister Eden sent out a Constitutional Commission under Lord Radcliffe, the latter's terms of references excluded the key imponderable of final status.[71] In the disastrous backwash of the Anglo-French military assault on Egypt, the British government's ability to evade fundamental issues concerning Cypriot governance declined sharply. In facing up to the real Cyprus Question, its manner of proceeding was to make prospective self-determination subject to the option of partition. This was the 'pledge', in effect made at the behest of Turkey, enshrined in a ministerial statement in the House of Commons on 19 December 1956.[72] What the British Foreign Office tellingly called 'the Turkish-political factor' began in this way to escape its constraints.

This does not mean that the British veered towards partition in order to allow what became characterized as 'double self-determination' to be actually implemented. Rather the nub was to find a means of frightening the Greek Cypriots into reconsidering the merits of the status quo. The minority (and Turkey) were not so much to be ingratiated, as that the majority (and Greece) were to be coerced. Yet even members of the British Cabinet were quick to see the grim possibility of ending up like British mandatory administration in Palestine—scorched between two fires, and able to put out neither.[73] Partitioning ethnically plural societies, furthermore, was inherently a bloody business, and all the more so in Cyprus where the various communities often lived intermixed with each other. When the Cyprus government carried out a planning exercise, the conclusion emerged that partition might be implemented peacefully if staggered over fifteen years, but that otherwise it could only be enforced 'by fire and sword'.[74] Partition for British policy makers might harbour powerful attractions, therefore, but it also possessed a strong element of repulsion.

---

[70] Harding to Lennox-Boyd, 25 June 1956, CO926/551.

[71] For the conclusions of the Radcliffe Commission see Hatzivassiliou, *The Cyprus Question*, 59–63.

[72] *Hansard Parliamentary Debates,* 3rd Series, vol. dlxii (Commons), 19 Dec. 1956, cols. 1268–78.

[73] Cyprus: Cabinet Conclusions on Plan for a Constitutional Settlement, 11 Dec. 1956, CAB128/30/2.

[74] The Cyprus Government's 'Report on the Methods, Costs and Consequences of Partition' is in CO926/1042.

For Harold Macmillan, who succeeded Eden as Prime Minister in January 1957, the situation he inherited regarding Cyprus was an albatross around his neck. Conscious of his predecessor's fate, Macmillan was acutely aware of the island's role as a potential lightning rod for domestic right-wing impulses. For this reason he expressed very early on the hope that a way out of the Cypriot impasse could be found 'in the lifetime of this Parliament'.[75] The immediate necessity was to buy time and American goodwill on the matter, which he did by releasing Makarios from his Indian Ocean prison in early April (though the Archbishop was refused a return to his homeland, and had to kick his heels in Athens). This 'act of grace, or of contempt', as Macmillan presented this decision to appease those Tories for whom it was intensely distasteful, was designed to put off any negotiation with Cypriots, not assist one.[76] His essential goal was to manoeuvre towards the kind of 'internationalized' solution which he had first begun to sketch as Foreign Secretary at the London Conference of September 1955. Such a solution would integrate Greek (and, much more importantly, Turkish) 'co-sovereignty' as a means of perpetuating continuing British rule in the island. *Plus ça change, plus c'est la même chose* was to be the spirit of the exercise. There could be no real possibility of any Greek government collaborating in such an outcome, however, unless confronted directly not just with the alternative of partition, but with the war with Turkey which partition was bound to unleash. Letting the shadow of partition settle ominously over Cypriot minds was thus part and parcel of Macmillan's evolving strategy.

It was the incipient linkage between war and partition which redefined the struggle for mastery in Cyprus from a largely colonial construct to a regionalized and ethnic confrontation. As such, it became too destabilizing for the Eisenhower administration in the United States to continue to turn a half-blind eye to the vagaries of British policy. 'Good grief,' one State Department official in Washington scribbled on the telegram conveying the first intimations that partition featured in British thoughts, with its recent Indian— and, given the legacy in Kashmir, by no mean comforting—parallel.[77] Some less explosive means of approaching a Cypriot settlement was called for, and it was out of this recognition that the concept of a self-standing, unitary, and independent Cyprus emerged. To effect such a compromise all the main protagonists would need to make sacrifices—the Greeks of *enosis*, the Turks of partition, and the British of their sovereignty. Furthermore, there was no a priori reason why such a status for Cyprus should be unwelcome in London. But in the circumstances of 1957 independence was tantamount to 'handing Cyprus over to Makarios' and as such *worse even than enosis*, since the latter at least had the compensation that hostile elements would be subject to (admittedly unpredictable) Athenian restraints.[78] Through the summer and autumn of 1957, therefore,

[75] Harold Macmillan to Selwyn Lloyd, 4 Feb. 1957, PREM11/1757A, National Archives of Great Britain.   [76] For Macmillan's decision to release Makarios see Holland, *Revolt in Cyprus*, 175–81.
[77] Holland, *Revolt in Cyprus*, 170.
[78] Thompson minute, 7 Aug. 1957, FO371/130084.

Macmillan ordered his officials to do everything possible to sideline mediation inspired by American and NATO sources, until an opportunity arrived to put his own favoured outcome into operation.

Frustrated at the failure to provide a 'fixed visible light' on the path to pacification, and facing a renewed campaign of violence by EOKA, Governor Harding resigned from his post on 22 October 1957. Harding believed that he had at least 'proved that terrorism could be mastered in a physical sense'.[79] The fault that the achievement had not gone further lay, he thought, with others—with the Greek Cypriots for not rallying to 'moderation', but also (as he confessed indiscreetly to an American confidante) with Her Majesty's government for turning aside whenever a window of opportunity for negotiation had offered itself.[80] Macmillan had for some while been under pressure to send out a new governor with a more sympathetic and healing persona than the incumbent. This advice he now followed in selecting Sir Hugh Foot, currently Governor of Jamaica, and a member of a distinguished family with strong liberal beliefs. The appointment, however, was made with the same traces of grace mixed with contempt which had accompanied the release of Archbishop Makarios. 'Wheel on the Idealist,' Macmillan was afterwards wont to quip whenever Foot arrived in London for talks on the rapidly deteriorating situation in Cyprus.[81] British liberalism had often enjoyed a very ambiguous relationship to the world of Hellenic politics, and the governorship of Sir Hugh Foot—the last in colonial Cyprus—was to capture that complexity in perfect miniature.

Foot arrived in the island with an incipient plan of his own. The new Governor's notions had nothing to do with self-determination—given the role of Cyprus in British politics, he would not have been appointed if they had. Indeed, he firmly believed that it was only by 'freezing' the whole question of ultimate status that inter-communal tension could be moderated and an opportunity created for an experiment in local self-government under continuing British sovereignty. In other words, Foot's goal was that of 'calming things down', rather than searching for a definitive solution which, it was widely held, could only divide rather than unite the inhabitants.[82] It was to start the process of calming that Foot inaugurated what he characteristically called 'a time of gestures', ranging from dispensing with the tight personal security which had surrounded his predecessor, and even riding out on horseback into country districts with minimal protection, to the release of the first batches of inmates from the overcrowded detention camps.[83] Both personally and politically these actions were brave enough, but from the first they were open to Greek suspicions that gestures were all they

---

[79] For Harding's valedictory assessment see his speech to the District Security Committees, 21 Oct. 1957, CO926/1074.   [80] Holland, *Revolt in Cyprus*, 209.

[81] Ibid. 212.

[82] Sir Roger Bowker (British Ambassador, Ankara) to Selwyn Lloyd, 10 Jan. 1958, FO371/136328.

[83] For Foot's own account of his governorship, see *A Start in Freedom* (London, 1964), 143–87.

were—not a light at the end of a tunnel, but the merest flicker of hope on a distant and deceptive horizon.

In the ensuing months a sharp division also appeared between the Governor and his senior administrative and army colleagues in Nicosia. The latter believed that any renewed search for an internal compromise between Greeks and Turks was wholly illusory—nor, perhaps, even desirable. 'Basically', Foot's chief adviser on Cypriot politics, John Reddaway, summed things up, 'the Cyprus problem has always been ... [a] simple choice of evils.'[84] That is, since the British were clearly incapable of governing the island alone, they had to do so in alliance with either the Greek majority or the Turkish minority. Too many bridges had been burned with the former to make that option viable, whilst the security force machine had now become completely dependent on Turkish Cypriot co-operation. In the many permutations of the old Eastern Question and its latter-day variants, the British had indeed been pulled back and forth between Hellenic and Turkish imperatives. Never was the choice between these polarities posed in such a crude and compelling manner as in Cyprus after late 1957. The key to the prolonged final phase of these troubles lay, indeed, in the fact that, however unintended, British policy ended up, not pursuing clearly defined United Kingdom goals, but providing a vehicle for the interests of Ankara. Although this bitter irony was not lost on some in Whitehall,[85] arresting the process once it started was sure to be very rocky.

This process began in earnest with the Turkish Cypriot riots in Nicosia during early January 1958. A simultaneous visit to Ankara by Foot and Lennox-Boyd was a humiliating disaster—the Turkish premier, Adnan Menderes, would not even meet the Governor, however much he supplicated. Ominous rumours began of Turkish Army divisions massing on the Anatolian coast, ready to invade Cyprus if the Turkish authorities decided that the British were sliding away from previous commitments. By the early spring the so-called Foot Plan—which had never been a real plan so much as some tentative suggestions—imploded, whilst in the island a new security assessment concluded that the British had more to fear from the new Turkish Cypriot subversive organization, TMT (Turkish Defence Organization), than from EOKA. Far from the logical deduction being made that the time had come for the British Army to nip Turkish terrorism in the bud, the lesson derived was that the risks in the situation had to be assessed, as General Kendrew, the British Commander-in-chief, stated, in terms of 'how they [the Turks] choose to see it'.[86] In this manner the 'Turkish-political factor' emerged as the dominant factor in shaping events.

The extremity of these circumstances, nevertheless, offered possibilities as well as risks to Macmillan. By mid-1958 he was more eager than ever to find a way out of

[84] Reddaway note, 6 May 1958, 181/12, Box 5, Foot Papers. Reddaway's sometimes bitter retrospective account can be found in his *Burdened with Cyprus* (London, 1986).

[85] Holland, *Revolt in Cyprus*, 276.

[86] 'The Security Implications of the "Peace" Plan', 23 Dec. 1958, 181/4, Foot Papers, Rhodes House Library.

the Cypriot maze before the next general election, not least because other colonial problems—principally in Eastern and Central Africa—looked likely in combination with Cyprus to provide the Labour Party with powerful ammunition against their Conservative opponents. Macmillan had always believed—like Foot's officials in Nicosia—that it was only by seeming to readmit a Turkish presence into the island that the Greeks could be cowed into accepting something less than *enosis*. This was the nub of a plan for a 'modified tridominium' bearing Macmillan's name which took shape after June 1958, the chief modification being that, instead of unwieldy joint sovereignty, Greece and Turkey would be 'associated' with British administration by the appointment of representatives in Nicosia. The whole point of the plan was not that it should be accepted by Greece—since this was most unlikely—but that it should be accepted by Turkey, and implacably applied under Anglo-Turkish accord. Admittedly, this proposition fell short of the unvarnished partition which fervently nationalist demonstrations in many Turkish cities demanded through that summer. But it did offer what Macmillan, with his taste for indirect methods of securing tricky outcomes, termed 'metaphysical partition', by which was meant a solution so permeated by guarantees for Turkish Cypriots that it could be converted into full partition as and when the Greeks refused to submit.[87] That such a scenario might lead to 'the ultimate disappearance of the whole regime' in Greece itself, and even precipitate a move to dictatorship, did not seem to dismay London, since it was only thereby that the backwash of an eventual Cypriot carve-up might conceivably be contained.[88]

Even Field Marshal Harding had regarded partition, or quasi-partition, as 'a counsel of despair',[89] and it was now by ramming despair down Greek throats that the plan had to be pushed towards fruition regardless of calls to halt elsewhere. So it was that the gestures of hopefulness integral to the governorship of Sir Hugh Foot were subverted, and a new security drive implemented which restocked the detention camps with Greek suspects even when the main source of violence had transparently shifted around to the Turkish Cypriot community—indeed, Grivas had decreed a truce by EOKA some months before. For Macmillan, one benefit of unfolding partition was that it was popular with his party's right wing, who were now (as the Chancellor of the Exchequer, R. A. Butler, privately complained to the US Ambassador in London) 'more Turkish than the Turks'—the resurfacing of the phrase was an unconscious but telling echo of British policy over Cretan affairs after 1908.[90] There remained the possibility of opposition from Washington, where it was feared that the British were bracing themselves to 'pull a Palestine' by evacuating with minimal notice, leaving chaos and bloodshed behind.[91] But even here Macmillan calculated that against the background of a wider crisis in the Middle East the Eisenhower administration could be coaxed in the British wake. Joint

---

[87] Holland, *Revolt in Cyprus*, 285.
[88] R. Allen (British Ambassador, Athens) to Selwyn Lloyd, 25 Sept. 1958, FO371/136313.
[89] Harding to Lennox-Boyd, 16 Oct. 1956, PREM11/1756.
[90] Quoted in Holland, *Revolt in Cyprus*, 225.   [91] Ibid. 248.

Anglo-American interventions in Jordan and the Lebanon in mid-July 1958 had set a new pattern of co-operation, and relegated the bad transatlantic blood of Suez to an unpleasant memory not for repetition.

Yet, just as over Crete in 1911–12, a sudden regional *bouleversement* had left British policy stranded and irrelevant, so it did over Cyprus in 1958/9. Since mid-1957 tensions had been rising along Turkey's border with the loose Syrian-Egyptian union known as the 'United Arab Republic'. Then in July 1958 occurred the seismic shift of the Iraqi Revolution, and the replacement of the pro-Western Hashemite monarchy by an erratic republican and nationalist regime. At first it was reckoned in London that what had happened in Baghdad would increase Turkish leverage across the board. But there was a limit to the amount of anxiety along borders that Turkish diplomacy could tolerate, and voices began to be heard in Ankara to the effect that the time had arrived to take what profits had already been won over Cyprus as the fortuitous result of British actions, and thereafter to cool it. On 1 October, as designated under the Macmillan Plan, the Turkish representative assumed his place in Nicosia, so providing a renewed lodgement inside the island's affairs which had always been the essential Turkish aim. After that, however, Menderes and his Foreign Minister Fatin Zorlu turned their attention, not to co-operating with Macmillan to ensure the full-blown application of his controversial plan, but to finding a bilateral compromise with Greece. This crucial turnaround was at first conducted in discreet secrecy, but as evidence of it mounted, the British government began to fear that whatever leverage it retained over Cyprus was in danger of liquidation.

A framework for a compromise between Ankara and Athens lay conveniently to hand in the proposition of Cypriot independence which both American policy makers and Paul Henri-Spaak, the NATO Secretary-General, had continued to press as an alternative to the Macmillan Plan. The credibility of independence as a solution had received a major boost in late September when Archbishop Makarios accepted it, in principle at least, during the course of an interview with the British Labour MP Barbara Castle—though the implicit distancing from *enosis* earned him the enmity of Grivas.[92] It was true that, with the exception of the Americans, all of the parties drawn to the independence option had in mind something other than the conventional article. Zorlu told Selwyn Lloyd, the British Foreign Secretary, in Paris, for example, that what was under consideration was 'not really independence...The island [of Cyprus] must be Turkish-Greek, not Greek or Cypriot.'[93] But this was not inherently unacceptable to Athenian ministers, now as keen as the British and the Turks to clip the wings of Makarios. It was the concept of an 'independent', Greek-Turkish island under international guarantee which lay at the heart of the settlement reached, seemingly out of the blue, when the Greek and Turkish Prime Ministers met at a conference at Zurich on 6–11 February

[92] For Castle's involvement with Cyprus, see Ann Perkins, *Red Queen: The Authorized Biography of Barbara Castle* (London, 2003), 152–9.
[93] R. Jebb (Paris Embassy) to Foreign Office, 18 Dec. 1958, FO 371/136410.

1959. Given the animosities which had surrounded the conflict over Cyprus, the outcome could not be anything but fragile. 'The agreement reached', one senior Turkish official remarked afterwards, 'was like a *soufflé* which must be eaten at once, otherwise it will collapse.'[94]

The dish hurriedly concocted at Zurich was certainly bitter-sweet to the British palate. After all, a Greek-Turkish island was not likely to be very British. For this reason the latter showed an inclination to cling to the Macmillan Plan for Cyprus—just as Royal Navy warships had once stubbornly continued to patrol residual Ottoman sovereignty in Crete—even when everybody else had deserted the exercise. Legislation for the election of separate municipal councils—a key demand of the Turkish Cypriot leadership—was prepared in order to demonstrate to Ankara in particular that the various elements of the plan were still being rolled out. Yet how British did Cyprus now really need to be? '[W]e only need our Gibraltars,' Macmillan commented when he first heard that the Greek and Turkish Foreign Ministers were travelling to London directly from Zurich to inform Her Majesty's government, somewhat ironically, of the fate of one of its own colonies.[95] The essential requirement had indeed shrunk from Cyprus as a base to bases on Cyprus, though it was clear on the British side, not only that these areas must be sovereign, but that their proper working would require very extensive rights (including a series of 'protected sites' beyond the bases themselves). It was only by providing clear guarantees relating to the retention of territory—the size of which, however, remained as yet imprecise—that the Greek and Turkish governments ensured that Macmillan and his senior Cabinet colleagues agreed to go through the motions of hosting the Lancaster House Conference on 17–19 February 1959 to rubber-stamp the real decision which had, in truth, already been taken by others.

There was one critical imponderable hanging over the Lancaster House proceedings, however, which was by no means cut and dried: would Archbishop Makarios accept the resulting ageements on behalf of the Greek Cypriot people? Ministers in Athens had been careful to keep the Archbishop closely involved in their own decisions, but there was no certainty that when it came to the decisive moment he would sign on the dotted line. The conference was a tense affair, made all the more so by the tragic crash as the aeroplane carrying the Turkish delegation had attempted to land in London (the Turkish premier, Adnan Menderes, survived).[96] Virtually throughout the ensuing conference, Selwyn Lloyd, as chairman, sought to harry Makarios into acceptance, looking not least to the Greek Foreign Minister, Evangelos Averoff, to help him. That the Archbishop with deep reluctance eventually added his imprimatur to the document foreshadowing a new republic of Cyprus has sometimes been interpreted as a devious attempt to

[94] Record of meeting at Carlton House Gardens, 11 Feb. 1959, FO371/144640.
[95] Quoted in Alistair Horne, *Macmillan, 1957–1986*, ii (London, 1989), 691.
[96] Following a new revolution in Turkey during 1960, however, both Menderes and Zorlu were to be hanged, the charges including that of instigating the anti-Greek riots in Istanbul during 1955.

distance himself from what in Cypriot terms could easily be interpreted as a crushing defeat. Evanthis Hatzivassiliou has argued 'that the Archbishop's hesitation should rather be attributed to the very human difficulty of the ethnarch of Cyprus, the guarantor of the Hellenic tradition of the island ... signing a settlement which, however necessary, was not ideal and which ... excluded *enosis*'.[97] This rings true. No representative of Hellenic aspirations in the Ionian Islands or Crete (with the possible exception of Prince George's abject departure from the latter in 1906) had been penned into a similar corner by British diplomacy exploiting a political opportunity which had fortuitously opened up. The resulting sense of bitterness could not easily be wiped away thereafter.

Viewed as a problem in the 'demission of empire', however, the Cypriots (both Greek and Turkish) were able to inflict a collective defeat on the British, since this turned out to be one case where in departing from a dependency the latter were accorded no role in shaping the independence constitution. The drafting of this took place within a purely Graeco-Turkish committee, assisted by a Swiss jurist. As Averoff rather bluntly stated, the 'psychological conditions'—or moral standing—of the British government in relation to the future of Cyprus had become too compromised for it to be otherwise.[98] British negotiators could not be similarly frozen out when it came to delimiting the bases that were to remain on the island. The Greeks and the Turks were happy to leave the British and the Cypriots to their squabbles over that. The original British demand was for two sovereign zones the combined extent of which was larger than Malta. At bottom, as a Colonial Office official frankly admitted, this inflated requirement was dictated 'by domestic political factors rather than by strategic or international considerations'[99]—that is, by Macmillan's need to be able to wave some 'trophy' before the United Kingdom Parliament. By the same token, however, the contest over base areas was the one aspect of the Lancaster House agreements where the Cypriots could tenaciously fight their own corner, and as a result of these pressures the initial date for independence (19 February 1960) had to be repeatedly put off. The resulting interregnum exacerbated underlying inter-communal issues. Only when the British and Cypriot delegates finally settled in April 1960 on a total area of 99 square miles to remain under British control was the way open for the inauguration of an independent republic of Cyprus on the coming 16 August.

At its very inception, indeed, old misunderstandings were renewed, and some new ones were being formed. Precisely because the British remained embedded in the Cypriot scene by virtue of their residual territorial stake on the island, the Greek Cypriots continued to ascribe to them capacities which in truth they no longer possessed. Indeed, the first British High Commissioner in the new state, Arthur Clark, was viewed as a kind of governor-in-reserve, and Greek Cypriot overestimation of

---

[97] Hatzivassiliou, *The Cyprus Question*, 83.
[98] Record of meeting at the Foreign Office, 13 Feb. 1959, FO371/144640.
[99] Holland, *Revolt in Cyprus*, 330.

his influence and advice was to play a part in the fatal crisis which gripped the new arrangements after December 1963.[100] Even more importantly, the emergence of anti-agreement factions within the Greek Cypriot community, and the growing intransigence amongst Turkish Cypriots under the influence of Rauf Denktash, further corroded the equipoise on which the chances of the new polity depended. In the other cases we have studied in this book, the pivotal climaxes represented by King George I's triumphant arrival in Corfu on 2 June 1864, the appearance of a Greek Governor, Stephanos Dragoumis, in Crete on 25 October 1912, and Admiral Ionnides' establishment as Greek military administrator in the Dodecanese on 31 March 1947, were each distinctive in their atmosphere and meanings. Yet they shared one clear implication in common: the definitive ending of an era, and the hopeful start of a new one. Such was not the atmosphere in Cyprus on 16 August 1960. One description states that

The ceremony of the inauguration was conspicuously low-key. There were no foreign dignitaries, no ministers from the governments of the guarantor powers. People turned out to celebrate in large numbers, although it was not always clear what they were celebrating, for the birth of the Republic of Cyprus attracted far less enthusiasm than, on the one hand, the return of the EOKA exiles, or, on the other hand, the arrival of the Turkish army. The Cyprus flag was little in evidence. Street decorations, according to the area, were either of Greek or Turkish flags.[101]

In short, what had emerged was what a Greek historian has described as an unstable 'dualism',[102] or, as Sir Hugh Foot had himself neatly summed up the impending regime, 'Agreement rule' rather than independence proper.[103] This was, indeed, the sort of anomalous system of government, capable of arousing no real loyalty amongst its citizens, and even subject to a crippling form of statelessness, which had once characterized the old Ionian states under British protection, and Cretan autonomy under European occupation after 1898. Those unfortunate polities had not ultimately proved sustainable, and in retrospect the odds on the survival of the new Cypriot dispensation were not much greater. The travails which followed, from which the British could not disengage themselves as they might have hoped, go beyond our present concerns. From the perspective of this account, however, what stands out is that just as the approach of Cypriot independence was 'a special and mangled form of decolonization',[104] so it constituted the most distorted and enduring experience in the modern Anglo-Hellenic encounter.

[100] Clark's role in the 1963, crisis is traced in Markides, *Cyprus*, 129–57.

[101] Ibid. 43. Under the Lancaster House Agreement the Greek and Turkish governments were both permitted to station troops on the island. It was symptomatic that whereas Turkish Cypriots enthusiastically welcomed the arrival of the garrison sent by Ankara, the Greek Cypriots reserved most of their warmth for returning EOKA fighters, not the contingent from Greece.

[102] Hatzivassiliou, *The Cyprus Question*, 90.

[103] Higham minute, 4 June 1959, CO926/928.   [104] Holland, *Revolt in Cyprus*, 335.

10

Love, Deception and Anglo-Hellenic Politics

Lord Londonderry declares 'No one had been more deceived in the Greeks than the English', but the Greeks should feel no difficulty in returning the compliment.

('Mr. Gladstone and the Greek Question', 1876)

The range of historical experience covered in these pages has been very considerable. In navigating a path across it, we have sought to draw out the comparative dimension in essentially four intense island experiences. This conclusion will be restricted to rehearsing some of the common threads. An outstanding feature has been the ideological sensitivity which issues of Hellenic irredentism caused in British policy making. The uncomfortableness of the British position in the Ionian Islands arose, as one Lord High Commissioner observed, because they constituted 'a stage very open to the observation of Europe', and as such vulnerable, as more distant possessions were not, to Britain's international detractors.[1] A couple of decades later Lord Salisbury identified the same weakness when forewarning a newly appointed High Commissioner of Cyprus that the principal challenge surrounding this new acquisition came from 'the reflex operation on the public feeling of the island when thrown back, in a magnified and distorted form, by the exaggeration of European controversy'.[2] Such magnification was experienced during the European occupation of Crete after 1897, when the criticisms of local Christians concerning British peacekeeping in Candia interacted with wider attacks on England's 'splendid isolation' and unilateral diplomacy. But Salisbury's concern that Cyprus in particular might prove an embarrassment was to be all too amply fulfilled at the end of our period. A Colonial Office official, minuting in early 1950 on appeals by the Governor in Nicosia for more anti-sedition powers, pondered:

Whatever may have been true in 1878, how far is a repressive regime in this European island practicable today in the light of the political ideals of the Commonwealth and the

[1] Sir John Young to Labouchere, 1 Dec. 1855, Young Papers, Add. 62940, BL.
[2] Salisbury to Biddulph, 4 July 1879, FO421/32.

Atlantic Powers? ... Cyprus is ... a vulnerable salient in the present world ideological struggle.[3]

From the international ideological struggle of the 1850s, through to its counterpart of the 1950s, the situations we have dealt with were all perched on awkward salients, and it is this which helped to import a uniform fragility into British calculations and actions.

By a logical corollary, what Gladstone called the 'real point of danger' for British interests came when forces of Hellenic irredentism were able to breach the limits of their insularity and hook their own aspirations to wider flows.[4] In fending off such pressures the British strove to attain their ideal of achieving the 'tranquillity' which was for them the best of all possible worlds when engaged with rumbustious Greek societies. This meant, as much as circumstances allowed, sealing these islands off from regional environments and influences. Political safety for local expatriate administration lay in obscurity, including keeping Ionian, Cretan, and latterly Cypriot affairs out of the newspapers, British parliamentary debates, and international congresses, and later the United Nations. The natural rhythms of these narratives have therefore lain in British attempts to keep Hellenic populations boxed into frameworks short of union with Greece, and the counter-effort of *enosis* movements to connect with wider worlds. The latter's opportunity always came, as an Ionian radical hailed the *bouleversement* of 1862–63, amidst 'an epoch of movement, eagerness and action',[5] and it is on British dilemmas in such eras of renewed Greek revolution, climactic insurrections, regional conflict, and colonial liquidation that we have concentrated our gaze.

It was built into the structure of the resulting sequences that their evolution was bound up with controversial comings and goings, sometimes covert, sometimes celebratory, sometimes voluntary, sometimes enforced. If the stories above could be usefully consolidated and abbreviated into a single mass, it might therefore best be by some multi-coloured pictogram displaying the arrivals and departures of kings and queens, archbishops and bishops, commissioners and governors, rebels and refugees, Ottoman troops and administrators, British marines and Greek gendarmes, amongst many others. The trajectory of these movements—whether it was the 'one continuous triumph' of King George's tour of his new Ionian province in 1864, Cretan deputies successfully evading British warships to reach the Athenian Parliament in 1912–13, the emotional visit of Regent Damaskinos to Rhodes on 14 May 1945, or Archbishop Makarios' return to an ecstatic welcome in his native Cyprus during February 1959—embodied many defeats and victories along the way for the contending parties.

---

[3] Quoted in Ronald Hyam, *The Labour Government and the End of Empire, 1945–51*, part 3: *Strategy, Politics and Constitutional Change* (London, 1992), 111.

[4] William Gladstone to Bulwer Lytton, 7 Feb. 1859, CO136/165.

[5] See article by the radical leader Monferrato, enclosed in Storks to Newcastle, 10 Jan. 1862, CO136/177.

For the British, there was in these situations one central and recurring defeat: the failure to identify and encourage the forces of 'moderation' within the corpus of Hellenic nationalism. Just as in the Ionian Islands there was never really a 'Party for the Protectorate', so there was never a party 'for' the British connection else-where (with the telling exceptions of Muslim minorities in Crete and Cyprus). Deprived of a compact and reliable body of friends, the British never found the political security they craved. A tense and unstable equilibrium was their optimal achievement. This was not for want of trying: the sporadic dispatch of sympathetic proconsuls and overseers, the provision of honours and occasional knighthoods for the more co-operative leading men in local society, or the composi-tion of liberal constitutions and 'offers'. In twentieth-century Cyprus the British expended not inconsiderable sums on colonial welfare and development, and by 1950 had eradicated malaria, perhaps the greatest Cypriot boon in modern times. Yet none of it helped. Moderation remained the 'missing ghost in the machine' wherever the British sought to exercise over Hellenes that happy knack of supervising other people which often worked (at least up until the Second World War) in other political and cultural settings.[6]

Of the various reasons for this incorrigible Hellenic obduracy, there was one that was simple and sufficient: experience taught 'unredeemed' Greeks that mod-eration rarely paid. The more impartial British commentators frequently had cause to remark that Ionians, Cretans, and Cypriots were 'behaving very well', as the Dodecanesians certainly did under British military administration, but little good it often did them in terms of their national claim. Illustrations could be made *ad nauseam* but let us take one report in *The Times* on 10 December 1898 shortly after the eviction of the Ottoman Army and administration from Crete.

The situation [here] is...far better than could have been anticipated six weeks ago. Those who knew the Cretans best thus shook their heads gravely when the subject of surrendering arms or the rehabilitation of Mussulmans was mentioned...As it happens, the Cretans have carried out their obligations [to the powers] most loyally.

But where did acting 'most loyally' actually get the populations concerned? Rarely much nearer where they ultimately wanted to go. Instead their prize was to inhabit a twilight zone of indeterminate sovereignty. It was all very well for some *éminence grise* in Whitehall to argue that inhabiting a kind of juridical and emo-tional no man's land called autonomy constituted 'no hardship whatever' for Greeks.[7] But for dominant communities whose consciousness and modernity had, in an age of cultural and political nationalism, been defined by Hellenic attachment, such an unsatisfactory terminus was viable only for very short periods before agitation was inevitably renewed. So it was that when outside forces led by Great Britain strove to get Greeks 'to see that they must govern themselves' outside

[6] Holland, *Revolt in Cyprus*, 40.   [7] Hardinge minute, 30 July 1910, FO371/883.

their chosen motherland,[8] the latter often preferred to skirt the edge of chaos, and even to plunge for a while into its 'heart of darkness', than be fobbed off with something less than what Sir Henry Elliot had once stated was 'the dream that in more or less intensity haunts every Greek brain'.[9] There was in all of this a distinctive Anglo-Hellenic shadow play, but a catastrophic roulette was often built into the game, the effects of which were to be most damaging in Cyprus. In sum, 'moderation' remained beyond the British grasp because what Englishmen and Greeks meant by the term differed so radically, with the result that whenever an experiment was tried, the gulf of understanding was all too soon revealed.

The psychology surrounding the resulting encounters was inevitably brittle, and sometimes poisonous. Indeed, the rot had set in very early. Capodistrias, President of Greece between 1828 and 1831, was said to 'hate England like an Ionian'. The alienation was entirely mutual. 'The people are all cowards here,' Storks reported to the Duke of Newcastle from Corfu in 1862 without needing qualification,[10] whilst in 1908 Sir Edward Grey concluded, 'what very undesirable people the Cretans are'.[11] A few decades later pejorative expressions about Greek Cypriots in British official circles became endemic. By extension, British characterizations of *enosis* movements in Whitehall conventionally adopted metaphors of disease, with references to the Greek 'malady' or 'fever' generally to the fore. Such usages reflected what evolved on the ground as deeply *personalized* contests in which the principal agents of British policy found themselves at the eye of the storm. Thus one observer once commented that Storks, like every Lord High Commissioner before him, led 'a dog's life' in his Ionian post,[12] whilst at the other end of our chronology Sir John Harding was reckoned (with only a touch of hyperbole) to have endured the worst experience of any colonial governor in living memory.

This takes us back to the 'inexplicable suspicion' which Sir Alfred Biliotti once lamented always hovered over the British consulate in the Cretan capital,[13] and which was a factor throughout these episodes. Just as in the Ionian archipelago during the mid-nineteenth century the British sought to dispel such clouds by reiterating that they had 'no selfish interests of their own',[14] so they did later on. It was, by contrast, axiomatic amongst Greeks, just as it was amongst competing Great Powers, that the British were driven by those 'maritime dreams' pervading their national policy. British denials of such 'selfishness' were not wholly without sincerity. As early as 1849 Lord John Russell described himself as happy to hand over the Ionian Islands to Austria (though not, at that stage, to Greece) if only a chance to do so arose.[15] As for Cyprus, professional naval and military opinion in Britain was initially very sceptical about the merits of possessing the island; at the

---

[8] Nicolson minute, 5 Aug. 1911, FO371/1351.

[9] Elliot to Russell, 29 May 1862, PRO30/22/64.

[10] Storks to Newcastle, 20 Sept. 1862, Storks Papers, NAM.

[11] Grey minute, 7 Sept. 1906, FO371/52.   [12] Quoted in Dasent, *Delane*, 73.

[13] See above, 88.   [14] Scarlett to Russell, 12 Aug. 1862, FO32/303.

[15] Spencer Walpole, *The Life of Lord John Russell* (London, 1889), 4.

end of the nineteenth century a senior Admiralty official reaffirmed baldly that it 'had no harbours and no strategic value'.[16] That island did come to be ascribed more utility after the Great War of 1914–18, not least due to technological changes. 'Gibraltar, Malta, Suez, Cyprus represent a chain', Benito Mussolini, formulating his own grand Mediterranean dream, lamented in 1926, 'that permits England to encircle [and] ... imprison Italy.'[17] Yet on the eve of 1939 some strategists in London were in favour of abandoning much of the area, and however important the wider Mediterranean became as a British theatre in the ensuing conflict, Cyprus itself remained an operational backwater. All in all, the slippery quality of military justifications for policies obstructing the attainment of Hellenic ideals compounded other misunderstandings and confusions.

That special interests underlay the actions of British governments is undoubted—it could hardly be otherwise. But the motivation involved was more subtle and indistinct, perhaps, than crude stereotypes might suppose. Here the frequent, seemingly offhand, analogies made to Gibraltar are suggestive. British debates about the Ionian Islands were littered with such references. In occupying Cyprus in 1878 Salisbury was moved, not so much by strategic criteria proper, as by the inherently political attraction that the island might reprise the role of Gibraltar—that is, provide a 'Rock' to which the metropolitan public could be made to cling, and in so doing provide an emotional and political pivot in the 'British' Mediterranean.[18] At bottom, what British officialdom yearned for in this context was 'a Gibraltar in the East', so that even as late as 1958 Macmillan was exploiting the analogy, with its appeal to British populism, when articulating the United Kingdom's continuing requirement for Cypriot bases.[19] The search for such an iconic benchmark was never to succeed. Indeed, the very different geopolitical circumstances in the eastern Mediterranean compared to the west made sure this was so.[20] It is, however, important for our study that the Anglo-Hellenic tie was caught up in aspirations defined as much by the national myth inherent in the British Mediterranean 'lake' as by discrete and rational ends.

It stands out from our account that the British never developed a conscious methodology for dealing with Hellenic irredentist claims. There was instead a constant improvisation in which old lessons, sometimes painfully acquired, had

---

[16] Sir John Hopkins to Secretary of the Admiralty, 5 Apr. 1898, ADM121/75.

[17] Quoted in Stephen Morewood, *The British Defence of Egypt, 1935–40* (London, 2004), 25.

[18] Lee, *Great Britain*, 75 and Steel, *Lord Salisbury*, 133. At a slightly earlier period Stratford Canning reflected the dominance of political over military factors in shaping British actions in the area when he wrote that 'Our [British] fleets and military stations in the Mediterranean were so many *pledges* of a determined policy.' See Lane-Poole, *Stratford Canning*, i., 91. Italics added.

[19] See above, 238.

[20] *The Times*, 5 Aug. 2004 ('The Rock Comes out to Party'), reported that 'A thin red line looped around the Rock of Gibraltar yesterday as the population joined hands to celebrate 300 years of British rule', whilst in the public gallery of the colony's legislature were gathered the Minister of Defence representing Her Majesty's government, the First Sea Lord of the Royal Navy, and the leader of Her Majesty's opposition. It is inconceivable that a similar celebration of British loyalism could take place at the other end of the Mediterranean.

to be relearned with the help of the old mistakes. The easiest recourse was simply to contend that declarations of an irrevocable commitment to Hellenic nationality were purely tactical, or even wholly artificial. After Sir Henry Storks' first tour of the Ionian Islands he recorded in his official dispatch that he 'never heard mention' of any desire amongst the inhabitants for union with Greece.[21] When the course of events described earlier nonetheless made that union imminent, it became a fixed assumption in British circles that ordinary Ionians would swiftly regret a transformation which 'exchanged Paradise for Hell'.[22] The wish became father to the thought. As late as 1892 Sir George Bowen could write to Sir James Lacaita, both veterans of earlier Ionian controversies, that

Nothing can be more untrue than what many Englishmen allege viz. that the majority of the Ionians regret their union with Greece. The sentiment of nationality is as strong amongst the Greeks as amongst the Italians.[23]

It is, indeed, fundamental to our treatment that in British—and more broadly Western—perspectives the process of Greek unification never did attain the moral or political legitimacy of the Italian *Risorgimento,* despite the fact, once underlined by Douglas Dakin, that it extended over a longer period, overcame greater hurdles, and cost a great many more lives in contexts which extend beyond the range of this study.[24] What Britons alleged for so long and against a great deal of evidence about Ionians was later applied to Greek Cypriots. Just as it was said that sophisticated Ionians could surely not wish to join themselves to a rude and poverty-stricken kingdom scarcely free from its Ottoman past, so it was repeatedly stated a century later that most Greek Cypriots did not really wish to merge them-selves with a Greece sunk in the legacy of a bitter civil war. The real difference between these cases, however, was that the Cypriots ultimately proved more vulnerable to the orchestration of a complex denouement in which the struggle for mastery, far from being resolved, was simply transplanted onto a different, and even more contorted, basis.

A more reflective and calculated British response when facing challenges posed by Hellenic irredentism was to make their superintendence as delicate and sym-pathetic as possible. British Ionian Protection unavailingly sought the safety of the shadows. As Ioannis Stefanidis has pointed out, in Cyprus the British never sought to administer the territory 'colonially', apart from a brief interlude in the 1930s.[25] So light was the British touch in this territory, indeed, that Greek Cypriot schools fell under the remit of the Ministry of Education in Athens, and the atlases of Greek Cypriot schoolchildren featured their island in the blue and white of Greece, not the red and white of the British Empire. Successive governors with Hellenic sympathies were dispatched from London to Cyprus, as Gladstone had once been

[21] Storks to Newcastle, 17 Apr. 1860, CO136/169.
[22] Storks to Newcastle, 10 June 1863, CO136/181.
[23] Quoted in Lacaita, *Italian Englishman,* 235.
[24] Douglas Dakin, 'The Greek Unification and the Italian *Risorgimento* Compared', *Balkan Studies,* 10 (1968), 1–10.   [25] Stefanidis, *Isle of Discord,* 111–12.

coaxed to go to Corfu, in the hope of smoothing Greek feelings. Yet such conciliation not only met invariably with failure, but according to some profound conundrum was actually counter-productive. 'The enlightened sway of a [British] High Commissioner', it was ironically recalled in the 1870s of past Ionian experience, 'was as unpalatable to Pan-Hellenism as the infamous rule of the most despotical Vali in the Greek border provinces.'[26] In like vein some Greek Cypriots were later to claim, tongue only partly in cheek, that they preferred the 'despotical Vali', Sir John Harding, to the subtle and deceptive liberalism of his successor, Sir Hugh Foot.[27]

Why, then, did this light touch to the British presence so consistently fail? For one thing it was aways prone to being compromised. Sooner or later the British were confronted with a choice between exercising authority and full-blooded retreat. In the heat of such moments lightness of touch often instantly departed. Even when at the higher levels of policy making there was an assumed commitment to what we might today define as 'soft' power, British officialdom on the ground had an innate tendency to act more directly, and to attempt to sink yet deeper roots. We saw that even British military administrators in the Dodecanese after 1945 were apt to display a grating 'colonial' style, accentuated by the hubris of the recent war. According to the canon of British imperial historiography, this bankruptcy of informalism may be set in a broader Mediterranean framework. An equally 'light touch' was tried at different times in Egypt and Palestine, but in those countries the British ended up causing more alienation than in the great majority of territories where their oversight took a plain, unvarnished form. Overall, the British never effectively *penetrated* eastern Mediterranean societies as they did the Afro-Caribbean, or even south Asian, worlds at elite level. As such, they could not control or divert the tensions which their own presence helped to generate. Britain's Hellenic experience simply highlights this failure arguably in its most acute form.

Yet if British informalism usually wilted under eastern Mediterranean conditions, repression did not work either. British authority in the Ionian Islands never recovered from the severity with which the Cephalonian rebellion of 1849 had been put down. Sir Edward Grey pressed for European military reintervention in Crete to the very eve of integration into Greece, but everybody else drew back from the use of force against armed Greeks. As for British conduct of the 'Emergency' in late colonial Cyprus, Harding himself realized by mid-1957 that it had failed—the problem he saw was how to withdraw with honour intact. It was the 'honour of England' which had, indeed, been Gladstone's chief concern in dealing with Ionian problems, and led him to take up so closely the history of the Cephalonian disturbance (with considerable implications for the evolution of his later thoughts over Ireland).[28] The capacity of Anglo-Hellenic discourse to resonate within constituent

---

[26] 'Mr. Gladstone and the Greek Question', *Diplomatic Sketches*, 3 (1878), 137.

[27] George Grivas, *Memoirs* (London, 1964), 210.

[28] See Gladstone's Third Report in PRO30/6/22.

political cultures was therefore powerful, and scarcely less so for being complex and indirect. Meanwhile we need only note that although physical force was a recurring temptation, it was one which more often than not was passed over as unsustainable and self-defeating.

Where brute force was abjured the imperial British were often accused of seeking a cheaper, if not necessarily less dangerous, method through divide and rule. The island societies we have studied certainly contained disparate and combustible elements which lent themselves to such tactics. In the Ionian archipelago social division arose from class and landownership, not religion or communal identity. Sir Henry Storks was deeply aware of this potential for internal divisiveness, and to some extent took account of it in his actions. He sought to tap into 'country' opinion outside the traditional connection between British Protection and the old Venetian nobility which he was convinced would fall victim to a bloody jacquerie once English troops left. Yet in fact even under the pressures of 1863/4 Storks showed no sign of exploiting class feeling (with its capacity to turn Ionians against each other) as a diversion from *enosis*. He finally bent himself, whatever his feelings of Ionian betrayal, to hand over the island in one piece to Greek sovereignty, and this was an achievement fully recognized by ministers in London as well as by the entourage of King George I.

In Crete there was, of course, a significant Muslim minority, but during the final insurrection against Ottoman domination the two groups of religionists came to live adjacent to each other across hostile cordons, not intermingled. Under these conditions the allegation to which the British were subject in their Candian zone was that they simply threw in their lot with the *bashi-bazouks*. In fact it was the danger that they would end up tarred with an Ottoman brush in a largely Greek island which led the local British authorities to make in the summer of 1898 a last desperate attempt to revitalize an older pattern of inter-communal trade and coexistence. The British commanding officer referred to the racial divide as follows during July 1898, on the eve of the Great Massacre of Candia:

> I have suggested that Englishmen (preferably an officer) should be placed in each district as a referee—he will probably be as popular as a Football referee. I believe that I shall get them to live alongside each other again (till next time) before very long.[29]

There was in this both *naïveté* and cynicism, but nothing of the ruthless tactical sophistication of a divide and rule policy setting competing elements in local society against each other. After the transition to autonomy the British may have done little to assist the reintegration of an ethnically diverse Crete, holding back from offering the financial aid essential to facilitate a 'return to homes', and ensuring little more than a basic level of law and order. Nevertheless, a renewal of communal rivalry within the island was the last thing that first Lord Lansdowne and then Sir Edward Grey at the head of the British Foreign Office desired, if only

---

[29] Captain Mainwaring to Chermside, 13 July 1898, FO78/4969.

because of the catastrophic implications for stability elsewhere in the Balkans and Asia Minor. Indeed, had a cycle of *extermination* ever truly got underway in the island up to the summer of 1912, it is fairly sure that British troops would have flooded back into the island to clap the lid back on the Cretan boiler.

Perhaps inevitably in the light of recent history, it is with regard to Cyprus that the British finally laid themselves open to the accusation of stimulating communal strife for their own selfish purposes. Despite inevitable accusations to the contrary, there was in fact little in the general run of British rule in the island to suggest any such thing, beyond the finessing of differences between Christian and Muslim representatives in the Legislative Council. The British clung to the ideal of being 'masters of their own house' in Cyprus, and that ideal could only be jeopardized by exciting communal violence. Sir John Harding remained true to this tradition, explicitly stating that exploiting communal animosities was beneath his dignity.[30] It was only after his departure, when all else failed, that the British strove not to divide and rule, since that was beyond their power, but to survive by linking up with a Turkish government committed to division, and although they soon realized the danger this created, it was too late to stuff the genie back into its bottle. It was inherent in the tragedy of Sir Hugh Foot's governorship that his liberal credentials were from the first undermined by the high-risk game which Harold Macmillan as Prime Minister was bent on playing. Here, as in some other respects, Cyprus was the exception which proved the rule in Anglo-Hellenic encounters.

Given the very limited efficacy of all these improvisations and possibilities, then, there were only two other recourses for British policy makers faced with the task of defeating Hellenic irredentism. One was to browbeat Greek governments into doing the job for them. Translated into the prevailing metaphor in Whitehall, this meant getting Athenian officialdom to 'turn off the tap' which supplied *enosis* movements with encouragement, cash, and sometimes arms. But the British capacity to bend Athens to its own requirements proved fitful and partial at best. Even the Glücksburg dynasty—given its origins, the most Anglophile institution in Greece—felt bound to play a double game, and anyway lost its stabilizing role over time. In the end British officialdom was reduced to the crudest verbal browbeating, on the grounds that if one shouted loud enough, the seriousness of one's intent would sink in. When the British Ambassador in the Greek capital asked his superiors at home during 1953 how he could be expected to persuade local ministers that the status of Cyprus was not for negotiation, he was told to make 'a shew of impatience. You know the sort of thing: a little foot-tapping, lip biting and a changing of the subject in what P. G. Wodehouse called "a marked manner".'[31] There was a lot of 'foot-tapping' and marking of manners in these histories, and those British ambassadors in the Greek capital who occasionally rebelled, and told

---

[30] For Harding's attitude to partition see Holland, *Revolt in Cyprus*, 156–7, 198–9.
[31] Quoted in Stefanidis, *Isle of Discord*, 117.

London plainly that Greek governments were in no position to do what was asked of them, could always be written off—as Sir Francis Elliot was over Crete, and later Sir Charles Peake over Cyprus—as having gone native, of being in the repeated phrase 'more Greek than the Greeks'.[32] Here was a charge absolutely fatal to further advancement up the British diplomatic ladder. Still, yelling at 'official Greece', as Anthony Eden once did at Prime Minister Papagos over Cyprus, never got very far either, and was soon seen to have made things worse rather than better.

This leads us to the final option for British policy when all other avenues had proved fruitless in the asphyxiation of Hellenic irredentism. This was to coax Turkey into the centre of the picture. 'It's a much more difficult question to settle by frontal attack,' this thought was summarized in early 1909 in the British Embassy in Constantinople 'and the easiest if not most automatic solution [over Crete] may lie in allowing Turkey to growl at and threaten Greece. The latter may then ... swallow her *amour propre* and ... tell the Cretans to let sleeping dogs ... lie.'[33] Subsequently, the codes and metaphors of British policy were sometimes amended, but what lay behind them was generally consistent: a desire to stifle or deflect the impulse of Greek expansiveness, without the need to intervene too overtly or messily oneself. Anthony Eden, first as Foreign Secretary, and then as premier, reverted frequently to the pressing necessity of 'letting the medicine work' on Greece and the Greek Cypriots, the medicine being a painful recognition that in any all-out fight with Turkish opponents they would be the certain losers. Letting Graeco-Turkish relations take the strain, and in so doing 'freeze' the status quo for fear of more drastic outcomes, gelled with the oblique preferences of British officialdom facing these dilemmas.

Yet Turkish aggression was not something that could be turned on and off at British instigation. Ironically, whenever the British sought to turn up the pressure emanating from Turkey, the effect on Britain's relations with that country was subject sooner or later to an inverse process. As one historian has noted, the British may often have proved 'the most energetic champions of Turkish interests' over Crete, but curiously they ended up incurring most of the odium in Constantinople.[34] The same paradox was refracted through Cypriot events after 1957, when the British government bent over backwards to satisfy Ankara, only to find that both the Turkish government and the Turkish Cypriots held them to a brutal political ransom. The key to this puzzle is not too far to seek. Turkish political leadership had a profound suspicion, rooted in Ottoman experience, of Western powers playing on their susceptibilities. That leadership displayed an ingrained consciousness that although Great Britain appeared often enough to patronize Turkey against Greece, British tactics were just as likely to snap back in the opposite direction once the Greeks had been manoeuvred into line. Indeed, it

[32] Grey minute, 12 Nov. 1908, FO371/445.
[33] G. H. Fitzmaurice to Tyrrell, 11 Jan. 1909, Gooch and Temperley (eds), *Origins of the War*, v., 271.
[34] Hinsley, *British Foreign Policy*, 186.

was because Greeks and Turks *shared* a dislike of being bullied and condescended to by powers from outside their region that they were sometimes capable, to the surprise of others, of sinking their differences and resolving hitherto intractable issues between them. And although, as with regard to the future of Crete and the Dodecanese, the British often stressed how keen they were for direct agreement between Greece and Turkey, when this did eventually occur—as over Cyprus at the end of 1958—the consternation in London could not easily be disguised.

The British, then, might *in extremis* encourage Turkey into and out of the 'centre of the picture' as it suited their passing interests in eastern Mediterranean politics, but they were never really able to do the job without mishap. What did often affect events more decisively was not so much the manipulation of Greek fears of the Turks, but Turkish fear for the security of their own borders. It may well be that had the Young Turk regime after 1909 fully realized the reality of the threat to them posed by a Balkan Christian alliance, it might have sought to cut a deal with Greece, with a Cretan resolution to the fore. Certainly it was fear of Soviet ambitions on the Straits and in Asia Minor that led the Inönü government to look benignly on the transfer of the Dodecanese to Greece after 1946. Likewise, the regional crisis triggered by the Iraqi Revolution of July 1958 renewed acute Turkish anxiety over borders and led the government of Adnan Menderes to reduce its goal from a slice of partitioned Cyprus to a solution which, whilst in theory sovereign, was in practice a 'Greek-Turkish' protectorate rather than a truly independent entity. Such analysis merely underlines the banal but unerring truth that in the struggles narrated in this book it was the unpredictable play of events, rather than deep calculations, efficient strategies, or 'national' predestination, which determined outcomes.

Finally, what of the legacy of these events on the Anglo-Hellenic tie? The first instinct was always to turn the page, since all had an interest in doing so. 'Farewell, Brave Sons of England,' the municipal council of Corfu town stated in an address sent to the commander of the English garrison on 2 June 1864. 'Forget, as we do, whatever tends to mar our mutual love. Love us, as we love you, and desire that we may imitate your national virtues.' Something of the same valedictory atmosphere surrounded the British departure from Candia on 28 July 1909, though the euphoria on that occasion proved extremely short-lived. Given what later happened in Cyprus, nineteenth-century verities did not come quite so easily when the Union Jack was finally taken down from its place in the great Venetian moat of Nicosia on 16 August 1960, in an era when the national virtues of Great Britain were anyway less widely recognized. Nevertheless, Archbishop Makarios had felt able to assure the Colonial Office well in advance of that event that 'byegones would be byegones' between the Greek Cypriots and the British.[35]

These sentiments have not been wholly belied by time. Cricket is still played on the Esplanade of Corfu town, where the greenest and most tranquil

---

[35] Quoted in Holland, *Revolt in Cyprus*, 334.

nook—meticulously maintained by its dedicated Greek superintendent—
remains the British Military Cemetery. In September 1998, when the centenary of
the Great Massacre of Candia was commemorated, the local municipal authorities did not omit a special genuflection towards the British servicemen whose
deaths had been 'the true cause of the ending of the Turkish occupation of the
island'. As for Cyprus, there are few countries with whom, proportionate to size,
the United Kingdom enjoys today a closer interaction at a variety of levels—the
fact that the British team arrived in Greece for the 2004 Olympics on board
Cyprus Airways, not its eponymous British equivalent, testified to this.
Gladstone's bust, meanwhile, retains its favoured position in front of the imposing
Athenian Academy, if more in his guise as a universal Hellenic icon than a past
British statesman. Yet in all of these places, in varying degrees of acuteness, continuing public issues or merely chance personal encounters can still reveal significant
traces of the Anglo-Hellenic contests we have explored.

Sources and Bibliography

UNPUBLISHED SOURCES

Official Records

(i) The National Archives of the United Kingdom
The following record classes were used:

Admiralty

ADM 121	Mediterranean Station: Correspondence and Papers.
ADM 116	Secretariat Papers.

Cabinet

CAB41	Cabinet Letters in Royal Archives.
CAB121	Information Files.
CAB128	Cabinet Conclusions.

Colonial Office

CO67	Original Correspondence, Cyprus.
CO136	Original Correspondence, Ionian Islands.
CO537	Original Correspondence, 1939–1955.
CO883	Confidential Print, Mediterranean.
CO926	Mediterranean Department, 1938–1966.
CO1035	Intelligence Files.

Foreign Office

FO32	General Correspondence, Greece, 1827–1905.
FO78	General Correspondence, Ottoman Empire, 1780–1905.
FO195	Embassy and Consulate Files: Turkey, 1808–1962.
FO286	Embassy and Legation Files: Greece, 1813–1973.
FO371	General Correspondence since 1906.
FO421	Confidential Print: South-Eastern Europe, 1812–1947.
FO800	Private Papers (Lord Lansdowne, Ernest Bevin).
FO930	Foreign Publicity Files.

War Office

WO32	Overseas Files.
WO106	Directorate of Military Operations.
WO30	Miscellaneous Papers.

Other Classes

PREM11	Prime Minister's Office, 1951–1964.

(ii) Archive of the Foreign Ministry of Greece, Athens

(iii) State Archives of Cyprus, Nicosia (Secretariat Papers)

Unofficial Records

(i) Private Papers

British Library	Papers of William Gladstone, Sir Austen Layard, Sir John Young, Lord Carnarvon.
British School at Athens	Papers of George Finlay.
Genadius Library, Athens	Papers of Stephanos Dragoumis.
Institute of Commonwealth Studies, London,	Papers of Sir Ellis Ashmead-Bartlett.
National Army Museum, London	Papers of Sir Henry Storks.
News International Archive, London	Papers of J. T. Delane and J. D. Bourchier.
Rhodes House Library, Oxford	Papers of Sir Hugh Foot and John Reddaway.

(ii) Other Collections

Municipal Library of Rethymno, Greece.

Municipal Library of Rhodes, Greece.

State Archive and Library of Chania (Canea), Greece.

(iii) Photographic Sources

Benaki Museum, Athens.

Cultural Foundation of the Laiki Bank, Nicosia.

Genadius Library, Athens.

Hulton Archive, London.

Imperial War Museum, London.

National Historical Museum, Athens.

PUBLISHED SOURCES

(i) Parliamentary Debates

Hansard   House of Commons.

——————   House of Lords.

(ii) British Government Publications

State Papers, lxxxii: *Correspondence Relating to the Affairs of Crete, 1890.*

State Papers, lxxxvii: *Correspondence Relating to the Affairs of Crete, 1889.*

State Papers, xcvii: *Further Correspondence Relating to the Affairs of Crete, 1890–91.*

Cmd. Paper 4045, Disturbances in Cyprus in October 1931 (London: HMSO, 1932).

(ii) Newspapers

London

The Times.

Athens

Vima.

Crete
Enosis.
Kyrix.
Lefka Ori.
Metarythmisis.
Nea Erevna.
Patris.

Cyprus
Alithia.
Cyprus Mail.
Eleftheria.
Enosis.
Phonis tis Kiprou.
Times of Cyprus.

Rhodes
I Dodekanisi Epitheorisi.
I Elliniki Simaia.
O Chronos.

(ii) Books

ABBOTT, G. C., *Greece and the Allies, 1914–22* (London, 1922).

AHMAD, FEROZ, *The Young Turks: The Committee of Union and Progress in Turkish Politics* (Oxford, 1969).

ALASTOS, Doros, *Venizelos: Patriot, Statesman, Revolutionary* (London, 1942).

—— *Cyprus Guerrilla: Grivas, Makarios and the British* (London, 1960).

ALEXANDRIS, ALEXIS, *The Greek Minority of Istanbul and Greek–Turkish Relations, 1918–74* (Athens, 1983).

APOSTOLOS, Bishop of Carpathos and Cassos, *To Chronikon tis Italokratias tis Rodhou* (Athens, 1973).

APOSTOLOS, Bishop of Rhodes, *Apomnimonevmata: Chronographiki Istoria tis Ekklesiasatikis Eparchias, Rodhou epi Italo-Yermano-Anglokratias, 1912–1947* (Athens, 1947).

ARNOLD, PERCY, *Cyprus Challenge: A Colonial Island and its Aspirations* (London, 1956).

ARTHUR, GEORGE (ed.), *The Letters of Lord and Lady Wolseley, 1870–1911* (London, 1922).

AUCHMUTY, JAMES, *Sir Thomas Wyse, 1791–1862: The Life and Times of an Educator and Diplomat* (London, 1939).

AUGUSTINOS, GERASIMOS, *Consciousness and History: Nationalist Critics of Greek Society, 1897–1914* (Boulder, Colo., 1977).

AVEROFF, EVANGELOS, *Lost Opportunities: The Cyprus Question, 1950–63* (New York, 1986).

BELL, H. L. F., *Lord Palmerston* (London, 1936).

BÉRARD, VICTOR, *Les Affaires de Crète* (Paris, 1898).

BICKFORD-SMITH, R. A. H., *Cretan Sketches* (London, 1898).

BIKELAS, DEMETRIOS, *Seven Essays on Christian Greece* (Edinburgh, 1890).

BLAKE, ROBERT, *Disraeli* (London, 1966).

BLAZOUDAKI-STAVROUDAKI, Athina, *O Souris ke I Kriti* (Canea, 1998).

BOURNE, KENNETH, *Palmerston: The Early Years, 1784–1841* (London, 1982).

BOWER, LEONARD, and BOLITHO, GORDON, *Otho I: King of Greece* (London, 1939).

BOWKER, GORDON, *Through the Dark Labyrinth: A Biography of Lawrence Durrell* (London, 1998).

BRYANT, REBECCA, *Imagining the Modern: The Cultures of Nationalism in Cyprus* (London, 2004).

BUCKLE, G. A. (ed.), *The Letters of Queen Victoria*, iii: *1896–1901* (London, 1932).

CATTERALL, PETER (ed.), *The Macmillan Diaries: The Cabinet Years, 1950–57* (London, 2003).

CAVENDISH, ANNE (ed.), *Cyprus 1878: The Journal of Sir Garnet Wolseley* (Nicosia, 1991).

CHESTER, S. B., *The Life of Venizelos* (London, 1921).

CHRISTMAS, WALTER, *The Life of King George I of Greece* (London, 1914).

CLOGG, RICHARD, *Anglo-Greek Attitudes: Studies in History* (London, 2000).

CLOSE, DAVID H., *Greece since 1945: Politics, Economy and Society* (London, 2002).

CROUZET, FRANÇOIS, *Le Conflit de Chypre, 1945–59*, vols. i and ii (Brussels, 1973).

CUNNINGHAM, ALAN (ed.), *Eastern Questions in the Nineteenth Century: Collected Essays* (London, 1993).

DAKIN, DOUGLAS, *The Greek Struggle in Macedonia, 1897–1913* (Thessaloniki, 1966).

—— *The Unification of Greece* (London, 1972).

DARWIN, JOHN, *The End of the British Empire: The Historical Debate* (Oxford, 1991).

DASENT, ARTHUR, *John Thadeus Delane: His Life and Correspondence*, ii (London, 1908).

DETORAKIS, THEOCHARIS, and KALOKERINOS, ALEXIS (eds.), *I Teleftaia Fasi tou Kritikou Zitimatos* (Heraklion, 2001).

DIVANI, LENA, and CONSTANTINOPOLOU, PHOTINI (eds), *The Dodecanese. The Long Road to Union with Greece: Diplomatic Documents from the Historical Archive of the Ministry of Foreign Affairs* (Athens, 1997).

DIXON, C. W., *The Colonial Administrations of Sir Thomas Maitland* (London, 1969).

DOUMANIS, NICHOLAS, *Myth and Memory in the Mediterranean: Remembering Fascism's Empire* (London, 1997).

DRIAULT, EDOUARD, *Histoire diplomatique de la Grèce*, ii: *La Règne d'Othon* (Paris, 1926).

DURRELL, LAWRENCE, *Bitter Lemons* (London, 1957).

—— *Reflections on a Marine Venus* (London, 1951).

DUTKOWSKI, JEAN-STANISLAW, *L'Occupation de la Crète, 1897–1909* (Paris, 1953).

ENGLEZAKIS, BENEDICT, *Studies in the History of the Church of Cyprus 4th–20th Centuries* (Aldershot, 1995).

FINLAY, GEORGE, *A History of Greece: From its Conquest by the Roman to the present Time, B.C. 146–A.D. 1864*, vii (Oxford, 1877).

—— *A History of the Greek Revolution*, i and ii (London, 1861).

FOOT, HUGH, *A Start in Freedom* (London, 1964).

FORD, RICHARD, *UNRRA Assistance to the Dodecanese*, Operational Analysis Papers, No. 15 (London, 1947).

FRANGOUDIS, George, *Kibris* (Athens, 1890).

GALLANT, THOMAS W., *Experiencing Dominion: Culture, Identity and Power in the British Mediterranean* (New York, 2000).

GARDIKAS-KATSIADAKIS, Helen, *Greece and the Balkan Imbroglio: Greek Foreign Policy, 1911–13* (Thessaloniki, 1992).

GEORGHALLIDES, G. S., *A Political and Administrative History of Cyprus, 1918–1926* (Nicosia, 1979).

—— *Cyprus and the Governorship of Sir Ronald Storrs: The Causes of the 1931 Crisis* (Nicosia, 1979).

GOOCH, G. P. (ed.), *The Later Correspondence of Lord John Russell, 1840–1878*, ii (London, 1925).

—— and Temperley, Harold (eds), *British Documents on the Origins of the War, 1898–1914*, v: *The Near East* (London, 1928).

—— (eds), *British Documents on the Orgins of the War, 1898–1914*, ix: *The Balkan Wars*, part 2: *The League and Turkey* (London, 1934).

GRAVES, PHILIP, *Briton and Turk* (London, 1941).

GREEN, MOLLY, *A Shared World: Christians and Muslims in the Early Mediterranean World* (Princeton, 2000).

GRIVAS, GEORGE, *Memoirs* (London, 1964).

GROGAN, LADY, *The Life of J. D. Bouchier* (London, 1926).

HARDINGE, LORD, *Old Diplomacy* (London, 1947).

HASLIP, JOAN, *The Sultan: The Life of Abdul Hamid* (London, 1958).

HATZIVASSILIOU, EVANTHIS, *The Cyprus Question, 1878–1960: The Constitutional Aspect* (Minneapolis, 2002).

—— *Britain and the International Status of Cyprus, 1955–59* (Minneapolis, 1997).

HICKMAN, TOM, *The Call-Up: A History of National Service* (London, 2004).

HILL, GEORGE, *A History of Cyprus,*, iv: *The Ottoman Province. The British Colony, 1571–1948* (London, 1953).

HINSLEY, F. H., *British Foreign Policy under Sir Edward Grey* (Cambridge, 1977).

HOGARTH, D. G., *Accidents of an Antiquary's Life* (London, 1910).

HOLLAND, JEFFREY, *The Aegean Mission: Allied Operations in the Dodecanese, 1943* (London, 1988).

HOLLAND, ROBERT, *Britain and the Revolt in Cyprus, 1954–59* (Oxford, 1998).

—— *The Pursuit of Greatness: Britain and the World Role, 1900–1970* (London, 1991).

HOWARD, ESME, *Theatre of Life, 1905–1936* (London, 1936).

HUSSEY, J. M., *The Journals and Letters of George Finlay*, ii (Athens, 1995).

IATRIDES, JOHN O. (ed.), *Ambassador MacVeagh Reports: Greece, 1933–1947* (Princeton, 1980).

JELAVICH, BARBARA, *History of the Balkans: Eighteenth and Nineteenth Centuries* (Cambridge, 1983).

KATSIAOUNIS, ROLANDOS, *Labour, Society and Politics in Cyprus during the Second Half of the Nineteenth Century* (Nicosia, 1996).

—— *H Diaskeptiki, 1946–8* (Nicosia, 2000).

KELLING, GEORGE H., *Countdown to Rebellion: British Policy in Cyprus, 1935–55* (New York, 1990).

KIRKWALL, VISCOUNT, *Four Years in the Ionian Islands*, i and ii (London, 1864).

KITROMILIDES, PASCHALIS, *Enlightenment, Nationalism, Orthodoxy: Studies in the Culture and Thought of South-Eastern Europe* (London, 1994).

KOLIOPOULOS, JOHN, *Brigands with a Cause: Brigandage and Irredentism in Modern Greece, 1821–1912* (London, 1987).

—— *Greece and the British Connection* (Oxford, 1977).

—— and Veremis, Thanos, *Greece: The Modern Sequel* (London, 2002).

KOUMOULIDES, JOHN, *Cyprus and the Greek War of Independence* (London, 1974).

KYPRIOTIS, PHOTIS, *Dodekanisiaki Ethniki Antistasi sta Chronia tis Italo-Yermano-Anglokratias, 1912–1948* (Rhodes, 1988).

LACAITA, CHARLES, *An Italian Englishman, 1813–1895: Sir James Lacaita* (London, 1933).

LANE-POOLE, STANLEY, *The Life of Stratford Canning*, i and ii (London, 1888).

LANGER, WILLIAM, *The Diplomacy of Imperialism, 1890–1902* (New York, 1935).

LANITIS, N. K., *O Akritas tou Ellinikou Noto* (Athens, 1945).

LEE, DWIGHT E., *Great Britain and the Cyprus Convention Policy of 1878* (Cambridge, Mass., 1934).

LEE, SIDNEY, *King Edward VII: A Biography*, i (London, 1925).

LEVENTIS, YIORGOS, *Cyprus: The Struggle for Self-Determination in the 1940s* (Frankfurt, 2002).

LHÉRITIER, MICHAEL, *Histoire diplomatique de la Grèce à nos jours*, iii: *La Règne de Georges I avant le traité de Berlin* (Paris, 1926).

LOUIS, WM. ROGER, *The British Empire in the Middle East, 1945–51: Arab Nationalism, the United States and Postwar Imperialism* (Oxford, 1984).

LUKE, HARRY, *Cities and Men: An Autobiography*, ii (London, 1953).

MACGILLIVRAY, J. ALEXANDER, *Sir Arthur Evans and the Archaeology of the Minoan Myth* (London, 2000).

McHENRY, JAMES, *The Uneasy Partnership, 1919–1939: The Political and Diplomatic Interaction between Great Britain, Turkey and the Turkish-Cypriot Community* (New York, 1987).

McKERCHER, B. J. C., *Esme Howard: A Diplomatic Biography* (Cambridge, 1989).

MACMILLAN, HAROLD, *War Diaries: The Mediterranean, 1943–1945* (London, 1984).

MANETAS, I. K., *Iepos Lochos, 1942–1945* (Athens, 1977).

MARKIDES, DIANA, *Cyprus, 1957–63: From Colonial Conflict to Constitutional Crisis. The Key Role of the Municipal Issue* (Minneapolis, 2001).

MARTINIÈRE, H. de La, *La Marine Française en Crète* (Paris, 1911).

MATHEW, H. C. G., *Gladstone, 1809–1874* (Oxford, 1988).

—— *The Gladstone Diaries*, v: *1855–60* (Oxford, 1978).

MAYES, STANLEY, *Makarios: A Biography* (London, 1981).

MAZOWER, MARK, *Inside Hitler's Greece: The Experience of Occupation, 1941–44* (London, 1988).

—— *Salonica: City of Ghosts; Christians, Muslims and Jews, 1430–1950* (London, 2004).

MEDLICOTT, W. N., *The Congress of Berlin and After: A Diplomatic Study of the Near Eastern Settlement, 1878–1880* (London, 1938).

MELAS, SPYROS, *I Epanastassi tou 1909* (Athens, 1972).

MILLER, WILLIAM, *The Ottoman Empire and its Successors, 1801–1922* (London, 1923).

MITCHELL, LESLIE, *Bulwer Lytton: The Rise and Fall of a Victorian Man of Letters* (London, 2003).

MONTIS, COSTAS, *Closed Doors: An Answer to Bitter Lemons* (Minneapolis, 2004).

MORLEY, JOHN, *The Life of Sir William Ewert Gladstone*, i (London, 1903).

PADOUVA, COSTA E., *Kriti 1897–1913: Poliethnikes Enobles Dhinamis Katochi-Autonomia-Enosi me tin Elladha* (Athens, 1997).

PAPAPOLYVIOU, PETROS, *Fainon Simeion Atichous Polemou: I Simmetochi tis Kiprou ston Ellinotourkiko Polemo tou 1897* (Nicosia, 2002).

—— *I Kipros kai I Valkaniki Polemi: Simvoli stin Istoria tou Kipriakou Ethelontismou* (Nicosia, 1997).

PAPASTRATIS, PROCOPIS, *British Policy towards Greece during the Second World War* (Cambridge, 1984).

PAXIMAPOLOU-STAVRINOU, MIRANTA, *I exergerseis tes Kephallenias kata ta etei 1848 kai 1849* (Athens, 1980).

PEARS, EDWIN, *The Life of Abdul Hamid* (London, 1917).

PENZOPOULOS, DIMITRI, *The Balkan Exchange of Minorities and its Impact on Greece* (Paris, 1962).

PERSIANIS, PANAYIOTIS, *Church and State in Cyprus Education* (Nicosia, 1978).

PERKINS, ANN, *Red Queen: The Authorized Biography of Barbara Castle* (London, 2003).

PERRIS, G. H., *The Eastern Question of 1897 and British Policy in the Near East* (London, 1897).

PRATT, LAWRENCE R., *East of Malta, West of Suez: Britain's Mediterranean Crisis, 1936–39* (London, 1975).

PRATT, MICHAEL, *Britain's Greek Empire* (London, 1978).

PREVALAKIS, ELEFTHERIOS, *British Policy towards the Change of Dynasty in Greece* (Athens, 1953).

PREVELAKIS, PANTELIS, *To Chroniko mias Politias* (Athens, 1938).

REDDAWAY, JOHN, *Burdened with Cyprus* (London, 1986).

REINACH, A.-J., *La Question crétoise vue de Crète* (Paris, 1910).

ROBBINS, KEITH, *Lord Grey of Falloden* (London, 1971).

ROBERTS, ANDREW, *Salisbury: Victorian Titan* (London, 1999).

RUMBOLD, HORACE, *Recollections of a Diplomatist* (London, 1902).

SAAB, ANN POTTINGER, *Reluctant Icon: Gladstone, Bulgaria and the Working Classes 1856–1878* (Cambridge, Mass.: 1991).

SHERRARD, PHILIP, *Edward Lear: The Corfu Years* (Athens, 1988).

SKINNER, J. HILARY, *Roughing it in Crete in 1867* (London, 1868).

SMITH, MICHAEL LLEWELLYN, *Ionian Vision: Greece in Asia Minor, 1919–22* (London, 1973).

STEEL, DAVID, *Lord Salisbury: A Political Biography* (London, 1999).

STEELE, E. D., *Palmerston and Liberalism, 1855–1865* (Cambridge, 1991).

STEFANIDIS, IOANNIS D., *Isle of Discord: Nationalism, Imperialism and the Making of the Cyprus Problem* (London, 1999).

STORRS, RONALD, *Orientations* (London, 1937).

SVOLOPOULOS, CONSTANTINE, *O Eleutherios Venizelos ke I Politiki Krisis eis tin Autonomon Kritin 1901–1906* (Athens, 1974).

—— (ed.), *Greece and Great Britain during World War I* (Thessaloniki, 1985).

TATSIOS, THEODORE, *The Megali Idea and the Greek–Turkish War of 1897: The Impact of the Cretan Problem on Greek Irredentism, 1866–1897* (Boulder, Colo., 1984).

TZIOVAS, DIMITRIS, (ed.), *Greece and the Balkans: Identities, Perceptions and Encounters since the Enlightenment* (London, 2003).

VEREMIS, THANOS, *The Military in Greek Politics: From Independence to Democracy* (London, 1997).

—— and Dragoumis, Mark, *Historical Dictionary of Greece* (London, 1995).

VICKERS, HUGO, *Alice: Princess Andrew of Greece* (London, 2000).

WAGSTAFF, J. M., *Greece: Ethnicity and Sovereignty, 1820–1994. Atlas and Documents* (London, 2002).

WEBER, FRANK, *The Evasive Neutral: Germany, Britain and the Quest for a Turkish Alliance in the Second World War* (Columbia, Mo., 1979).

WIEDE, M. G. (ed.), *Benjamin Disraeli: Letters, 1857–59* (Toronto, 2004).

WRATISLAW, A. C., *A Consul in the East* (London, 1924).

XYDIS, STEPHEN, *Cyprus: Reluctant Republic* (The Hague, 1973).

—— *Cyprus: Conflict and Conciliation, 1954–58* (Columbus, Oh., 1967).

(iii) Articles and Chapters

ALEXANDRIS, ALEXIS, 'Turkish Policy towards Greece during the Second World War and its Impact on Greek–Turkish Détente', *Balkan Studies*, 23/1 (1982), 185–7.

ANAGNOSTOPOULOU, SIA, 'I Eklissia tis Kiprou kai o Ethnarchikos tis Rolos', *Sichrona Themata*, 68–70 (1998–9).

AUGUSTINOS, GERASIMOS, 'Hellenism and the Modern Greeks', in Peter Sugar (ed.), *Eastern European Nationalism in the Twentieth Century* (Washington, D.C., 1995).

BOURNE, KENNETH, 'Great Britain and the Cretan Revolt, 1866–1869', *Slavonic and East European Review*, 35 (1956–7).

CARABOTT, PHILIP, 'Italy's "Temporary" Acquisition of the Dodecanese: A Prelude to Permanency', *Diplomacy and Statecraft*, 4-2 (1993).

DAKIN, DOUGLAS, 'The Greek Unification and the Italian *Risorgimento* Compared', *Balkan Studies*, 10 (1968).

FISHER, JOHN, 'Lord Curzon and Cyprus in British Imperial Strategy, 1914–23', *Journal of Byzantine and Modern Greek Studies*, 23 (1999).

GARDIKAS-KATSIADAKIS, Eleni, 'I Elliniki Kivernissi ke to Kritiko Zitima, 1908', in *Afieroma ston Panepistimiako Dhaskalo, Vas. Bl. Sfiroera* (Athens, 1992).

—— 'O Stephanos Dragoumis Ke I Oristiki Lisi tou Kritikou Zitimatos', in Theocharis Detorakis and Alexis Kalokerinos (eds), *I Teleftaia Fasi tou Kritikou Zitimatos* (Heraklion, 2001).

GEORGHALLIDES, G. S., 'Church and State in Cyprus, October 1931 to November 1932', *Epiteris*, 19 (1992).

—— 'Cyprus and Winston Churchill's Visit', *Thetis*, 3 (Mannheim, 1996).

—— 'The Cyprus Revolt and the British Deportation Policy, October 1931–December 1932', *Journal of the Society of Cypriot Studies* (Nicosia, 1995).

—— and Markides, Diana, 'British Attitudes to Constitution-Making in Post-1931 Cyprus', *Journal of Modern Greek Studies*, 13-1 (1995).

GEORGIS, GEORGIOS, 'O Antichtipos tis Enosis tis Eptanisou me tin Ellada stin Kipro', in *Proceedings of the Third Conference of Cypriot Studies* (Nicosia, 2000).

HICKS, GEOFFREY, 'Don Pacifico, Democracy and Danger: The Protectionist Party Critique of British Foreign Policy, 1850–52', *International History Review*, 26/3 (Sept. 2004).

HOLLAND, ROBERT, 'Never, Never Land: British Colonial Policy and the Roots of Violence in Cyprus, 1950–1954', *Journal of Imperial and Commonwealth History*, 21-3 (1993).

—— 'Greek–Turkish Relations, Istanbul and British Rule in Cyprus, 1954–59', *Deltio: Bulletin of the Centre for Asian Minor Studies*, (1994).

KNOX, BRUCE, 'British Policy and the Ionian Islands, 1847–1864: Nationalism and Imperial Administration', *English Historical Review*, 99 (1984).

KOLODNY, ÉMILE, 'La Crète: mutations et évolutions d'une population insulaire grecque', *Revue de géographie de Lyon*, 43/3 (1968).

LOIZOS, PETER, 'Ottoman Half-Lives: Perspectives on Particular Forced Migrations', *Journal of Refugee Studies*, 3-12 (1999).

MARKIDES, DIANA, 'Britain's "New Look" Policy for Cyprus and the Harding–Makarios Talks, January 1955–March 1956', *Journal of Imperial and Commonwealth History*, 23-3 (1995).

MARKOPOULOS, GEORGE, 'King George I and the Expansion of Greece, 1875–1881', *Balkan Studies*, 9 (1968).

—— 'The Selection of Prince George of Greece as High Commissioner in Crete', *Balkan Studies*, 10 (1969).

MAZARAKIS-AINIAN, IOANNIS K., 'The Cypriot Exhibition of 1901', in *Cypriot Costumes in the National Historical Museum: The World of Cyprus at the Dawn of the Twentieth Century* (Athens, 1999).

SANDIFORD, KEITH, 'W. E. Gladstone and Liberal-Nationalist Movements', *Albion*, 13-1 (1991).

SMITH, RAYMOND, and ZAMETICA, JOHN, 'The Cold Warrior: Clement Attlee Reconsidered, 1945–7', *International Affairs*, 61-2 (1985).

SVOLOPOULOS, C., 'Anglo-Hellenic Talks during the Axis Campaign against Greece', *Balkan Studies*, 23-1 (1982).

TEMPERLEY, HAROLD, 'Disraeli and Cyprus', *English Historical Review*, 46 (Apr. 1931).

XANALATOS, DIGENIS, 'The Greeks and the Turks on the Eve of the Balkan Wars', *Balkan Studies*, 3 (1962).

(iv) Theses

CALLIGAS, ELENI, 'The "Rizopastoi": Politics and Nationalism in the British Protectorate of the Ionian Islands, 1815–1864' (doctoral dissertation, University of London, 1994).

CARABOTT, PHILIP, 'The Dodecanese Question, 1912–1924' (doctoral dissertation, University of London, 1991).

KYRIAKIDES, KLEARCHOS A., 'British Cold War Strategy and the Struggle to Maintain Military Bases in Cyprus, 1951–60' (doctoral dissertation, University of Cambridge, 1996).

Index